BRITAIN

FODOR'S TRAVEL PUBLICATIONS, INC.

NEW YORK • TORONTO • LONDON • SYDNEY • AUCKLAND

WWW.FODORS.COM

Copyright © 2000 The Automobile Association
Maps copyright © 2000 The Automobile Association

Published in the United States by Fodor's Travel
Publications, Inc.
Published in the United Kingdom by A.A. Publishing

Fodor's is a registered trademark of Random House, Inc.

ISBN 0-679-00473-4
Fourth Edition

Fodor's Exploring Britain

Authors: **Tim Locke, Richard Cavendish,
Barnaby Rogerson**
Accommodations and restaurants revised by
Elizabeth Carter
Series Adviser: **Ingrid Morgan**
Joint Series Editor: **Susi Bailey**
Revisions Editor: **Grapevine Publishing Services Ltd**
Cartography: **The Automobile Association**
Cover Design: **Tigist Getachew, Fabrizio La Rocca**
Front Cover Silhouette: **Bob Krist/Blackstar**

Printed and bound in Italy by Printer Trento srl.

10 9 8 7 6 5 4 3 2 1

How to use this book

ORGANIZATION

Britain Is, Britain Was
Discusses aspects of life and culture in contemporary Britain and explores significant periods in its history.

A–Z
Breaks down the country into regional chapters, and covers places to visit, including walks and drives. Within this section fall the Focus On articles, which consider a variety of subjects in greater detail.

Travel Facts
Contains the strictly practical information vital for a successful trip.

Accommodations and Restaurants
Lists recommended establishments throughout Britain, giving a brief summary of their attractions.

ABOUT THE RATINGS
Most places described in this book have been given a separate rating. These are as follows:

▶▶▶   **Do not miss**

▶▶   **Highly recommended**

▶   **Worth seeing**

MAPS
To make each particular location easier to find, every main entry in this book has a map reference to the right of its name. This comprises a number, followed by a letter, followed by another number, such as 176B3. The first number (176) refers to the page on which the map can be found, the letter (B) and the second number (3) pinpoint the square in which the main entry is located. The maps on the inside front cover and inside back cover are referred to as IFC and IBC respectively.

Contents

How to use this book 4

Contents pages 5–7

My Britain 8

BRITAIN IS 9–22
Variety 10
Government 11
The British people 12–13
The economy 14
The pub 15
Gardens 16–17
Events 18–19
The industrial past today 20–21
The semi-detached house 22

BRITAIN WAS 23–41
Man and the landscape 24–25
Castles and manors 26–27
Churches and monasteries 28–29
Domestic architecture 30–31
Kings and queens 32–33
A maritime nation 34–35
Writers and places 36–37
Landscape artists 38–39
The Industrial Revolution 40–41

A–Z

London 42–59
Walks
Covent Garden, royal London, and
  Westminster 52–53
Along the South Bank to Tower
  Hill 53

The West Country 60–85
Focus On
The north Cornish coast 68–69
The south Cornish coast 70–71
English place-names 81
Walks
West Country walks 64
Bath 66
Drive
Thomas Hardy country 76

6

Southern England 86–109
Focus On
Seaside resorts 94–95
Houses of the Weald 102–103
Walks
Southern England walks 92
Drive
The Weald 106–107

The Heart of England 110–133
Focus On
The Cotswolds 118–120
Ironbridge Gorge 123
The canal system 128–129
Walk
Oxford walk 127
Drive
The Cotswolds 121

Eastern England 134–149
Focus On
The north Norfolk coast 142
Preserving the landscape
144–145
East Anglian artists 149
Walk
Cambridge walk 139
Drive
Constable country 148

Wales 150–171
Focus On
The Valleys 156
Welsh culture and politics
160–161
Walks
Wales walks 158
Drive
Snowdonia National Park 170

Northwest England 172–189
Focus On
The Lake District 178–179
Revitalizing the cities 184–185
Port Sunlight 188
Walks
Northwest England walks 175
Drive
The Lakes 180–181

Northeast England 190–209
Focus On
The Brontës 198
Walks
Northeast England walks 193
York city highlights 205
Drive
The Yorkshire Dales 207

Southern Scotland 210–233
Focus On
Clans and tartans 233
Walks
Southern Scotland walks 214
Edinburgh walk 225
Drive
The (Scottish) Borders 217

Northern Scotland 234–262
Focus On
Bonnie Prince Charlie 246
Highland land use 262
Walks
Northern Scotland walks 238
Drives
Loch Ness and the Black Isle 243
Oban and Argyll 249

TRAVEL FACTS 263–274

ACCOMMODATIONS AND RESTAURANTS 275–284

Index 285–288

Acknowledgments 288

Maps and plans
Regions and 3-star sights IFC
London 42–43
London walks 52
The West Country 60–61
Bath walk 66
Thomas Hardy country drive 76
Southern England 86–87
The Weald drive 106
The Heart of England 110–111
The Cotswolds drive 121
Oxford walk 127
Eastern England 134–135
Cambridge walk 139
Constable country drive 148
Wales 150–151
Snowdonia drive 170
Northwest England 172
Lake District drive 180–181
Northeast England 190–191
York city highlights 205
Yorkshire Dales drive 207
Southern Scotland 210–211
The (Scottish) Borders drive 217
Edinburgh walk 224–225
Northern Scotland 234–235
Loch Ness and the Black Isle drive 243
Relief map of Britain IBC

My Britain

From my house in Sussex I can look upon Lewes Castle, an administrative headquarters set up in Norman times. The town's main thoroughfare slopes down between numerous Georgianized half-timbered buildings, past the White Hart Hotel—where Tom Paine held meetings in the 18th century—to family-run Harvey's brewery, little changed in over a hundred years. A short walk away are the sheep-grazed slopes of the South Downs, dotted with ancient remains. On one slope is the site of the Battle of Lewes, where in 1264 Simon de Montfort defeated Henry III, forcing him to grant rights that paved the way for parliamentary democracy.

I find this sense of continuum an impressive aspect of Britain: its landscapes, both rural and urban, pockmarked with historical incident. I sometimes wonder what else would strike me about Britain if I had never seen it before. I imagine being confronted with a series of cameos: a sheep auction in Mid Wales, with cloth caps and ruddy Celtic faces in abundance; the landscapes of East Anglia, where the quality of light imparts subtle differences each time a view is encountered; a county cricket match at the spa town of Tunbridge Wells; or the hypnotic patter of a dealer at London's Brick Lane market.

Britain, as much as any other corner of the Earth, has been much traveled in and much written about. This book is our selection of the most rewarding places in the kingdom. It doesn't include every city or attraction, but aims to be a balance between the well known and the less obvious.

It constantly surprises me that, in an age ever tending toward standardization, so many aspects of Britain have survived intact: its communities, its lifestyles, its idiosyncracies. The pressure to change is still there, but there has been a realization that we need our heritage as a point of reference to tell us who we are. It would take a great deal to erode that national persona.
Tim Locke

Tim Locke has contributed to *Boston and New England*, *Thailand* and *Germany* in the Fodor's *Exploring* series, as well as to other guides on Britain. Richard Cavendish—who wrote most of the Britain Is, Britain Was and Focus On features—has written numerous books on Britain. Travel writer Barnaby Rogerson, the author of *Exploring Britain*'s Scottish chapters, is also the author of AA *Essential Scotland*.

Britain's

9

N.T. = *National Trust (see page 102)*

E.H. = *English Heritage (see page 124)*

Cadw = *Welsh Historic Monuments Commission (see page 167)*

H.S. = *Historic Scotland (see page 124)*

N.T.S. = *National Trust for Scotland (see page 102)*

Britain is by no means a uniform entity: the more you travel around this compact island, the more there is for you to see and enjoy. Within the boundaries of its 88,000 square miles Britain shows an astonishingly rich variety of landscape, architecture, climate, regional accents and cuisine, cultural traditions, social make-up, and economic activity.

Britain constantly reminds us that it is an island. Once a mighty naval power and the center of a huge empire, it still has a rich heritage of its historic past, and plenty of unmistakably British hallmarks. The Industrial Revolution began here, as did punk rock, railways and soccer, and it's only in this country that you will find the quintessentially British village *fête* complete with striped tents and bring-and-buy stalls, the seaside pleasure pier, the pub, the English stately home in its landscaped park, Scottish haggis, Welsh cakes, and leafy suburbs dotted with Tudor-style semi-detached houses and the odd fish and chip shop. British contributions to world culture include an incomparable and all-embracing literary output, from Shakespeare to Winnie-the-Pooh.

THE DIVERSITY Many newcomers to Britain are surprised by how quickly the urban scene gives way to beautiful rural landscapes. Factors include the compactness of many urban centers, restrictive zoning laws, and the constant variations in the natural environment: low-level arable fens, rolling hedgerow-lined pastures, craggy dales, blustery moorland, post-glacial mountain scenery, and shingle shores. This has given rise to numerous types of local architecture: sometimes the bedrock itself supplies the building material, as can be seen in the Cotswolds, Cornwall, rural Wales, the Scottish Highlands, and the Pennines, while elsewhere wood and/or bricks predominate.

Twentieth-century progress has inevitably eroded some of the finer distinctions in various locales (high-tech agriculture today blankets vast tracts of farmland, and chain stores dominate small towns' main shopping streets), but in spite of this, much has been carefully preserved or has survived. Regional accents, for instance, continue to thrive to a surprising degree: a well-trained ear can distinguish from which side of the Pennines, part of Scotland, or even district of London the speaker comes.

Britain's greatest assets for visitors include its sense of history and variety, all of which are packed into one accessible island where the driving distances are never too long between distinctively different landscapes and cultures. Britain has a confusing variety of names.

Market day (this one is Norwich)— a colorful experience in every way

The British system of government is that of parliamentary democracy, based on principles of common law. Led by its prime minister (since 1997 Tony Blair, of the Labour party), the country is a "constitutional monarchy," although there is no written constitution, since it has evolved over the centuries. Queen Elizabeth II gives royal assent to Acts of Parliament, but this is really a mere formality. Universal male suffrage in Britain dates only from 1918, and women did not get the vote until as recently as 1928.

❏ "Let not England forget her precedence of teaching other nations how to live."
—John Milton (1644) ❏

The British Isles are the two islands of Britain and Ireland. Britain, or Great Britain, means England, Wales, and Scotland. Wales was conquered by England in the 13th century. The King of Scots succeeded the English throne in 1603, and the political union of England and Scotland dates from 1707.

The United Kingdom is comprised of England, Wales, Scotland, and Northern Ireland, the latter being the six counties of Ulster (predominantly Protestant) that refused to join the rest of Ireland when it broke away from Britain in 1921.

Scotland, Wales, and Northern Ireland are ruled, like England, from London but in 1999 powers were devolved to Scotland and Wales, with the Scottish Parliament in Edinburgh and the Welsh Assembly in Cardiff.

THE SEAT OF POWER The head of state is officially the Queen. Much of the ceremony of British life revolves round **the monarchy**, dating from a time when the monarch ruled the country. Today, power rests with the democratically elected government answerable to **parliament** and to the **House of Commons**, the chief legislative body. The unelected **House of Lords** is the secondary chamber. Britain's relationship with the European Union, however, and the consequences for British sovereignty and parliament are under debate.

❏ "Great Britain has lost an empire and has not yet found a role."
—Dean Acheson (1962) ❏

11

Class distinctions are still profoundly impor- tant in British life. They involve the most acutely discriminating judgments—concern- ing people's houses and furnishings, clothes, cars, jobs, education, manners, and personal tastes. The simplest clue to someone's class is usually gained by listening to their accent—as George Bernard Shaw once remarked, an Englishman cannot open his mouth without making some other Englishman despise him.

The population of Great Britain numbers about 56 million. A small and densely populated country, it would fit neatly inside the American state of Oregon, which has a popula- tion of only 3 million. Or, keeping the comparison within Europe, the coun- try has about the same number of people as France, in an area less than half the size.

EARLY ANCESTRY The British are a nation of mongrels, principally a mixture of Germanic and Celtic strains. The original "English," or Anglo-Saxons, came across the North Sea in their dragon-prowed

longships from northwest Germany and southern Denmark some 1,500 years ago. They subjugated most of the native Celtic people on the island, whom they dismissively called Welsh, meaning "foreigners."

More Germanic invaders came from Denmark and Norway in the Viking Age. Then the famous Norman Conquest of England in 1066 eventually gave all areas of the British Isles a new and initially French-speaking ruling class. From the 16th to the 18th centuries, thousands of French Protestants, known as Huguenots, came to England to escape the religious persecution of Europe. The 19th century brought substantial Irish immigration to Britain and an influx of Jewish families fleeing from perse- cution in Russia and Eastern Europe. After World War II fresh waves of immigrants came from the West Indies, the Indian subcontinent,

Cyprus, and many other countries of the former British Empire that now form part of the Commonwealth association of nations.

ETHNIC AND RELIGIOUS MIX Despite the presence of many ethnic and religious minorities, statistics show that more than 80 percent of the U.K. population is still classified as English, about 10 percent as Scottish, 2½ percent as Irish and 2 percent as Welsh. Britain is 95 percent white, with West Indians, Indians, and Pakistanis now numbering about 1 percent each. There are also tiny percentages of Bangladeshis and Chinese. Of the ethnic minority population, close to 50 percent is British by birth.

The population is overwhelmingly Christian, or thinks of itself that way. More than 85 percent of the British people regard themselves as Christians, but less than one person in five goes regularly to church or chapel. The Muslim population is about 2 percent, and practicing Jews total 1 percent.

Male and female members of the population are nearing equality in numbers. In the 20th century the birth rate increased slowly; during the 1970s population fell for a time.

❏ Arthur Koestler, a notable foreign writer who lived in Britain for many years, described the average Englishman as an attractive hybrid between an ostrich and a lion: keeping his head in the sand for as long as possible, but, when forced to confront reality, capable of heroic deeds. ❏

A NATIONAL CHARACTER? Whether there is anything that can be called a British national character is open to question. The Scots, the Welsh, and the Irish have retained their separate identities despite (or because of) English domination. Even in England itself, people from London, Yorkshire, Lancashire, the Northeast, the West Country, and other areas cherish their regional identities.

Class distinctions are being steadily eroded, but certain national traits live on: reserve, politeness, a sense of fair play, a genius for compromise and a gift for understatement to name but five. Voluntary work plays a major role in the everyday life of many people, with thousands of charity shops, civic societies, women's institutes and fund-raising ventures spread across the country. The British are fond of gardens, dogs, and horses. Although they love the countryside, most of them do not actually live in it; walking or hiking in the countryside is by far their most popular activity. They love sports, and taught the rest of the world organized games, such as soccer and cricket.

Perhaps the most fundamental trait that all the British have in common is an ironic sense of humor which allows them to make fun of themselves with good grace.

13

If anything causes the British more complaint, anxiety, and frustration than the weather, it is the economy. In the Victorian Age, Britain was the most powerful industrial nation on Earth, with a mighty economy based on coal, iron, and steel, heavy machinery, textiles, shipbuilding, and foreign trade. Queen Victoria ruled the largest empire in history. This commanding position has since been lost, and with it the self-confidence of that era.

The British economy today is based on private enterprise; in the 1980s many of the nationalized industries were restored to private ownership. Heavy industry has declined while the service sector has grown. Britain used to import raw materials for its factories. Now it is a net importer of manufactured goods from countries that make them better and cheaper. The fishing industry has shrunk after over-fishing led to E.U. and government restrictions. Inflation, high in the 1970–1980s, is now under control.

❏ The change that has come over Britain can be observed in the mining valleys of South Wales, where King Coal once raised his grimy scepter above teeming pits and slag heaps. Today not a nugget of coal is mined in the Rhondda Valley, and the valleys are being extensively "greened." ❏

TRADE AND RESOURCES A strong financial sector brings in more wealth from overseas. Less food is imported today and more grown at home, but only 2 percent of the population is employed in agriculture. In 1973, Britain joined the European Union (E.U.), which accounts for more than half of its trade, but did not join the European Monetary Union when the Euro was launched as the European currency in 1999. That year, the trade gap reached a new record with the strength of sterling and a collapse in demand from countries hit by the global economic crisis.

The U.K. was the sixth richest country in the world in 1950, while in 1980 it was only the 22nd richest. All the same, in the 1990s, with two-thirds of British households owning their homes and two-thirds owning cars, Britons had a higher standard of living than ever before.

The Bank of England, at the heart of the City of London

Pubs are much more than places in which to drink. They are enclaves of laughter and gossip, arenas for playing games, and havens of sympathy in times of trouble. A good pub has its own distinctive atmosphere, complete with its own resident cast of characters.

❏ "When you have lost your inns drown your empty selves, for you will have lost the last of England."—Hilaire Belloc (1870–1953) ❏

Some pubs are dedicated to thoughtful imbibing and peaceful conversation, others to deafening taped music and clattering slot machines. There are venerable half-timbered Tudor hostelries, leaning at an angle and apparently held up as much by the strength of the ale on tap as they are by their massive black timbers. There are broad-fronted Georgian coaching inns, glittering Victorian "gin palaces," and dubious little backstreet taverns. There are pubs with romantic tales to tell of smugglers and highwaymen, rose-wreathed pubs idyllically set by rivers and canals, lobster-potted inns gazing over picturesque fishing harbors and patronized by sailing enthusiasts, while grim-faced pubs accustomed to wind and weather and perched high on remote moors are frequented by ramblers in thick boots and waterproof parkas.

THEN AND NOW Today's neighborhood pub is descended from the local alehouse of Anglo-Saxon and medieval England, an ordinary house whose occupants brewed and sold ale. In the 12th and 13th centuries inns began to open up, providing overnight accommodations for travelers. In recent years, the traditional pub has found a new identity: serving food—"pub grub"—has become more important, and there has been a comeback of

There are town pubs, village pubs, country pubs...and boaty pubs

"real ale," meaning old-fashioned beer, once threatened with extinction by the big commercial brewers. Most pubs have become less aggressively masculine, and women can feel quite comfortable in them.

WHAT'S IN A NAME? Pubs have picture-signs hanging above their doors, illustrating their names—a custom dating from days when few people could read. Some names are derived from heraldry, like the White Hart and the Red Lion. Others are named for royalty, as in the Crown or the King's Head. Other names reflect country life—the Plough or the Fox and Hounds. There are New Inns that are centuries old, and there are strange and enigmatic names: the Pig and Whistle, the Cat and Fiddle. All are part of the richness and variety that keep the British pub a vital institution.

15

Gardens and gardening are a national passion. Whether they possess the tiniest cottage garden or live on the grandest estate, the green-thumbed British have always found opportunities for self-expression and creativity. This selected list of gardens that are open to the public gives you an idea of the scope and diversity of the nation's "backyards."

The British garden dates from Roman times, when every upwardly mobile villa owner aspired to have an atrium with a small garden. Monastic gardens were merely practical affairs for growing food or cultivating herbs and plants for dyes or for medicinal purposes. With the first great houses of the 16th century came the first true pleasure gardens, with their "knots" of herbs and flowers. In the next century the aristocratic classes toured France and Italy and saw the formal creations of Le Nôtre; topiary and water parterres were the rage.

The classical age of English landscaping in the 18th century saw formality rejected in favor of the naturalistic contrivances of Lancelot "Capability" Brown and others, who designed green expanses fringed by woodlands, interrupted by lakes, and punctuated by classical follies. Victorian times saw formal rockeries, ferneries, roseries, and other horticultural extravaganzas back in fashion. Meanwhile the working classes tended small plots in allotment gardens where they grew their own vegetables, and middle-class suburban villas sported lawns and herbaceous borders. In their back gardens, people found a private haven from the outside world.

THE WEST COUNTRY Subtropical species thrive in the gardens of **Tresco Abbey**, on the Isles of Scilly. On the mainland of Cornwall **Glendurgan** (N.T.), **Penjerrick**, and **Trebah** are neighboring subtropical havens; **Trelissick** (N.T.) is noted for rhododendrons and azaleas with color all year round; paths wind down to the waterside with glimpses of Pendennis Castle. At **Trewithen**

magnolias, rhododendrons, and rare shrubs surround a Georgian mansion, while the **Lost Gardens of Heligan** is Europe's largest garden restoration project, begun in 1991 in a neglected Victorian estate. In Wiltshire, **Stourhead** (N.T.) is a splendid example of traditional 18th-century landscaping.

SOUTHERN ENGLAND and London **Kew Gardens** in London is the king of all botanic gardens. The collection of rare specimens from all over the world owes much to the 19th-century botanist Sir Joseph Banks. Don't miss the elegant Palm House and the Princess of Wales Conservatory. **Wisley Garden**, Surrey, was set up in 1904 as experimental gardens for the

Stourhead in Wiltshire, the quintessential landscaped garden

Late spring at Sissinghurst

Royal Horticultural Society: it has many scarce species and an excellent garden center. **Winkworth Arboretum**, Surrey, is a great tree collection, splendid for spring and fall colors. Sussex gardens to head for are **Sheffield Park** (N.T.), with azaleas and rhododendrons backed by a lake, **Nymans Garden** (N.T.), full of romantic vistas, **Wakehurst Place** (N.T.), an outpost of the Royal Botanic Gardens at Kew and of interest year-round, and **Great Dixter**, the manor house garden of the gardening writer David Lloyd. In Kent the gardens of **Hever Castle** are strongly Italian in feel, and those of **Scotney Castle** (N.T.) are of the picturesque-romantic style in a lake and island setting. **Sissinghurst Garden** (N.T.) is the wonderful 1930s creation of Harold Nicholson and Vita Sackville-West.

THE HEART OF ENGLAND Barnsley House, **Hidcote Manor** (N.T.), **Kiftsgate Court**, **Miserden Park**, **Painswick Rococo Garden,** and **Westonbirt Arboretum** are all in the Cotswolds, each offering something different (see panels, pages 118 and 120). **Rousham House**, Oxfordshire, is an example of an 18th-century romantic rural idyll by William Kent.

WALES Powis Castle in Powys is set amid fine 18th-century terraces. At

Bodnant, Conwy is based on five Italianate terraces with the mountains of Snowdonia as a beautiful backdrop.

NORTHERN ENGLAND Chatsworth in Derbyshire is a masterly marriage of parkland, landscaped by Lancelot "Capability" Brown, and gardens full of surprises that owe much to Joseph Paxton, head gardener from 1827 and later designer of Crystal Palace. **Studley Royal** (N.T.), North Yorkshire, is an ultra-romantic creation around Fountains Abbey.

SCOTLAND Culzean Country Park, in South Ayrshire, is landscaped park and woodland. At **Edzell Castle**, in Stirling, is a 17th-century "pleasaunce," while **Branklyn**, near Perth, is a modest-sized, amazingly stocked suburban garden. **Crathes Castle**, in Aberdeenshire, is enchanting and innovative. In the wilds of the Highlands, **Inverewe** is a spectacular oasis in a mild gulf-stream climate.

❏ The National Gardens Scheme is an umbrella organization for gardens throughout Britain. Included are many private gardens whose owners open them to the public just one or two days a year. See the booklet *Gardens of England and Wales.* ❏

The national calendar of events ranges from the local customs of Mayday dancing and Shrove Tuesday pancake-racing to the royal pageantry of Trooping the Colour and the great sports events held at Wembley Stadium, Royal Ascot, and Lord's Cricket Ground. Local tourist information offices stock details of what's on where and when.

PAGEANTRY AND SPECTACLE

Trooping the Colour, which is the celebration of the Queen's official birthday, takes place in June in Horse Guards' Parade in London and shows off the best of royal pageantry. The Lord Mayor's Show in November features the new mayor of the City of London in procession in a gorgeous golden coach.

18

Other spectacles include Cruft's Dog show (March, Birmingham), the International Air Show (September, even-numbered years, Farnborough, Hampshire), and the Chelsea Flower Show (May, London).

The Randwick Wap, a Cotswolds mayoral swearing-in

ARTS FESTIVALS

The major arts festival of the year is the Edinburgh Festival in August/September; other sites include Bath, Brighton, and Glasgow, plus Gloucester, Herefordshire or Worcestershire for the Three Choirs Festival (see page 117) and Llangollen for the International Eisteddfod in Wales (see page 163). The Promenade Concerts ("Proms") at London's Royal Albert Hall take place from July through September, with classical music, old and new, being performed.

SPORTS

Professional soccer matches are held every Saturday between August and April; the F.A. (Football Association) Cup Final in May is the big match. Cricket, the summer game played with bats, balls, and wickets, is subtler than it looks at first sight; try a one-day county game first. The Wimbledon Lawn Tennis Championships are held in London late June to early July. As for horse racing, the Grand National is a notoriously tough steeplechase run at Aintree near Liverpool in April, and the ultra-fashionable Royal Ascot takes place in June. Regattas are rowed at Henley and Fowey, and a round-the-island yacht race takes place at Cowes on the Isle of Wight. In March the University Boat Race (Oxford versus Cambridge) is rowed on the Thames in west London.

Numerous traditional sports get an annual revival: variants of medieval football are played in the streets of St. Columb Major in Cornwall and Ashbourne in Derbyshire, while Cumberland wrestling takes place in the Lake District. In Scotland the summer Highland Games at Braemar and elsewhere feature caber-tossing, mountain races, and pipe bands.

SHOWS AND FETES

County shows have an agricultural emphasis, with livestock and horticultural competitions attracting the nearby farming communities, but also include sports and entertainment.

Village *fêtes* (fairs) are in many ways miniature versions of these, with tombolas (raffles), cake competitions, produce and bric-à-brac stalls, and sometimes sheep-dog trials—essential for anyone wanting to see the real rural Britain.

FOLK AND RELIGIOUS CUSTOMS

The only nationally celebrated event unique to this country is Guy Fawkes Night, on November 5, when fireworks are set off and effigies of Guy Fawkes, the anarchist caught attempting to blow up the Houses of Parliament in 1605, are burned on the top of big bonfires.

Locally, an amazing variety of folk customs are celebrated. Some of the oldest owe their origins to Mayday fertility rites, including maypole dancing around the country and, in Cornwall, the Furry Dance in Helston and the 'Obby 'Oss Festival at Padstow. Elsewhere, you can take your pick from such oddities as oyster-blessing at Whitstable (Kent), a pancake (crêpe) race at Olney (Buckinghamshire), or face-pulling through a horse-collar at Egremont (Cumbria). Church customs include rush-bearing (dating from times when churches needed rushes to cover earthen floors) and, in the Peak District, well-dressing, when wells are decorated with pictures made of flowers, etc.

The 'Obby 'Oss Festival, Padstow

The Industrial Revolution began in Britain, in a phenomenal burst of innovation in the late 18th and 19th centuries. In the new millennium, even as Britain's heavy industrial base continues to decline, museums that explore this aspect of the national heritage are a boom industry—and you don't have to be a fan of rusty sprockets and cogwheels to appreciate and learn from them.

Listed here is a selection of the best museums to visit. You can also see evocative reminders of Britain's industrial past—though they haven't been turned into museums as such—in the textile mill towns of West Yorkshire, the valleys of South Wales, the factory villages of Port Sunlight and Saltaire, and numerous abandoned mining landscapes such as the tin mines of Cornwall and the lead mines of Swaledale. Many of the sites and museums mentioned below are described more fully in the A-Z section of the book.

THE WEST COUNTRY Coldharbour Mill at Cullompton in Devon is an old wool mill that recalls the heyday of the Devon wool industry; the processes of carding, drafting, and spinning are shown, and there are some fine old machines. **Poldark Mine** at Wendron in Cornwall includes an underground tin mine tour, reconstructed cottages, and children's amusements. At **Wheal Martyn**, St. Austell, Cornwall's

still-surviving china clay industry is explained, with a tour around an abandoned site and a view of the moonscape of working pits nearby.

SOUTHERN ENGLAND At **Amberley Chalkpits Museum**, West Sussex, visitors see craftsmen at work in a former chalk pit and lime works. The **Historic Dockyard** in Chatham, Kent, is the world's largest Georgian dockyard. At Hove in East Sussex, the **British Engineerium** evokes the age of steam power, within a Victorian water pumping station.

THE HEART OF ENGLAND The **Black Country Living Museum**, Dudley (West Midlands), is a skillful reconstruction of an industrial Black Country community of yesteryear, with a colliery, redbrick cottages, a canal where you can try "legging" along the tunnel in the time-honored fashion, and an old-style fairground. The **Ironbridge Gorge Museum** (in Shropshire), considered the birthplace of the Industrial Revolution, is the undoubted star of Britain's distinguished industrial museums.

WALES Visit the **Big Pit Museum**, Blaenavon, Torfaen, to get the full experience of going down into a coal mine in the heart of the Welsh valleys. **Sygun Copper Mine** in Beddgelert, Gwynedd, and **Llechwedd Slate Caverns** in Blaenau Ffestiniog, Gwynedd, offer imaginatively conceived tours of the old mines, and the **Welsh Slate Museum**,

The Museum of Iron at Ironbridge Gorge, a World Heritage Site

The Black Country Museum

Llanberis, is an evocative semi-abandoned slate quarry. **The Museum of the Welsh Woollen Industry**, at Drefach Felindre in western Wales, has fabric-making demonstrations, factory trails, and bygone tools and machinery; you can even try your hand at spinning.

NORTHWEST ENGLAND Cromford Mill, in Cromford, Derbyshire, is an exciting monument to Richard Arkwright on the site of his first water-powered cotton mill. In the Potteries area (around Stoke-on-Trent), the **Royal Doulton**, **Wedgwood**, and **Spode** factories are open to visitors. The **Gladstone Pottery Museum** is an authentic Victorian pottery, with demonstrations of traditional methods (numerous Staffordshire pottery factories can also be visited, see page 189). The **Paradise Silk Mill and Museum** in Macclesfield, Cheshire, gives the story of the town's heyday when anyone who was anyone wore Macclesfield silk buttons. **Quarry Bank Mill**, Styal, Cheshire, is an excellent restoration of an 18th-century water-powered cotton mill in a fine verdant setting. Authentically clanking old machines can be seen, and heard, at the **Helmshore Textile**

Museums, in the heartland of the former Lancashire cotton-making country. At **Stott Park Bobbin Mill** in Finsthwaite, Cumbria, former mill workers explain the process of one of the last bobbin mills to be operational in England; it functioned from 1835 until as recently as 1971.

NORTHEAST ENGLAND At **Abbeydale Industrial Hamlet**, Sheffield, South Yorkshire, a courtyard is surrounded by 18th-century workshops where scythes were forged in the River Sheaf. The sense of period and sheer atmosphere are very impressive. The **North of England Open Air Museum**, Beamish, Co. Durham, is a clever evocation of the early 1900s.

SOUTHERN SCOTLAND New Lanark Mills at Lanark, South Lanarkshire, is a remarkably well-preserved factory village with working machinery, a period store and house, and craft workshops; the village has a dramatic setting near waterfalls. At Newtongrange, Midlothian, the **Scottish Mining Museum** has a fine working steam engine used for winding. Ambitious displays cover the lives of the miners, and some of the colliery buildings can be visited.

21

Gladstone Pottery Museum

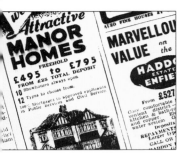

Although it is often taken for granted, the "semi" is a major component of British cityscapes. Rapidly and cheaply built during the 1930s, semidetached houses were laid out in neat rows, avenues, and crescents. Within two decades a large part of Britain's countryside had given way to suburbanization. The semi may never have been chic, but over the years it has adapted well for modern living, and is still going strong today.

Mention the word suburbia in Britain and it is the semi that springs first to mind. The length and breadth of the country, pairs of mirror-image houses under a single roof line the roads that lead into every major town. At first glance, each semi is identical, but closer inspection will reveal certain marks of individuality. For an Englishman's home is his castle, and none more so than his semi.

RISE OF THE SEMI Terraced houses, similar to the American row house, had been the dominant feature of 19th-century popular housing in England and Wales (Scottish cities specialized more in tenements); inexpensive and quick to build, the terrace provided housing for the artisan classes. Wealthier folk aspired to semidetached or detached (separate) properties.

The semidetached was a feature of the urban scene in Victorian and Edwardian times, but it was in the 1930s Depression years that it really came into its own. Labor was low-cost and plentiful, cheap materials readily available. Speculative builders were creating new subdivisions in the verdant fringes of major cities, and improved rail and road links made commuting more feasible. Advertisements promised a rural idyll.

THE BUILDING BOOM With this boom came the mass-produced semi: a square plan, a common pitched roof, one party wall, a front and back garden, often a garage built onto one side. Since only a modest down payment was needed, the semi was available to virtually anyone with a reasonable income. Rustic and fanciful flourishes were added to the basic design: leaded windows, gables sporting Tudor-style half-timbering, tile-covered walls, stained-glass windows, sunrise motifs. Interior plans varied little: three or four bedrooms and a bathroom, a living room and a small kitchen (in the new labor-saving age of convenience foods, after all, who needed a big kitchen?). "Three-piece suites" (a sofa for the children, an armchair for each parent) in the living room exemplified Edwardian solidity.

And more than half a century later, the semi has shown itself readily adaptable, with new porches, and extra rooms over the garage being frequent alterations.

A typical semi, in Basingstoke

22

Britain was

England's "green and pleasant land" is not a natural phenomenon, but the product of 200 generations of hard work. To oversimplify matters, imagine Britain's underlying geology as dividing the country into a highland zone in the north and west, including Scotland, the Pennines, the Lake District, and Wales, and a lowland zone in the south and east. No matter what the geology, however, hardly any part of the landscape is unaltered by human hand.

The first people to make a mark on the landscape were the mesolithic people, nomadic hunters who burned forests and cleared large areas of land in order to gather herds of wild animals together. This lifestyle gradually became more settled over the years as neolithic peoples introduced crops, farming, and domesticated animals. In order to make the necessary cropland and pasture for their cattle, sheep, and pigs, they made permanent clearings, creating landscapes that were not unlike those we see today, although the actual use of the land was substantially different. Generally, small groups lived in hamlets of a few huts surrounded by an earth bank or a wooden palisade (a tall fence), with fields outside. These were the forerunners of subsequent centuries of village life.

A well-preserved Roman road on Wheeldale in the North York Moors

❑ The stone axes with which neolithic farmers cleared the land were far more effective implements than is generally realized. Experiments indicate that one man working alone could have cleared a half acre a week. ❑

THE EARLIEST COMMUNITIES Over many centuries, villages grew up where there was fertile soil and an adequate water supply. The "typical" English village of houses clustered around a village green and duck pond is only one of several types (in Wales and Scotland the green is not a common feature). Other villages are stretched out along a road or have more than one center or sprawl about in a congenial muddle.

Each village was a service center for the surrounding countryside, providing a church, a drinking house, craftsmen, a market for produce. The more successful ones usually had some geographical advantage—they were located at a ford or an important road junction, for instance—and they grew into towns. Other towns were founded by landowners looking for profit.

TRACKS AND ROADS The earliest roads were created by farmers and their livestock, and many of today's country lanes, lying deep between high banks, may be thousands of years old. Trade also had its part to play, and a network of prehistoric "high roads" can still be traced.

❏ Britain's human history stretches back over a vast period of time to the arrival of manlike beings over 300,000 years ago. It is conventionally divided into the periods shown here, but the dates should be taken only as extremely rough approximations.

Period	Dates	Outstanding example
Paleolithic (Old Stone Age)	to 12000 BC	
Mesolithic (Middle Stone Age)	12000–4500 BC	
Neolithic (New Stone Age)	4500–2500 BC	Belas Knap tomb
Bronze Age	2500–750 BC	Stonehenge
Iron Age	from 750 BC	Maiden Castle hill fort
Roman invasion of Britain	AD 43	Roman Baths, Bath ❏

Oak woodlands near Butts Lawn in Hampshire's ancient New Forest

25

The Romans introduced the first centrally planned road network—dig a few feet beneath a long, straight stretch of today's highway and you'll find Roman road. The Roman network sufficed until a new era of road-building began in the 1700s.

❏ "The great charm ... of English scenery is the moral feeling that seems to pervade it. It is associated in the mind with ideas of order, of quiet, of sober well-established principles, hoary usage and reverend custom. Everything seems to be the growth of ages of reverend and peaceful existence."
—Washington Irving (1820) ❏

FOREST AND WOODLANDS As well as clearing forest for agriculture, neolithic people managed woodlands very successfully. Coppicing is a good example: the tree is cut down to ground level so that several shoots grow up to replace the lost one. Over several years this produces a crop of poles of just the right size for whatever use the woodsman decides upon. And coppiced trees live on almost indefinitely so long as coppicing continues. It is a perfect self-regenerating system. After World War II, men were still using and refining skills such as these, first learned over 4,000 years ago.

Today, however, most woodlands are unmanaged since management is seen as expensive. Wildlife actually suffers as a result: flowers are shaded out, butterflies lose their habitat.

LANDSCAPE TODAY Despite the changes of the 20th century, the British landscape presents a remarkable historical tableau. Early settlers slashed and burned down the primeval forests, exhausting the soil and leaving moorlands that still cover much of upland Britain. Agricultural and much common land was subject to enclosure from medieval times to the 19th century; the old "open field" system, where several farmers worked strips within a large single field, was abandoned in favor of smaller enclosures. During that period the hedges (now themselves being removed in many areas) and drystone walls that dominate so much of the lowlands today changed the face of the country.

Gaunt and gray in the British countryside, the shells and ruins of formidable medieval strongholds still defy time and weather. They were sited at strategic points—to control a river crossing, a hill pass, or a harbor, for example. Many of them saw little or no action, which is testimony to their effectiveness. They were not built to provoke attack, but to deter it.

26

The Norman Conquest of England made 1066 one of the key dates of British history. The triumphant William the Conqueror—known in his own time, though not to his face, as William the Bastard—parceled England out among his Norman, French, Breton, and Flemish followers. The more important built castles to secure their grip on their new estates, and by 1100 there were some 500 of these strongholds in England. The early ones consisted of a mound of earth (the motte), built by conscript labor, with a yard (the bailey) around its base, enclosed by an earth rampart and ditch. Wooden buildings housed the castle's lord, his family, and his small private army. The local villagers could take refuge in the bailey in time of danger.

BASTIONS OF STONE Many of these primitive fortresses were soon replaced by daunting strongholds built of stone. A hulking keep was erected on the mound, its walls as

Stark and strong, Corfe Castle in Dorset was built by the Normans

much as 100 feet high and 20 feet thick at the base, pierced by tiny windows through which archers and crossbowmen could fire. The living quarters were in the keep, with the ground floor used for storage and dungeons. Outer walls kept besiegers at a distance, and around them might be a water-filled moat crossed by a drawbridge. Castles became ever more elaborate as time went by. The

> ❏ "The rich man in his castle,
>   The poor man at his gate,
> God made them high and lowly,
>   And ordered their estate."
> —19th-century hymn ❏

Tower of London, originally built for William the Conqueror himself, is a particularly impressive specimen.
   In Wales, both Norman and native warlords built themselves castles. When Edward I of England conquered the country, a chain of powerful fortresses that could be supplied by sea cemented his hold. **Caernarfon**, **Harlech**, **Conwy**, and **Beaumaris** castles still testify to the skill of his military engineer, James of St. George. Scotland, where central authority was never as strong, bristles with ferocious and romantic strongholds, led by **Edinburgh** and **Stirling**, high on their lofty crags.

THE MANORIAL ESTATE Castles were extremely costly and only the richest nobles could afford them. In medieval England the basic landholding unit was the manor, ruled by its lord, who lived in the large manor house. Often a manor was a village with its surrounding countryside, but some manors

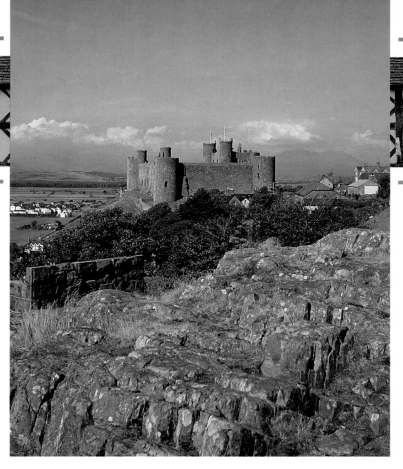

*Harlech Castle, impregnable monument
to King Edward I*

contained more than one village,
while others covered only part of
one. The villagers cultivated the land,
while the lord's function was to protect them and to keep order. Above
the lord, in what is now called the
"**feudal system**," a chain of greater
lords led up to the king himself, each
link in the chain owing support to
the one above it and protection to
the one below.

The lord's manor house was at first
just a bigger version of the wood-
and-mud hovels of his villagers. By
the 13th century, though, manor
houses were being built of stone, and
the fortified manor house appeared
—cheaper and more comfortable
than a castle, but defensible. They
centered on one main room, the hall,
where the household ate and slept,
while the dogs gnawed bones on the
straw- or rush-covered floor and
smoke from a central hearth drifted
out through a hole in the roof.

Over the centuries the medieval
lord of the manor became the less
powerful, though still dominant,
country squire. Just as the power of
kings has ebbed away, so the title of
lord of the manor has become a
picturesque but empty honor.

> ❏ Perhaps England's best
> example of a fortified manor
> house is Stokesay Castle, near
> Shrewsbury in Shropshire (see
> page 124), which has preserved
> its medieval atmosphere to a
> remarkable degree. ❏

At the same time as being beautiful and satisfying to the senses, churches were originally built as earthly houses for God; symbols of the God-given order of the world and the true purpose of human life. Through the centuries, generations of Christians have worshipped in them, joined in the community's spiritual life, been baptized and married and finally, after life's fitful fever, have been laid to rest in eternal peace in the churchyard.

From the humblest parish church to the most sumptuous cathedral, in country and town alike, churches are an essential element of the British scene. Almost all of them have been altered, enlarged, or rebuilt many times over.

STYLES OF ARCHITECTURE A few **Anglo-Saxon** churches are still standing. Small and plain, they are the oldest English ecclesiastical buildings to survive. The **Normans** built on an altogether more massive and powerful scale, notably with thick round columns supporting the roof and round arches above small doors and windows.

Movingly simple, the Saxon church at Greensted is built of split logs

The **Gothic** style, which arrived in Britain in the 12th century, was lighter, airier, more slender, more uplifting to the spirit. Its earliest phases, Early English and the more ornate Decorated, introduced the pointed arch, the flying buttress, and the tall spire that directed worshippers' eyes and thoughts heavenward. These churches were alive with elaborate decoration, carvings in wood and stone, stained-glass windows, statues, and wall paintings—the religious textbooks of an age that could not read. (Much of this decoration, unfortunately, was destroyed or painted over by the Puritans when they took over the government in the 17th century.) In the 14th century came the Perpendicular style, named after the strong vertical lines that carry the eye up to the roof. Tall, soaring shafts support a web of fan-vaulting and enormous windows of the most delicate tracery, while graceful towers rise to a riot of pinnacles. The style reached its apogee in the amazing stone cobweb of **King's College Chapel**, Cambridge. In the 19th century the values of medieval architecture were upheld by such architects as Augustus Pugin in the form of the Gothic Revival style.

THE MONASTIC MOVEMENT Among the most haunting legacies that the Middle Ages left to Britain are the now ruined monasteries—**Fountains**, **Rievaulx**, **Glastonbury**, **Tintern**, and many more. Medieval abbeys and priories ran a virtual welfare system for the poor, treated the sick, kept scholarship and art alive, and gave hospitality to travelers, but their primary function was as centers of prayer and worship. With eight services a day, from matins before dawn to vespers at sunset and compline at bedtime, the monks paid humankind's tribute of devotion to God.

The church was always the biggest and finest building in a monastery, usually standing at one side of a quadrangle. Around the other sides were the domestic buildings—the refectory for meals, the kitchen, the dormitory, the infirmary. The monks themselves took vows of poverty, but monasteries accumulated large estates, ran farms, and raised sheep.

The soaring ruins of Tintern Abbey

Fountains Abbey in Yorkshire, for example, was the North of England's biggest producer of wool.

The **Reformation** of the 16th century created the Church of England as a separate body, no longer owing allegiance to the Pope, and in the 1530s the monasteries were all closed down (the church, however, was often retained by the community as a parish church). Most of the monastic land ended up in the hands of the aristocracy and the country gentry, not only enriching them but making it quite certain that the Dissolution of the Monasteries would never be reversed. Today empty, roofless shells stand quietly where generations of monks once lived and prayed.

❏ Guidebooks often use the following terms for styles of church architecture in Britain. The dates should be considered as rough indications only.

Style	Dates	Outstanding example
Saxon	650–1066	St. Laurence's, Bradford on Avon
Norman (or Romanesque)	1066–1190	Durham Cathedral
Gothic: Early English	1190–1275	Salisbury Cathedral
Decorated	1275–1375	Exeter Cathedral
Perpendicular	1375–1485	King's College Chapel, Cambridge
Classical	17th–18th centuries	St. Paul's Cathedral, London
Gothic Revival	early 19th century	All Saints, Margaret Street, London W1
Victorian	1837–1901	St. Mary's Cathedral, Edinburgh ❏

A long era of peace on British soil since the 1500s has left Britain virtually without equal in the number of grand historic houses open for visitors to enjoy. They're packed from floor to ceiling with treasures of art and triumphs of decoration—paintings, sculptures, furniture, carpets, porcelain, books, clocks. Surrounded by exquisite gardens and sumptuously land-scaped parks, they testify to five centuries of wealth, taste, and social prominence.

30

Britain retains a notable number of timber-framed houses dating from medieval times, though most have been adapted and precise dating is difficult; more important buildings were often constructed in stone. Grander medieval examples include **Haddon Hall** in Derbyshire and **Ightham Mote** in Kent.

Tudor Chenies Manor House, near Amersham in Buckinghamshire

THE VERNACULAR The houses of the ordinary people in particular, but also their agricultural and industrial buildings—were constructed following local traditions and in whatever material was readily at hand, be it stone, flint, or cob, thatch, slate, or pantile.

THE ELIZABETHAN AGE The Tudor era was one of peace and prosperity in which the rich Englishman's home no longer needed to be a fortified castle. The wealthy built ostentatious

houses, Cardinal Wolsey and Henry VIII leading the way with the huge brick palace of **Hampton Court**. Capacious bay windows gazed out upon the countryside, while the fan-tastically elaborate chimneystacks of grand houses of the 16th and 17th centuries joined the gables, turrets, and balustrades that enlivened the roofline to impress the neighbors with the owner's wealth.

Much Tudor building was in brick, but in areas where there was plenty of lumber—as in the Southeast and the western Midlands—houses were half-timbered, with rectangular wooden frames enclosing panels of whitewashed plaster or brick. The most lavish examples, like **Little Moreton Hall** in Cheshire, are a riot of zebra-striped patterns.

THE CLASSICAL IDEAL Outside these houses, a formal symmetrical garden was evidence of the Renaissance enthusiasm for classical Greek and Roman ideals. The first really famous British architects—**Inigo Jones** and **Sir Christopher Wren** in the 17th century—were influenced by classi-cal architecture. Inigo Jones's Queen's House (1616–1635) in Greenwich was the first house in Britain to be designed on classical principles. The typical house of Queen Anne's reign was a simple, symmetri-cal red-brick mansion with large sash windows and a four-sided roof behind a parapet. As the 18th century unfolded, **Sir John Vanbrugh** piled the colossal baroque palaces of **Castle Howard** and **Blenheim** upon the groaning earth, with their splendid domes and porticoes. Most of the English upper class, however, preferred the restrained elegance of the Palladian style of mansion, with its straight lines and pleasing proportions, its classical pillars and pediments. Around the house would stretch a noble park, where smooth lawns escorted the eye to carefully positioned groups of trees, an artificial lake, a bridge, and a temple, such as William Kent's **Holkham Hall**, Norfolk. Horace Walpole's **Strawberry Hill** was play-fully picturesque "Gothick" style.

GEORGIAN ELEGANCE The same style, imposing a calm order upon unruly Nature, created some of Britain's most satisfying townscapes in Bath, London, Edinburgh, and other cities. From the 1760s the interiors of Georgian houses were opulently enriched by the genius of **Robert Adam** and his many imitators, who introduced delicate ornamentation into mansions like **Syon House** in Middlesex, in rooms never intended for living in, but for entertaining. In the early 19th-century Regency period John Nash created the flamboyant **Royal Pavilion** in Brighton and the stucco row houses around **Regent's Park.** His contemporary John Soane adopted a highly original style, exemplified by **Sir John Soane's Museum** in London.

VICTORIAN EXUBERANCE A powerful enthusiasm for medieval Gothic Christian architecture gave many Victorian houses an ecclesiastical

Kiftsgate Court, Gloucestershire: a Georgian house in a lovely garden

❏ All through the 19th century the Gothic and the classical styles vied for supremacy. In Yorkshire, for instance, the city fathers of Leeds built a magnificent classical temple as their town hall, while rival Bradford erected a Gothic town hall of mammoth proportions. ❏

look, with turrets, pointed windows, and stained glass, while Scots magnates built themselves mock baronial palaces. Victorian architects and their patrons took the whole past as their province. They adopted whatever architectural style took their fancy and blended characteristics from different styles to romantic and sometimes wildly excessive effect. In the early 1900s **Richard Norman Shaw** introduced stylized "vernacular," or countryside, styles (as at Cragside, Northumberland), and **Sir Edwin Lutyens** revived the classical style (as at Great Maytham, Kent).

CHANGING IDEALS A fierce reaction against Victorian and Edwardian "pastiche" followed in the 20th century as the modern movement in architecture adopted an austere simplicity of straight lines and concrete, often criticized as concrete monstrosities and provoking a more varied approach from the 1980s on, ranging from neo-classical to mock-vernacular. Yet some high-rise blocks are coming back into fashion: Erno Goldfinger's once-hated and much-vandalized 31-story **Trellick Tower** (1972) in west London is now loved by many residents, and acclaimed a masterpiece.

In 1066 William the Conqueror, the Duke of Normandy, invaded from France and became the hugely influential William I of England. The last medieval king was Richard III, who wrested power from Edward V whom he declared illegitimate. Richard was killed at the Battle of Bosworth (1485), and Henry Tudor seized the throne to become Henry VII.

Britain's modern history begins in 1485, when the marriage of **Henry VII** of Lancaster to Elizabeth of York ended the 30-year Wars of the Roses—an inheritance dispute between the dukes of Lancaster and York. His son, **Henry VIII**, with a massive frame and small eyes so famously depicted in the Holbein portrait, is best known for his six wives. Two he divorced—breaking from the Catholic Church in Rome in the process—and two he executed, one died in childbirth, and the sixth outlived him.

ELIZABETH TUDOR It was typical of Henry's daughter **Elizabeth I** that when a deputation arrived at Hatfield House in Hertfordshire in 1558 to tell her she was queen, the 25-year-old princess was found sitting under an oak tree demurely reading a book. She always had a genius for public relations. A consummate politician, with her father's physical and intellectual vigor combined with feminine grace

Henry VIII, with Anne of Cleves

Elizabeth I, "Virgin Queen"

❑ "I know I have the body of a weak and feeble woman, but I have the heart and stomach of a king, and of a king of England too."—Queen Elizabeth I, speech to the troops on the approach of the Armada, 1588 ❑

and charm, she successfully steered her country safely through 44 dangerous years.

THE STUARTS Scotland, meanwhile, had seen a long succession of kings of the Stuart dynasty, who since 1371 had struggled to impose their authority on their rebellious aristocracy. The beautiful **Mary, Queen of Scots** was forced to abdicate in 1567. She escaped to England, where she was politely kept prisoner for 20 years until execution in 1587.

Her son, **James VI of Scotland**, succeeded the childless Elizabeth I in 1603 as **James I of England**. The

32

A Van Dyck portrait of Charles I

house of Stuart fared little better in England than in Scotland. **Charles I**, attempting to uphold royal power against Parliament, was defeated by the Puritans under **Oliver Cromwell** in the **Civil War** and executed in London in 1649. **Charles II** was restored to the throne in 1660, after an interregnum of republican rule that proved deeply unpopular. He is remembered for his charm, his cynicism, and his sex life. His brother was **James II**, who had a brief anti-Protestant reign before fleeing the throne in 1688; Parliament offered the crown, in the bloodless "Glorious Revolution," to the Dutch prince **William of Orange**, who reigned jointly with his wife **Mary**, James's daughter. Queen Anne was the last Stuart ruler.

THE HANOVERIANS On Anne's death in 1714, the Elector of Hanover became king as **George I**. Although he was a German who could not speak a word of English, as a Protestant he was preferred to the Stuart claimants, who made a dashing but unsuccessful last bid for the lost throne in 1745, led by Prince Charles Edward, sentimentally known as **Bonnie Prince Charlie**.

George III, who was much liked for his hearty geniality, was king when the American colonies broke away to become an independent nation. His son, ultimately **George IV**, acted as regent during George III's mental illness and became influential in fashion, architecture and the arts, while his grand-daughter, **Queen Victoria**, enjoyed the longest reign of any British sovereign—64 years from 1837 to 1901. Clad invariably in black after the death of her beloved Prince Consort, Albert, in 1861, the widowed queen was ruler of the largest empire in history.

THE HOUSE OF WINDSOR Victoria's grandson, **George V**, sensitive during World War I about the dynasty's German connections, decided to change his family's name (Saxe-Coburg-Gotha) to the House of Windsor. His son **Edward VIII** caused an international scandal by abdicating within months of coming to the throne in 1936, following his marriage to the American divorcée Wallis Simpson, leaving his shy and unprepared brother to rule as **George VI** throughout World War II. Since 1952, **Queen Elizabeth II** has reigned, but the future of the monarchy is constantly under debate.

The fact that Britain is an island has formed and colored its history and character. Britain's greatness was built on seaborne trade, and the British Empire rested on the Royal Navy's command of the sea, celebrated in popular patriotic songs from Rule Britannia *to the Gilbert and Sullivan parody* HMS Pinafore. *The sea and seafaring are in Britain's blood.*

Nelson's flagship, H.M.S. Victory

34

The sea has played contradictory roles in British history, as both barrier and bridge. Britannia has always needed her "towers along the steep"—coastal fortifications against attack by sea. They can be seen bristling along England's southern and southeastern shoreline, ranging from Roman forts of the Saxon Shore to medieval and Tudor castles, 19th-century Martello towers and Palmerston forts against the French, and World War II defenses.

OVERSEAS TRADING At the same time, while the sea has served Britain as a defensive moat, it has also been by sea that people, ideas, and trade have moved between Britain and the rest of the world. Far back in prehistoric times, ships from the Mediterranean came to Cornwall for

tin. In Roman days, Britain exported slaves, oysters, and hunting dogs to the Continent and imported wine.

The great medieval "wool churches" of England stand as testimony to the wealth generated by the export trade in wool and cloth. It remained a major factor in the economy into the 16th century, when merchants forged thriving trade links with the world beyond Europe—Asia, Africa, and the Americas. The piratical **Sir Francis Drake** sailed away in 1578 in a cockleshell of a ship, which was only the second to circumnavigate the globe. Gleefully plundering Spanish possessions on the way, he returned in 1580 with loot estimated at $37½ million in today's money.

IN COMMAND OF THE SEAS The British navy can trace its history back to **Alfred the Great** in the 9th century; he was the first English king to lead his own squadron in battle, against the Danes. In medieval times, ships and crews were supplied for the royal fleet by the **Cinque Ports** of southeast England—Dover, Sandwich, Hythe, New Romney, and Hastings. The Tudor and Stuart kings built up a more effective and powerful force. Along with two other formidable Elizabethan seadogs, Hawkins and Frobisher, Drake

❏ "Britannia needs no bulwarks,
No towers along the steep;
Her march is o'er the mountain
    waves,
Her home is on the deep."
—Thomas Campbell,
"Ye Mariners of England"
(1800–1801) ❏

helped defeat the ponderous Spanish Armada in 1588.

Between 1700 and 1780 Britain's foreign trade almost doubled. The port of Bristol took a leading part in the slave trade, which shipped millions of Africans to the American plantations. Meanwhile, Britain became the world's leading colonial power in a struggle against the French in which command of the sea was of paramount importance. The French were driven from India and North America, and the British built up the empire on which the sun never set. The "wooden walls"—the Royal Navy's implacable three-deckers—kept **Napoleon** at arm's length. "I do not say they cannot come," said Admiral Lord St. Vincent of the French invasion barges, "I only say they cannot come by sea."

ILLUSTRIOUS NAMES The navy was the guardian of British liberty, and a succession of naval heroes etched their names on the British conscious-ness—Anson, Rodney, Hood, Howe, St. Vincent, Collingwood, Cochrane. The most admired and loved of them all was **Horatio Nelson**, killed at the Battle of Trafalgar in 1805 as the HMS *Victory* bore down upon the foe. The great ship is lovingly preserved in Portsmouth.

A martello tower on the south coast, one of many built to counter the threat of Napoleonic invasion

35

❏ A willing foe and sea room. —The Royal Navy's Friday night toast ❏

The British Empire eventually covered a quarter of the land surface of the globe, stretching across the world's heaving waters from Canada to India, Australia, New Zealand, as well as remote islands in the Pacific. It could not be sustained however, and World War II demonstrated that command of the sea had eventually passed from Britain to the mightier United States.

Many places in Britain are linked with famous writers and their work. The village of Chawton in Hampshire shelters the modest house where Jane Austen wrote, hiding her papers when any of the household came in. Nearby at Selborne is the home of Gilbert White, the nature writer. Each year, Rochester in Kent honors Charles Dickens, who lived nearby. You can explore George Bernard Shaw's home at Ayot St. Lawrence in Hertfordshire, as well as Lord Byron's and D.H. Lawrence's houses near Nottingham, Rudyard Kipling's at Bateman's in Sussex, and Samuel Johnson's in Lichfield and London.

36

No writer in English is more admired than **William Shakespeare**, and his birthplace town of Stratford-upon-Avon in Warwickshire is the most visited British tourist destination outside London. The Bard's birthplace attracts more than half a million visitors a year.

LITERARY SHRINES In West Yorkshire the once grim little town of Haworth is thronged with pilgrims to the parsonage where **Charlotte**, **Emily**, and **Anne Brontë** and their brother **Branwell** lived. Out on the desolate moorland is the ruined farmhouse that may have been the original *Wuthering Heights*.

The Lake District also draws literary pilgrims, to **William Wordsworth**'s homes at Dove Cottage and Rydal Mount and the Lakeland scenes which inspired his poetry. **John Ruskin**, the Victorian art critic and social reformer, owned a house with a magical view over Coniston Water. **Beatrix Potter** also lived at Near Sawrey.

At Laugharne in South Wales the most famous Welsh poet of the 20th century, **Dylan Thomas**, is fondly remembered at **his studio**, the Boathouse. Scotland's national poet, **Robert Burns**, is cherished at the humble cottage where he was born in the outskirts of Ayr, and also in Dumfries, where he spent his last years. **Sir Walter Scott**'s engaging collection of historical curios—Rob Roy's sword, a lock of the Young Pretender's hair, and so on—can be admired at Abbotsford, his home in his beloved Borders, while at Kirriemuir is the birthplace of **Sir James Barrie**, author of *Peter Pan*.

John Bunyan's iron violin is on show in the Bedford museum devoted to the author of *Pilgrim's Progress*. At Coxwold in North Yorkshire is the house where **Laurence Sterne** wrote *Tristram Shandy*, and **Milton** completed *Paradise Lost* in a cottage at Chalfont St. Giles in Buckinghamshire.

> ❑ Earth has not anything to show more fair:
> Dull would he be of soul who could pass by
> A sight so touching in its majesty:
> This City now doth like a garment wear
> The beauty of the morning; silent, bare,
> Ships, towers, domes, theatres, and temples lie
> Open unto the fields, and to the sky;
> All bright and glittering in the smokeless air.
> —William Wordsworth (1770–1850),
> *Upon Westminster Bridge* ❑

RESTING PLACES Interesting literary connections can frequently be found in churchyards. **T.S. Eliot** is buried at East Coker in Somerset, **John Buchan** at Elsfield near Oxford. The country churchyard of **Thomas Gray**'s famous *Elegy* can be found at Stoke Poges in Buckinghamshire. The memory of the evil Count Dracula, **Bram Stoker**'s creation, vampirishly haunts the Yorkshire graveyard of Whitby. In London, Westminster Abbey's south transept is affectionately known as **Poets' Corner** because Chaucer, Edmund Spenser, Lord Tennyson, Robert Browning, and many other famous poets are buried or have memorials there. Monuments to Shakespeare, Milton, Wordsworth, Burns, Keats, and Shelley cluster close to memorials to Lord Byron, T.S. Eliot, W.H. Auden and Dylan Thomas.

> ❏ The first fire since the
>   summer is lit, and is smoking
>   into the room;
> The sun-rays spread it through,
>   like woof-lines in a loom.
> Sparrows spurt from the hedge,
>   whom misgivings appal
> That winter did not leave last
>   year for ever, after all.
> —Thomas Hardy (1840–1928),
> *Shortening Days at the
> Homestead* ❏

Sometimes it is the characters more than the author who cast the spell. It is hardly possible to explore Exmoor without recalling Lorna Doone, Cornwall without thinking of the heroes and heroines of **Daphne du Maurier** and **Winston Graham** or Dartmoor without memories of Sherlock Holmes, Doctor Watson and the hound of the Baskervilles.

37

Thomas Hardy's statue at the end of the high street in Dorchester, the "Casterbridge" of his novels

> ❏ The curfew tolls the knell of
>   parting day,
> The lowing herd winds slowly
>   o'er the lea,
> The ploughman homeward plods
>   his weary way,
> And leaves the world to
>   darkness and to me.
> —Thomas Gray (1716–1771),
> *Elegy in a Country Churchyard* ❏

" ...MY COUNTRY STILL" Some writers are associated with a whole area of countryside, seen through their eyes and peopled with their own characters. **Thomas Hardy** Country extends over much of Dorset, and the museum in Dorchester has an excellent Hardy collection. The "blue remembered hills" of Shropshire are inseparably linked with the melancholic poetry of **A.E. Housman**.

Tennyson is particularly cherished in his native county of Lincolnshire, and there is a noble statue of him outside Lincoln Cathedral. The center of the **George Eliot** industry is Nuneaton in Warwickshire; the southern part of Tyne and Wear now calls itself **Catherine Cookson** Country in homage to the best-selling romantic novelist.

Britain's most characteristic contribution to Western art lies in a long tradition of landscape painting, which inspired such artists as Gainsborough, Constable, and Turner. It is this tradition which created the British idea of what the landscape looks like—or at least of what it ideally ought to look like. Visitors enjoying the British countryside today still tend to see it through the eyes of the great painters of the past.

The British tradition of landscape painting was founded by **Richard Wilson**, who was born in Wales in 1714 and was deeply impressed by the work of the French painter Claude Lorraine. Unappreciated and poverty-stricken, he struggled to convince the British eye that wild scenery could be beautiful; his paintings of his native Welsh mountains looming above limpid lakes have a classic grandeur and serenity.

THE GREAT NAMES Far more successful financially was **Thomas Gainsborough**, who originally came from Suffolk. He made his money as a fashionable portrait painter in Bath and London, but his true passion was for landscapes—often generalized and idyllic, rather than depicting a particular place. The great Victorian art critic John Ruskin said of him: "His touch was as light as the sweep of a cloud and swift as the flash of a sunbeam."

John Constable, arriving on the scene 50 years later, came from the Suffolk–Essex border, and his paintings of hayfields, church towers, river scenes, carthorses, and wagons have remained hugely popular ever since. Salisbury Cathedral, Hampstead Heath and the South Coast were also favorite subjects of his. He believed in the most minute study of Nature, to render, as he said, "light—dews—breezes—bloom—and freshness" with loving accuracy, and he broke free of the formal Claude-inspired landscape.

Constable's contemporary, the prodigious **Joseph Mallord William Turner**, traveled all over Britain, painting romantic landscapes, castles, cathedrals, and great houses. He followed in Richard Wilson's footsteps in Wales, painted extensively at Petworth in Sussex and in the Thames Valley, and rejoiced in the scenery of the Lake District and Wharfedale in Yorkshire. As he grew increasingly fascinated by effects of light, his paintings of Norham Castle in Northumberland depict the ruined fortress and the grazing cattle almost disappearing into abstraction in the glowing sunlit mist.

❑ Britain's country houses and London's National Portrait Gallery harbor a rich legacy of portraitists. Foreign artists were patronized in earlier times: **Holbein** painted Henry VIII and his court, and **van Dyck** depicted Charles I. In the 18th century the English artists **Sir Joshua Reynolds** and **George Romney** achieved much success. **Sir William Hogarth** created portraits as well as moralizing commentaries such as *The Rake's Progress*. ❑

PLACES OF INSPIRATION Other painters drawn to the Lake District were **Philippe de Loutherburg** and **Joseph Wright**. **L. S. Lowry** painted Lake District scenes, too, though he is better known for his northern industrial townscapes. Over the centuries, the Thames at London has inspired many foreign artists, including **Canaletto**, **Whistler** and **Monet**.

Flatford Mill in Suffolk, still recognizable from Constable's paintings

The young J.M.W. Turner

Some areas have inspired groups of artists, like the **Norwich School** of painters in the early 19th century. **Bristol**'s school of artists was dominated by **Francis Danby** in the 1820s. The **Newlyn School** of artists, based in Cornwall's fishing port, was led by **Stanhope Forbes** from the 1880s, while **St. Ives** in Cornwall was a base for **Barbara Hepworth**, **Ben Nicholson**, and the potter **Bernard Leach**.

Mystical painter **Samuel Palmer** settled at Shoreham, Kent in the 1820s to explore his "Valley of Vision." **John Singer Sargent** painted Worcestershire landscapes in the 1880s, **Graham Sutherland** painted in Pembrokeshire pre and post World War II. **Cookham**, Berkshire owes its fame to the works of **Sir Stanley Spencer**.

❑ The Pre-Raphaelite Brotherhood of 19th-century English artists painted religious and moralistic scenes, steeped in romantic medievalism and brilliantly hued. Leading figures included **Burne-Jones**, **Rossetti** and **Millais**. London's Tate Gallery and the Birmingham Museum and Art Gallery have superb collections. ❑

39

Crowded, noisy, dirty, and packed with life, Manchester was the archetype of the new cities created in Britain by the Industrial Revolution. Instead of a skyline of church spires, hundreds of factory chimneys belched out smoke and fumes. Though horrified by the city's abominable slums and its turbid rivers crawling with filth, many visitors saw Manchester as the symbol of a dawning new age of intense creativity and vitality.

40

The Industrial Revolution was revolutionary not so much in its speed, but in its consequences. The century between 1750 and 1850 ushered in the machine age of factories, mass production and the assembly line, the industrial town and the industrial working class. Why it should all have started in Britain is a disputed question, but the country had certain obvious advantages: ample resources of coal and iron, and a growing empire overseas that provided a captive market for British-made products.

THE TEXTILE INDUSTRY The industries most affected in the early stages were textiles, iron and steel, coal mining and pottery. In textiles, a succession of inventions made it possible to increase output while using less human energy. This transformed the making of cloth from a small-scale operation, carried on by skilled workmen and their families at home, to large-scale production in factories where unskilled workers, many of them women and children, toiled as acolytes of the insatiable machines. In 1765 **James Hargreaves** patented the "Spinning Jenny"—named after his wife—which could spin several threads simultaneously. Four years later a formidable Lancashireman named **Richard Arkwright**, the first great industrial tycoon, patented a spinning frame powered by water. He built a cotton mill and company town at Cromford in the beautiful Derbyshire valley of the Derwent, where his workers labored in 12-hour shifts as the machines clattered on day and night.

Titus Salt's vast 1853 mill and his model village at Saltaire, Bradford

❏ "And if here man has made of the very daylight an infamy, he can boast that he adds to the darkest night the weird beauty of fire and flame-tinted cloud. From roof and hill you may see on every side furnace calling furnace with fiery tongues and wreathing messages of smoke."
—Arnold Bennett, *The Potteries* (1898) ❏

THE POWER OF STEAM Arkwright's machinery was powered by water, but in 1779 **Samuel Crompton** invented the so-called mule, a spinning machine that could be powered either by water or steam. Steam was the driving force of the Industrial Revolution, and the most important figure in its development, the Scottish inventor **James Watt**, patented the first modern steam engine in 1769. Steam was used to drive all kinds of machinery in factories and mines, and was later to propel locomotives and ships, as a transportation revolution developed in the 19th century.

❏ "Since the introduction of inanimate mechanism into British manufactories, man, with few exceptions, has been treated as a secondary and inferior machine."
—Robert Owen, *A New View of Society* (1813) ❏

COAL AND IRON Steam required coal. Britain's coal production doubled between 1750 and 1800, and then grew by 20 times by the end of the 19th century. **Abraham Darby** initiated the mass production of iron ore at Ironbridge, and new industrial regions grew up close to the principal coalfields in the **Midlands**, the **North of England**, Scotland's **Clydeside**, and **South Wales**. The flow of coal from the valleys turned sleepy little fishing villages like Cardiff, Barry, and Swansea into busy, blackened ports. At the entrance to the Great Exhibition of

1851 in London's Hyde Park, there stood, appropriately, a towering 24-ton block of coal.

Towns like Manchester, Birmingham, Glasgow, Leeds, Bradford, and Sheffield covered their surrounding countryside with row upon row of back-to-back workers' housing. Many a lush valley became an inferno of blast furnaces, slag heaps, and "satanic mills". A new Iron Age introduced iron buildings, iron machines, iron bridges, iron boats, even iron tombstones—as well as the iron regimentation of the assembly line.

Victorian Britain was "the workshop of the world," but other countries soon and began to overtake it, notably Germany and the United States. In the 1880s Britain enjoyed 37 percent of the world's trade in manufactured goods, but by 1913 the figure was down to 25 percent. A new phase of the Industrial Revolution had opened, based on steel, chemicals, and electricity, and Britain was unable to keep up.

41

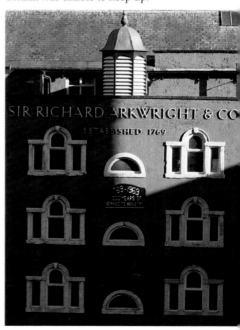

The cotton mill built by Richard Arkwright in Cromford, Derbyshire

London

[Map of London showing the West End area, including landmarks such as Regent's Park, London Zoo, Hyde Park, Kensington Gardens, Buckingham Palace, Westminster, the River Thames, and various neighborhoods including Bayswater, Mayfair, Soho, Bloomsbury, Knightsbridge, Chelsea, Pimlico, and Belgravia.]

LONDON CONTENTS
Overview 42–46
Museums and art
  galleries 47–49
Houses 50–51
Walks 52–53
Churches 54
Nightlife 55
Shopping 56–57
Accommodations 58
Eating out 59

LONDON With a population of seven million, London sprawls across a great basin bisected by the River Thames, which provides classic views, such as Big Ben and the Houses of Parliament from Westminster Bridge, and the Tower of London and Tower Bridge from the South Bank. It is not an easy city in which to get your bearings—many Londoners think of the capital in terms of the Underground map rather than the street network—but its sudden changes of mood are the key to its appeal.

THE WEST END The bulk of the capital's attractions are to be found in the **West End**. **Trafalgar Square▶▶▶** is the undisputed center of London, where a statue of Admiral

Nelson stands high on a column guarded by lions modeled by the artist E.H. Landseer. **St. Martin-in-the-Fields►** and the **National Gallery►►** take up two sides of the square; Admiralty Arch leads through the third into The Mall, the grand approach to **Buckingham Palace►►** (begun 1825), the chief residence of the Queen with some rooms open in August and September. Adjacent are the **Queen's Gallery** (closed until 2002) and the **Royal Mews**. Flanking the Mall are tree-shaded **Green Park** and **St James's Park►►**, an alluring expanse with a lake and bandstand concerts in summer.

The hub of **Westminster** is Parliament Square, dominated by the clocktower housing the huge Big Ben

Taking a break by the fountains of Trafalgar Square against the backdrop of the National Gallery (left) and St. Martin-in-the-Fields Church (right)

▶▶▶ CITY HIGHLIGHTS

British Museum
pages 45 and 47

Covent Garden
pages 44 and 52

Greenwich
pages 46, 47, and 57

Hampton Court *page 51*

Museum of London
pages 46–49

St. Paul's Cathedral
pages 46 and 54

South Kensington museums
pages 48–49

Tate Britain and Tate Modern *page 49*

Tower of London and Tower Bridge
pages 45, 49, and 53

Trafalgar Square
pages 42–43, and 52

bell, which is part of London's most photographed building, the splendid Gothic Revival **Houses of Parliament▶▶▶**. The symbol of the seat of government, they were remodeled by Charles Barry and Augustus Pugin after fire destroyed an earlier building in 1834. When Parliament is in session you can view from the Strangers' Gallery (for times and details of guided tours tel: 020-7219 3000). Across the square is **Westminster Abbey▶▶▶**.

To the west, some of the best addresses in London are in **Mayfair**, chic **Chelsea**, elegant **Knightsbridge**, and **Kensington**. Here there is a preponderance of 19th-century stucco in addition to the familiar yellow-gray London stock brick. **South Kensington** is the primary museum quarter. **Hyde Park** and adjacent **Kensington Gardens** constitute a green swath north of the Royal Albert Hall and the mildly preposterous Albert Memorial.

Covent Garden▶▶▶, the former fruit and vegetable market hall, has been imaginatively revamped as a lively piazza, with boutiques, street musicians, and craft stalls—the scheme was inspired by the renaissance of Faneuil Hall in Boston, Massachusetts. Covent Garden Piazza, laid out by Inigo Jones in 1631, was the first true square in London. The name Covent Garden also denotes the Royal Opera House. **Soho▶▶**, farther west, is the center of the Chinese community (around Gerrard Street the street names are in Chinese) as well as an amalgam of Italian delicatessens, high-class restaurants, nightclubs, and sex shops.

Bloomsbury▶ represents the hub of intellectual London: blue plaques (placed on buildings throughout London) indicate the former houses of the famous, including the homes of Charles Dickens (a memorial museum is at 48 Doughty Street) and Virginia Woolf and her "Bloomsbury Set." Bloomsbury still has a gracious atmosphere, and is a good illustration of how residential London developed into formal squares and terraces in

Georgian and Regency times; Bedford Square continues to be as fashionable as when it was first laid out in 1775. Landmarks include the **British Museum▶▶▶** and the unusual **British Telecom Tower**, built in 1964.

Regent's Park▶▶ is a gracious tract laid out by Regency architect John Nash in conjunction with the supremely elegant stucco row houses on its east side; within the park is **London Zoo**, a boating lake and an open-air theater.

Legal London revolves around **Holborn**, with its Gothic Revival High Courts on the Strand and the Central Criminal Courts in the Old Bailey; both have public galleries within the courtrooms. Barristers are attached to chambers within the **Inns of Court and Chancery▶▶** (Gray's Inn, Middle Temple, Inner Temple and Lincoln's Inn), medieval foundations that originally gave lodging to lawyers and legal students; you can wander into the court-yards on weekdays. In Chancery Lane, the **Public Record Office▶** is open weekdays and exhibits the *Domesday Book*—the detailed survey of England made by William the Conqueror in 1086.

THE CITY The "square mile" of the ancient city of London, the City is where the major financial institutions are concentrated; it retains its medieval street pattern, and though the city wall has largely disappeared, its gateways live on in place-names (Ludgate, Aldersgate, Moorgate, etc.); these gates, plus plinths bearing the City griffin, still mark the City boundaries. It is best approached from London Bridge, which has a picture-postcard view of **Tower Bridge▶▶▶** and the **Tower of London▶▶▶**. The **Monument▶**, designed by Sir Christopher Wren to commemorate the Great Fire of 1666, is a good viewing platform for those fit enough to manage the narrow steps up. Richard Rodgers' **Lloyd's Building▶** on Lime Street is London's most innovative contribution to high-tech architecture. The **Bank of England** (museum inside), the central

45

WHITEHALL
Linking Trafalgar Square and Parliament Square, this street contains grandiose 19th-century government offices. London's main royal residence was Whitehall Palace until it was destroyed by fire in 1698; the Banqueting House (designed by Inigo Jones in 1622), with its superb painted ceiling by Rubens, is the sole survivor. In 1649 Charles I walked across the hall and through a window to face his execution. The archway at the Horse Guards is the former entrance into the palace: traditionally dressed soldiers still keep watch; the Changing of the Guard occurs Apr–Aug, daily at 11 AM; Sep–Mar, every other day.

St. Paul's Cathedral was begun in 1675 and completed 35 years later

Canary Wharf Tower, completed in 1991, rises to 800 feet

46

GETTING AROUND
Forget the car and use public transportation. Day travelcards can be purchased at Underground and railroad stations, and from many newsdealers ("newsagents"), and entitle you to unlimited travel by train, Underground, and bus (but not night bus services); Zone 1 tickets cover the center. The Underground (or "tube") is easiest to understand, but the double-decker buses give excellent views (bus route 11 is recommended); free bus maps are available from tourist offices.
For organized tours see page 271.
The London *A–Z Street Atlas* is especially useful for exploring the center and suburbs.

bank of the U.K., stands opposite the Mansion House, the official residence of the Lord Mayor; Lombard Street, leading east, is London's Wall Street. Close by **St. Paul's Cathedral▶▶**, the somewhat bleak-looking Barbican complex comprises 21 high-rise concrete apartment blocks and a confusing maze of walkways; within is the **Barbican Arts Centre**, home of the London Symphony Orchestra and London base of the Royal Shakespeare Company, and the **Museum of London▶▶**. To the west and outside the City proper, the quiet streets of **Smithfield▶** are a different world, with an endearingly workaday look. The Central London Markets (Smithfield) is an outstanding example of a Victorian market building; adjacent Cloth Fair has a rare wooden house, a survivor of the Great Fire, while the **Church of St. Bartholomew the Great▶▶** represents London's most impressive Norman church architecture.

THE SUBURBS Docklands▶ is Europe's biggest urban development area. Once the East End district around the river docks, now a cityscape of gleaming office blocks and Dutch-looking waterside housing, the area covers the Isle of Dogs, North Woolwich, and Rotherhithe on the south bank. The best way to see it is from the elevated Docklands Light Railway (D.L.R.), running from Island Gardens to **Canary Wharf Tower**, Britain's tallest building. Pulling in the crowds, the **Dome** houses the **Millennium Experience** (see sidebar on page 47).
   Greenwich▶▶▶ The former center of the maritime world (see also panel, page 47), Greenwich Park occupies a hillside above the Thames, and within it are the Greenwich meridian line and the old **Royal Observatory▶▶** of 1676, which houses instruments of navigation and astronomy. Just below, the **National Maritime Museum▶▶** and **Queen's House** (begun in 1616) form a supreme early classical composition by Wren and Inigo Jones. The former Royal Naval College was designed by Wren, and the **painted hall▶▶**, open in the afternoons, has a superb painted ceiling by Thornhill.
   Hampstead and Highgate▶▶ Hampstead Heath remains pleasantly countrified, with hollows, glades and grassland. Parliament Hill Fields, in the southeast corner of the heath, has a wonderful view over central London. Hampstead village developed as an 18th-century spa and is one of the most fashionable residential districts; psychologist Sigmund Freud and poet John Keats were among its residents—both men's houses can be visited. **Highgate Cemetery▶▶** (*Guided tours*) has a spectacular derelict area where many rich and famous Victorians are buried.
   Richmond and Chiswick▶▶ These charming riverside suburbs, are best seen by taking the summer boat service (from Putney Bridge, Kew Bridge, and Richmond Bridge) or by walking along the river, for example westward from Hammersmith Bridge along Chiswick Mall and on to **Chiswick House▶** (see page 51) or from Kew to Richmond. The towpath continues westward past **Ham House▶** (see page 51). Another excellent boat trip is to **Hampton Court▶▶▶** (see page 51). **Richmond Park▶▶** is a former royal hunting park, fenced in by Charles I in 1635 and still inhabited by deer; within is the Isabella Plantation, famous for azaleas and heathers. For **Kew Gardens▶▶▶** see page 16.

Museums and art galleries

This is a list of London's top museums and galleries, arranged by area. The London White Card gives entry to 15 major ones for three or seven days for individuals or families (on sale at participating museums).

TRAFALGAR SQUARE The **National Gallery**►►► (*Guided tours* daily at 11:30 and 2:30, Sat 2 and 3:30 plus Wed 6:30 PM from the lobby of the Sainsbury Wing. *Admission free*), in Trafalgar Square, WC2, has a superb collection of paintings, many of which will be instantly familiar, from early Renaissance to the French Impressionists. Around the corner, in St. Martin's Place, WC2, is the **National Portrait Gallery**►► (*Admission free*), as complete a collection of faces of British history as you will find.

COVENT GARDEN AND BLOOMSBURY The art gallery of the **Courtauld Institute**►►, Somerset House, The Strand, WC2, contains one of Britain's finest selections of French Impressionist paintings. The **London Transport Museum**►►►, in the Piazza, Covent Garden, WC2, is an enthralling place which traces the development of

London's buses, trams, trains, and "tubes," with exhibits you can board. Nearby, the **Theatre Museum**►, 1e Tavistock Street, Covent Garden, WC2, is a home for stage memorabilia.

The **British Museum**►►► (*Admission free; introductory and specialist tours daily*), Great Russell Street, WC1, is one of the greatest collections in the world. The most famous of its artifacts ancient and modern include the Rosetta stone (which helped historians to decode hieroglyphics) and Egyptian mummies, the Elgin marbles from the Parthenon in Athens, and the Mildenhall and Sutton Hoo treasure hoards. The famous Reading Room, where Marx wrote *Das Kapital*, has been transformed into a reference library, surrounded by the Great Court, spanned by a huge glass roof. The **British Library**►► (*Admission free*) outgrew this space and was moved to 96 Euston Road (by St. Pancras rail station); its John Ritblat Gallery has many great treasures, including the oldest wall map of the world and Beatles music manuscripts. **Pollock's Toy Museum**►, Scala Street, W1, has tin soldiers, mechanical curios, and toy theaters.

GREENWICH
Greenwich Pier, SE10, is home to the "tea-clipper" **Cutty Sark**, launched in 1869 and the last of her kind to survive. She is preserved in dry dock as a museum. In Greenwich Park, the **National Maritime Museum**, Romney Road, celebrates Britain's long maritime history, with a fine array of nautical clocks, sea paintings and ship models. The **Old Royal Observatory**, was designed by Wren, with astronomical and navigational exhibits. Adjacent is the **Greenwich Meridian** (0° longitude), where you can have one foot in each hemisphere. On the north bank in Docklands, the **Dome** houses the huge **Millennium Experience**, covering 14 "zones": Work, Learn, Transaction, Body, Play, Mobility, Local, National Environment, Atmosphere, Communicate, Spirit, Rest, Mind and National Identity.

The London Transport Museum

EXCURSIONS
The number of possible day trips from the capital is endless. Here we highlight some recommended excursions that can easily be made by train.
Castles: Dover, Windsor.
Historic cities: Cambridge, Canterbury, Oxford, Salisbury, Winchester.
Industrial, railroad, and naval interest: Amberley Museum, Bluebell Railway (near East Grinstead), Chatham Dockyard, Portsmouth, Watercress Line (Alton to Alresford).
Roman remains: Fishbourne Palace (near Chichester), Lullingstone Villa (near Eynsford), Verulamium (St Albans).
Coastal resorts: Brighton, Broadstairs, Eastbourne, Hastings.
Small towns: Arundel, Lewes, Rye, Sandwich, Tunbridge Wells.

CHANGING EXHIBITIONS OF ART AND DESIGN
Major sites for art exhibitions are the Hayward Gallery on the South Bank, SE1, the Royal Academy on Piccadilly, W1, the I.C.A. on the Mall, SW1, and the Barbican Centre, Silk Street, EC2. The latest aspects of design are on show at the Design Centre on Haymarket (*Admission free*). The Serpentine Gallery in Kensington Gardens has exhibitions focusing on younger contemporary artists (also free).

The Natural History Museum's pattern of colored terra-cotta and French Romanesque elements was the creation of architect Alfred Waterhouse

GREAT SPORTS VENUES
London's major sporting venues double as tourist attractions. The Wimbledon Lawn Tennis Museum (Southfields rail station) recalls the sport's great moments. The soccer FA Cup Final and internationals are played at Wembley Stadium (Wembley Park tube); there are guided tours (10 AM–3 PM winter, 10 AM–4 PM summer), but the stadium is to be rebuilt, probably during 2000, so check first on tel. 020-8902 8833. For Rugby Union fans, the Twickenham Experience (Twickenham rail station) includes a museum and a stadium tour, while Lord's Cricket Ground (St. John's Wood tube) has a museum open on match days.

REGENT'S PARK AND BAKER STREET London Zoo►► in Regent's Park, NW1, is one of the world's great animal collections and an important research center. It places emphasis on breeding endangered species and on education. On Marylebone Road, NW1, **Madame Tussaud's►** wax museum tops the charts as a paying tourist attraction; be photographed alongside politicians, pop stars, and sports celebrities. Lines can be long—some may feel the wait and steep admission aren't worth it. Its annex, the **Spirit of London►** is a "sight, sounds, and smells" journey in replica London taxicabs through 400 years of London. Next door at the **Planetarium►** the night sky is projected onto a dome as you are guided around the constellations. The **Sherlock Holmes Museum** at 221b Baker Street, W1, displays memorabilia of the great sleuth at the address used in Arthur Conan Doyle's stories. The **Wallace Collection►►** (*Admission free*), has Frans Hals's *The Laughing Cavalier*, plus a superb collection of French paintings and porcelain. In Portland Place, the **BBC Experience►** charts the work of the BBC, showing how radio and TV programs are made; you can try recording a three-minute play of the radio soap *The Archers* or present the weather forecast.

SOUTH KENSINGTON Prince Albert headed the Royal Commission that purchased the museum sites in what was dubbed Albertopolis. The **Victoria and Albert Museum►►►** (the "V & A"), Cromwell Road, SW7, is a treasurehouse of decorative art and design, displayed by theme (musical instruments, costume, furniture, etc.) and by civilization (Japan, China, India, etc.). There is something for everyone but too much for one visit. Meanwhile, across the road at the **Natural History Museum►►►**, Cromwell Road, SW7, dinosaurs, evolution, blue whales ... just about everything is here in this splendid Victorian building. Transferred from antiquated glass cases to high-tech displays, the collection is extremely popular with enthusiasts, semi-enthusiasts, and children. The **Science Museum**▶▶, around the corner on Exhibition Road, SW7, is a hit with children, but with plenty for adults, science buffs and non-experts alike.

CHELSEA AND WESTMINSTER The **National Army Museum** (*Admission free*), Royal Hospital Road, SW3, tells a 500-year story of soldiers through the ages. The **Cabinet War Rooms**▶ on King Charles Street, SW1, were the subterranean emergency accommodations for Winston Churchill and his cabinet in World War II; the Map Room and the Transatlantic Telephone Room remain intact.

    Tate Britain▶▶▶ on Millbank, SW1, is the nation's greatest collection of British and modern art. Entry is free but admission is charged for special exhibitions. **The Queen's Gallery**▶ at Buckingham Palace, SW1, has items from the royal collection (closed until 2002), while the **Royal Mews**▶ contains the spectacular State Coaches and the Royal Family's sleighs.

SOUTH OF THE RIVER The **Imperial War Museum**▶▶, Lambeth Road, SE1, covers the wars that Britain has been involved in since 1914. There is a Blitz reconstruction and a trench dug out, in addition to weapons, memorabilia, uniforms, and (from May 2000) a Holocaust exhibition. Near Westminster Bridge, County Hall is home to the **London Aquarium**▶ and the **Football World of Experience**, and the new British Airways London Eye rises from Jubilee Gardens. Further east, by Waterloo Bridge, is the Royal National Theatre complex.

    In Southwark, on Bankside, the thatched, circular **Globe Theatre** is a faithful rebuilding of the venue where many of Shakespeare's plays were performed in his own lifetime. There are guided tours, an exhibition, and summer performances. **Tate Modern**▶▶▶ is the new branch of the Tate Gallery (*Admission free*). The **Design Museum**▶ at Butler's Wharf, 28 Shad Thames, SE1, is a stylish riverside building housing changing thematic exhibitions of 20th-century design. At the **London Dungeon**▶ in Tooley Street, SE1, gloomy vaults reveal the dark stories of punishment, torture, and witchcraft in times past. Next door, the **Britain at War Experience**▶ evokes London at the height of the Blitz, with the smells and sounds of an air raid. Moored on the Thames close by (reached from Tower Bridge, The Thames Path) is **H.M.S. Belfast**▶, the last of the Royal Navy's big World War II gunships, launched in 1938.

TOWER HILL AND THE CITY The **Tower of London**▶▶▶ on Tower Hill, EC3, is the greatest Norman castle in the kingdom, standing silent sentinel in the shadow of adjacent Tower Bridge; the locale has had a long and gory history from Roman times on. Traditionally dressed Beefeaters still patrol the grounds. The White Tower is the main Norman feature, housing St. John's Chapel while the Crown Jewels are in the Jewel House.

    At the **Museum of London**▶▶▶, London Wall, EC2, is a time-walk display beginning with Roman London, passing a cell door from Newgate Prison, a panorama of the Great Fire, and a street of Victorian shops.

THE EAST END
The **Bethnal Green Museum of Childhood** (*Admission free*), Cambridge Heath Road, Bethnal Green, E2, is an entertaining offshoot of the Victoria and Albert Museum. Toys of all ages and countries are here; among the exhibits are a wonderful collection of dollhouses, a surreal display of dolls' heads, and a group of puppet theaters. The **Geffrye Museum** occupies a row of early 18th-century almshouses on Kingsland Road, Hackney, E2. Each of a series of rooms is furnished in a different period style, from the Elizabethan era to the 1960s. It is a succinct summary of furniture styles through the ages.

49

SUBURBAN MUSEUMS AND GALLERIES
The **Royal Air Force Museum**, Grahame Park Way, Hendon (Colindale tube) has dozens of aircraft, plus an interactive Fun 'n' Flight Gallery, a Red Arrow flight simulator and a Battle of Britain Experience. The **Dulwich Picture Gallery**, Dulwich, SE21, is England's oldest public gallery (1814), and housed in a neoclassical building by Sir John Soane. There are works by Gainsborough, Reynolds, Rembrandt, and others.

The White Tower, the Tower of London

London

A SUBURBAN OVERVIEW: COMMUTERDOM

Most Londoners live outside the center; commuterdom extends far into the Home Counties (that is, the counties adjacent to London). The suburbs are much-expanded villages, joined together for the most part by somewhat anonymous 19th- and 20th-century fill-in, but seen from the air it is the greenery that really stands out. Several ancient commons (originally common grazing grounds) have been retained as public open spaces, and there are literally millions of trees in backyards, suburban roads, and parks.

WHERE THE FAMOUS LIE AT REST

The churchyards of Inner London were so crowded by the early 1800s that they had become revoltingly unsanitary. To relieve pressure, massive cemeteries were created farther out, which are the resting places of some of London's most famous dead. Emmeline Pankhurst, the suffragette leader, is buried in Brompton Cemetery; the music-hall queen Marie Lloyd in Hampstead Cemetery; Isambard Kingdom Brunel and Anthony Trollope at Kensal Green; George Eliot and Karl Marx in Highgate Cemetery.

Houses

London has a wide range of houses open to the public, from grand palaces built for monarchs to the more personal homes of the famous or eccentric. Hundreds of buildings in London carry blue plaques. These mark houses where famous people lived and died, such as 25 Brook Street, W1, where Handel lived for 25 years until his death in 1759, or 45 Berkeley Square, W1, where Clive of India cut his throat in 1774.

CENTRAL LONDON Sir John Soane's Museum►► (*Admission free*), 13 Lincoln's Inn Fields, WC2, is wonderfully eccentric; it was designed by the architect Soane (1753–1837), to contain his collection of mostly architectural artifacts. The house is full of inventive lighting effects and quirky details, as well as some great treasures, in particular the paintings of *A Rake's Progress* and *An Election* by Hogarth. At **Dickens' House►**, 48 Doughty Street, WC1, Charles Dickens wrote *Oliver Twist*, the *Pickwick Papers* and *Nicholas Nickleby*. **Dr. Johnson's House**, 17 Gough Square, EC4, hidden away down an alley off Fleet Street, is the house where Samuel Johnson lived between 1749 and 1759, and where he completed his celebrated dictionary. Now it is a museum, with mementoes of Johnson's life and work.

Apsley House►►, Hyde Park Corner, W1, was the London home of the Duke of Wellington, built in 1778 by Robert Adam with 19th-century alterations by James Wyatt. Its grand interior houses mementoes of the Iron Duke and his campaigns, as well as his impressive collection of paintings.

Kensington Palace►► Kensington Gardens, W8, was remodeled by Christopher Wren and later William Kent.

Hampton Court's Pond Gardens started life as fish ponds supplying the royal kitchens

It was the birthplace of Queen Victoria; it is now the residence of Princess Margaret, and was that of Diana, Princess of Wales. It has the royal collection of pictures and furniture, and magnificent court costumes.

Spencer House▶ (1756–1766) was built for the first Earl of Spencer, an ancestor of the Princess of Wales, and has sumptuously gilded interiors.

Buckingham Palace▶▶, the official residence of the Queen, is open Aug–Sep, giving a glimpse of the state rooms and garden; try to book ahead on 020-7321 2233.

HAMPSTEAD Kenwood House▶ (*Admission free*), Hampstead Lane, NW8, is handsomely situated on the edge of Hampstead Heath. Robert Adam gave the house its classical proportions; within is a collection of old masters and portraits, including works by Reynolds and Gainsborough. Outdoor summer concerts, often with fireworks, attract big crowds on Saturday evenings. Hampstead's oldest house, and one of the grandest, is **Fenton House▶** (N.T.) on Windmill Hill, NW3; it contains antique keyboard instruments, paintings, and furniture. You can visit the houses of the poet **John Keats** and the psychoanalyst **Sigmund Freud**. The great Modernist architect Erno Goldfinger designed **2 Willow Road** in 1939 for himself; it is now owned by the National Trust.

Kensington Palace became a royal residence when asthmatic William III elected to move away from the unhealthy riverside air of Whitehall Palace

SOUTH AND WEST Hampton Court▶▶▶, East Molesey, Surrey, is best reached from London by riverboat from Westminster Pier. The palace was begun in the early 16th century by Cardinal Wolsey and later presented to Henry VIII; it is an enjoyable potpourri of styles and history, with a hammer-beamed hall, Wren's Fountain Court, an Orangerie with Mantegna cartoons, and carvings by Grinling Gibbons. The grounds contain a famous maze.

Ham House▶▶ (N.T.), Ham Street, Ham, near the Thames towpath close to Richmond Park, is, for London, an outstanding example of Jacobean architecture, built in 1610.

Kew Palace▶▶ was built in 1631 for a London merchant and subsequently leased by George II for Queen Caroline. Since its purchase in 1781 by George III, the house has changed little and retains its old paneling and portraits. A visit here ties in nicely with **Kew Gardens** (see page 16) and a walk along the Thames towpath to Richmond.

On the other side of the river is **Syon House▶**, Isleworth. Founded in 1415 as a monastery, the house underwent a remodeling in the 18th century, being given crisp interiors by Robert Adam and grounds by Capability Brown. Adjacent in Syon Park are a major gardening center, a butterfly park, and a collection of historic vehicles. **Chiswick House▶** (N.T.), Chiswick Park, Chiswick, W4 is a small, formal Palladian villa (1729) once used for soirées and as a library rather than a house. Modeled on Palladio's Villa Capra in Italy, it stands in delightful parkland, naturalistically landscaped in what came to be regarded as the English manner.

Osterley Park▶▶ (N.T.), off Great West Road (A4), Osterley, is a gracious manor house set in parkland, all but engulfed by the suburbia of London's western fringes. Osterley provides an excellent opportunity to see Robert Adam's interiors at their richest. Adam's work dates from 1761 to 1780; the house itself has Tudor origins.

ROBERT ADAM
The state rooms at Syon House and Osterley House are among the finest sets of Robert Adam interiors in the country. The brilliant Scottish designer was born at Kirkcaldy in 1728 and was trained, along with his three brothers, by his architect father, William. He set up practice in London in 1758 and three years later was appointed principal architect to George III. His elegant and graceful classical interiors, lightening the austere accepted Palladian style, were soon all the rage and widely copied. He pioneered several architectural features, notably elliptical rooms. Charlotte Square in Edinburgh (see page 224) is one of his most notable works in his native Scotland. He died in London in 1792.

51

LONDON WALKS

Walk

Covent Garden, royal London, and Westminster

Start from Covent Garden tube station. Walk down James Street to **Covent Garden►►**, the former fruit and vegetable market, now transformed into a stylish shopping piazza and popular meeting place. The **Theatre Museum►** and **London Transport Museum►►** are close by. From Henrietta Street, an archway on the right leads into the churchyard of St. Paul's, the innovative design of Inigo Jones. At the heart of London's theaterland, St. Paul's is known as the **actors' church►** and its

interior walls are covered with plaques in memory of stars of stage and screen. Leave the churchyard via a gate onto Bedford Street; off the next street to the west, Bedfordbury, an arch leads into Goodwin Court, where bow-windowed houses have changed little since the 18th century. As you reach St. Martin's Lane, opposite is Cecil Court, part of the secondhand bookshop quarter. Enter **Trafalgar Square►►►** at the end of St. Martin's Lane, the great pigeon-populated piazza fronted by the church of **St. Martin-in-the-Fields►►** and the **National Gallery►►►**. Cross over to Admiralty Arch and enter the Mall. Steps lead up to the right past the Duke of York's column. Walk along Pall Mall, past the long-established concentration of fashionable gentlemen's clubs, distinguished by unobtrusive signs at the entrances.

Big Ben: not the tower, not the clock, but the massive bell inside

Take a detour to look at the east side of St. James's Street with its trio of old-fashioned shops—Lock's the hatmakers, Berry and Rudd's wine merchants, and Lobb's, makers of custom-fitted shoes. Adjacent Pickering Place was once used for sword duels.

Cleveland Row skirts **St. James's Palace▶**, residence of Prince Charles and others; leave by gates onto Queen's Walk, along the edge of Green Park. Return to the Mall: **Buckingham Palace▶▶**, the main residence of the Queen, is to the right; the Changing of the Guard takes place Apr–Aug, daily at 11:30 AM; Sep–Mar, every other day. Cross the Mall and enter St. James's Park, keeping left. Pass through the arch into **Horse Guards' Parade▶▶** and on to Whitehall; Downing Street, to the right, has at No. 10 the house of the prime minister. In Parliament Square is Big Ben, part of the **Houses of Parliament▶▶▶**. Across the square is **Westminster Abbey**. Return from Westminster tube station.

Walk

Along the South Bank to Tower Hill

Start from Westminster Bridge. The above walk can be extended by following the South Bank (which has a walkway for much of the way) from Westminster Bridge to the **Royal Festival Hall▶**. Further on is the **Globe Theatre▶▶** (see page 49). The walkway continues east of Waterloo Bridge past an impressive modern office complex, with outstanding views of the City. At **H.M.S. *Belfast*▶** it is necessary to detour away from the river to Tooley Street, but a path leading through a small park takes you to **Tower Bridge▶▶** (the Tower Bridge Experience inside the bridge explains its workings and gives access to the high-level walkway, or cross at street level for free); to the right you can see Canary Wharf, Britain's tallest building. On the other side, circle around the moat of the **Tower of London▶▶▶**. Signs to the World Trade Centre lead you to **St. Katharine's Dock▶** yacht haven. Return from Tower Hill tube station.

St. Katharine's Dock

54

Southwark Cathedral is noted for the many monuments that survived from its days as a monastic church. That of poet John Gower, above, is dated 1408

SIR CHRISTOPHER WREN (1632–1723)

Wren, one of the most celebrated of English architects, was responsible for the rebuilding of St. Paul's Cathedral (in which his monument appears as *lector, si monumentum requiris, circumspice*— "reader, if you seek my monument, look around") and the City churches. He drew up an ambitious plan for the rebuilding of London with Continental-style avenues, but the complexities of land ownership prevented it from being carried out. M.P. for Weymouth in Dorset, he used the local Portland stone liberally in his buildings. The other great architect of the day was Inigo Jones, who designed Covent Garden piazza, the first piazza in London.

The dome of St. Paul's Cathedral

Churches

Although the Great Fire of 1666, the Blitz of 1940, and constant rebuilding have changed London's face repeatedly, it still has an impressive legacy of church architecture, dating from Norman times. There are particularly fine examples of designs of the master architects of the 17th and 18th centuries: Wren, Hawksmoor, and Inigo Jones.

THE EARLIEST CHURCHES The only large-scale church of the Norman period in London is **St. Bartholomew the Great►►** in West Smithfield, EC1. It is the survivor of a 12th-century Augustinian priory and although the apsidal east end is a 19th-century rebuilding, the atmosphere is one of great antiquity. **Southwark Cathedral►►**, Montague Close, the cathedral for the South Bank, was founded as the Augustinian priory church of St. Mary Overie in 1106. Although much restored in the 19th century, it is the most substantial medieval artifact in the district of Southwark. The building attained cathedral status in 1905. Previously it was known as St. Mary Overie (meaning "over" the water from the City).

SIR CHRISTOPHER WREN Wren's domed masterpiece, **St. Paul's Cathedral►►►**, Ludgate Hill, EC4, replaced an earlier Gothic cathedral that perished in the Great Fire of 1666. It no longer dominates the skyline as it did until the mid-20th century, but when seen close up the proportions are overwhelming. Inside the dome, the Whispering Gallery plays acoustic tricks (whispered sounds carry around the great void) and gives splendid interior views. There are tombs of Wren, Nelson, Wellington, Turner, and Reynolds in the crypt, views from the Golden Gallery, woodwork by Gibbons, and ironwork by Tijou.

After the Great Fire, Sir Christopher Wren graced the City with 51 **churches**. Among the most celebrated of **Wren's City churches►►** are St. Bride's (Fleet Street), St. Margaret's (Lothbury), St. Martin Ludgate (Ludgate Hill), St. Mary Abchurch (Cannon Street), St. Mary-at-Hill (Eastcheap), and St. Stephen Walbrook (Walbrook).

OTHER GREAT CHURCHES St. **Martin-in-the-Fields►**, Trafalgar Square, WC2, is an 18th-century rebuilding by James Gibbs, and a particularly satisfying example of the temple-like architecture of the period, with a characteristic galleried interior.

At **Westminster Abbey►►►**, Parliament Square, SW1, British sovereigns are crowned and many great men and women are buried, among them monarchs, statesmen, poets, and scientists. It also has a cloisters, treasury, brass-rubbing center, and the oldest garden (*Open* Thu only) in the country. **Westminster Cathedral►**, in Ashley Place, off Victoria Street, SW1, is Britain's premier Roman Catholic cathedral, a Byzantine brick creation finished in 1903; incense fills the cavernous interior.

Nightlife

THEATER There are dozens of theaters to choose from, offering everything from Shakespeare to Andrew Lloyd Webber musicals; the capital has an impressive legacy of Victorian theater architecture. Discount tickets for the day of performance are available from the S.W.E.T. ticket booth in Leicester Square (see panel).

NIGHTSPOTS Soho and Covent Garden constitute the heart of clubland with clubs like the Hippodrome and Empire discotheque by Leicester Square, and The Wag in Wardour Street. Ronnie Scott's (47 Frith Street, W1) is a well-established jazz spot, and Heaven (under Charing Cross Station) is a leading gay club. Cabaret and alternative comedy are performed at The Comedy Store in Leicester Square. Away from the center of town is the highly esteemed Fridge, at Town Hall Parade, Brixton Hill, SW2. Watch listings (see panel) for pop/rock concerts at the Hammersmith Odeon and Brixton Academy.

CLASSICAL MUSIC London has five resident orchestras. The Royal Festival Hall on the South Bank (plus the smaller Purcell Room and Queen Elizabeth Hall), and the Barbican Hall, Silk Street (Moorgate subway), are major concert halls. Wigmore Hall, Wigmore Street hosts performances by up-and-coming artists. Summer visitors should try to take in a Promenade Concert ("the Proms," see page 18), Europe's biggest music festival, at the Royal Albert Hall. Operas at the Royal Opera House in Covent Garden are performed in the original language with "subtitles" projected above, while the English National Opera in the Coliseum, St. Martin's Lane, gives performances in English. Many churches host lunchtime recitals; most are free, with a collection made at the end.

MOVIES The big first-run movie house is the Odeon on Leicester Square, which still boasts an organ. The National Film Theatre (N.F.T.) on the South Bank near Waterloo is the leading repertory movie theater; programs change daily; one-day memberships are available.

LISTINGS AND BOOKINGS
The weekly magazine *Time Out* gives listings for all London's entertainments, events, and exhibitions, and has excellent previews. The *London Theatre Guide*, updated every two weeks, lists theatrical events and is available free of charge from West End theaters, libraries, and tourist information centers. Buy tickets directly from the box office to avoid paying commissions. Ticket agencies include Ticketmaster (tel: 020-7344 4444); check for credit card surcharges. Never buy tickets from scalpers on the street or unofficial agencies. The S.W.E.T. (Society of West End Theatres) ticket booth opens at noon for matinées and 2:30 PM for evening performances for the same day.

The lights of Leicester Square

55

James Smith's redoubtable stick and umbrella store

LONDON VIEWS
Take the elevator up the bell tower of Westminster Cathedral, ascend in the fixed hot-air balloon near the Oval Cricket Ground in Vauxhall (tel: 020-7587 1111), or climb the steps to the top of St. Paul's Cathedral or the Monument (both in the City). There are superb views for free from Waterloo and Hungerford bridges, Primrose Hill (north of Regent's Park), and Parliament Hill Fields (Hampstead Heath).

Shopping

PRINCIPAL SHOPPING AREAS Major West End department stores are clustered along **Oxford Street**, with Selfridges the biggest of them. John Lewis (whose "never knowingly undersold" policy guarantees a refund if you find the same goods on sale cheaper elsewhere) has a fine stock of furnishings, fashions, and decorative items, while the ubiquitous Marks and Spencer is known for good-value clothing and good food halls. Virgin Megastore and H.M.V. have big selections of CDs and cassettes.

Around the corner, **Regent Street** comes into its own in the weeks before Christmas when the illuminations are switched on; during this period, Hamleys, the undisputed king of the toyshops, fills to bursting and has spectacular displays. Nearby is Liberty, renowned for Liberty print fabrics and stylish clothes; the mock-Tudor building itself is worth a look at.

Stereos and electrical goods are available at discount prices in the shops along **Tottenham Court Road**. The **British Museum** shop has stylish reproductions of some of its treasures; nearby at 53 New Oxford Street, **James Smith's** umbrella store has an eye-catching Victorian shopfront boasting "Life Preservers, Jagger Canes and Swordsticks."

Charing Cross Road constitutes the heart of London's bookstore territory. Foyles, the largest bookstore, has an impressive stock though the layout can be confusing. There is a particularly fascinating array of specialist secondhand bookshops just off Charing Cross Road on Cecil Court. Round the corner in Trafalgar Square, the **National Gallery shop** has a good selection of art posters, cards and books. **Soho** is densely packed with ethnic food stores, including

Chinese supermarkets in Chinatown, and numerous Italian delis.

Covent Garden has an absorbing variety of stores and boutiques, including the Tea Shop in Neal Street, a cheese shop and bakery in Neal's Yard, and a dollhouse shop in the piazza itself.

St. James's Street, off Piccadilly, has old-fashioned shops: Berry and Rudd wine merchants, Lock's the hatmakers, and Lobb's the shoemakers.

Kings Road in Chelsea is the place for chic fashions, stylish interior design stores and people-watching; a smart antique market (Monday to Saturday) extends along one part.

GREAT FOR WINDOW SHOPPING Harrods, Brompton Road, is the grandest department store of them all; many visitors go just to collect a shopping bag. Harrods prides itself on its range and quality of stock; the food halls conjure up Edwardian splendor. **Burlington Arcade**, off Piccadilly, is a perfectly preserved Regency shopping arcade, retaining its early 19th-century air with considerable dignity. An immaculately attired beadle patrols the alley, and notices forbid "hurrying or whistling." **Fortnum and Mason**, on Piccadilly, is the food store *par excellence*. The famous exterior clock features Mr. Fortnum and Mr. Mason, who bow to each other on the hour.

Street markets always provide good entertainment. Easily the most atmospheric is **Brick Lane** (Sunday mornings only), off Bethnal Green Road in the heart of Cockney London, now the Bengali community. It is unashamedly shabby and hugely crowded, and the mishmash of wares is bizarre, ranging from cheap stereos to bargain CDs to secondhand junk. Note this is not the same as the nearby (and overrated) Petticoat Lane Market. Weekend-long antiques markets are at **Camden Lock** and **Greenwich**. **Portobello Road**, W11, operates Monday to Saturday (junk stalls on Friday, antiques on Saturday); both get absolutely packed. Grays Antique Market (Mon–Fri) at 1–7 Davies Mews, W1, has some 180 dealers within two Victorian warehouses.

Below: some chic window displays verge on the inscrutable

57

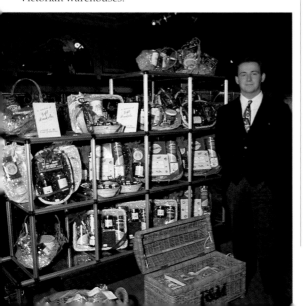

Only the best: a selection of Fortnum and Mason's gift baskets while a frock-coated assistant looks on

London

RESERVING ACCOMMODATIONS

London Tourist Board has lists of accommodations and operates a reservation service. For recorded information, tel: 0891 505487. For bookings tel: 020-7932 2020. You can also rent a flat; the tourist board has details of agencies. For inspected and approved B & B accommodation, bookable in advance of arrival, contact U.K. Bed and Breakfast, (tel: 0800/852 2632).

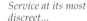

In a city of pricey accommodations, London's top hotels can be a very expensive experience

Service at its most discreet...

Accommodations

HOTELS London is one of the most expensive European capitals for hotel rooms. Those who can afford high prices will appreciate the style and service at such long-established and prestigious establishments as the Ritz, Claridge's, the Savoy, the Dorchester, and the Connaught; be prepared for lots of British formality, however, and do not expect air-conditioning as a matter of course. The top modern hotels are generally all in the same price bracket. Among the best areas to stay in the capital are the West

End (W1, NW1, SW1, WC2), Bloomsbury (WC1), Kensington (SW7, W2, W8, W11), Knightsbridge (SW1), and Chelsea (SW3).

BED AND BREAKFAST More modest B. & B. accommodations roughly cost twice what you would pay outside London. There is a reasonable selection around Victoria (SW1) and Bloomsbury (WC1); the King's Cross area (also WC1) is cheap and drab (Argyle Street WC1, is a reasonable bet if you're really stuck). Out to the west, Hammersmith (W6) is an unprepossessing area but has some large hotels and good Underground connections to central London. Small hotels and B. & B.s exist in many suburbs, and can cut your hotel costs; aim for a location convenient to the Underground, and check the journey time and the timing of the last train back.

HOSTELS AND CAMPGROUNDS The central locations for youth hostelers are on Noel Street, W1, Bolton Gardens, SW5, Holland Park, W8, Euston Road, N1, and Carter Lane, EC4; three farther-flung hostels are on Highgate West Hill, N6, Wellgarth Road, NW11, and Salter Road, Rotherhithe, SE16. Reservations are advised (national Y.H.A. tel: 01727 855215). Additionally, numerous colleges offer accommodation in the summer. The St. Dorothy's International Student Hostel at 99 Frognal, NW3 (tel: 020-7794 6893), is a females-only establishment in Hampstead. Campgrounds are obviously farther out; Crystal Palace Caravan Site, SE19, is pleasantly located, with good public transportation links.

Eating out

BREAKFAST For a leisurely start to the day, splurge on **breakfast** at one of the big hotels such as the Savoy (the Strand, WC2; tel: 020-7836 4343). Devotees of Chinese dim sum brunch should look no farther than New World (1 Gerrard Place, W1; tel: 020-7734 6631).

LUNCH For quick lunches, sandwich bars and no-frills restaurants are a good bet; there are several of these in the West End. Many pubs and wine bars offer food, though some get crowded and smoky; the long-established Gordon's Wine Bar (47 Villiers Street, WC2; tel: 020-7930 1408) is set in a subterranean vault by the Thames. Look around Soho and Covent Garden for Asian restaurants, which offer good-value lunches. You can lunch at some top restaurants for roughly half the price of an evening meal. Big museums and galleries, including the National Gallery, Tate Gallery, and Festival Hall, have good self-service cafeterias. A number of inexpensive southern Indian vegetarian restaurants, along Drummond Street, NW1, are handy for Regent's Park. Panton Street, WC2, off Leicester Square, has several budget eateries.

AFTERNOON TEA Tea is served with considerable flair at such prestigious hotels as the Ritz (reservation advisable; Picadilly, W1; tel: 020-7493 8181) and Brown's (Dover Street, W1; tel: 020-7493 6020), although prices are high and there is a formal dress code. Less expensive options are Fortnum and Mason's (tel: 020-7734 8040) and the Charing Cross Hotel (Strand, WC2; tel: 020-7839 7282).

THE EVENING For a treat, try one of the great French restaurants such as Bibendum (Michelin House, 81 Fulham Road, SW3; tel: 020-7581 5817) in the eye-catching Michelin Building, or Nico Central (35 Great Portland Street, W1; tel: 020-7436 8846). Those who wish to live it up without breaking the bank may like Kettner's (29 Romilly Street, W1; no reservations), in the heart of Soho, part of the Pizza Express chain. London's residential districts Hampstead, Camden Town, Islington, Bayswater, Kensington, and Chelsea have a good choice of places to eat. See also hotels and restaurants, pages 281–282.

PUBS IN LONDON
Pubs of special character include the **Cittie of York** (with Britain's longest bar, 22 High Holborn, WC2); the **Lamb and Flag** (in Covent Garden, 33 Rose Street, WC2); the **Museum Tavern** (near the British Museum, Museum Street, WC1); the **Princess Louise** (spectacular Victorian tiled interior, 208 High Holborn, WC1); the **Lamb** (Bloomsbury, with old fittings, Lamb's Conduit Street); **Ye Olde Cheshire Cheese** (ancient tavern, former haunt of writers Dickens and Johnson, Wine Office Court, 145 Fleet Street, EC4; the **George Inn** (London's last galleried inn, Borough High Street, SE1); the **Black Friar** (London's finest Art Nouveau pub interior, 174 Queen Victoria Street, EC4, opposite Blackfriars station,); and the **Dove** (riverside pub with terrace, 19 Upper Mall, Chiswick). Fuller's and Young's are two excellent "real ale" London brews.

59

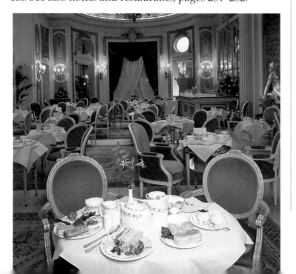

The Ritz was London's very first steel-framed building, erected in 1906

The West Country

ISLES OF SCILLY
Tresco St Martin's
Bryher
Hugh Town
St Agnes St Mary's

St Just Penzance
Newlyn
Land's End St
Porthcurno Buryan

Saundersfoot
Tenby Carmarthen Bay
Caldey Llanrhidian
Rhossili
Worms Head Culture Hole
Oxwich
Swansea Bay
Porthcawl

Burry Port Pontarddulais Glyn
Neath
Llanelli Swansea Neath Port Talbot Pontypridd
Killay Mumbles Head M4 Pencoed
Bridgend
Cowbridge
Llantwit Major

Aberdare
Mountain Ash

Bristol Channel

Lundy

Ilfracombe
Woolacombe
Braunton
Westward Ho!

Hartland Point
Hartland Quay Clovelly
Hartland
Morwenstow

Lynton Countisbury
Lynmouth Porlock Minehead
Watersmeet 519m Dunster
Exmoor Dunkery
National Park Hill Winsford
Exford
Withypool Tarr Steps

Bideford South Molton Dulverton
Great Torrington Chulmleigh Witheridge
Tiverton
Cullompton
Bickleigh Castle

Bude
Holsworthy
Hatherleigh Coppleston
Clawton Okehampton Crediton

CORNWALL
Boscastle
Tintagel
Port Isaac Launceston
Polzeath 419m Altarnun
Trevose Head Rock Brown Willy
Padstow Blisland
Wadebridge St Neot
Bedruthan Steps Bodmin
Newquay Lanhydrock House
Trerice St Keyne
Lostwithiel
St Agnes Head St Austell Lanreath
Wheal Coates Charlestown
Cornish Truro Trewithen
Engines Redruth Garden
St Ives Hayle Camborne Mevagissey
Zennor Chysauster Penryn Portloe
Pendeen Trengwainton Garden St Just in Roseland
Carn St Michael's St Mawes
Euny Penzance Mount Falmouth
Land's Mousehole Penjerrick
End St Buryan Helston
Porthcurno Mount's Mullion
Bay Lizard Cadgwith
Peninsula Lizard
Lizard Point

DEVON
Bridestowe
Lydford 821m
Gorge High Willhays Chagford
Dartmoor Bovey
National Tracey
Tavistock Park Ashburton
Cotehele Buckfastleigh
Buckland Dartington
Abbey
Saltash Plymouth Totnes
Antony Yelverton
House Torpoint Plympton Modbury
Looe Polperro Kingsand Wembury
Fowey Bigbury-on-Sea
Hope
Salcombe
Prawle Point

Castle Drogo Topsham
Exeter
Exmouth
Dawlish
Newton Teignmouth
Abbot
Torquay
Paignton
Brixham
Kingswear
Dartmouth
Kingsbridge Start Bay

Eden Project
Redruth

60

C

B

A

1 2 3

★ Walk start point

| 0 | 10 | 20 | 30 | 40 | 50 km |
| 0 | | 10 | | 20 | 30 miles |

4   5

61

THE WEST COUNTRY The tapering southwestern peninsula of England culminates in the rugged clifflands of western Cornwall, where Land's End forms the big toe of Great Britain. Called the West Country, the area offers perhaps a fuller range of activities, landscapes, and experiences than any other in Britain, and as a result, you'll find many other visitors here, especially during the summer, when the crowds are sometimes overwhelming. People from all over Britain spend their vacations here, in indolent ease or in a whirl of activity. For many of them, the region's diversity is the key to its appeal.

The climate is mild and the sprawling resorts of Torquay and Bournemouth head the sunshine league; this is also a major retirement area. To many, the West Country is synonymous with dairy country; the locals are big cheese-eaters, and you can indulge in a cream tea or even mail home some delicious "clotted" cream, a cholesterol-watcher's nightmare. Another regional specialty is lardy cake, a gooey raisin-topped bakery product largely confined to the southern and western counties.

Land's End, Cornwall
(far left)

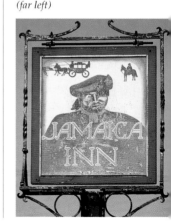

RECOMMENDED COASTAL TOWNS AND VILLAGES
Cornwall: Boscastle, Port Isaac, Padstow, St. Ives, Mousehole, Cadgwith, St. Anthony in Roseland, Portloe, Mevagissey, Charlestown, Fowey, Polperro, Kingsand.
Devon: Lynmouth, Clovelly, Sidmouth, Dartmouth, Salcombe, Newton Ferrers, Plymouth.
Dorset: Lyme Regis, Abbotsbury, Weymouth.

SMALL TOWNS INLAND
Cornwall: Launceston
Somerset: Dulverton, Wells, Dunster, Glastonbury.
Dorset: Beaminster, Sherborne, Shaftesbury.
Wiltshire: Marlborough, Bradford on Avon, Devizes.

HISTORIC CITIES
Bath, Bristol, Exeter, Salisbury.

COASTAL FEATURES
Cornwall: Tintagel Castle, Bedruthan Steps, Gurnards Head (near Zennor), Porthcurno open-air theater, Logan Rock (near Treen), St. Michael's Mount, Mullion Cove, Fal Estuary, Dodman Point, Rame Head.
Devon: Valley of Rocks, Baggy Point (near Croyde), Hartland Quay, Hobby Drive (near Clovelly), Hooken Cliffs (near Beer), Bolt Head, Bolt Tail (both near Salcombe).
Somerset Porlock Toll Road, Selworthy Beacon, Brean Down
(continued on page 63)

62

▶▶▶ **REGION HIGHLIGHTS**

Avebury *page 65*
Bath *pages 65 and 66*
Cheddar Gorge *page 85*
Cornwall *pages 68–71*
Dartmoor *pages 73–74*
Dorset coast *page 77*
Exmoor National Park *pages 78–79*
Salisbury *pages 82–83*
Stonehenge *page 84*
Wells *page 84*

CORNWALL Until the opening of the Tamar railway bridge on the Devon border in the 19th century, Cornwall was the remotest county in England. That may be hard to believe at the peak of summer, as tourists descend upon the coastal villages and the narrow lanes jam with traffic, but the area still has a distinct sense of locale—partly real, partly manufactured by the tourist industry. The Cornish language has gone, the last tin mine has now closed, and Tintagel has but a tenuous link with King Arthur's Camelot. But plenty is real enough: Cornish place-names live on, and the superlative coastline encompasses awe-inspiring headlands and secret coves that bring to life tales of smugglers and shipwrecks. Cornwall is a summer playground, ideal for water sports and family fun, less promising for scenic drives (the roads seldom follow the coast close enough) and more interesting for its archeology, holy wells (structures built over springs that have supposed miraculous curative properties), and ancient stone crosses than for its architecture. Cornish villages are plain, sturdy-looking affairs of granite walls beneath Delabole slate roofs. There is nothing very ancient-feeling about much of central Cornwall, which largely grew up around the mining and china clay industries. However, no part of the county is more than a half-hour away from the coast (in normal driving conditions!), where you can usually walk along a coastal path in comparative solitude, surrounded by unrivaled beauty.

DEVON South Devon has the best beaches (such as Blackpool Sands near Stoke Fleming and Bigbury-on-Sea) and some popular coastal resorts—Torquay, Paignton, Teignmouth, Dawlish, Brixham and Exmouth, each pleasant enough at the shore but not worth going out of your way to see. Sidmouth has a conspicuously well-preserved Regency seafront. Much of the action focuses around the estuaries, notably the grand finale of the River Dart at Dartmouth, and the Kingsbridge Estuary. Of central Devon, Dartmoor is by far the best-known part, a world of windswept wastes and wilderness, tors and relics of early settlers. Granite is the predominant building material, although on the edges you will see cob walls and thatched roofs, a Devon vernacular hallmark. Exeter, unfortunately, was bombed in World War II, and you have to search around for its best corners; but the city repays such exploration (particularly the cathedral) and makes a good base. The rest of central Devon is less well known, a terrain of hilly farmlands, sandstone walls, and swift-flowing rivers. In the far north, moorland meets the sea in Exmoor, which has primeval grandeur, England's highest cliffs, and Devon's longest stretch of unspoiled coast—but a damp climate.

SOMERSET While the **Somerset** coast has little to speak of outside Exmoor (which straddles the Devon border), there is much to explore inland. The little-visited Quantock Hills have a fine heritage of country churches; the Mendip Hills are dull-looking until you encounter Wells, the Cheddar Gorge, and Burrington Combe. Southward lie the Levels, a flat, drained marshland once beneath the sea; Glastonbury Tor and the low-rise Polden Hills protrude above the far side. Taunton, the main town in the heart of (hard) cider-making country, has a bland streetscape redeemed by an impressive church and an absorbing museum.

Bath is the obvious first choice among cities to visit in Somerset (although until recently it was in the county of Avon, named after the river that flows through it, but now renamed). It is a delightful city for wandering around, but hellish to drive in. Bristol (now in its own county of Bristol) is a large port with a great maritime heritage and an elegant suburb called Clifton.

DORSET The home of Dorset Blue Vinny cheese, the county often has the tag "Hardy's Wessex" applied to it, though the ancient kingdom of Wessex in fact extended into Wiltshire, Somerset, and Hampshire. There is scarcely a corner of Dorset that does not appear under a pseudonym in Thomas Hardy's literary output. Although over three-quarters of the county's heathlands have disappeared since 1945, the inland areas still have an ancient, primitive look, with sweeping downs, clumps of beech trees, thatched villages, and prehistoric burial sites (tumuli) and hill forts. Villages such as Abbotsbury and Corfe Castle make delightful bases for the best of the remarkably varied and largely undeveloped coast.

RECOMMENDED
(continued from page 62)
Dorset: Lyme Regis under-cliff, Chesil Beach, Portland Bill, Lulworth Cove, St. Albans Head, Old Harry Rocks, Poole Harbor.
WALKING
The 500-mile South West Coast Path follows the coast from Minehead (Somerset) to Poole (Dorset); Exmoor, north Cornwall, and east Dorset are the most dramatic parts; Dartmoor is best for inland walking; otherwise inland Exmoor, the Dorset Downs, the Mendips, the Quantocks.
OFFSHORE ESCAPISM
Isles of Scilly, Lundy Island.
PREHISTORIC SITES
Wiltshire Downs, west Cornwall.

63

WILTSHIRE An inland county, Wiltshire has a gentle landscape of prairie-like chalk downlands, with its northern reaches of honey-stone villages just in the Cotswolds. Most of its interest is manmade—as in the curious hill "carvings" of horses and regimental badges on the hillsides. More famous is the legacy of early inhabitants, notably at Stonehenge and perhaps even more memorably at Avebury. Salisbury Cathedral is the pinnacle of the Early English style; a bus service from Salisbury station to Stonehenge helps make it a feasible day-trip from London. Wiltshire's largest town, Swindon, grew up in the railroad era (its railroad museum is a magnet for train buffs) and witnessed an economic boom in the 1980s; smaller places, including Devizes, Marlborough, and Bradford on Avon, are much more attractive.

Thatched roofs and whitewashed walls in Lustleigh: the unspoiled face of Devon

"There is in the Cornish character, smoldering beneath the surface, ever ready to ignite, a fiery independence, a stubborn pride."
—Daphne du Maurier, *Vanishing Cornwall* (1967)

Walks

Cheddar Gorge, Somerset   61C4

Parking lot adjacent to Butchers Arms near gorge entrance. Walk along the road at the bottom of the gorge; at the far end (1 mile) across from the gate into a nature reserve, take the West Mendip Way on the right, up through woods. Fork right to follow the top edge of the gorge; the views are impressive. Drop down by steps at Prospect Tower. (2 hours)

Lizard, Cornwall   60A1

Start at Lizard village. For the best of this celebrated coast, take the road east to Church Cove and turn right along the coastal path, past Lizard Point, the southernmost point on the mainland, and to idyllic Kynance Cove. Follow the toll road inland, branching right by a National Trust sign onto a path back to Lizard village. (2 hours)

Lulworth Cove, Dorset   61B5

Parking lot at Lulworth Cove. Take the broad path from the car park, joining the coast to reach Durdle Door, a wave-eroded natural arch; on return-ing, keep along the coast past Stair Hole, for a view of Lulworth Cove. The rugged coast east of the Cove towards Kimmeridge is army training land (open most weekends, Easter and all of August); a path heads down to the cliff where there is a fossil forest. (1 to 2 hours)

Lydford Gorge, Dartmoor   60B3
National Park, Devon

Parking lots by gorge; entrance fee. Walk through this densely wooded gorge with the White Lady Waterfall at one end and the Devil's Cauldron, where the River Lyd swirls in a gloomy chasm, at the other. The full trail takes 1½ hours, or you can take short walks from the parking lots.

Valley of Rocks, Exmoor   60C3
National Park, Devon

Start at Lynton. Take the small road between the Valley of Rocks Hotel and the church; it becomes the coastal path. The Valley of Rocks and its wild goats soon come into view. Climb Castle Rock, the most prominent fea-ture, for the view and return along the road, branching left after ¼ mile by a stone shelter to ascend Hollerday Hill and then drop into Lynton. (1½ hours)

Avebury's stones stand silent as daily life goes on around them

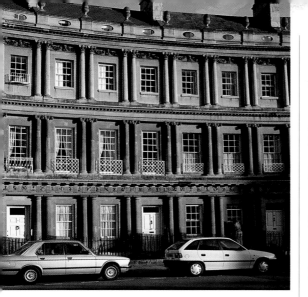

Bath's elegant Circus is built in a perfect circle around a covered reservoir

PREHISTORIC LANDMARKS AT AVEBURY

Avebury's stone circle, which can be walked around in its entirety, connects to the so-called **Stone Avenue**, parallel rows of stones that lead south to the site of another circle, the **Sanctuary**. Across from the parking lot, a path leading south passes close by **Silbury Hill**, the largest prehistoric earth-work in Europe; it is thought to have played an astronomical or religious role. The path continues south of the A4 to **West Kennet Long Barrow**, an ancient burial chamber, which can be entered.

BATH REVIVES ITS SPA

Bath's major Millennium project funded by the National Lottery is the rein-statement of its spa. The Hot Bath and the Cross Bath in the city centre have been restored and from 2001 visitors can once again take the waters. The Cross Bath will be for bathing, while the Hot Bath will house the Preventorium—a medical treatment center.

▶▶▶ **Avebury**   *61C5*

(tel: 01672 539425)

Avebury is encompassed by a huge Bronze Age stone circle—the largest such monument in Europe—which, like Stonehenge (see page 84), seems to have been erected for a mystical or ceremonial purpose (see panel). The Alexander Keiller Museum (N.T./E.H.) explains Avebury's archeology; a manorial barn houses the Great Barn Museum of Wiltshire Life. Avebury Manor (N.T.), dating back some 900 years, is open to visitors.

▶▶▶ **Bath**   *61C5*

(tel: 01225 477101)

A spa center since Roman times, Bath regained its popularity in the 18th century as a place for "taking the waters," and it remains the finest Georgian townscape in Britain. Parks, terraces, squares, an architectural "circus," and a Royal Crescent—much of it the design of John Wood the Elder and Younger (father and son)—were laid out in that heyday when Beau Nash, the archetypal English dandy, led fashionable society. The city has elegant uniformity thanks to the use of the golden-hued Bath stone.

Museums include the **Museum of Costume**▶▶▶ in the Assembly Rooms, the **Museum of East Asian Art**, the **Bath Postal Museum**, the **Bath Industrial Heritage Centre**▶▶ with a re-created Victorian factory, the **Building of Bath Museum**▶, the **Victoria Art Gallery**, the **William Herschel Museum**▶ (former home of the astronomer Herschel, who discovered Uranus from his garden), the **Holburne Museum**▶ of fine arts. At Claverton Manor the **American Museum in Britain**▶ has 17th–19th-century New World interiors. When not hosting functions, you can look inside the **Guildhall Banqueting Room**▶, for its Adam-style décor. The **Pump Room**▶▶, the **Roman Baths**▶▶▶ and **Bath Abbey**▶▶ form the historical core (see page 66). Set in a valley overlooking the city, **Prior Park Landscape Garden**▶▶ (N.T.) is an 18th-century creation by Capability Brown; take bus 2 or 4 (there is no car park).

BATH

Walk

Bath city center

At the **abbey►►**, look at the west front depicting Bishop Oliver's dream of angels that inspired him to rebuild the abbey in 1499. Then walk past the **Roman Baths►►►**, Britain's finest Roman remains: baths, cold plunges, a hypocaust room, and part of a Temple to Sulis Minerva, goddess of the springs, can be seen. Adjacent is the **Pump Room►►**, the epitome of Bath's timeless spirit; you can sip afternoon tea to the strains of chamber music by the statue of Beau Nash.

Continue along Old Lilliput Alley. **Sally Lunn's House**, a bakery producing the original Sally Lunn cakes from a secret recipe, is the oldest house in Bath (1482); a kitchen museum tells the story. Follow Grand Parade as far as **Pulteney Bridge►►** (1774, designed by Robert Adam), with stores along both sides. On Milsom Street pass the **RPS Octagon Galleries**.

Walk up Saville Row past the **Assembly Rooms** and **Museum of Costume►►►**. Walk around **The Circus►►►** (John Wood the Elder, begun 1754), and continue onto **Royal Crescent►►►** (John Wood the Younger, 1767–1774), No. 1 is open to the public. Go through Royal Victoria Park, past the **Georgian Garden►** (recreated from its 1770 plan), and on past **Queen Square** (1729–1736). Return via Bath Street to the abbey.

▶ Bodmin Moor   60B2
(tel: 01566 772351)

The top of Cornwall resembles a smaller version of Dartmoor, its bleak open moors dotted with granite tors, ponies, and sheep. Brown Willy (1,377 feet) is the county's highest point. Tracks onto the moor from the windswept hamlet of **Minions** give excellent views and lead past the **Hurlers Stone Circle▶** (Bronze Age).

At nearby Darite, **Trethevy Quoit▶** is a Bronze Age burial chamber with its capstone still in place. Villages ringing the moor are well off the beaten path. AltarnunP is a tranquil haven off the busy A30; its church has magnificent 16th-century bench ends with carvings of jester, piper, and dancers, while **St. Neot** Church has the finest medieval stained glass in Cornwall.

Launceston▶ occupies a hilltop crowned by a Norman castle keep; twisting streets, a town-wall gateway, and a steam railroad head its other attractions. **Lanhydrock House▶** (N.T.) epitomizes high living at the turn of the 20th century.

▶▶ Bradford on Avon   61C5
(tel: 01225 865797)

A charming base for the southern Cotswolds, the stone-built town rises steeply, terrace by terrace, with flagged

steps connecting its narrow lanes. Former cloth merchants' mansions and humble medieval and 18th-century weavers' cottages set the tone; oddly named Top Rank Tory is the street with the best views. In Barton Farm Park stands a splendid 14th-century barn.

Lacock Abbey▶ (N.T.), some 9 miles northeast, retains 13th-century cloisters, chapter house, and sacristy. A barn houses the Fox Talbot Museum, in memory of the pioneering photographer who lived here from 1827 to 1877. The village itself has an 18th-century time-warp feeling, and is National Trust property.

BODMIN MOOR: THREE CURIOUS COLLECTIONS
Jamaica Inn (look for signs on the A30) is the setting for Daphne du Maurier's eponymous novel of lawless days and smugglers. Its upper story is home to Potter's Museum of Curiosities, a collection of oddities that includes tableaus of stuffed animals playing cricket, attending village school, and so on. At Lanreath is an ever-growing folk museum of familiar and not-so-familiar objects of everyday and yesterday. Near St. Keyne, the Paul Corrin Musical Collection focuses on old-style mechanical musical instruments—pianolas, fairground organs, and the like—demonstrated by the owner.

67

Bradford on Avon's nine-arched Town Bridge dates from the 14th century; two of its original arches remain

A LOST CHURCH
Bradford on Avon's Church of St. Laurence, thought to be 7th–8th century, is one of Britain's most complete Saxon churches, yet it lay completely forgotten for many years. Looking over the town from a house above the church, a 19th-century vicar noticed the cruciform shape of the building, parts of which had been incorporated into a school, a house, and a factory wall. In 1858, restoration was carried out and its interior can once more be seen.

The harsh Atlantic winds buffet a wild, rocky coast, a graveyard for hundreds of wrecked ships. Eerie ruins of tin mines perch on treeless hillsides. The long coast is popular for its beautiful scenery, sights, and excellent swimming and surfing beaches. Accordingly, you have to be prepared for crowds at the peak of the season, and also for some unsightly resort development, especially between Padstow and Newquay. But it is still remarkably easy to get away from it all if you are prepared to walk for a mile or two along the coastal path.

PENWITH'S RICH ARCHEOLOGY

Inland Penwith is peppered with reminders of early peoples. Major sites include two Iron Age villages, Carn Euny and Chysauster. Chûn Castle is an Iron Age fort, while Lanyon Quoit is a good Bronze Age burial chamber and Men-an-Tol is a stone hoop of unknown purpose, used in recent times as a folk remedy for rickets; all three sites lie near the Madron–Morvah road. Close by St. Buryan, near the road, Merry Maidens stone circle is Bronze Age, the maidens supposedly turned to stone for dancing on the Sabbath.

ARTHUR'S FABLES

The deeds of King Arthur—his castle Camelot, the sword Excalibur, his Knights of the Round Table and his quest for the Holy Grail—mix fact and fiction. He was a real 6th-century chieftain (reputedly born in Tintagel and buried at Glastonbury). But later writers embroidered his exploits—the anonymous *Sir Gawayne and the Greene Knight* (1346), Sir Thomas Malory's *Le Morte d'Arthur* (1485), Tennyson's *Idylls of the King* (1857–1885), and works by T.H. White and Mark Twain.

The Devon border to Padstow The village of **Morwenstow▶** bears the indelible stamp of Rev. Robert Hawker, Celtic poet and priest here from 1834 to 1875. He adorned the vicarage with chimneypots in the form of miniature church towers and, on the cliffs nearby, erected a driftwood shack for meditation and opium-smoking (it still stands). His memorial is in the church, which has Norman arches and 16th-century bench ends.

Bude is an unremarkable resort town and a major surfing base, with a large beach; a small museum on the quay tells the story of the Bude Canal, which ends here. Inland, **Launcells Church▶**, standing all by itself, escaped the fervor of Victorian restorers, and little has changed since the 15th century.

Boscastle▶ occupies a craggy, precipitous creek; the best views are from the clifftop just west of the harbor. **Tintagel▶** achieved fame for its legendary connections with King Arthur; the ruined medieval castle postdates Arthur, but the site is nevertheless magnificent, atop an impregnable headland, reached by a steep staircase. The adjacent village is a tourist trap of the tackiest kind, redeemed somewhat by the Old Post Office (N.T.), a small-scale manor house preserved as an outstanding example of Cornish domestic architecture. **Port Isaac▶ ▶** may stake a claim as the most authentic-feeling Cornish fishing village, a hodgepodge of cottages and narrow alleyways, with a wholesome whiff of seaweed.

Padstow▶ is a busy resort town of considerable charm. It lacks a beach (try Harlyn Bay, west of town) but has a harbor packed with brightly painted craft; fresh fish are on sale at quay warehouses and served at a number of good seafood restaurants. Prideaux Place, at the top of the town, looks Elizabethan, but house tours in the summer months reveal whimsical Strawberry Hill Gothic alterations (see Shobdon, page 122) as well as the original Elizabethan plaster ceilings. The adjacent Camel Estuary offers sailing and gentle walks.

Bedruthan Steps to Land's End West from Padstow the summer crowds thicken rapidly. Many of Cornwall's safest and cleanest beaches are found between Padstow and Newquay. The immediate hinterland is spoiled by modern development, but **Bedruthan Steps▶ ▶** is an impressive coastal feature, comprising massive rock buttresses detached from the cliff itself. **Newquay** has a brash bustle: nightspots, loud-music pubs, theme parks, and surfers' stores. It also offers good beaches, a well-stocked zoo, and a pretty harbor. Out of town, **Trerice▶** (N.T.) is a handsome Elizabethan manor house with a minstrels' gallery and intricate plasterwork ceilings.

St. Ives▶▶, a delightful port turned resort, has attracted artists and beach-loving vacationers for a century. Although it has been considerably cleaned up since its heyday as a fishing port, its back streets have unmistakably Cornish character. Sculptress Barbara Hepworth was one of many 20th-century artists who settled here; her studio is now a museum with her sculptures gracing its garden. A branch of the Tate Gallery features the St. Ives school of artists in one of the most striking settings of any gallery.

Cornwall's westernmost knob of land is known as **Penwith▶▶▶** and has some of the most dramatic coastal scenery in England, with lonely heather moors inland. At **Zennor** the folk museum has an appealing selection of Cornish bygones while the church is home to a legendary mermaid, carved on an ancient bench end. **Land's End**, Britain's southwesternmost mainland point, is the place to come if you collect geographical extremities. A signpost gives distances to places throughout the world (add your home town and pose for the photo); the crowds and theme park dwindle to nothing within ten minutes' walk along the cliff southward, where the scenery gets better and better. The impressive outdoor **Minack Theatre▶** clings to a breathtaking cliff site at Porthcurno, while eastward the headland of **Treryn Dinas**, near Treen, is one of the most dramatic features of Cornwall's coastline. **Mousehole** (pronounced "Mouzal"), as quaint as its name suggests, was the home of the last solely Cornish speaker, Dolly Pentreath, who died in 1777.

A shopkeeper holds some Cornish pasties (hefty meat and vegetable turnovers)

69

MINING IN CORNWALL
Until the 19th century Cornwall was a world leader in copper and tin production (lead was also produced), when Redruth, Camborne and St Just were busy centers. The industry has gone, but there is a striking legacy of abandoned mines and engine houses, such as Wheal Coates near St Agnes Head. At Pool, near Redruth, the National Trust preserves two huge beam engines that pumped water from the mines. In medieval times tin was weighed and stamped at stannary towns, which included Penzance and Truro. Mine accidents were numerous. Cornish innovations which made the job easier included Sir Humphry Davy's miner's safety lamp, Richard Trevithick's steam-powered beam engine, and the rock drill.

St. Ives' distinctive Mediterranean light qualities attracted artists such as Naum Gabo, Ben Nicholson, and Bernard Leach

Eastward from Penzance, the coast gets more sheltered; the cliffs are less mighty, the seaboard is lusher and more populated than the north coast. Deep-water harbors are packed with craft: industrial ships, private yachts, and ferries—every village and town seems to have a sign advertising fishing and sharking trips by boat. Visitors in spring and early summer will be on time for Cornwall's famous gardens.

LIZARD TRANSMITTERS
The Lizard Peninsula is an important past and present telecommunications center. A memorial near Poldhu Cove commemorates the birth of transatlantic transmissions—it was from here that in 1901 Marconi sent three dots (a morse "S") to Newfoundland; his first message which followed was " What hath God wrought." Inland, "the Lizard" is dominated by the space-age form of the Goonhilly Downs Earth Station, the receiving center for satellite-relayed telephone calls. A tour of the site takes you into an old control tower, and you can see the nerve center of the whole operation.

Penzance to Falmouth The town of **Penzance** has been knocked about by the 20th century, but it retains corners of Georgian streetscape, at its best on Chapel Street with its capricious Egyptian House, an early 19th-century precursor to art deco. The National Lighthouse Centre records the essential function of lighthouses on a perilous coast. Surveying the main street is the statue of Sir Humphry Davy, inventor of the miner's safety lamp and the town's foremost son in its tin-mining heyday.

    St. Michael's Mount▶▶▶ (N.T.) shimmers ethereally in the sea, an isle capped by a castle. Those who have seen Mont St. Michel in Brittany can be excused a sense of *déjà vu*, and in fact it was the Benedictines from Brittany who founded a church on the site, which became a fortress after Dissolution in 1539. The owners today are the same family that snatched possession after the Civil War. At low tide you can walk to it along a causeway across the sands; at other times take the little ferry. It has a tremendous view from the roof terrace and an intriguing warren of rooms inside.

    The **Lizard Peninsula** juts out to form Britain's southernmost acres. Its inland portion is flat and bleak. **Kynance Cove▶** epitomizes the best of the tumbledown cliffscape of the western Lizard, with a wonderfully sited beach amid the so-called Serpentine Rocks. There are several rock workshops at **Lizard** village, which is itself of little appeal. Eastern Lizard, beyond **Cadgwith▶**, with its thatched

These days fishing boats in Mevagissey are still busy, but tourism is the main source of income

cottages stepping down to the sea, has hidden, verdant creeks in the vicinity of the **Helford River**, including around the tiny waterside village of Helford itself.

Falmouth, Cornwall's largest town, is no great beauty but it's the base for boat trips up Carrick Roads, alternatively known as the Fal Estuary▶ including excursions upriver to **Truro**, the Cornish capital (not itself of major interest, although it has a 19th-century cathedral). Perfectly preserved Tudor castles, St. Mawes and Pendennis, guard the great estuary. Subtropical plants abound at the delightful churchyard of **St. Just in Roseland**▶, which dips down to the water's edge.

Portloe to the Tamar Portloe▶ is an unspoiled fishing hamlet, hard to get to—and long may it continue to be; it has real character and nothing to attract large-scale commercialization. **Veryan**, inland, is known for its five early 19th-century round houses. **Charlestown**▶, a carefully preserved port, is still used by the china clay industry, whose white refuse heaps dominate the area.

Fowey▶▶ rises terrace by terrace above the deep-anchorage Fowey Harbour, with Polruan across the water. Blockhouses that used to guard the harbor stand silent sentinel. An appealing resort town, Fowey comes to life during the late summer regatta.

Mevagissey has become too popular for some people's tastes, with busloads of visitors cramming into its little harbor, but the place resumes its quiet charm when they have gone; ice cream, fish and chips, a model railroad, and the Gardens of Heligan—a Victorian garden being restored—are attractions for tourists. **Polperro**▶▶▶ is even prettier and more groomed, though no less popular, with a maze of alleys around its photogenic harbor; park at Talland Bay to the east and walk in along the level coastal path rather than struggle with traffic jams.

The **Tamar Estuary** forms the Devon/Cornwall border; the river can be explored by boat trip from Plymouth. **Antony**▶ (N.T.) is the earliest and finest classical-style house in Cornwall, with fine woodland gardens. **Cotehele**▶▶ (N.T.) is an extraordinary medieval relic, a completely unmodernized house; its estate buildings (saddler, smithy, wheelwright, etc.) are well preserved. By the Tamar is moored *Shamrock*, the last Tamar barge in existence. The **Mount Edgcumbe estate**▶, tucked in the far corner of southeastern Cornwall, is a country park looking across to Plymouth; paths through its grounds lead toward quietly characterful Kingsand and Cawsand.

Rising like a dream from Mounts Bay, St. Michael's Mount acquired its monastery after the Archangel Michael appeared in a vision to local fishermen

SUBTROPICAL GARDENS 71

Penjerrick, Glendurgan (N.T.), and Trebah gardens, close together west of Falmouth, were all the creation of the Foxes, a Quaker family, who aimed to create Paradise on Earth. For other gardens to visit in south Cornwall, see Gardens, page 16—do not miss the Lost Gardens of Heligan. Opening in full in 2001 (visitor center open from Easter 2000), the exciting Eden Project near St. Austell recreates Mediterranean and tropical plant life in "biomes."

Looe, a lively resort in a pleasant setting

CLIFTON

Venture out to the Georgian suburb of Clifton when visiting Bristol. It resembles a mini-Bath with its handsome stone-built squares, crescents and terraces (notably Royal York Crescent). Brunel's majestic Clifton Suspension Bridge (built 1836–1864) spans the Avon gorge. Nearby, an 18th-century camera obscura offers views over the city.

When Brunel's superlative Clifton Suspension Bridge was completed in 1864, its 702-foot span was the world's greatest

▶▶ Bristol   61C4

(tel: 0117 926 0767)

The city center was badly bombed in 1940 and postwar planning was unimaginative. However, a huge facelift has been made for the new millennium, with construction of tree-lined avenues, and the restoration of Queen Square as a traffic-free haven. The city preserves many gems, among them **Christmas Steps**, a 17th-century relic; the **Church of St. Mary Redcliffe▶** with its majestic proportions; the **cathedral▶** (begun 1142), notable for its Norman chapter house and organ case carved by Grinling Gibbons; and the **New Room**, Britain's first Wesleyan (Methodist) chapel. A curious architectural folly, the **Cabot Tower▶** provides an excellent city view.

Docking activity is now concentrated in Avonmouth, but the revamped dockland area still has a July regatta, and boat tours around the harbor. Here too is the **Industrial Museum**, which acknowledges the life of Isambard Kingdom Brunel, the 19th-century engineer who designed the world's first ocean-going propeller ship, the **S.S. *Great Britain*▶ ▶**. Launched in 1843, it is now on show in the dry dock where she was built. Entrance covers the **Maritime Heritage Museum**, which charts the city's shipbuilding, the replica of *Matthew* (in which Cabot voyaged to Newfoundland) and the **Bristol Blue Glass Workshop**. From 2000 the harbor will also be home to **Explore@Bristol** (a hands-on science center) and **Wildscreen@Bristol** (looking at wildlife photography, with IMAX theater and interactive exhibits).Here also is the **Arnolfini** arts center.

▶ Clovelly   60B2

A captivating fishing village, overrun in summer, Clovelly is so steep that cars must park at the top. The Hobby Drive was built by a 19th-century owner of Clovelly Court as a scenic road; it's well worth the modest toll. Donkeys and sleds make the descent through its cobbled, time-warp main street, which ends at steps that zigzag down to the harbor.

Hartland Quay▶ ▶, to the east, gives access to some of the most formidable cliffs in the West Country, the strata fantastically contorted into bizarre cross-sections.

AN L OF AN ACCENT

The hallmark of Bristol speech is the adding of the letter *L* to the ends of words. Thus *area* becomes *areal*, *Australia* becomes *Australial* and *Bristowe*, the old city name, becomes *Bristol*.

►►► Dartmoor National Park 60B3
(tel: 01822 890414)

Southern England's largest area of wild country, Dartmoor is a great expanse of blustery moors punctuated by weathered granite outcroppings known as tors. Sheep and Dartmoor ponies graze the open grasslands, wandering between Bronze Age hut circles and burial mounds. The moor can be a bleak place—there is no higher place in England south of the Pennines—but there are cozy cob-and-thatch villages to come down to in the lusher valleys (some offering Devon cream teas), and several fine country-house style hotels. Indoor attractions are few: this is a place to be outdoors—picnicking, touring, walking, or riding horseback.

On Dartmoor's east side, lush farmland meets the barren moors. **Hay Tor►►** is the most visited viewpoint, easily accessible. **Hound Tor►►**, close by, is well marked by signs and lies next to a well-preserved abandoned medieval village, where you can still make out the fireplaces. West of **Buckland**, whose church clock has the letters MY DEAR MOTHER instead of numerals, **Bel Tor** presides over the Webburn Valley. The **Dart Valley►** is full of choice corners, including Combestone Tor and the medieval "clapper" bridge, made of great granite slabs, at Dartsmeet, the confluence of the West and East Dart rivers.

Widecombe in the Moor► draws visitors for its valley setting, its fame from the folksong "Widecombe Fair" and for its church, the "cathedral of the moor." **North Bovey►** is much quieter and quite uncommercialized, with a pretty green, thatched cottages, a stone cross, and a village pump. **Chagford** is a large but sleepy village; **Moretonhampstead**, a crossroads town, is a shade busier and has a fine row of 17th-century almshouses; to the west, on the B3212, the **Miniature Pony Centre** shows several rare farmyard breeds (not just ponies).

In northeast Dartmoor the River Teign has carved a course through a deep valley with an enchanting deciduous forest. From **Fingle Bridge►**, an old packhorse bridge, paths lead along the river and up onto moorland viewpoints; the Hunter's Path passes the back entrance to **Castle Drogo►►** (N.T.), architect Edwin Lutyens' early 20th-century masterpiece, an improbable marriage of granite medievalism and Edwardian Arts and Crafts style. The main entrance is near **Drewsteignton**, which has a charming village square.

Two main roads cross the central moor; the B3212 passes through **Postbridge**, with its notable medieval "clapper bridge," and grim **Princetown**, dominated by a high-security prison originally built for Napoleonic prisoners of war. For an overview of Dartmoor, go to the High Moorland Visitor Centre in Princetown. (Access to the high northern moor is restricted due to military training.)

Two outstanding features justify a visit to the western fringes: **Brent Tor►**, a plain church atop a huge rock and looking far into Cornwall, and **Lydford Gorge►►** (see Walks, page 64. *Admission charge*), a deep and tortuous ravine with a waterfall and whirlpool.

The towns encircling Dartmoor National Park are not of great interest, although **Ashburton** has some attractive streets and **Buckfastleigh** boasts a modern Benedictine abbey, a butterfly park and otter sanctuary, and the

Hound Tor: weathering has attacked the joints in the great granite outcrops that dominate the wastes of Dartmoor

73

DARTMOOR'S MAILBOXES
Many visitors to Dartmoor in the 19th century liked to try to locate Cranmere Pool, scarcely more than a puddle and remotely situated in the moors above Chagford. Someone had the idea of placing a mailbox here, so that a self-addressed postcard would be left here by one walker and picked up and sent on by the next. The fad caught on and now there are some 6,000 official, unofficial, and mobile boxes in various places. Today you can record your visit with the rubber stamp provided.

PREHISTORIC PROCESSIONAL ROUTES
Rows of stones erected in the Bronze Age are believed to have marked processional routes. Above the Erme Valley in south Dartmoor, one of these stretches 2 miles from Stall Moor to Green Hill.

EARLY SETTLERS ON DARTMOOR

The moorland gravels yielded copious quantities of tin, exploited by Bronze Age settlers. Among the most striking of their relics are **Scorhill Stone Circle**, on Shovel Down above Gidleigh (near Chagford), a Bronze Age stone circle of 23 uprights, and **Spinsters' Rock**, off the A382 south of its intersection with the A30, a neolithic tomb with its capstone held in place by three uprights.

Grimspound, between Widecombe in the Moor and the B3212, reached by a path up from the road onto Hamel Down, consists of a large walled enclosure with 24 discernible hut circles.

74

terminal of the steam-powered South Devon Railway which wends its way 7 miles to Totnes. The **Museum of Dartmoor Life** at **Okehampton** tells of country life and ways; a fragment of a medieval castle (E.H.) caps a hillock on the edge of town.

Buckland Abbey►, a former Cistercian monastery, was once home to Sir Francis Drake, born at nearby Tavistock. The house has some relics from his famous ship, *Golden Hind* (including a drum and banners), but it was more Sir Richard Grenville, an earlier occupant, who stamped his character on the house; he added the intricate plasterwork in the Great Hall.

►► Dartmouth   60A3
(tel: 01803 834224)

An old naval town, set on steep slopes which drop to the River Dart, Dartmouth has real atmosphere, with small craft on the river and harbor and a maze of back streets. The August regatta sees the town at its most exuberant.

Beside Duke Street is the arcaded **Butterwalk**, a former dairy market and now a local museum. In the quayside gardens stands the world's first steam pumping-engine, built in 1725 by Thomas Newcomen, a Dartmouth resident. Two Tudor castles guard either side of the harbor entrance; **Dartmouth Castle►** has a magnificent view from its roof terrace.

Dartmouth is a good base for excursions, including **Totnes►** with its Norman castle and steep medieval streets, and **Salcombe►**, a yachting center with a handsome location on an estuary. Ferries cross the Dart to Kingswear, where steam locomotives haul trainloads of day trippers along the **Paignton and Dartmouth Steam Railway**.

Dartmouth quay: boat trips can be taken up river or out to sea

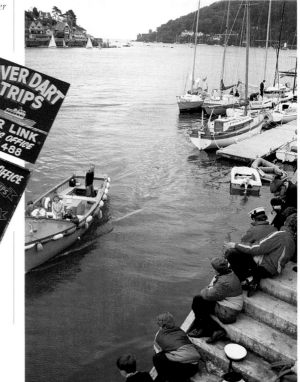

▶ Dorchester

61B4

(tel: 01305 267992)

Although not outstandingly attractive, Dorchester is the center of the countryside of Thomas Hardy's novels, in which the town features as Casterbridge; it is often visited for that reason. It has a good museum celebrating aspects of the county and displaying Hardy's study and a collection of material relating to him. Hardy was also a trained architect and designed **Max Gate** (N.T.), open to the public; he lived there from 1885 until his death in 1928.

Dorchester, a typical country town, is still recognizable as Thomas Hardy's "Casterbridge"

Maiden Castle▶▶ is a huge earthwork on the south-western edge of Dorchester; its massive concentric ramparts date from the 1st century BC.

Hardy's Birthplace▶, the humble thatched cottage where Thomas Hardy was born in 1840, is furnished as it may have looked in his lifetime. Start from the car park at Higher Bockhampton; either walk along the main track or take the longer Thorncombe Trail, a nature walk through woodland and a fragment of the "untamed and untamable wild" of Egdon Heath in Hardy's work. Although Hardy is buried at Westminster Abbey, his heart is buried in the family plot at **Stinsford Church▶**, Mellstock Church of his novel *Under the Greenwood Tree*.

A prominent tower some 5 miles southwest of Dorchester, confusingly called the **Hardy Monument▶**, commemorates Admiral Thomas Hardy, Nelson's flag-captain at the Battle of Trafalgar. From here there's a view over Chesil Beach and Portland Bill.

THOMAS HARDY COUNTRY

Drive

Thomas Hardy country

This tour (about 70 miles in total) explores the heartland of the countryside immortalized in the writings of Thomas Hardy. Local life has changed beyond recognition, but many elements are still there—thatched villages, rolling downlands, manor houses, ancient monuments.

From **Dorchester** take the A35 east, branching off for **Stinsford▶** and detouring to Hardy's Birthplace at **Higher Bockhampton▶** (see page 75). At **Tolpuddle** the cottage museum pays homage to the Tolpuddle Martyrs who formed a trade union and were transported for their pains.

Take minor roads heading northward to **Milton Abbas▶ ▶**, an 18th-century estate village of rustic thatch and whitewash: the owner of Milton Abbey house nearby (which is now a school) had the village rebuilt here to improve the view from his house. The abbey church and finely roofed Abbot's Hall are open.

Take lanes west to **Cerne Abbas▶ ▶** to look at the famous Giant, best seen from a vista point on the A352 road north. Follow the A352 to **Minterne Magna**, where a turn-of-the-century house harbors a fine collection of trees and shrubs (open in season).

❏ Looming over the demure village of Cerne Abbas is an extraordinary prehistoric hill-carving of a naked club-bearing man (known as the Cerne Giant) revealing all for the world to see. Its origins and purpose are unclear, but it is thought to be a fertility or cult symbol. ❏

Continue west to **Beaminster▶**, a delightful scene of small-town rural England with an attractive square, and past **Parnham House▶**. Drunken lanes meander southeast through **Powerstock**, attractively placed on a hillside, and past **Eggardon Hill▶**, an impressively bleak Iron Age hill fort site. Continue on through Littlebredy and up to the **Hardy Monument▶** (see page 75). Drive east via the B3159 and minor roads to pass **Maiden Castle▶** (parking lot on Dorchester side). The A354 leads northward into Dorchester.

THE FOWLES CONNECTION
At Lyme Regis a sinuous sea wall known as The Cobb gained fame through the movie of John Fowles's novel *The French Lieutenant's Woman*, where crazed Sarah Woodruff stared out to sea in despair while Charles Smithson explored natural history in the undercliff just west of town. The Cobb is of medieval origin, and the undercliff, still a wild place and riddled with landslips, is designated a National Nature Reserve.

▶▶ Dorset Coast   61B4–B5

(tel: 01305 267992 for west; 01929 552740 for east)

Beyond Dorset's mighty cliffs lie unspoiled hinterlands that seem to have emerged only recently from the primeval past. The coast is famous for fossils, no place more than **Lyme Regis▶▶**, a charming resort beloved of novelist Jane Austen. The narrow lanes and Regency seafront cottages have changed little since her visits at the turn of the 19th century. Huge ammonite fossils can be seen in garden walls, in **Dinosaurland** (a museum which also gives guided fossil walks along the beach) and in special fossil stores. The thatched honey-stone village of **Abbotsbury▶▶** crouches beneath a hillock crowned by a lone chapel; dedicated to St. Catherine, it was once the property of the Benedictine abbey which gave the village its name. A tithe barn and the swannery (very much alive) are other abbey leftovers.

Close by, **Chesil Beach** (or Bank) is one of the most extraordinary features of the British coastline (see panel). **Weymouth▶**, an elegant resort with an early 19th-century flavor, made popular by George III, lies behind a curving bay. Further east lies **Lulworth Cove▶▶▶**, abutted by amazing cliffs that offer ideal cross-sections for the aspiring geologists who flock here along with fishermen, skin-divers, and walkers heading for **Durdle Door** (see Walks, page 64), a fine natural arch. East of Lulworth, army ranges permit only occasional access to rugged cliffs as far as Kimmeridge. **St. Aldhelm's Head** juts into the sea and has a primitive chapel on its summit. Beyond the coastal resort of **Swanage** lie **Old Harry Rocks▶**, chalk stacks detached from the cliff, and the multicolored sands of **Studland**, with its fine Norman church; the village lies near the largest remaining heathlands in Dorset. Seaward, views extend to the Isle of Wight. The **Purbeck Ridge** offers a panorama of Poole Harbour and the largest of Dorset's heathlands. The ridge is interrupted dramatically at **Corfe Castle▶▶**, where the pinnacle of a Norman castle rises above the village.

THE CHESIL BEACH NATURAL PHENOMENON
The 18-mile shingle bank was created by the deposit of millions of pebbles through the process of long-shore drift, the lateral shift of material as a result of the waves meeting the shore at an oblique angle. The beach links Portland Bill to the mainland and encloses a lagoon known as the Fleet, a peaceful haven for birds. Because of the steeply shelving seaward side of the beach, it attracts anglers (but swimmers must stay clear: this is one of Britain's most dangerous beaches). The pebbles increase in size from west to east.

Tarr Steps was allegedly built in a single night by the Devil

78

A LA RONDE

At Exmouth, south of Exeter, A la Ronde (N.T.) is a delightfully eccentric 16-sided house of 1796, built by Jane and Mary Parminter on returning from a Grand Tour of Europe. It is based on the Byzantine church of San Vitale in Ravenna, Italy, and displays many items the sisters collected on their travels.

LUNDY ISLAND

A popular day-trip by ferry from Bideford (in summer also from Barnstaple) is to Lundy, a little island some 39 miles north of Hartland Point. Its cliffs are a major site for birdlife; over 400 species are recorded, including puffins (*lunde* being Norse for puffin).
From 1925 to 1954 Lundy's owner Martin Harman tried to make it a separate kingdom; he did not succeed, but the island still issues its own stamps. Lundy's isolation in the Bristol Channel has given it a long history of smuggling. The Marisco Tavern serves beer brewed on the island.

▶ Exeter   60B3
(tel: 01392 265700)

Prior to destruction in a World War II air raid (one of a series targeted on historic sites), Exeter was among southern England's most attractive cities. Amazingly the **cathedral▶▶▶** escaped almost unscathed, and makes it worth the effort to visit the otherwise largely rebuilt center. The twin towers are Norman, and its nave displays the longest span of Gothic vaulting in the world. Look too for the astronomical clock in the north transept, the bishop's throne, and the intricately carved misericords.

The porticoed **Guildhall** on the High Street is England's oldest municipal building. Within Boots Arcade is the entrance to a 13th-century subterranean water system known as the **Underground Passages▶** (guided tours).

▶▶ Exmoor National Park   60C3
(tel: 01398 323665)

A small but varied national park, Exmoor encompasses unspoiled coast, moors, and quiet farmland straddling the Devon and Somerset borders. The coast is the main focus of interest, but inland there are lonely moors and fine river valleys. Unusually for England, the moors often reach the clifftops, and the Exmoor coast is a fine place for walks, where you can set off on the coastal path and return over windswept hillsides.

THE COAST ROAD (A39) In the northwest of the national park, **Parracombe's Church of St. Petrock▶** is a completely unaltered medieval building, threatened with demolition in the last century but preserved thanks to a campaign led by John Ruskin, influential writer, critic, and social reformer. **Trentishoe Church** has a tiny musicians' gallery (notice the notch cut out to allow for a double bass's bow); just east, **Heddon's Mouth** is a charming, walkers-only valley which leads from the isolated Hunter's Inn to an abandoned lime kiln on a pebbly beach. At **Lynton**, a dozy but amiable resort, strangely shaped crags adorn the **Valley of Rocks▶▶**, where wild goats sniff the sea breezes (see Walks, page 64); **Heddon Valley** is another popular area for walks. A cliff railroad connects Lynton with **Lynmouth** below, prettily situated by a small harbor and, in season, it's more animated than its neighbor. Eastward, the River Lyn lines a magnificent wooded valley; you can walk along the river to an idyllically sited café at **Watersmeet▶▶**, at the joining of the East Lyn River and Farley Water, or head for the hills for the best views; close by, the cliffs near **Countisbury** exceed 1,000 feet and are some of England's highest. **Oare** and **Malmsmead** are at the heart of Doone Country, the setting of R.D. Blackmore's *Lorna Doone*, based on a real family of outlaws (see panel). **Culbone**, north of the main road, boasts England's smallest church, alone in the woods. **Allerford►** has a pretty packhorse bridge and a fascinating local museum within its old school, while tiny **Selworthy►** has a group of immaculate thatched cottages and a large church with a fine wagon roof.

INLAND EXMOOR Sheep and ponies roam the breezy hills, red deer the eastern forests. Over the years the moors have dwindled in extent, encroached upon by farmland and pastures, but recent National Park measures have safeguarded what remains. A road tour from Dunkery Hill to Exford, then to Dulverton and west along the Park boundary to Twitchen, gives a good idea of the moor. **Winsford►**, **Exford**, and **Withypool** are three attractive villages in this area; **Dulverton►** has lots of small-town charm. South of Withypool, **Tarr Steps►** is a 1,000-year-old clapper bridge spanning the River Barle. **Dunkery Beacon► ►** is an easily climbed hill, a 10-minute walk from the road, which on a clear day offers a far-ranging view across Devon and Somerset and over the Bristol Channel into South Wales. **Dunster► ►** rates as one of the most perfect small towns in England, with its ancient yarn market at the hub of its tapering street of medieval buildings, and the **Dunster Castle► ►** (N.T.) towering above. The fashionable 19th-century architect Salvin upgraded the castle interior, but it retains earlier features, including a 17th-century staircase and leather wall-hangings that tell the story of Antony and Cleopatra. On the edge of town is a working 18th-century watermill (N.T.), and there are glorious walks through Dunster Park and along the ridge of Grabbist Hill.

A storefront in Dunster, an important cloth center in the 16th century

LORNA DOONE

Blackmore's Victorian adventure novel takes place in the wilds of Exmoor. The hero, John Ridd, seeks revenge on the Doones for shooting his father, and is in love with Lorna Doone, whom the Doones have kidnapped for her large inheritance. Tragedy later strikes at Lorna's wedding at Oare Church. Despite failing to sell for more than a year after publication, *Lorna Doone* has become a minor classic that for many is synonymous with Exmoor.

English schoolchildren are often taught how Francis Drake insisted on finishing a lawn bowling match on Plymouth Hoe before turning his attention to the Spanish Armada. Devon-born, he was the first Englishman to sail around the world and, as a darling of Elizabeth I, he was knighted for his efforts. In 1588 he achieved the great victory over the Armada; the weather played a major role—a third of the Spanish vessels were shipwrecked. This was Drake's last great naval exploit, although he pioneered a leat (channel) bringing fresh water from Dartmoor to Plymouth.

80

Gilded ceilings and other adornments at Longleat House were added in the 19th century by the 4th Marquess of Bath

▶▶ Glastonbury   61C4
(tel: 01458 832954)

The town huddles around the base of Glastonbury Tor, a hillock capped by St. Michael's Chapel. Visible from afar, the Tor was an island in early times, when the sea extended across the Somerset Levels. The **abbey▶** has long been a place of pilgrimage: the Legend of Glastonbury records Joseph of Arimathaea burying the chalice used at the Last Supper. There are links too with Arthurian legend: Arthur's corpse was brought here by Sir Lancelot.

▶▶ Longleat   61C5
(tel: 01985 844400)

In 1949 Longleat was Britain's first country house to open its doors full-time; side attractions include a Mirror Maze and a safari park. The house, completed in 1580, was ahead of its time: it looks out to its park rather than gazing into a courtyard. Inside are some 16th-century tapestries, portraits, and rare manuscripts; 19th-century embellishments—marquetry, fireplaces, and gilded ceilings—were added by Italian craftsmen after the 4th Marquess of Bath returned from a Grand Tour. The kitchen dates from this period. Capability Brown landscaped the grounds in 1757 with the world's largest maze.

▶ Plymouth   60A2
(tel: 01752 264849)

A major naval base for centuries, Plymouth sprawls in a natural harbor. After World War II bombing, much of the center was rebuilt in a monolithic style. Head for the Barbican, west of Sutton Harbour, with the **National Marine Aquarium▶**, the timber-framed **Elizabethan House**, the **Plymouth Gin Distillery** (in operation since 1793) and the **Pilgrim Fathers Memorial**. Carry on past the **Royal Citadel** to **The Hoe▶▶** waterfront area: **Plymouth Dome▶** is a hi-tech evocation of the city's past; entrance covers **Smeaton's Tower**, a re-erected 18th-century lighthouse. On Finewell Street is 15th-century **Prysten House** (with a model of 17th-century Plymouth). The **Tamar Bridges** cross into Cornwall: the 1961 road suspension bridge and Brunel's 1859 railroad bridge.

In Dorset you can walk from Ryme Intrinseca to Beer Hackett; in Kent you can try getting your tongue around Trottiscliffe (pronounced Trozlee); in County Durham you can go to Pity Me; while in Worcestershire, there is a village called Upton Snodsbury. England's place-names have long amused and bemused visitors and locals alike, inspiring both affectionate parody and rhapsodic poetry.

Historical pointers By the time of the Norman invasion in 1066, the settlement pattern in England was already largely established. Place-names give a host of clues as to how and when England developed. Generally the suffix gives the key element, with the prefix acting as a descriptive defining element—Doncaster, for example, tells us of a Roman camp (*castra*) on the River Don.

Settlers from the East As Saxons began to settle in England, they introduced their own place-names rather than using the existing Celtic ones—the only native place-names to have survived adopted natural features such as hills, rivers, and valleys. Early Saxon names included heathen names such as those of gods, for instance Woden (Wednesbury) and Thunor (Thunderfield). The suffix *-ing* survives from that period, particularly in Surrey and East Anglia, while later Saxon names included the commonest suffixes, *-ham* (home) and *-ton* (enclosure, farm, or manor).

Scandinavian settlers ensconced themselves in eastern England, where today there are still many names ending with *-by* (Grimsby, Whitby, Wragby, etc.): the vast majority are in the eastern counties. Remote areas had names unto themselves: Lympne and Lyminge in east Kent and numerous Cornish names (Trelissick, Marazion, Nanjizal) are unique to those parts. The suffix Chipping (Chipping Campden, Chipping Sodbury, Chippenham, etc.) indicates a marketplace; the word is related to the German *kaufen* (to buy) and appears to be the root of Copenhagen.

Later changes In the 19th century, mining and other industrial settlements created new names—ranging from matter-of-fact New Mills to the intriguing likes of Indian Queens and Booze. The Somerset coastal resort of Weston upgraded itself into Latin, and was renamed Weston-super-Mare. The odd euphemism evolved—the Devil's Arse cave was tamed to Peak Cavern, and Pigg Hill became Peak Hill. Craven Arms in Shropshire was originally just a pub; a railroad town grew around it and the name stuck.

PLACE-NAME QUIRKS
● Some places were merely mapmaker's accidents: Unnear appears on several early 19th-century maps of Mid Wales, but was no more than the corruption of a mapmaker's query—Quaere.
● Few 20th-century place-names exist; the new towns of Peterlee (named after a trade union leader) and Telford (after Thomas Telford, a Scottish civil engineer) are exceptions.
● Westward Ho! is Britain's only place-name bearing an exclamation mark.
● Coldharbour (meaning a shelter from bad weather) is the commonest minor place-name.

81

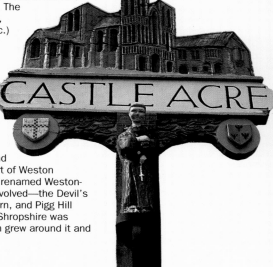

The West Country

THE LYRIC POETS IN SOMERSET

The Quantocks and hills near Culbone inspired *The Lyrical Ballads* (1798) of William Wordsworth and Samuel Taylor Coleridge. Dorothy Wordsworth recorded: "There is every-thing here; sea, woods wild as fancy ever painted, brooks clear and pebbly as in Cumberland, villages so romantic." Coleridge wrote *The Rime of the Ancient Mariner* and Part One of *Christabel* at Nether Stowey. His great poem *Kubla Khan* was written at a cottage near Culbone in Exmoor and was inspired by an opium dream, rudely broken off by the alleged arrival of a "person from Porlock" about some minor matter. The work was never completed.

82

Salisbury Cathedral

► **Quantock Hills**   *61C4*
(tel: 01823 336344)

A forgotten corner of rural England, if there ever was one. The hedges grow high around the sunken, crooked lanes, the churchyards hide behind banks of cow parsley, and manor houses lurk behind estate walls. Villages are sleepy, typically of sandstone and color-washed cottages. Dense woodlands cloak the lower slopes. On the top is a plateau of heather moors crossed by ancient trackways.

Medieval wool-trade prosperity left a legacy of fine churches in the Quantocks: 16th-century carved bench ends are a specialty; the best include those at **Broomfield**, **Spaxton**, **Crowcombe**, and **Bicknoller**.

William Wordsworth and his sister Dorothy stayed in 1797 at Alfoxton Park at **Holford**, keeping fellow poet Samuel Taylor Coleridge company (see panel). The latter lived for some years at **Nether Stowey**►, where his cottage has been restored by the National Trust and filled with mementoes of his life and works.

The **West Somerset Railway**►, the longest private line in Britain, operates steam and diesel trains along the track from Bishop's Lydeard (near Taunton) to Minehead on the coast. Washford station has a small museum devoted to railroad memorabilia.

►► **Salisbury**   *61C5*
(tel: 01722 334956)

Painted by Constable, Salisbury's **cathedral**►►► is all of one style, being built between 1220 and 1258 in Early English Gothic. Its noble spire, added in 1334–1380, soars 404 feet, higher than any other in the country. On clear days, it's worth the effort to climb the tower to the base of the spire. Reached through the cloisters, the octagonal chapter house boasts a medieval carved frieze depicting scenes from the books of "Genesis" and "Exodus" and the best-preserved of four manuscripts of the Magna Carta, the first bill of rights foisted by barons on King John in 1215. England's largest **cathedral close** surrounds the precincts; houses open to the public are the 13th-century **King's House**, now home to the **Salisbury and South Wiltshire Museum** (exhibits relate to Stonehenge, Old Sarum, ceramics, and a pre-National Health Service doctor's office),

Redcoats in the Wardrobe (regimental museum), **Malmesbury House**, and **Mompesson House▶** (N.T.), a Queen Anne house with a walled garden, period furnishings and a rare collection of English drinking glasses. The rest of town, laid out on a spacious grid plan by Bishop Poore in the 13th century, has many attractive corners.

Wilton House▶▶ The 17th-century home of the Earls of Pembroke in nearby Wilton is not on the grandest scale but shows exemplary taste; Inigo Jones designed most of it, including the Double Cube Room, hung with Van Dyck portraits. Here too is the room where some of the D-Day invasion planning took place.

▶▶ Scilly, Isles of   60C1
(tel: 01720 422536)

An idyllic retreat beyond the southwestern tip of the British mainland, the Scillies, as they are often known, comprise five inhabited islands. Each is surprisingly different from the other and there is much to interest the naturalist, particularly birdlife. Daffodils, narcissi, iris, and tulips are commercially grown.

Hugh Town is the principal township on **St. Mary's**, the largest island (with a maximum width of only 3 miles); Star Castle, built in 1593–1594 as a fortress against a possible Spanish invasion, is now a hotel. Paths follow the coastline; there is a remarkable concentration of prehistoric burial chambers to explore, while at Peninnis Head are curiously weathered rocks. The island of **Bryher** is windswept, with simple facilities and gorse-clad hillsides. **St. Agnes**, the smallest inhabited island, has an old lighthouse of 1680 (now a private house but still providing flashes). Troy Town Maze, a piece of folk art with stones laid out on the turf, may have been created by an 18th-century lighthouse-keeper with time on his hands. **St. Martin's** is treeless, with a prominent day-mark cone (1683) on its highest point, and has splendid beaches; Higher and Lower Towns between them muster a population of around 100. **Tresco▶▶** is renowned for its subtropical gardens of Tresco Abbey, the major attraction of the Scillies, created by Dorrien Smith. The island is fun to explore (no cars, just tractors), with forts and several white-sand beaches.

83

Stonehenge, compellingly immense and silent, is thought to have been constructed in three phases

STONEHENGE —THE FACTS

Stonehenge began as a simple ditch and bank (2800 BC); sarsen stones from Wiltshire and stones from the Preseli Hills in Wales were added around 2000 BC. In the Bronze Age, around 1600–1500 BC, the whole was remodeled with uprights and cross-lintels. The central axis aligns with the sun on Midsummer's Day, and other alignments may have enabled the circle to function as a kind of calender.

STONEHENGE —THE ENIGMA

Archeologists may never know the precise mystical, religious, or ceremonial significance of Stonehenge. More extreme theories have included notions of inspirations from beings from outer space, a creation by King Arthur and his circle of models of male and female sexuality, a bird trap, a model of the solar system, and a cosmic scheme related to the Egyptian pyramids and built by the people of Atlantis.

▶▶▶ Stonehenge   61C5
(tel: 01980 624715)

Britain's most famous prehistoric stone circle (E.H.), a World Heritage Site, stands alone on Salisbury Plain, a sparsely populated area of chalk downland studded with mementoes of early inhabitants. Its origins remain a mystery (see panel). Entry includes an audio tour. Visitors flock here in the thousands; there are plans to reroute the main road and for an upgrade facilities.

▶▶ Stourhead   61C5
(tel: 01747 841152)

In 1741, inspired by a Grand Tour of Europe, Henry Hoare II, the son of a wealthy banker, returned home to Stourhead and decided to re-landscape his grounds with classical temples, a triangular lake, and rare plants. He created one of the highest achievements of English landscape gardening. The Palladian mansion suffered a fire in 1902 but still has good Chippendale furniture, paintings, and a library. This and the adjacent village of Stourton are owned by the National Trust.

▶▶▶ Wells   61C4
(tel: 01749 672552)

England's smallest cathedral city is set near the eastern end of the Mendip Hills. The streets of limestone houses are dwarfed by the **cathedral▶▶▶**, significant above all for the richness of its early 13th-century west front (recently restored), adorned with 356 statues. Building started on the choir in about 1180 and finished with the cloisters in 1508, following the designs of Bishop Reginald de Bohun. A problem of subsidence at the crossing was resolved by the innovation of inverted "scissor" arches, which despite the obvious Gothic provenance look timeless in style. Here too is the world's second oldest clock, with its 14th-century face showing phases of the moon and the position of the sun. The stained glass, chapter house, and carving deserve time to be savored.

Close by is the moated **Bishop's Palace▶▶** with its drawbridge, turrets and medieval hall; a rope dangles for swans to pull when they want to be fed (a trick passed down from one generation to another). Just off the cathedral close, an archway leads into **Vicars Close▶▶**, a medieval street dating from 1381.

84

Cheddar Gorge▶▶▶ is the most outstanding feature of the Mendip Hills, themselves a gently rolling whaleback plateau perforated with limestone caverns, some of which have collapsed to form gorges. A road follows the bottom of Cheddar Gorge beneath the massive gray cliffs; fanciful names have been given to many of the crags. A staircase at the entrance to the gorge, on its south side, leads up to a ramshackle tin prospect tower; views are even better from above. (See Walks, page 64.) Also by the gorge entrance are the **Cheddar Caves▶**, of which Gough Cave is recommended for its weird limestone formations. Cheddar itself has a fine medieval market cross.

Axbridge▶ is a pleasing, small town that sees far fewer visitors than Cheddar Gorge or Wells. Its fetching, rather irregular central square is overlooked by the half-timbered King John Hunting Lodge, a 15th-century merchant's house that is home to a local history museum.

Burrington Combe▶ is a lesser version of Cheddar Gorge. During a storm here in 1792, Reverend Augustus Toplady sheltered beneath a rock and composed the hymn "Rock of Ages." **Dolebury Warren▶**, a grassy ridge between Burrington Combe and the A38, has good views from its Iron Age hill fort, extending over the Severn Estuary to South Wales and southward toward Bath. Jutting out into the Severn Estuary south of Weston-super-Mare, **Brean Down▶▶** gives phenomenal views of hills and estuary; this too has the site of an ancient hill fort on its summit. **Wookey Hole▶** is a colorfully lit cavern, said to have housed the Witch of Wookey (her alabaster ball and comb and the bones of her goat are in the town museum in Wells). It's a fun place to bring children, with wax figures and vintage penny-in-the-slot machines by the exit, and Britain's oldest complete skeleton—with a re-creation of his world 9,000 years ago. Near Wookey Hole, Ebbor Gorge is a secretive limestone ravine with a nature trail through charming woods.

CHEDDAR CHEESE
Cheddar itself is of course best known for Cheddar cheese. The hard cows'-milk cheese was first made here in the early 12th century, perhaps even earlier. The traditional method is to "cheddar" or cut the firm curd into small pieces and to drain the whey before packing the residual matter into cylinders some 12–15 inches in diameter; the cheese is then wrapped in cheesecloth and coated with wax. It is left to mature (originally this was done in local caves) for anything from three months to two years according to the strength desired. The Cheddar Gorge Cheese Co. Rural Village, Cheddar, makes the authentic product.

85

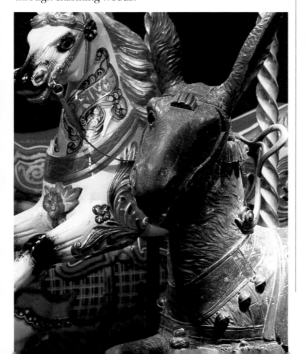

A genre of folk art: antique merry-go-round horses in the old Paper-mill at Wookey Hole

Highworth · Shrivenham · Uffington · Wantage · Didcot · Wallingford · Stonor Park · M40 · Marlow · Beaconsfield · Cookham · M25 · Harrow · Uxbridge · **LONDON** · Swindon · M4 · Lambourn · Goring · Henley-on-Thames · **Maidenhead** · Eton · **Slough** · **Richmond** · Kew Gardens · Greenwich · Barl

Wootton Bassett · Avebury · **BERKSHIRE** · Mapledurham · Theale · **Reading** · Windsor Great Park · **Windsor** · **Staines** · **Kingston upon Thames** · **Brom** · Marlborough · Hungerford · **Newbury** · M4 · Wokingham · **Bracknell** · Hampton Court Palace · **Sutton** · **Croydon**

WILTSHIRE · Burbage · Kingsclere · Tadley · Sandhurst · M3 · **Camberley** · **Woking** · **Epsom** · Down House · **Caterh** · Charts

Salisbury Plain · Ludgershall · Whitchurch · **Basingstoke** · **Aldershot** · **Farnborough** · **Farnham** · **Guildford** · Polesden Lacey · **Leatherhead** · **Reigate** · M25 · Redhill · Oxted · Edenbridge · Eas Grinst

B · Stonehenge · North Tidworth · **Andover** · Godalming · Dorking · Winkworth Arboretum · **SURREY** · Horley · M23 · Amesbury · **HAMPSHIRE** · Alton · Cranleigh · Mole · **Crawley** · Standen · Wakehurst Place · Blue Railwa

Old Sarum · Stockbridge · M3 · Watercress Line · New Alresford · Liphook · Haslemere · **Horsham** · Nymans · Sheffield Park · **Wilton House** · **Salisbury** · **Winchester** · Petersfield · Liss · **WEST** · Billingshurst · Petworth · Cuckfield · Hayward's Heath · Burgess Hill · 248m

Romsey · **Eastleigh** · Bishop's Waltham · Midhurst · **SUSSEX** · Pulborough · Henfield · Ditchling Lewes · Fordingbridge · M27 · **Southampton** · Wickham · Horndean · Bignor Roman Villa · Parham House · Amberley · South Downs · Benson

Ringwood · Lyndhurst · New Forest · Hythe · Netley · M27 · Waterlooville · Weald & Downland Museum · Arundel · Shoreham-by-Sea · **Hove** · **Brighton**

A · Ferndown · Brockenhurst · Sway · Bucklers Hard · Beaulieu · Hamble-le-Rice · Exbury · **Fareham** · **Havant** · Kingley Vale · Fishbourne Palace · Chichester · Littlehampton · **Worthing** · Newhaven · Seafo

Bournemouth · **Christchurch** · New Milton · Lymington · Cowes · Osborne House · Solent · **Gosport** · **Portsmouth** · South Hayling · Bosham · **Bognor Regis** · Selsey · Selsey Bill

Yarmouth · Freshwater · The Needles · Newtown · Carisbrooke Castle · Godshill · Ryde · Bembridge · Nunwell · Sandown · Shanklin · **Appuldurcombe** · **ISLE OF WIGHT** · St Catherine's Point · Ventnor

86

| 1 | 2 | 3 |

★ Walk start point

SOUTHERN ENGLAND The southeastern counties make up a comparatively affluent corner of Britain. Proximity to the capital and a green-belt policy restricting growth around London have pushed up property prices in this cherished ring of countryside, so that the villages have become affluent commuter caches; beyond the green belt spreads a sizeable stretch of suburbia. Yet for all the urban pressures, the region has surprisingly deep pockets of rural countryside; west Kent, southern Surrey, and much of Sussex represent some of the most varied lowlands in Britain.

THE WEALD AND THE DOWNS Many of the region's lushest gardens (see pages 16–17), finest country houses (see pages 102–3) and most appealing villages are found in the Weald, a term given to a somewhat ill-defined area stretching south of London towards the coast. Geologically it is identifiable as being between the North and South Downs, two ranges of chalk hills—or "downs"—that run west to east and end spectacularly at sheer, crumbly cliffs at Dover (the famous White Cliffs) and at Beachy Head near Eastbourne. The Downs rise to no great height, but are much-loved weekend walking grounds, with the long-distance North Downs Way and South Downs Way benefitting from wide views over the Weald itself.

Weald comes from a word meaning "wood", and though many of the trees have been cleared, it has the character of a wooded area, with clumps of trees and hedge-lined fields. Here the villages tend to be traditional

Opposite: Wye Down, part of the North Downs, in Kent

looking, many with timber framed structures, some hung with pantiles and others exposing their beams, plus cottages built with flints, brick or local stone. In Kent you will see oast houses—circular brick kilns built for drying hops for brewing, and now converted to other uses; regimented poles of hops growing in "hop gardens," as well as apple and cherry orchards, are also particularly Kentish. Jutting between the North and South Downs are the hills (of a Wealden sandstone known as greensand) of the High Weald, which include the Ashdown Forest, the wonderfully timeless heathland landscape of the Winnie-the-Pooh stories of A. A. Milne.

KENT, EAST AND WEST SUSSEX, AND SURREY Kent is a mixed bag; the north coast is part marshy, part industrial, although the historic dockyard in Chatham and the center of Rochester are attractive. Inland Kent has numerous pretty villages such as Penshurst, Chiddingstone, Chilham, and Shoreham; of its inland towns, Canterbury, Sandwich, Cranbrook, Tunbridge Wells, and Tenterden stand out the most.

On the coast, Dover deserves more than a fleeting glance for its castle, and Broadstairs and Folkestone are pleasant resorts. The Channel Tunnel runs from Folkestone to Sangatte (see panel, page 98).

The **Sussex** shoreline is almost entirely built up, much of it with 20th-century residential development, and the beaches are not in the least bit remarkable; one interesting place to visit is the assembly of houseboats on the tidal mud flats at Shoreham, in West Sussex, or the De La Warre Pavilion, a Bauhaus-inspired design, in the unlikely setting of Bexhill.

The most appealing coastal towns by far are Hastings and Eastbourne, in contrasting styles but both abutting fine cliffs; and Brighton, a semi-shabby seaside resort, still has tremendous atmosphere, with its Royal Pavilion rating as one of the country's most extravagant follies. Chichester Harbour is the big yacht haven for Sussex. Chichester, West Sussex's cathedral city, lies within easy reach of the county's finest Roman monuments—Fishbourne Palace and Bignor Villa.

RECOMMENDED HISTORIC CITIES
Canterbury, Rochester, Winchester.
CASTLES AND ROYALTY
Berkshire: Windsor.
Hampshire: Portchester, Solent defenses at Portsmouth, Southsea, etc.
Isle of Wight: Carisbrooke, Osborne House.
Kent: Deal, Dover, Rochester, Walmer.
Sussex: Bodiam, Pevensey.
ROMAN REMAINS
Kent: Lighthouse and painted house at Dover, Lullingstone Villa (near Eynsford), Richborough Castle (near Sandwich).
Sussex: Bignor Villa (near Amberley), Fishbourne Palace (near Chichester).
SMALL TOWNS Arundel, Chichester, Cranbrook, Faversham, Lewes, Petworth, Rye, Sandwich, Tunbridge Wells.
SEASIDE TOWNS
Brighton, Broadstairs, Eastbourne, Hastings. Naval heritage Chatham, Portsmouth.
COASTAL SCENERY
East/West Sussex:
Seven Sisters and Beachy Head (near Eastbourne), Fairlight Cove (Hastings). **Kent**: Cliffs between Folkestone and Walmer.

Oast houses are unique to Kent and the Hereford and Worcester areas

A number of small-scale vineyards are now well established in the south

"In quitting the great Wen [London] we go through Surrey ... There are erected within these four years, two entire miles of stock-jobbers' houses on this one road, and the work goes on with accelerated force! ... What an at once horrible and ridiculous thing this country would become, if this thing could go on only for a few years!"
—William Cobbett (1822), *Rural Rides*

Much of inland Sussex is genteel, with tiny villages and lots of historic buildings, tearooms, and antique shops. Highlights include Arundel, with its massive castle towering over its steep main street; Battle, the historic battlefield of 1066 and the abbey founded by William the Conqueror; Lewes, with its architectural variety and Norman castle; and Alfriston, memorably set beneath the South Downs.

Surrey, Britain's most wooded county, has been largely developed into affluent commuter suburbs, but it has some delicious countryside, ideal for walking—notably in the greensand country around Haslemere and the vicinities of Shere and Leith Hill, at 965 feet the highest point in the Southeast.

HAMPSHIRE AND BERKSHIRE The county of **Hampshire** rolls gently inland, the best of its country in the far east around Selborne and in the far west by the heaths and woodlands of the New Forest. Winchester has a compact but fascinating medieval center. The coast doesn't have much to offer aesthetically, but Portsmouth has an important naval heritage. Southampton, a large industrial and commercial center that was heavily bombed in World War II, has a few corners of historic interest (medieval town walls, Tudor House, and the oldest bowling green in the world) as well as aviation and maritime museums and a fine art gallery. Both these towns, and Lymington, have ferries to the **Isle of Wight**, a pleasant base, with plenty of attractions and scenery to tempt families and walkers, despite the suburbanization along its eastern coast. The island has an excellent public transportation system (some may wish to leave the car on the mainland to avoid the expense of taking it on the ferry), and its south coast is one of Britain's sunniest spots.

Berkshire has a split identity, divided into north–south by the M4 motorway, with downlands merging into Wiltshire and Hampshire to the west, while its flatter eastern edge is Windsor Great Park. At Windsor Castle you can see inside the state apartments of the Queen's favorite residence. Crowds throng the town all year round; you can escape from the bustle by taking a boat trip along the Thames or a walk into Eton or the park. The Thames defines Berkshire's northern border from Windsor to Streatley; the river, which runs down from Buckinghamshire and Oxfordshire, has a placid beauty and a boating scene that can only be found in England.

▶▶▶ **REGION HIGHLIGHTS**

Beachy Head *pages 98–99*

Brighton *pages 90–91*

Canterbury *page 93*

Dover Castle *page 98*

Portsmouth *page 104*

Rye *pages 104–105*

The Weald *pages 102–103, 106–107*

Winchester *pages 107–108*

Windsor *page 109*

I will go out against the sun
Where the rolled scarp retires,
And the Long Man of Wilmington
Looks naked toward the shires;
And east till doubling Rother crawls
To find the fickle tide,
By dry and sea-forgotten walls,
Our ports of stranded pride.
—Rudyard Kipling (1865–1936), on the Sussex landscape

Horsted Keynes Station on the Bluebell Line— so-called because of the bluebell woods through which the railway passes

BRIGHTON'S PAST
In 1754 Dr. Richard Russell came to the fishing village of Brighthelmstone and prescribed seawater as a cure for a variety of complaints; many people took his advice and the village acquired spa status. Georgian and Regency terraces followed as the élite arrived in the footsteps of the Prince Regent. Brighton later got a reputation as a rendezvous for lovers' illicit weekends; the railroad added a sleazy element. Graham Greene's novel *Brighton Rock* is set in the world of 1930s gang warfare. Brighton hosts a Festival in May, and on the London to Brighton Veteran Car Run in November gleaming old machines that last the trip end at the beach.

▶▶ **Bluebell Railway**   *86B3*
(tel: 01825 722370)

In 1960 the Bluebell was the first standard-gauge steam railroad to be reopened as a tourist attraction; in many ways it is the pick of the bunch, with some of its carriages dating from the 1890s and stations furnished with Victorian advertising signs, fire buckets, and gas lamps. Its 18-mile round trip takes an hour (special restaurant trains and other events on weekends) and runs between Sheffield Park and Kingscote via Horsted Keynes (there are bus links to East Grinstead rail station, where the line may eventually extend). Sheffield Park Garden (see page 17) makes a pleasant destination.

▶▶▶ **Brighton**   *86A3*
(tel: 01273 292599)

This is the oldest and most interesting British coastal resort. The Prince Regent, later King George IV, came here after his secret marriage to Mrs. Fitzherbert and initiated the fashion for seaside vacations and bathing. He converted a farmhouse bought in 1784 into his capricious **Royal Pavilion**▶▶▶, an oriental extravaganza covered with minarets and onion domes (see sidebar, page 91).

Despite the obvious decay (itself a Brighton hallmark) of the **seafront**▶▶, you can still see traces of its elegant heyday. **West Pier**, Britain's finest such structure, has long been derelict, but a National Lottery award has been allocated to help restore it. Meanwhile, the newer **Palace Pier** is very much alive, with fish-and-chips shops, tacky souvenir booths, and fortune-tellers. Summer weekends still draw the crowds to the amusements, aquarium, and privately run seafront train, one of the oldest electric trains in the world. The nude beach, Britain's first, lies out of sight from the pier; the main beach is shingle. Cream- and sky-blue period streetlamps and rows of white stucco houses and hotels proliferate. The best streets lie to the east at **Kemp Town►**, an example of early 19th-century town planning, with Lewes Crescent at its far end. Toward Hove to the west there are elegant bow-fronted Regency terraces, in Brunswick Square and above Western Road.

The Lanes►► survive from the once humble fishing village of Brighthelmstone; ironically this is now the most chic area of Brighton, with expensive antique shops, sidewalk cafés, and galleries in its warren of narrow alleys. Brighton's main **museum►►** (*Admission free*), housed in the former stable block of the Royal Pavilion and similarly fantastic in style, has some eye-catching furniture, including Art Nouveau pieces and a sofa by Salvador Dali representing Mae West's lips. The **North Laine** (between the station and North Street) is the vibrant heart of funky Brighton, with buskers and alternative shops.

A conspicuously attractive town by the South Downs, to the northeast of Brighton, **Lewes►►** is graced with some very pleasing streets and paths known as "twittens", which include steep, cobbled Keere Street. The hilltop castle is Norman and was adapted into a romantic garden feature in the 18th century; it gives a fascinating rooftop view. Many of the half-timbered houses were given a fake brick veneer, fashionable in the 18th century, with the widespread use of "mathematical tiles," thin fascia tiles resembling bricks. The town is famed for the best and heartiest November 5 fireworks night in the country. On a more genteel note, Lewes also has a notable concentration of antique stores and auction rooms.

►► Broadstairs   87C5
(tel: 01843 862242)

The prettiest of the coastal resorts in Thanet in East Kent is Broadstairs; all its charm is concentrated on the seafront, with seven sandy coves beneath low cliffs. It's a combination of sedate resort and fishing port; you can still watch fish being unloaded and eat shellfish on the harbor wall. The town has a pleasantly old-fashioned air. Charles Dickens knew Broadstairs well; he spent several summers at what has since been named "Bleak House," with the desk at which he wrote *David Copperfield*.

Nearby **Ramsgate►** is more run down, but it's worth a stroll for the Regency streets. The coastal walk from Broadstairs to Ramsgate takes about 30 minutes.

THE ROYAL PAVILION
The Prince Regent employed the great architect John Nash to transform an unspectacular house into a fantasy palace that formed the nucleus of his flamboyant social life—centered on parties, horse-racing, concerts and vast dinners. The building takes its inspiration from India externally and China internally. Queen Victoria was unenthusiastic about the Pavilion and Brighton: "There were far too many of the wrong sort of people, and they were all staring at me." She sold the building in 1850.

91

BLOOMSBURY CONNECTIONS
Three places associated with the Bloomsbury Group are found in the South Downs around Lewes. **Monk's House** at Rodmell (south of Lewes) was the home of Leonard and Virginia Woolf. **Charleston Farmhouse**, near Alciston, was the home of Duncan Grant and Clive and Vanessa Bell (the latter being Virginia's sister), and its walls and furniture are still decorated with their paintings; the garden is reminiscent of the Bloomsbury days. The Group added further decorations in the form of murals in **Berwick Church**.

At this desk at "Bleak House," Dickens completed David Copperfield

Walks

Tennyson Down,   86A1
Isle of Wight

Start from Freshwater Bay. The coastal path leads west along a grassy ridge, with sea views on three sides. Pass the Tennyson monument and continue to the island's western tip; an old fort, Needles Old Battery, gives views of The Needles, a set of rock pinnacles battered by the waves. Return the same way. (2½ hours)

Ditchling Beacon,   86A3
West Sussex

Start from parking lot adjacent to Ditchling Beacon. Here the South Downs rise to their third highest point and are capped by the site of an Iron Age hill fort. Follow the South Downs Way west along the escarpment edge. After 2 miles you reach the famous Jack and Jill windmills. Return the same way. (2½ hours)

Bewl Water, Kent/East   87B4
Sussex border

Start from visitor center parking lot. An attractive reservoir, Bewl Water is the largest lake in Southeast England and is circled by a well-marked and scenically varied path. It is too long for an entire day's walk, but very pleasant for strolls.

Lullingstone Park, Kent   87C4

Start from parking lot at visitor center off the A225. Trails from the center take in landscapes of river, woodland, and grassland plus Lullingstone Roman Villa and Lullingstone castle (about 1½ hours). Longer walks can incorporate the pretty villages of Shoreham, Otford, and Eynsford.

Ashdown Forest,   87B4
East Sussex

Start at the Poohsticks Bridge parking lot in Ashdown Forest (take the B2026 south of Hartfield 1¼ miles, turn west at intersection with minor road; the parking lot is 200 yards on north side of road). This is the heartland of A. A. Milne's *Winnie the Pooh* stories. A path leads to the bridge where the game of Poohsticks was once played; return to the parking lot and follow the gravel track eastward; ignore left forks. Cross the road and take a path rising onto heathland (where Piglet supposedly lived). Walk up to the monument to Milne on Gill's Lap: this is the Enchanted Place of the stories, an ideal picnic spot with a view encapsulating the splendor of the "forest." Return the same way. (1½ hours)

Poohsticks Bridge, Ashdown Forest

▶▶▶ **Canterbury**   87B5
(tel: 01227 766567)

Canterbury has witnessed two very dark hours. One was the murder of Thomas à Becket in the cathedral in 1170, the other a World War II "Baedeker raid" in 1942 (so called because targets were historic rather than military). The medieval city center was destroyed, but the cathedral, seat of the Archbishop of Canterbury and the premier church of England, was miraculously unscathed.

Yet today the city's sense of history is as compelling as ever. You can walk through the **West Gate** (museum inside), as pilgrims have done for eight centuries, and pass a number of charitable hospitals founded in medieval times as places to accommodate pilgrims (St. Thomas's Hospital and the **Poor Priests' Hospital** are open to the public, the latter housing the hi-tech **Canterbury Heritage**▶ museum).

The old city center is largely contained within the **city wall**, but just outside lie **St. Augustine's Abbey** (E.H.), founded in 597, its church and cloister foundations still apparent, and **St. Martin's Church**, England's oldest

CANTERBURY'S STREETSCAPE
The city's surviving older streets show a rich mixture of medieval, Georgian, and Victorian styles. Some of the first buildings in the center are: Queen Elizabeth's Guest Chamber, a former inn with a wonderfully over-the-top stucco facade; The Weavers, which is ancient, although its "half-timbering" is fake and relatively modern; and the Beaney Institute, an elaborate library, a statement of high Victorian exuberance. The major Roman remains are within the Roman Museum in Longmarket.

Canterbury's rich architectural heritage is in evidence around the early 16th-century Christ Church Gate

93

church in continuous use and once the headquarters of St. Augustine—shallow red Roman bricks can be seen in the walls.

The **cathedral**▶▶▶ precincts are entered by Christ Church Gate. The cathedral, built in Caen limestone, boasts several outstanding features, among them Bell Harry, the 23-foot-high central tower, a collection of 12th- and 13th-century stained glass, a Norman crypt, and the Black Prince's tomb. Adjacent is the 15th-century Great Cloister, with a stone marking the spot where Thomas à Becket died. Behind the cathedral, Green Court is fronted by the Norman Staircase, ruins of the monks' dormitory, and the buildings of **King's School**. The **Roman Museum**▶ on Longmarket sets the scene of Roman Canterbury, with reconstructions of dealers' stalls and domestic interiors, before reaching a real Roman house with hypocaust system and mosaics. **The Canterbury Tales** brings Chaucer's characters to life in re-creations of medieval Canterbury.

To the southwest, the village of **Chilham**▶▶ has a half-timbered square, with church at one end and castle entrance at the other.

THE CANTERBURY TALES
In Chaucer's *Canterbury Tales*, the high point of English medieval literature, a party of pilgrims meet at the Tabard Inn, Southwark (now part of London). They agree to travel together and to tell stories to pass the time:
"And specially, from every shires ende
Of Engelonde to Caunterbury they wende."
Chaucer's works are brought to life in theme-park fashion, with tableaus and re-created sounds and smells, in *The Canterbury Tales* in St. Margaret's Street.

The seaside vacation is one of those great British institutions, which, like other good things, has spread down the class ladder. In the 18th century the only people who could afford a vacation of more than one day were the rich. Later, resorts like Bournemouth and Eastbourne were planned to attract middle-class business. The coming of the railroads and the invention of the nationwide "bank holidays" in Victorian times spurred the development of resorts for the working class— Blackpool, Margate, Skegness, and their like.

BEACH BELLES
When the fashion for "sea-bathing" began in the 18th century, men and women customarily swam naked, but as it spread, so did modesty. The "bathing machine" carried people, shielded from view, right out into the waves, but even so, women took to wearing all-enveloping flannel gowns tied with a drawstring at the neck. Elaborate Victorian and Edwardian costumes made of flannel, worsted, or serge looked much like day dresses, with frilly caps, stockings, even shoes. The one-piece swimsuit for ladies came in before World War I; it had sleeves and reached to the knees.

Before the 18th century Britons occasionally swam in rivers and lakes, but eyed the sea askance. It was dangerous and it tasted nasty. Even in the Royal Navy, a seaman who could swim was a rarity. When sea bathing began, it was for health rather than pleasure. A drawing of 1735 shows men and women in the sea at Scarborough, a health spa with a mineral spring on the Yorkshire coast. The spring enriched the local doctors, and it seems to have occurred to them then that perhaps the rolling brine so plentifully at hand, the salt-laden water, and brisk North Sea breezes might be profitably exploited as well.

"*So* bracing" Certainly this was what happened on the Sussex coast, where the obscure fishing hamlet of Brighthelmstone was transformed into glamorous **Brighton**, queen of the briny. A doctor named Richard Russell, who moved there in 1753, proclaimed the virtues of crabs' eyes, cuttlefish bones, and wood lice washed down with a hearty pint of seawater. His successor, an Irishman named Anthony Relham, opportunely discovered the salubrious qualities of fresh sea air, heightened, he said, by Brighton's fortunate lack of noxiously perspiring trees.

The effect of all this nonsense was to draw well-to-do invalids and hypochondriacs to the Sussex shore. When the Prince Regent took to visiting and built for himself the glamorous Royal Pavilion, the new resort's success was assured.

Some fishing villages and minor ports grew gradually into resorts, while others were planned for profit by shrewd local landowners and developers. **Llandudno** on the North Wales coast was laid out by the local Mostyn family and remains a charming Victorian resort, lording it over brash **Rhyl** and **Prestatyn**, which were developed later for Lancashire millhands. At Skegness on the Lincolnshire coast in the 1870s, the Earl of Scarborough built a resort with the intention of attracting the middle classes, but the Great Northern Railway brought hordes of tourists from the Midlands industrial towns and Skegness became a leading working-class resort. The first in a chain of Butlin's "holiday camps" opened there in 1937.

Places with a sandy beach naturally cashed in, as did towns with a mild climate and plenty of summer sunshine. The Thames Estuary resorts of Margate and Southend enjoy Britain's highest July/August temperatures, followed by those along the south coast from Torquay to Folkestone. The highest figures for hours of sunshine per day are held by Sandown and Shanklin on the Isle of Wight.

"Beside the seaside" Health remained a factor—"Skegness Is So Bracing," the posters proclaimed—but sheer fun took precedence as resorts sprouted piers and promenades, amusement parks, cliff railroads, zoos, excessively flowery gardens, bandstands, dance halls, freak shows, tattoo parlors, tacky postcards, fortune-tellers' booths, ice cream and rock-candy stands to spice up the simpler pleasures of swimming, sunbathing, sand castles, and donkey rides. The seaside landlady became a comic cliché, with her iron-bound notions of gentility, strictly regulated mealtimes, and green plants in a fussy parlor. On August Bank Holiday Monday in 1937 more than half a million people swarmed into Blackpool in 50,000 motor vehicles and 700 trains, the earliest of which arrived at 3:55 AM.

Since World War II, with growing affluence, more cars, and much longer vacations, patterns have changed. Some people still go faithfully to the same resort every year. Blackpool and Brighton are both going strong, but most British seaside resorts have found themselves unable to compete with the allure of the climate and competitive pricing of package tours abroad. Bad publicity about polluted beaches has not helped either. The traditional seaside vacation seems increasingly a pleasure of the past.

95

Above left: ice cream and beach huts, Walton on the Naze. Above: just sitting, Brighton Palace Pier

ALL THE WAY THROUGH
A traditional seaside delights is "rock," a stick of hard mint candy that is usually white in color with the resort's name in pink letters, mysteriously running through the stick's whole length. Blackpool and Morecambe both claim to have invented the treat, but there is also a tradition that it originated in the inland mining town of Dewsbury in the 1860s. As late as the 1970s Blackpool was manufacturing two tons of rock a day in the summer.

THE MEDWAY TOWNS
The three Medway towns of Rochester, Chatham, and Gillingham together form a large industrial sprawl in the north of Kent. The most historic of these is Rochester. Pre-industrial Rochester is compact but impressive, with a medieval cathedral, an absorbing museum within the Guildhall, and the ruins of a Norman castle (E.H.) giving mighty panoramas over the River Medway below. The writer Charles Dickens lived in Rochester for a period; the Charles Dickens Centre is in Eastgate House, which features in the *Pickwick Papers* and *Edwin Drood*.

FISHBOURNE'S UNEARTHING
What visitors see at Fishbourne—the mosaics, hypocaust and partition walls—is only one side of a vast palace of AD 75, the largest Roman building yet discovered in northern Europe. Part of the rest is under houses, and nearby excavations completed in 1999 have revealed a military building of similar date to the Roman Conquest in AD 43 that some historians believe confirms that the Conquest began at Fishbourne (where local tribes were friendly with the Romans) and not in east Kent as once thought.

Vernacular building styles on show at the Weald and Downland Open Air Museum at Singleton

►► Chatham Historic Dockyard   87C4
(tel: 01634 823800)
The historic dockyard here was once a naval center of ship-building and -fitting; today it incorporates Britain's largest concentration of landmarked buildings. The site includes warehouses, a rope works, shipbuilding sheds, a visitor center and three vessels—a destroyer, a submarine and a Victorian sloop—all part of the World Naval Base. Combined with Rochester (see panel), this makes an excellent day out (speedy train services from London).

►► Chichester   86A2
(tel: 01243 775888)
The cathedral city for Sussex, Chichester, is based on a simple criss cross layout centered on a fine 16th-century market cross and, with ancient city walls and handsome Georgian streets, it is an enjoyable place to explore. Its medieval **cathedral►** (early Norman with Early English additions) is unusual—it's not tucked away within its own close, and it has a freestanding belfry. The interior has some distinguished modern features: a tapestry by John Piper, a painting by Graham Sutherland, and glass by Chagall, and unusual older tombs (most famously the medieval Arundel Knight, who breaks with tradition and holds hands with his lady). The Mechanical Music and Doll Collection is the most offbeat of the city's museums, while Pallant House specializes in modern British art, displayed within an elegant early 18th-century house.

Fishbourne Roman Palace►►, on the edge of Chichester, is thought to have been built for one Cogidubnus, a Briton who supported the Romans and was made senator. Now much has been re-created, with a dining room, mosaics in full view; remarkably, excavations revealed the exact shape of the bedding trenches in the garden—this has been faithfully replanted, and there is a Roman herbarium, with the kinds of plants that would have been familiar to the Romans. (See also sidebar.)

To the southwest of the town, **Chichester Harbour►** is a big yachting center. Extending over a huge area, its east side is natural mud flats and complex, marshy inlets. **Bosham** is one of the best places to appreciate the setting: the much-painted village has a picturesque church steeple, waterfront cottages, and boating scenes. East Head juts into the southeast corner of the harbor: here sand dunes and salt marshes make a good setting for an exhilarating

Boat-building: one of several crafts found at Amberley Museum

KINGLEY VALE
Europe's largest yew forest spreads over a shoulder of the South Downs, a wonderful ancient-feeling place, dark and eerie, where trees have collapsed and then continued to grow from their horizontal positions, making a bizarre collection of shapes and forms. A nature trail circles the site. The forest's origins are a mystery; could it have been a plantation? Yews were once valued for making bows and arrows. The view from the Bronze Age bell barrows (burial mounds) on the summit extends over Chichester Harbour.

stroll. Daily boat tours (in season) from Itchenor take 1½ hours (for a recorded timetable tel: 01243 786418). Due north of Chichester is the **Weald and Downland Open Air Museum▶▶**, Singleton, a rural museum with reconstructed buildings rescued from Kent and Sussex—including a farmhouse, smithy, school, and water mill.

A sleepy, unblemished village, much of it thatched, **Amberley▶ ▶** is beautifully set beneath the South Downs some 13 miles northeast of Chichester. Glimpse through the churchyard gate to the 16th-century manor (private) within a massive medieval castle wall; the former residence of bishops of Chichester, the old castle was dismantled by Cromwell's men. It perches on the edge of Amberley Wild Brooks, an area of water meadows known for its rich birdlife and marshland plants. Near the station at the south end of the village, the Amberley Museum has displays of small-scale Sussex industries and crafts, located in a former chalk pit; here are a blacksmith, potter, boat-builder, printer, narrow-gauge railroad, vintage buses, wheelwright, and even a collection of antique radios. Nearby is the Elizabethan manor house **Parham House▶**, begun in 1577 by Sir Thomas Parham, who later sailed with Sir Francis Drake to Cadiz; its deer park has lakes and a walled garden.

Arundel▶ ▶ is a handsome, compact town. The main street climbs from the canalized River Arun up to the sprawling, much-restored medieval-Victorian castle—home of the Dukes of Norfolk and their ancestors for over 700 years—and the nearby superb Roman Catholic cathedral. The castle, rich in furnishings and art treasures, is open to the public, as is the adjoining park. At the **WWT Arundel▶** wildfowl reserve (just north of town), you can observe hundreds of geese, swans, and ducks at close quarters from specially constructed hides.

To the north, **Bignor Roman Villa▶**, one of Britain's largest Roman houses, has mosaic floors (depicting gladiators, Ganymede and the eagle, etc.). The villa was occupied during the 2nd to 4th centuries. Stane Street, a Roman road now turned into a path, cuts across the downland close by. Its finest section starts from the parking lot on Bignor Hill (reached by a dead-end lane).

Chichester: flint walls on St. Richard's Walk

THE CHANNEL TUNNEL
The project to build a link from England to France has been germinating since Napoleonic times. The final "Eurotunnel" was completed in 1994 at a cost of £10 billion; **Le Shuttle** takes cars between Folkestone and Calais, and the **Eurostar** passenger train runs non-stop from London Waterloo to Paris, Lille, and Brussels. The Eurotunnel Exhibition Center in Folkestone gives you an overview of the "Chunnel" (as it was originally called). The spoil created Samphire Hoe, Britain's newest land—a coastal grassland beautifully sited beneath the cliff, reached by road tunnel west of Dover.

Eastbourne's Victorian pier

▶▶ Dover   87B5
(tel: 01304 205108)

The major cross-Channel port since Roman times (when it was known as Dubris), Dover has long assumed a military role. It was badly bombed in World War II and redevelopment has been lackluster—a wasted opportunity, given its cliff and valley setting. But the famous white cliffs (a symbol of homecoming for Britons) still beckon across the Channel. The **castle▶▶▶**, high above the town, stands as one of Britain's finest examples of an intact Norman keep, within which are sight and sound experiences re-creating the castle under siege in 1216 and during a visit by Henry VIII in 1539. The castle has the longest history of any in the country, and has much scope for wandering around gun emplacements, watch towers, and parapet. Within the site a Saxon church stands beside the Pharos, a Roman lighthouse (Britain's tallest Roman building). Take the audio tour of the Battlements Walk and the medieval tunnels. Arrive early to reserve a tour of the Secret Wartime Tunnels, from where the evacuation of Dunkirk in 1940 was conducted; Cap Griz Nez on the French coast looks surprisingly near on a clear day. In the town center, a few Georgian and Regency terraces remain unscathed; the major sight is the **Roman Painted House▶**, with its central-heating system and painted walls. The **White Cliffs Experience▶** gives an interactive view of Dover's history: you can row a Roman galley and walk through a Blitz-damaged street.

THE FIRST CROSS-CHANNEL FLIGHT
The cliff walk northeast from Dover passes Blériot's monument, commemorating the first powered flight across the Channel. Louis Blériot (1872–1936), whose early flying experiments included towing gliders along the River Seine, made the historic flight from Calais to Dover on July 25, 1909.

Deal and Walmer▶ are both on the coast to the north of Dover, and both have castles built by Henry VIII in the plan of a Tudor rose. Walmer is all neat houses looking over a stony beach; Deal has a pretty ex-fishermen's quarter of narrow streets.

▶ Eastbourne   87A4
(tel: 01323 411400)

A town of chintz-decorated hotels, genteel stucco, and brass bands on the promenade, Eastbourne is a well preserved example of a 19th-century English seaside resort.

The South Downs end in style just west of Eastbourne at **Beachy Head** and the **Seven Sisters▶▶▶**. There's a sheer drop of 525 feet at Beachy Head, the chalk cliffs towering above a lighthouse. Farther west, the Seven Sisters are a series of dry valleys chopped off by the sea to form a roller-coaster cliff. There is access to the coastal path at **Birling Gap** and at the **Seven Sisters Country Park** by Cuckmere Haven. Beware of the unfenced edge.

Alfriston▶▶ is a village with a strong medieval atmosphere, with tile-hung and timber houses, cafés, and antique shops. The 14th-century Clergy House, a pre-Reformation vicarage, was the first building acquired by the National Trust and is a restored half-timbered house with its original clay floor. Adjacent, the church, dubbed the Cathedral of the Downs, has 14th-century features. The street also has two fine inns, the Star and the George, and the stump of a market cross is a memento of busier days. Nearby and best seen from south of Wilmington village is the **Long Man of Wilmington**▶▶, an enigmatic chalk carving on the downs of a man bearing a staff in either hand. It is probably Anglo-Saxon or earlier, although no written record before the 18th century has been found. Eastward along the coast is **Pevensey Castle**▶ (E.H.). Its 4th-century Roman walls enclose a medieval castle and keep. William the Conqueror landed here in 1066 to launch his invasion of Britain (see panel).

▶ Hastings   87A4
(tel: 01424 781133)

Dramatically hilly, Hastings is a mixture of a faded seaside resort and an old fishing port thick with character. The picturesque and warren-like **old town** lies in a valley east of the center; the former fishermen's quarter lies close to a group of tall wooden sheds, called deezes, built for storing fishing nets, and there are caves and a castle to visit. Pleasant walks onto the sandstone cliffs extend eastward to **Fairlight Cove** along a wild coastline, and a cliff-hugging train hauls you up the slope of the old town.

Battle▶▶ (see sidebars) is a handsome small town, famed for its abbey and battlefield (both E.H.); the medieval Almonry houses the Town Model, and the Battle Museum and Buckley's Yesterdays World (shop and room displays) justify a full day's visit.

Bodiam Castle▶▶ (N.T.), 12 miles inland from Hastings, dates from the 14th century—surrounded by a wide moat filled with water lilies and with walls at their original height. A visit can be combined with a nostalgic ride on the Kent and East Sussex Railway to Tenterden.

THE BATTLE OF HASTINGS
Every British schoolboy and schoolgirl knows the date 1066, when the Battle of Hastings between William of Normandy and King Harold took place at Battle (as it is now called). Oddly, the great turning point in English history was a surprisingly haphazard affair: the English (Saxons) should have trounced the French, who were vastly outnumbered and fighting uphill. However, the Saxons made a strategic blunder in storming downhill when they thought some of the Normans were retreating; this left a hole in the Saxon defenses on the top of the slope, which the Normans promptly filled.

BATTLE ABBEY
William I, "the Conqueror," vowed that if he was victorious he would found an abbey here, on the battlefield where he defeated Harold's English forces; the high altar marks the spot where Harold is said to have fallen, pierced in the eye with a Frenchman's arrow. Today a battlefield trail and an audiovisual display detail the story of the battle. Of the abbey, the gatehouse of 1338 and the east range are still intact.

Low tide at Birling Gap gives access to the beach below the brilliant-white Seven Sisters cliffs, which are slowly being eroded back

The Royal Yacht Squadron has its head-quarters at Cowes

SOME ISLAND HOUSES TO VISIT

Osborne House was built as a retreat for Queen Victoria, in 1845 and she died here in 1901. The State Apartments provide a rewarding insight into Victoria's lifestyle. Dating from the 18th century, **Appuldurcombe House** stands as a spooky skeleton, with a triumphal gateway to nowhere in its Capability Brown-landscaped grounds. **Arreton Manor** is a graceful stone house built around 1600, with furnishings and paneling of the period. Among several museums it incorporates is the **National Wireless Museum**, acknowledging the work of Marconi, who made his pioneering transmission experiments nearby.

THE TENNYSON CONNECTION

Alfred Lord Tennyson stayed at Farringford Park House (now a hotel) near Freshwater Bay; his Victorian fan club (autograph hunters and all) tracked him down here and he is still remembered by the monument on Tennyson Down.

Cowes High Street

▶▶ Isle of Wight   86A1
(tel: 01983 813818)

Just 2 miles (3 km) over the Solent from the mainland at its nearest point, the diamond-shaped island is reached by ferry or catamaran from Portsmouth (landing in Ryde and Fishbourne), Southampton (landing in Cowes), or Lymington (landing in Yarmouth). Although developed, the isle has plenty of scenic variety, with chalk downs and splendid coastal cliffs. Public transportation is excellent; many visitors leave their cars on the mainland.

On the south coast, grassy whaleback hills provide outstanding views for walkers; at the western end of **Tennyson Down▶▶** (see Walks, page 92) is a set of chalk pinnacles known as **The Needles**. Close by, the multicolored sands of Alum Bay are sold in souvenir glass bottles of every shape and size. The island's southernmost point, **St. Catherine's Point▶**, has a lighthouse open to visitors; St Catherine's Hill is capped by an oratory in the tower of a 14th-century chapel. Farther north, **Yarmouth▶** is the most appealing town on the island, a pretty port with whitewashed cottages and one of the numerous forts built by Henry VIII to defend the Solent. The coast and rivers have some attractive marshy landscapes, as found along the **River Yar** and **Newtown Estuary**.

The east coast is mostly developed: **Ryde**, **Shanklin**, **Sandown**, and **Bembridge** are good spots for low-key vacations. In spring 2001 the **Dinosaur Museum** will open in Sandown and promises to be one of the biggest on the subject. Shanklin has preserved it old village near Shanklin Chine, a gorge leading to the sea. **Cowes** has a sailboat atmosphere; in late June the Round the Island Yacht Race features over a thousand competitors, and in August Cowes hosts a regatta. **Ventnor** snuggles beneath an undercliff and has a subtropical **Botanic Garden▶▶**.

Near Newport, the island's capital, **Carisbrooke Castle▶▶** (E.H.) is one of the best-preserved Norman shells in the kingdom, with inner rooms dating from 1470; Charles I spent time here pending his execution. The castle has Britain's only surviving donkey wheel, used to haul water from a deep well. **Godshill** is a pretty village of stone and thatch; its church has a rare 15th-century wall painting of the "Lily Cross."

► New Forest 86A1
(tel: 01703 282269)

The New Forest, in western Hampshire, has survived into the 20th century surprisingly intact. Established in 1079 as a hunting forest for Norman royalty, it still feels incredibly remote. Essentially it is a tract of lowland heath and mixed forest; it is splendid territory for walking, camping, and picnicking. There are no major hills, but there is enough variety to spark interest; it tends to be more open on the west side. Wild ponies and red deer are commonly seen; the former graze on heathlands and are owned by commoners with historic grazing rights. The **New Forest Museum** at Lyndhurst sets the scene.

Lined with conifers planted in the 19th century, the **Bolderwood** and **Rhinefield ornamental drives►** are forest drives; species include giant fir, redwood, and swamp cypress. Lord Montagu's **National Motor Museum►►** at Beaulieu, the finest collection of its kind, celebrates the golden age of automobiles; adjacent are **Beaulieu Abbey►** (founded 1204) and **Palace House►** (the former abbey gatehouse), Montagu's stately home (complete with monorail and vintage bus rides). Downriver, **Bucklers Hard►** is a hamlet with a nautical flavor; the story of this former boat-building center is told in its Maritime Museum. **Exbury Gardens** includes a collection of azaleas, rhododendrons, magnolias, and camelias.

Rhinefield, in the New Forest

101

► Petworth 86B2
(tel: 01798 343523)

This attractive town, featuring clusters of timber and stone houses, stands adjacent to the park of **Petworth House►►**. This grand, late 17th-century mansion, built by the Duke of Somerset, has been Percy family property since Norman times. Today the National Trust maintains its interior, which includes virtuoso woodcarving and a collection of paintings unrivalled by any other National Trust property; there are works by Turner, Blake, Rembrandt, Reynolds and others. The grounds, landscaped by Capability Brown, offer delightful walks.

SQUATTERS' RIGHTS
A few scattered thatched hamlets are found in New Forest clearings. Typically such settlements owe their origins to squatters' rights, whereby common land could be occupied by anyone building a house within one day, provided smoke was seen to be rising from the chimney by dusk.

The counties of Kent, West Sussex, East Sussex, and Surrey boast a remarkably varied range of houses that are open to the public. Many of those described below make pleasant day-trips from London. Several are included in the Drive on pages 106–107. Some houses may be closed during the winter months, so it is always worth checking on opening times with local tourist information centers.

THE NATIONAL TRUST (N.T.)

The National Trust is a major landowner; it was formed in 1895 to safe-guard Britain's places of historic interest and natural beauty. Property it acquires is held in trust for the nation. Many of the N.T.'s hundreds of country houses, gardens, and other places of interest are open to the public. Cards giving free admission to any property are available, on payment of a membership fee, from these and from N.T. information centers, or by mail from Freepost MB1438, Bromley, Kent BR1 3BR; or tel: 020-8315 1111. Most properties close in winter. Membership also gives you free entry to properties owned by the National Trust for Scotland (N.T.S.), based at 5 Charlotte Square, Edinburgh EH2 4DU, tel: 0131-226 5922. In this book, N.T. and N.T.S. denote staffed properties that charge entrance fees.

102

The Italian Garden at Hever Castle: part of Astor's 20th-century design

Polesden Lacey▶ (N.T.), near Dorking, Surrey, was built by Thomas Cubitt in 1824 and remodeled in Edwardian times for Mrs Greville, a society hostess. Her furniture, porcelain, paintings, and silver are on display, and the house has a lovely rural view from its North Downs perch, and fine gardens.

Standen▶ (N.T.), near East Grinstead, West Sussex, is a delightful Arts and Crafts house, designed in the 1890s by Philip Webb, a friend of leading artist-craftsman William Morris. It still has its original electric light fittings and has a collection of ceramics by William de Morgan. Toward Tonbridge, **Penshurst Place▶▶**, Penshurst, Kent, lies amid charming lowland countryside, an outstanding example of 14th-century domestic architecture owned by the Sidney family, Earls of Leicester, whose forebears include Sir Philip Sidney, the Elizabethan poet. It has a splendid hall with a chestnut ceiling, and a fine, long gallery. Nearby **Hever Castle▶▶**, Hever, Kent, was the birthplace of Anne Boleyn, second wife of Henry VIII. The moated Tudor house owes much of its present appearance to the 20th-century renovation by William Waldorf Astor, a wealthy American. He added mock-medieval features and laid out delightful grounds with great avenues of chestnuts and lindens, a yew maze, yew topiary in the form of chessmen, and an Italian garden filled with sculpture. Some 5 miles north, **Chartwell▶▶** (N.T.), near Westerham, Kent, was Sir Winston Churchill's home from 1922 until his death in 1965. The house appears as it was when Churchill and his family lived here, a homely place filled with mementoes of one of the great men of the century. General Wolfe, general of the British army at the capture of Quebec from the French,

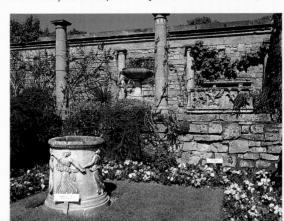

was born in 1726 at **Quebec House**▶ (N.T.), Westerham, Kent, close by; an exhibition illustrates the campaign that led to British supremacy in Canada.

Charles Darwin lived the last 40 years of his life at **Down House**▶ (E.H.) near Downe, Kent. Here he wrote

his seminal work *On the Origin of Species* (1859), the book that changed mainstream thinking on evolution.

Immediately southeast of Sevenoaks, Kent, **Knole**▶▶▶ (N.T.) is England's largest house, with 365 rooms, 7 courtyards and 52 corridors; little has been altered since the early 17th century. A former archbishop's palace which later fell into the hands of Henry VIII, Knole has been in the hands of the Sackvilles from the time of Elizabeth I. The huge deer park is always open to the public. **Ightham Mote**▶▶▶ (N.T.), near Shipbourne, Kent, is a 14th-century moated building of great character, with a Tudor chapel with painted ceiling, a splendid Great Hall, and a 14th-century chapel and crypt.

Close by the North Downs in northern Kent, **Owletts**▶ (N.T.), near Cobham, is a restrained red-brick 17th-century house, which boasts a plasterwork ceiling and a staircase of the same period. Do not miss the collection of memorial brasses in nearby Cobham Church. Near the village of Shoreham in Kent's Darent Valley, **Lullingstone Castle**▶ is a Tudor and Queen Anne family mansion with state rooms and one of the earliest brick gateways (*ca*1497) in the country; a visit can be combined with Lullingstone Roman Villa (see walk on page 92).

Leeds Castle▶▶, to the east of Maidstone, Kent, was once a residence of Henry VIII but is not as genuine a stately home as some: the furniture and contents were later brought in with the aim of re-creating a country house; but the grounds and building themselves are real enough, and the place has warmth and an idyllic lake setting. About 13 miles south near Goudhurst, Kent (not far from **Sissinghurst**, see Gardens, page 17), is **Finchcocks**▶, an early Georgian house noted for its collection of keyboard instruments, while 12 miles south again at Burwash, East Sussex, is **Bateman's**▶ (N.T.), the 17th-century house where author Rudyard Kipling lived from 1902 to 1936 and completed *Puck of Pook's Hill* and *Rewards and Fairies*. The mill next door houses one of the oldest water-driven turbines, still grinding flour for sale. Kipling's 1928 Rolls-Royce is on display.

The Arcadian beauty of Penshurst Place, famed for its medieval Baron's Hall

103

THE WEALDEN FORESTS
The Weald has not always been the countryside of fine mansions, charming villages, rich farms, and hop-fields that we see today. In centuries gone by, it was deeply forested, its oaks supplying the lumber that built the British navy. The trees were also felled by charcoal burners to smelt the Sussex iron. Patches of this ancient forest remain, in the forests of St. Leonards and Ashdown.

*Nelson's flagship,
H.M.S.* Victory

PORTSMOUTH'S HISTORIC SHIPS

H.M.S. *Victory* was Lord Nelson's flagship at Trafalgar, and is still in commission (thus manned by serving officers). Henry VIII's favorite battleship, the *Mary Rose*, keeled over in the harbor in 1545, in sight of the king. In 1982 the wreck was brought to the surface and is now kept under special conditions, an intriguing time capsule of Tudor life. H.M.S. *Warrior* (1860) was the world's first iron-hulled warship, now restored to its former glory; visitors are free to walk around the decks.

104

NAVAL DEFENSES AT PORTSMOUTH

Among those which can be visited are Southsea Castle, built in 1544, which still has tunnels (exhibits include fish-bone ship models made by Napoleonic prisoners of war); Spitbank Fort, out to sea and reached by a short boat trip, with a labyrinth of passages; and Fort Nelson at Fareham. In 1944 Portsmouth was the nerve center of the Normandy invasion, and in 1982 the South Atlantic Task Force was prepared here for battle in the Falklands War.

Church Square, Rye

▶▶▶ **Portsmouth**   86A2
(tel: 01705 826722)
A sprawling port and industrial city, heavily bombarded in World War II, Portsmouth is unique among British towns in being built on its own island. This has been a naval base since the 12th century, and in 1495 was host to the world's first dry dock. For the visitor, Portsmouth rates alongside Greenwich (see page 46) as the center for finding out about Britain's maritime history.

The **Historic Dockyard▶▶▶**, close to Portsmouth Harbour Station, is the chief attraction, where a trio of famous warships are berthed (see panel). The **Royal Naval Museum** (*Admission charge* separate, or combined with ticket for H.M.S. *Victory*) charts naval history from 1485 to the Falklands War, and features the stories of the Trafalgar campaign and the Siege of Malta. **Port cruises** operate between April through October, weather permitting. For the Millennium, Portsmouth has smartened up its waterside, with an ambitious development at **Gunwharf Quays**, public promenades beside the harbor, and the 500-foot **Millennium Tower**, for far-ranging views.

Eastward lies **Southsea**, an Edwardian coastal resort, where the **D-Day Museum▶** commemorates the Allied invasion of Normandy on June 6, 1944, with the sights and sounds of Britain at war and the 272-foot Overlord Embroidery (a latter-day Bayeux Tapestry). The **Royal Marines Museum** traces the 300-year history of the Marines and has an Arctic display, junior commando assault course, and Falklands multimedia theater. Also in Southsea, the **Portsmouth Sea Life Centre** is an aquarium with a ceiling-high "window onto the ocean."

Elsewhere in town are **Charles Dickens' birthplace** (Commercial Road), where the writer was born in 1812, now a three-room museum; **Portchester Castle▶▶** (E.H.), from which the Romans coordinated the defense of southeast England, and includes remains of a Norman church and a palace built by Richard II; and the **City Museum** (Museum Road) with old shopfronts and more.

▶▶▶ **Rye**   87B4
(tel: 01797 226696)
This small town of cobblestones and half-timbered houses perches on a rise above Romney Marsh. Mermaid Street is one of the prettiest thoroughfares in southeast England. Once a Cinque Port (see panel, page 105), Rye now lies inland by some 2 miles. In medieval times the town was

frequently attacked by the French, who set fire to it in 1377; the Ypres Tower is a rare pre-fire survivor and now houses the local museum. Medieval Landgate guards what was once the only landward entrance. The Gun Garden below looks down the River Rother toward Rye Harbour. The novelists Henry James and E. F. Benson lived at Lamb House (N.T.) at different times; many of Benson's Lucia stories are set in Rye. Antique hunters should head for the shops near the old quay.

To the northeast lies **Romney Marsh▶**. The sea has receded, leaving the marsh, now drained and fertile farmland grazed by chunky Romney sheep. A long way inland, the old Saxon shore is visible as an abrupt escarpment edge; at its foot runs the Royal Military Canal, built in Napoleonic times as a defense. Romney Marsh is sparsely populated but has some good medieval churches, including the drunkenly askew church at **Brookland**, with its freestanding belfry. **Camber Sands** offers one of the cleanest beaches in the southeast.

Winchelsea▶▶ is a quiet hilltop village just southeast of Rye, still ranged around its medieval grid plan, with many handsome old houses and a superb church. The original town was much plundered by the French in the 14th and 15th centuries. Three town gates survive.

Beyond Romney Marsh, the **Romney, Hythe,** and **Dymchurch Railway**, a mere 15-inch gauge, runs between the picturesque hillside town of **Hythe** (there's a bizarre collection of human skulls in the church crypt) and Dungeness, a most surreal place, where fishermen's shacks and converted train carriages crouch on a vast rocky bank beneath the shadow of Dungeness B nuclear power station (*Guided tours free*).

▶▶ Sandwich   87B5
(tel: 01304 613565)

Though it's of modest size, Sandwich has a remarkably intact medieval center, all the better for being off the tourist beat. Take a walk beside the river on the earth ramparts, visiting the Barbican, a toll bridge-cum-gateway. **Richborough Castle▶** (E.H.) was erected after the Roman invasion of AD 43, and a busy town once existed here, dominated by a huge gateway that greeted Roman legions at this threshold to Britain. The entrance fee includes an informative audio tour that explains the site.

THE CINQUE PORTS
During the reign of Edward the Confessor (1042–1066) a confederation of Channel ports was formed for the defense of the coast, and for 300 years these Cinque Ports (French for "five ports") had the monopoly on supplying ships and men for the royal fleet, enjoying privileges in return. The original five ports—Sandwich, Hastings, Hythe, New Romney, and Dover—were later joined by Winchelsea and Rye, and several other towns were also attached. After the 14th century, as harbors silted up and the coastline shifted, the Cinque Ports declined in importance. Today, only Dover is an active port.

105

MARTELLO TOWERS
A feature of the Kent and Sussex coasts is the string of 74 Martello towers (of a type formerly widespread in Europe, and named after Cape Mortella in Corsica, where the British Navy captured such a tower in 1794), built 1805–1812 to resist a possible French invasion; some are derelict, others are converted to private houses; English Heritage mainains one at Dymchurch, in Romney Marsh (Kent) and opens it to the public in summer.

Fishing boats on the beach at Dungeness

THE WELD

THE WEALD

North Downs
M26
Chevening
Dunton Green
Seal
Oldbury
Ightham
Borough Green
Great Comp
West Malling
M25
Darent
Sevenoaks
Stone Street
Old Soar Manor
A26
Brasted
Sundridge
Knole
Ivy Hatch
Plaxtol
Dunk's Green
Mereworth
Westerham
Emmetts Garden
Ightham Mote
West Peckham
Squerryes Court
Toy's Hill
Riverhill House
Shipbourne
Chartwell
Ide Hill
Sevenoaks Weald
Crockham Hill
A21
Hadlow
Golden Green
Marlpit Hill
Four Elms
Chiddingstone Causeway
Hildenborough
Medway
East Peckham
Edenbridge
Eden
Chiddingstone
Leigh
Tonbridge
Whitbread Hop Farm
Castle
Hever
Castle Penshurst
Penshurst Place
Five Oak Green
Paddock Wood
Marsh Green
Bidborough
Colt's Hill
Markbeech
Smart's Hill
Southborough
Cowden
Water
Fordcombe
Speldhurst
Pembury
Matfield
Kent
Rusthall
Langton Green
Kipping's Cross
Holtye
Ashurst
Tunbridge Wells
A21
Balls Green
Medway
High Rocks
Bayham Abbey
Owl House
Hartfield
Withyham
Groombridge
Bells Yew Green
Lamberhurst
Upper Hartfield
Eridge Green
Teise
Coleman's Hatch
Poohsticks Bridge
Chuck Hatch
The Weald
Outdoor Pursuits Centre
Cousley Wood
Ashdown Forest
A26
Crowborough
Wadhurst
Bewl Water
Camp Hill
Mark Cross
A22
Rotherfield
0 2 4 6 km
Duddleswell
0 1 2 3 miles

The Pantiles, an attractive shopping area in Tunbridge Wells

106

Drive

The Weald

Starting at Tunbridge Wells, this is a circular tour of approximately 70 miles. You'll see the weatherboarded and pantile-hung cottages, the undulating woodlands and farmland of the Weald, and you can visit a host of country houses and attractive gardens. Allow at least a day if you plan to stop at all the places mentioned.

Start at **Tunbridge Wells▶**, a very pleasant old spa town with echoes of its 18th-century heyday (evoked in the exhibition "A Day at the Wells"), including the delightful Pantiles, a Regency arcade. Leave by the A26, but soon fork right and then left to pass **High Rocks▶**, a popular place for climbers.

At **Groombridge** take the B2188 which rises onto the sandy heathlands of the **Ashdown Forest▶**, the landscape of A. A. Milne's *Winnie the Pooh* stories (see walk on page 92). Detour south along the B2026—just before the next road junction, Camp Hill on the right offers a fine viewpoint. Return north along the B2026 through **Hartfield** and turn off past Cowden railroad station to follow back lanes to **Penshurst▶▶**, known for its great house (see page 102) and picturesque cottages.

Continue on the B2176 and then a minor road to **Chiddingstone▶**, where a splendid half-timbered group of buildings owned by the National Trust includes the Castle Inn, close by an eye-catching Gothic castle.

Weave around minor lanes past **Chartwell▶▶**, Churchill's former house (see page 102), through pretty **Ide Hill** village, with its spacious green, around the south side of **Knole Park▶▶▶** and close to **Ightham Mote▶▶▶** (see page 103).

Return to Tunbridge Wells via **Plaxtol**, **Hadlow** with its ruined 19th-century folly tower, and **East Peckham**, where oast houses mark the site of Whitbread Brewery's **Hop Farms Country Park**.

King Arthur's "Round Table"

▶▶▶ Winchester   *86B1*
(tel: 01962 840500)

The capital of Saxon England, Winchester became a major religious and commercial center in medieval times. Its importance has ebbed, but its medieval core is well preserved. Its college is one of Britain's great schools.

Visitors will spend most of their time in the vicinity of the **cathedral▶▶▶**, the longest medieval cathedral in Europe. It has an outstanding Norman crypt, much

WINCHESTER COLLEGE
Students of Winchester College, one of the country's leading "public" (i.e. private) schools (see panel on Eton College, page 109), are known as Wykehamists, harkening to its 14th-century foundation by the Bishop of Winchester, William of Wykeham. Seventy scholars were taught classics and other disciplines here before studying at New College, Oxford (another Wykeham foundation). The school probably was used as a model for Eton College, founded by Henry VI. Both have quadrangles, a chapel, and a hall.

THE WATERCRESS LINE
Also known as the Mid-Hants Railway, the privately owned 10-mile railroad runs through the Hampshire countryside from New Alresford to Alton (where it connects with the main rail line), giving a good idea of train travel in the age of steam. The carriages are old British Rail ones, the staff dress in period costume, and the stations look and feel right. The watercress beds which gave the line its nickname can still be seen around New Alresford, and watercress soup is served on the line's evening diner train. For details, tel: 01962 734866.

Perpendicular work, and monuments to Jane Austen and to Isaak Walton, of *Compleat Angler* fame; the chantry of William Wykeham, who funded restoration work, is perhaps the finest monument of all. Walton resided in No. 7 in the **cathedral close**, a charming precinct abutted by the flying buttresses of the cathedral and by the rambling half-timbered Cheyney Court (dating from 1148). Close by is the **City Museum▶**, with a strong Roman section.

The **High Street** and **Broadway** have been the main axis of the city since Roman times. At the top end, **West Gate**, one of two surviving city gates, occupies a Roman site; a small museum upstairs has a drawing of Wren's scheme for a royal palace (which never got off the ground). Nearby is the Great Hall, where hangs "King Arthur's Round Table," which lists the names of all his knights but is actually a resplendent medieval fake made about 700 years after his death. Down along Broadway is a 1901 statue of King Alfred, King of Wessex, who is buried nearby, and the Abbey Gardens, a quiet haven close to the Gothic revival guildhall (1871) housing the Tourist Information Centre.

The half-timbered **City Mill** straddles the River Itchen nearby. On **College Street**, a plaque records the house in which Jane Austen died in 1817, aged 42. **Winchester College▶** (*Guided tours* Apr–Sep) has a "quad" like those found at the colleges of Oxford and Cambridge universities. **Wolvesey Castle▶**, a gaunt shell of a bishop's palace built in 1130 and dismantled by Parliamentarians in the Civil War, stands next to elegant **Wolvesey Palace** (1684), which superseded it.

A 15–20 minute walk along the riverside meadows to the south brings you to **St. Cross Hospital▶▶**, founded in 1136 as a charitable almshouse institution, an extraordinary time-warp place with cloistered seclusion, a fine Norman chapel, and an antiquated kitchen. By an ancient rule of the charitable trust, Wayfarer's Dole— bread and ale—is still given to anyone who asks for it specifically.

On the banks of the River Test, 10 miles southwest of Winchester, is the pleasant, small town of **Romsey**, well worth a visit for its wonderful Norman **abbey church▶▶**, built mainly in the 12th century by Henry de Blois, Bishop of Winchester, and with Saxon sculptures among its treasures.

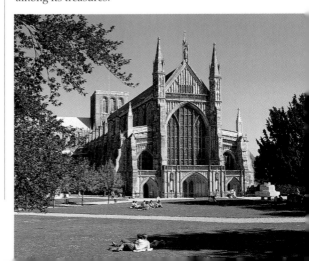

Winchester Cathedral, built of Quarr stone from the Isle of Wight

Eton College rowers with Windsor Castle beyond

TOO INNOVATIVE FOR SOME
Windsor's 17th-century guildhall, started by Sir Robert Fitch and completed by Sir Christopher Wren, needed no structural columns beneath its raised floor. The alarmed town burghers insisted that Wren supply some; this he did, but he deliberately built them too short, to prove they were actually unnecessary.

109

ETON COLLEGE
This is the most famous of Britain's public schools (i.e. those prestigious private, fee-paying establishments whose headmasters attend the Headmasters' Conference: they are actually quite independent of the state system). The high street has numerous barbers and tailors; one of them, T. Brown, has changed little over the years. Here, the boys are fitted out at the start of term in long-tailed jackets and wing-collars. "Old Etonians" include William Gladstone (19th-century prime minster), George Orwell (real name Eric Blair; author of *1984*), Ian Fleming (author of the James Bond books), and Thomas Arne (composer of *Rule Britannia*).

▶▶▶ **Windsor and Eton**   86C2
(tel: 01753 743900)

The two towns are a short walk apart, separated only by the Thames. Although within easy reach of London by train, Windsor and Eton demand a very full day if you want to get around all of the sights. Visitors often tie in a trip to the gardens at Wisley (see page 16).

The town of **Windsor** is dominated by the presence of **Windsor Castle**▶▶▶, Europe's largest, a royal family residence which opens its doors to visitors. The castle dates from the 12th century, but was extended over the next 700 years and was restored following a massive fire in 1992. St. George's Chapel (begun in the 15th century by Edward IV and a superb example of the Perpendicular style, with a fan-vaulted aisle and three-tier stalls), the State Apartments, and the extraordinarily detailed Queen Mary's Dolls' House are high points. During the restoration, parts of the building were re-discovered, including an undercroft and medieval well (restoration tours by appointment, tel: 01753 868286).

Another royal site is **Frogmore House** (*Open* occasionally), the 17th-century home of Queen Charlotte and Queen Victoria's mother and the burial place of Victoria herself, alongside Prince Albert. **Windsor Park**▶▶ is worth exploring on foot (there is public access to most of it), with follies, lakes, and a totem pole to discover. **Legoland** theme park includes a Lego driving school and a re-creation of Amsterdam, London, Brussels, and Paris; book ahead to avoid long waits in line (tel: 0990 040404).

Over the river lies **Eton**, its appealing main street fronted by **Eton College**▶▶ (see sidebar). Eton was founded in 1440 by Henry VI. The chapel is a fine example of the Perpendicular style, reminiscent of King's College Chapel, Cambridge. The quad also looks like Oxford or Cambridge University colleges. The **Museum of Eton Life** celebrates the life and times of Eton College.

From **Windsor**, boat trips run to **Boveney Lock** in the heart of the **Thames Valley**▶▶. At **Maidenhead**, villas and gardens back onto the river. **Cookham**▶ has been immortalized by the artist Stanley Spencer; a gallery here has a number of his works. **Henley-on-Thames**▶ is famed for its Royal Regatta, first rowed in 1839.

The Heart of England

THE ROBERT OPIE COLLECTION

THE
PACKAGE
REVISITED

ALBERT WAREHOUSE
GLOUCESTER DOCKS, GLOUCESTER

The Collection is open daily 10am-6pm, (last admission 5pm)
Open all Bank Holidays, except Christmas Day & Boxing Day.

110

GENUINE
BANBURY
CAKES

Made in Banbury by
R.S.Malcolm
Family Bakers & Confectioners

41 HIGH STREET
53 MIDDLETON ROAD
BANBURY

THE HEART OF ENGLAND This is a region that reflects, as deeply as any other, that elusively diverse nature of the English landscape: for it includes both the Cotswolds, the epitome of rural England, and the industrial "Black Country," the economic hub of the Midlands.

THE WEST MIDLANDS AND THE BLACK COUNTRY The Midlands is a nebulous term, often applied to the central industrial manufacturing belt encompassing the cities of Birmingham, Wolverhampton, Coventry, Leicester, Derby, Stoke-on-Trent and Nottingham (some of which fall outside the scope of this chapter). Most first-time visitors to Britain would give the bulk of the area a miss, but there is plenty of interest in the cityscapes, industrial sights, museums and even areas of unspoilt countryside.

The county of **West Midlands** encompasses the so-called Black Country, dominated by the conurbation of

RECOMMENDED HISTORIC CITIES AND COUNTRY TOWNS

Gloucestershire: Cheltenham, Chipping Campden, Cirencester, Gloucester, Painswick, Tewkesbury, Winchcombe.
Herefordshire: Bewdley, Hereford, Ledbury, Leominster
Worcestershire: Stourport, Worcester.
Oxfordshire: Abingdon, Burford, Dorchester, Henley, Oxford.
Shropshire: Bishop's Castle, Clun, Bridgnorth, Ludlow, Much Wenlock, Shrewsbury.
Staffordshire: Lichfield.
Warwickshire: Stratford-upon-Avon, Warwick.

INDUSTRIAL HERITAGE

Birmingham Black Country Living Museum, Didcot Railway Centre, Ironbridge, Severn Valley Railway.

WALKS

Abberley Hills, Cannock Chase, Chiltern Hills, Cotswold Hills (Cotswold Way and western escarpment), Clent Hills, Forest of Dean, Ironbridge Gorge, Lickey Hills, Malvern Hills, South Shropshire, Lower Wye Valley (page 171), the Wrekin, Wyre Forest.

VILLAGE-TO-VILLAGE DRIVES

Chiltern Hills, Cotswolds, Herefordshire, Shropshire.

Eastnor, below the Malvern Hills

Wolverhampton, West Bromwich and others, much of which developed in the 19th century through the exploitation of coal and iron deposits. Some towns developed specialized industries—leather in Walsall, glass in Stourbridge and locks in Willenhall. The industrial heritage is celebrated at the Black Country Living Museum in Dudley (see page 20), and at the Leather Museum in Walsall.

To the east the conurbation merges into **Birmingham** (nicknamed "Brum"), England's second city, and at first sight an unappealing jungle of highway overpasses and suburban and industrial sprawl. However, in the last decade or so a remarkable renaissance has come about in its downtown area, with a new lease of life for its canalside buildings and its Jewellery Quarter as well as its civic and industrial heritage. The City of Birmingham Symphony Orchestra, based at Symphony Hall, has emerged as one of the world's greatest orchestras, while the National Exhibition Centre and International Convention Centre bring in many business travelers. The heaths and woodlands of Cannock Chase and the modest heights of the Clent Hills have pleasant walks just outside the built-up area. East of Birmingham, **Coventry** had its heart knocked out by bombing in 1940, and the ruins of its medieval cathedral stand beside Basil Spence's innovative postwar replacement—endowed with some striking modern art, including glass by John Piper and a huge tapestry by Graham Sutherland.

THE ENGLISH MARCHES Shropshire, **Herefordshire** and **Worcestershire** encompass much in the way of unspoiled countryside, black-and-white and red-brick villages, and the assertive south Shropshire Hills; it is ideal for those who like to make their own discoveries. To the west it adjoins the even lesser-known, and much less populated, Welsh Marches or borderlands. Only the pleasant market town of Ludlow and Ironbridge Gorge, birthplace of the Industrial Revolution, are firmly on the tourist trail; Shrewsbury, Hereford, and numerous smaller towns and villages such as Much Wenlock and Ledbury are well-kept secrets. Walkers may like to head for the hills around Church Stretton and for the Malvern Hills. The russet-earthed territory of rural Herefordshire, its pastures grazed by docile Hereford cattle, is amiably sleepy and has a wealth of half-timbered "black and white" buildings as well as several outstanding churches, some tucked well away. **Worcestershire** has the cathedral city of Worcester for its centerpiece.

THE COTSWOLDS AND THEIR FRINGES East of the fruit and vegetable heartlands of the Vale of Evesham, the buildings change color dramatically as one climbs up into the **Cotswold Hills** (mostly belonging to **Gloucestershire** and **Oxfordshire**). Its honey-yellow stone villages and towns have enchanted generations of visitors; the area is rich in both places to visit and accommodations.

Non-Cotswold Gloucestershire includes Gloucester, Cheltenham, and the lowlands abutting the Severn Estuary, the final stages of Britain's longest river. On a waterside site, the naturalist Peter Scott set up the celebrated wildfowl reserve at Slimbridge. In the Forest of Dean, once a coal, and charcoal, producing area, the villages are not particularly attractive, but there are verdant walks, including the Sculpture Trail (west of Cinderford). The Lower Wye Valley (see under Wales) is close at hand.

The fringes of the Cotswolds harbor some of the greatest visitor attractions of central England, including Oxford, Blenheim Palace, and Shakespeare's Stratford-upon-Avon. These are close enough to London for day-trips. Notable arrays of stately homes and manor houses open to the public are found in **Warwickshire** (Baddesley Clinton, Charlecote Park, Coughton Court, Farnborough Hall, Kenilworth Castle, Packwood House, Upton House, Warwick Castle) and **Buckinghamshire** (Chenies Manor, Chicheley Hall, Claydon House, Nancy Astor's Cliveden, Dorney Court, Disraeli's Hughenden Manor, Wycombe Park, and above all the trio of Rothschilds' properties—Ascott House, Mentmore Towers, and Waddesdon). Closer to the capital lie the **Chiltern Hills**, whose gently rolling chalk hills and majestic beech woods have been carefully preserved by Green Belt legislation and whose villages look distinctly prosperous.

There are old musical instruments at Snowshill Manor as well as a collection of Japanese Samurai armour, toys, and bicycles

113

▶▶▶ REGION HIGHLIGHTS

Blenheim Palace
page 115
The Cotswolds
pages 118–121
Ironbridge Gorge Museum *page 123*
Ludlow *page 124*
Malvern Hills *page 125*
Oxford *pages 126–127*
Shropshire Hills
page 130
Stratford-upon-Avon
pages 131–132
Waddesdon Manor
page 132
Warwick *page 133*

OXFORD ALUMNI
Oxford University's many notable graduates include Sir William Walton (composer) and Lewis Carroll (author), both at Christ Church College; T.S. Eliot (poet), Merton College; Oscar Wilde (playwright) and Sir John Betjeman (poet), both Magdalen College; and T.E. Lawrence ("Lawrence of Arabia"), Jesus College.

*Birmingham Museum
and Art Gallery*

▶▶ **Birmingham**   111C2
(tel: 0212-693 6300)
England's second city, one of the largest manufacturing
centers in the country and a major convention venue, is
undergoing a dramatic facelift (trying to rid its image of
1960s brutalist architecture and run-down streetscapes).

SOHO HOUSE
Situated in Soho Avenue
off Soho Road, north of
central Birmingham
(buses 74, 78 and 79
from Bull Street), Soho
House was from 1766 to
1809 the home of
Matthew Boulton, one of
the industrial pioneers of
his day. He set up a huge
manufactory (where buck-
les, buttons, Sheffield
plate, silver and ormulu
objects were made) and
mint, and with James Watt
developed the steam
engine. Eminent scientific
luminaries from the Lunar
Society met here and the
house became a hotbed
of scientific thought. His
house has been pre-
served; it boasted such
comforts as central heat-
ing and a water closet.

At its heart, Victoria Square speaks of civic pride, with its
domed Victorian Council House (city hall), at the back of
which is the **Birmingham Museum and Art Gallery**▶▶
(*Admission free*), with one of the world's greatest collections of Pre-Raphaelite paintings, plus superb fossils,
silverware and wooden marquetry. A walk west from
here leads into Centenary Square, flanked by Symphony
Hall, which is the home of the City of Birmingham
Symphony Orchestra.

The canals are part of the city's renaissance, with a blend
of restored Victorian brick buildings and gleaming new
blocks; along the canals are the fish-shaped **National Sea
Life Centre**▶, with aquatic life from the River Severn displayed in a manner well-geared to children, and the **Gas
Street Basin**, with narrowboats moored near waterside
pubs. North of the city center, the Jewelry Quarter has
some 4,000 workshops and dozens of jewelry shops; the
Museum of the Jewellery Quarter▶▶ includes a tour of
Smith and Pepper's workshops, closed in 1981 and little
changed since starting business in 1899—production processes are shown by the guides.

At Birmingham University, the **Barber Institute for Fine
Arts**▶▶ (*Admission free*; train from New Street Station to

University) is a choice collection with many of the great European artists represented. **Aston Hall►►** (*Admission free*), after which Aston Villa Football Club is named, is a splendid Jacobean mansion of 1618–1635, with plaster ceilings and a fine Long Gallery. At Bourneville, the Cadbury family set up their chocolate factory in 1879 and near the original garden village built for workers is **Cadbury World►** (booking recommended, tel: 0121-451 4159)—not a factory tour, but you see handmade chocolates being made and sample the result; a history of the foodstuff is told in the attached museum.

►►► Blenheim Palace 111A3
(*tel: 01993 811325*)

This is more of a gilded palace than an English country house, impersonal in scale but undeniably impressive, with its sumptuous state rooms, furnishings, tapestries, and door-cases carved by Grinling Gibbons. It is considered the finest true baroque house in Britain.

Blenheim designed by John Vanbrugh for the 1st Duke of Marlborough, one John Churchill. It was a reward from Queen Anne in recognition of his crushing victory over the French at Blenheim in Bavaria in 1704. More recently, in 1874, it was the birthplace of Winston Churchill, and the contents include some fascinating Churchilliana. He is buried nearby in Bladon Church.

The palace stands in a great park laid out by Henry Wise, gardener to Queen Anne, and later modified by Capability Brown. Explore the numerous walks, beech woods, and formal features that include the Triumphal Way, Italian Garden, maze, ornamental bridge, and Column of Victory. Adjacent is the town of **Woodstock**, home to the Oxfordshire County Museum.

► Bridgnorth 110C2
(*tel: 01746 763257*)

Bridgnorth's high town perches on a sandstone cliff above the Severn, with a cliff railway connecting the low town. Stroll along Castle Walk past the slanting ruin of a Norman castle, blown up in 1646 during the Civil War. From here the **Severn Valley Railway►►** runs 16 miles to Kidderminster, recapturing the style of long-distance travel of yesteryear, with steam locomotives pulling carriages through a series of well-preserved stations. The journey takes just over an hour, and passes through **Bewdley►**, where the Old Shambles houses the local museum. To the east, on the A456, is the **West Midlands Safari Park**, which has themed rides in its Leisure Park.

THE RIDGEWAY
The eastern half of the long-distance Ridgeway Path follows the western escarpment of the Chilterns. Near Wendover it climbs over Coombe Hill, where a Boer War memorial marks the highest point in the Chilterns; close by you can glimpse Chequers, the country retreat of British prime ministers since 1921. Ivinghoe Beacon looks over the seemingly endless south Midlands plain. Walks here extend into the woodlands of the Ashridge Estate, past the monument to the 3rd Duke of Bridgewater, the 18th-century canal developer, and to the pretty village green at Aldbury.

115

MORE WALKS IN THE CHILTERNS
Between Luton and Whipsnade, the Dunstable Downs is a fine escarpment popular with walkers and kite-fliers; gliders and superb sunsets add to the pleasures. Near Tring, off the Chilterns proper, the Tring Reservoir National Nature Reserve provides plenty of interest in the way of birdlife and canal scenes. Burnham Beeches is a glorious place for fall colors (it is surprisingly easily to lose the way; look out for the helpful maps). The Chess Valley has very attractive walks, with the pretty villages of Chenies, Latimer, and Sarratt as focal points.

The Temple of Venus in the grounds of West Wycombe Park

WEST WYCOMBE AND THE DASHWOODS

The most notorious member of the Dashwood family was undoubtedly Sir Francis Dashwood (1708–1791), who set up the Hell Fire Club, a black-magic brotherhood more interested in drinking and whoring than satanic rites. Its meeting places included the West Wycombe Caves (open to the public, just north of the village street) and the hollow gold ball on top of the Church of St. Lawrence. The Dashwood memorials are within the curious roofless, hexagonal mausoleum (1764) next to the church.

Mapledurham Mill, the last working water mill on the Thames

WHIPSNADE WILD ANIMAL PARK

Planned by the Zoological Society of London, Whipsnade is one of Europe's foremost animal collections, located in a spacious park; close by, Whipsnade Tree Cathedral was created by Edmund Kell Blyth in 1931 as a war memorial, with trees laid out in aisles, transepts, and cloisters.

As one who long in
  populous city pent,
Where houses thick and
  sewers annoy the air,
Forth issuing on a
  summer's morn to
  breathe
Among the pleasant
  villages and farms
Adjoin'd, from each thing
  met conceives delight.
—John Milton (1608–
1674), *Paradise Lost*

▶ Chiltern Hills
(tel: 01494 421892)

Stretching some 50 miles from the Thames Valley west of Reading to the vicinity of Luton at their northern edge, the Chilterns are a rising of chalk downs to the northwest of London. Although the area is part of the City commuter belt, once you are clear of the suburban developments you find yourself in deep countryside, with pretty brick-and-flint cottages, fine manor houses, and country pubs. The beech woods that made the area an important furniture-making center are still a feature of the landscape.

At **Mapledurham▶**, by the Thames, you can visit a working water mill and Elizabethan Mapledurham House, while the 18th-century brick facade of **Stonor**

House▶, the home of the Stonors for 600 years, incorporates a private chapel and a medieval solar. Almost all of **West Wycombe▶** was purchased by the National Trust in 1929 to save it from a road-widening project; its main street has predominantly 17th- and 18th-century houses. Adjacent stands **West Wycombe Park** (N.T.), a mansion built in 1765 for Sir John Dashwood (see panel). Humphry Repton landscaped the park in 1803, adorning it with follies and classical temples. Benjamin Disraeli, the 19th-century prime minister, lived at **Hughenden Manor▶** (N.T.) north of High Wycombe; his library and study have been preserved. **Beaconsfield**, **Princes Risborough**, **Berkhamsted**, and **Wendover** are commuter towns today, but each has an old and attractive center.

In 1665 John Milton came to **Chalfont St. Giles** as an old and blind man, escaping plague-ridden London to a cottage (now a **museum▶**) where he completed *Paradise Lost* and began *Paradise Regained*. Close by, traditional Chiltern buildings can be seen at the **Chiltern Open Air Museum**; including an Iron Age dwelling, a 19th-century farm, and a 1940s prefab. **Chenies** is a tiny 19th-century village which was built for estate workers of the medieval step-gabled brick **manor▶** (*Open* to the public) of the Russell family.

▶ Gloucester

110A2

(tel: 01452 421188)

Gloucester's down-to-earth red-brick textures contrast sharply with the dreamy golden hues of the nearby Cotswolds, but offers rewards in its small yet absorbing medieval center and its revived 19th-century docks.

Just off the historic axis of Westgate Street, with its **Folk Museum**, lie the precincts of the **cathedral▶▶**. It became a place of pilgrimage after the installation of the tomb of Edward II, who was murdered at nearby Berkeley Castle in 1327. From the outside it is a pleasing medieval mishmash; within, its glory is the glass of its east window, one of England's largest, and the 14th-century fan-vaulting in the cloisters, England's earliest. Close by is the **Beatrix Potter Museum**, in the house featured in Potter's children's story *The Tailor of Gloucester*.

Meanwhile, in the **docks** the towering red-brick warehouses have been partly converted to offices, shops, and cafés; you can take 40-minute trips around the site on an old Thames craft. Here the **National Waterways Museum▶** charts the development of Britain's canals, the entertaining **Robert Opie Collection of Advertising and Packaging▶** wallows in nostalgia for vintage ephemera, and the **Soldiers of Gloucestershire Museum** details 300 years of regimental history.

Gloucester's neighbor, **Cheltenham▶**, is an elegant Regency spa, with its pump room designed in the best 19th-century Greek Revival tradition. A mineral spring was discovered here in 1715, allegedly by observing the comings and goings of a healthy-looking pigeon population; pigeons feature on the town's crest today. Cheltenham later received the royal approval of George III and acquired its handsome terraces, wrought-iron balconies, and leafy thoroughfares. Other attractions are the art gallery and museum, **Holst's Birthplace Museum** (where the composer of *The Planets* was born in 1874), the annual festivals of music (July) and of literature (October), and the racecourse.

To the northwest, **Tewkesbury▶**, where the Avon and Severn meet, is a handsome town of high-medieval and later facades. The **abbey church▶** is one of England's finest examples of Norman ecclesiastical architecture.

"Baker's bells," a distinctive carillon in Gloucester's Southgate Street

THREE CHOIRS FESTIVAL
This major music festival takes place in the last week of August and rotates in a three-year cycle between Gloucester, Worcester, and Hereford cathedrals. Its origins go back to the early 18th century; from the 1890s three organist-conductors (one from each cathedral) were appointed and a distinguished list of works by some of the country's greatest composers were given their first performance, including *Fantasia on a Theme of Thomas Tallis* (1910) by Vaughan Williams, the *Colour Symphony* (1922) by Bliss, and the *Choral Fantasia* (1931) of Holst. Elgar directed his own music here until his death in 1934.

Touring country par excellence, the Cotswold Hills are an area of beautiful honey-colored limestone villages, tucked-away manor houses, cottage gardens, russet-earth fields enclosed by drystone walls, and lonely, winding country roads leading to nowhere in particular.

118

SOUTH COTSWOLDS HOUSES

Buscot Park (N.T.), near Faringdon, is an 18th-century house renowned for its paintings and porcelain. Also near Faringdon is **Great Coxwell Tithe Barn** (N.T.), built by the monks of Beaulieu and considered one of England's finest: in medieval times a tenth of agricultural produce of each parish was taxed as a tax or "tithe" by the church, and was stored in tithe barns. **Owlpen Manor,** a Tudor manor in an old hillside garden of roses and box parterres was restored in the 1920s by Norman Jewson, a follower of the Arts and Crafts movement and is a fascinating mixture of centuries.

Cotswold architecture: honey-hued walls and stone-mullioned windows

SOUTH COTSWOLDS GARDENS

Among many outstanding gardens are the **Rococo Garden** outside Painswick, **Westonbirt Arboretum** (a Forestry Commission collection of over 17,000 trees), **Barnsley House Garden** (Georgian summerhouses, laburnum walk, herbaceous borders), **Batsford Arboretum** (rare trees) and **Miserden Park** (topiary, shrubs, borders, and more, in a woodland setting).

The Cotswolds present timeless tableaus of rural England. The scenery is pleasant rather than dramatic, with the best views from the western edges. There are plenty of hotels, some very high class indeed, and the area is strong on sights (with plenty for children). Wool was the key to the area's medieval prosperity, and the wealth it created is commemorated in a striking legacy of grand churches. Almost every town and village seems to have a Sheep Street.

The area is described in two parts, one lying south of the A40, the other north.

The south The undoubted capital of the south Cotswolds, **Cirencester►►** is a handsome town with more bustle than most of its neighbors, and plenty of specialty shops for browsing. In Roman times, only London (*Londinium*) was bigger than Cirencester (*Corinium*), and these and later days are celebrated in the excellent Corinium Museum, which displays mosaic paving and reconstructions of Roman domestic interiors. Dominating the market square is the cathedral-like parish church, with its fan-vaulted porch and grand interior. One of the finest streets is Cecily Hill, its far end leading into Cirencester Park (pedestrians only), the grounds of Lord Bathurst's stately home.

At **Bibury**▶▶ a triple-arched footbridge over the River Coln leads to Arlington Row, a group of former weavers' cottages. The village is full of unspoiled corners and pretty cottage gardens. The Victorian artist-craftsman William Morris, who with his pre-Raphaelite friends "discovered" the Cotswolds and in 1871 came to live at nearby Kelmscott, declared Bibury to be the most beautiful village in England. The former Arlington Mill houses the Cotswold Museum. More low-key, cozy charm is found in abundance in the **Colns** (Coln St. Aldwyn, Coln Rogers, and Coln St. Dennis) and the **Duntisbournes** (Duntisbourne Abbots, Duntisbourne Leer, and Duntisbourne Rouse, the latter having a little Saxon church). **Fairford**▶ prides itself on its splendid "wool church," famed for its late 15th-century stained glass.

Painswick▶▶ has an appealing, sloping knot of central lanes and gray-stone walls; grand houses jostle cheek by jowl with minute cottages. Best of all is the churchyard, dominated by 99 yews; an explanatory leaflet describes the fine 16th- to 19th-century tombstones. The surrounding area is lush and deep-set, the numerous viewpoints including **Painswick Beacon** and **Haresfield Beacon**. **Slad** was the village of writer Laurie Lee, who captured the pre-automobile age so evocatively in *Cider with Rosie*. **Stroud** is not particularly attractive, but the atmospherically derelict **Thames and Severn Canal**, near Sapperton, is worth exploring. Farther south are some finely sited towns and villages, including **Wotton-under-Edge** and **Dursley**, snug beneath the escarpment, and **Minchinhampton**, on a breezy hilltop site.

Chedworth Roman Villa▶ (N.T.), excavated 1864–1866, stands alone in the woods near Chedworth and gives an excellent insight into the period. Mosaics and bath and heating systems have been found; it is thought that the villa functioned like a hotel for people visiting its water shrine. Uley Bury, known as **Hetty Pegler's Tump**, after the wife of its 17th-century owner, is a neolithic burial mound with its stone slabs still in place.

The drystone wall is the main type of field boundary in the Cotswolds

FAMILY ATTRACTIONS (SOUTH)
South of Burford, the **Cotswold Wildlife Park** features white rhinos, tigers, and more. At **Prinknash Abbey**, a living community of Benedictine monks, there is a bird sanctuary and pottery. At Northleach are two absorbing attractions, **Keith Harding's World of Mechanical Music** (antique mechanical instruments) and the **Cotswold Heritage Centre** (exhibits from yesteryear housed in a former prison). Further afield, the **Wildfowl and Wetlands Trust** at Slimbridge on the Severn Estuary has a huge collection of wildfowl, and **Berkeley Castle** is famous for the dungeon in which Edward II was gruesomely murdered in 1327.

FAMILY ATTRACTIONS (NORTH)

The **Gloucestershire–Warwickshire Railway** operates steam trains between Toddington and Winchcombe, while the **Cotswold Farm Park** (west of Stow-on-the-Wold) is home to rare animal breeds. Just outside Witney, the **Cogges Manor Farm Museum** offers a look at rural Edwardian life in Oxfordshire, with craft and farming demonstrations.

Angular gables, stone roofs, and trim lawns: typical of many Cotswold manor houses

NORTH COTSWOLDS HOUSES

Stanway House is a good example of Jacobean architecture, while *Broughton Castle* near Banbury is a moated medieval manor, and **Snowshill Manor** (N.T.) contains a collection of bicycles, and Japanese Samurai armour. By contrast, **Sezincote** was remodeled in the 1800s as an Indian fantasy; the Prince Regent found in it inspiration for his Royal Pavilion in Brighton (see page 90). **Chastleton House** (N.T.) is a Jacobean manor (must book timed tickets, tel: 01608 674284). **Sudeley Castle**, an imposing part-ruined stately home at Winchcombe, was the burial place of Henry VIII's sixth wife, Catherine Parr.

NORTH COTSWOLDS GARDENS

The magically hidden-away gardens of **Hidcote Manor**, north of Chipping Campden, are pure joy: a 20th-century creation of a series of "rooms" bounded by hedges and walls. Close by, **Kiftsgate Court Gardens** have rare shrubs and a fine rose collection.

The north In the far north, **Chipping Campden▶▶** should not be missed for its showpiece main street, primitive open-sided market hall, and a fine church with Gloucester shire's largest memorial brass. The great manor house of Campden has gone, but its Jacobean lodges and gateway remain. Chipping Campden is just large enough to be a town, but its pace is unhurried and its charms preserved without being commercialized. By contrast, **Broadway▶** is a tourist magnet, its elegant (but traffic-ridden) main street well lined with gift boutiques and tearooms. The village lies beneath the Cotswold escarpment on the brink of the Vale of Evesham, a major fruit-growing area with roadside stalls selling produce in season; the abrupt transition from Cotswold stone to Midland red brick is quite striking.

Other quieter subescarpment villages nearby have charm in plenty, including **Buckland** and **Stanton**. Within the town center of **Winchcombe▶** you can find a gargoyle-covered church (look for the splendid

weathercock) and an old-fashioned ambience; attractions include a folk and police museum, and a museum of railroad memorabilia. Just out of town by the B4632, **Cleeve Hill▶** is a blustery highland (only 1,040 feet, but it feels higher), a place for strolls, kite-flying, and enjoying the view westward to the Malvern Hills (see page 125). Beautifully set beneath the Cotswold escarpment, the Cistercian ruin of **Hailes Abbey** (E.H./N.T.) was in its day a major pilgrimage site.

Stow-on-the-Wold and **Chipping Norton** are conveniently placed market towns, the latter with a superb 19th-century tweed mill. With its series of tiny bridges spanning the Windrush, **Bourton-on-the-Water** is almost too pretty to be believed; it is the most commercialized village in the Cotswolds, drawing crowds to its miniature model village, perfumery exhibition, model railroad, Birdland aviary, motor museum, and village life exhibition. By contrast, neighboring **Lower Slaughter▶** is an unspoiled delight, with cottages and an old mill overlooking a brook. **Burford** has an impressive church and a distinguished main street lined with stores and inns, sloping down to an ancient stone bridge. Close to Witney is **Minster Lovell▶** with its spooky, ruined 15th-century hall.

THE COTSWOLDS

121

Drive

The Cotswolds

This tour promises golden stone-built villages, dignified manor houses, and fine views (approx. 55 miles).

Start from **Burford▶**, descending the main street, and continue past **Stow-on-the-Wold** to branch off, past **Sezincote House▶▶** and **Blockley**, which still has a few of its old silk-throwing mills. Continue to **Chipping Campden▶▶**; head south-west to the A44 where you turn right (Broadway Tower, a famous scenic overlook, is soon off left) to **Broadway▶**. Take the B4632 to skirt peaceful **Buckland▶**; branch off left through **Stanton▶** and **Stanway▶** and rejoin the B4632 close to the turning to **Hailes Abbey▶**. Continue into **Winchcombe▶**, stopping off for **Sudeley Castle▶**. Pass **Belas Knap** prehistoric burial mound and **Guiting Power**. The villages of **Upper Slaughter** and **Lower Slaughter▶** lead up to busy **Bourton-on-the-Water**.

Finish by exploring the quiet countryside around **Great Barrington**.

CIDER IN HEREFORDSHIRE

The alcoholic apple drink has a venerable tradition in the county; in former days, many farms produced hard cider specially for farm laborers. True farm-house "scrumpy" cider is now a rarity, but the drink has enjoyed a revival in recent years. Bulmer's Cider, one of the largest operations, produces in Hereford (there is a factory shop; tours by appointment, tel: 01432 352000). Hereford's Cider Museum displays cider-making methods ancient and modern. Near Pembridge, a village on the Black and White Villages Trail, Dunkerton's Cider is an engagingly rustic outfit, operating from a barn, and Weston's, a much larger company, produces at Much Marcle.

The finely worked 900-year-old carving on the south doorway of Kilpeck Church

▶ Hereford   110B1

(tel: 01432 268430)

The capital of Herefordshire county, renowned for its eponymous cattle breed and for cider making, stands on the banks of the River Wye. An unfortunate ring road cuts too close to the center, but there are some good medieval streets. The highlight is the sandstone **cathedral▶▶** (begun in 1107) with its library of over 1,400 chained books and its priceless Mappa Mundi, a 13th-century map of the world.

Southwest of the town is **Abbey Dore▶**. Only a portion of what was a huge Cistercian abbey remains, but you can imagine it in its heyday. Nearby **Kilpeck Church▶▶** is a perfect Norman building, embellished inside and out with carvings of birds, beasts, and angels. Prudish Victorians failed to remove all of the more salacious ones.

The **Black and White Villages Trail▶▶** is a well-marked car tour west of Hereford through some beautiful, unspoiled half-timbered villages, including **Weobley**, **Pembridge**, **Eardisland**, and **Lyonshall**.

At **Shobdon▶** the stonework of the old church, which may well have been by the same person who sculpted Kilpeck, was turned into a garden ornament in the mid-18th century for a nearby house; the "new" church built in its place has an interior of wedding-cake "Strawberry Hill Gothick," a style of architecture named after that used in writer Horace Walpole's 1747 house at Strawberry Hill in Twickenham, near London. Farther north, **Croft Castle▶** (N.T.) is a fascinating mixture of medievalism and Georgian Gothic. Walks in the adjacent National Trust estate include the ascent of Croft Ambrey, a well-sited Iron Age hill fort with visible ramparts.

▶ Lichfield   111C3

(tel: 01543 252109)

The trio of sandstone spires of the mostly 12th- to 15th-century **cathedral▶** dominates a gracious close of 17th- to 19th-century buildings. There is much Early English and Decorated work. The west front has 113 statues, including 24 English kings. The city's most famous son was man of letters Dr. Johnson (1709–1784), subject of Boswell's biography; his birthplace is now a museum.

The wooded gorge of the River Severn gave birth to the Industrial Revolution in the early 18th century. What happened at Ironbridge signaled the emergence of Britain as the first industrial nation in the world, and was the catalyst for a dramatic change in the face of the country, as the Midlands and northern England became a great industrial heartland.

Here in 1709 Abraham Darby first smelted iron ore with coke instead of charcoal, making mass production of iron possible. The gorge soon filled with industrial activity. Today it is a picturesque area, and you have to imagine the din and smoke of the great ironworks and other industries—but the first-rate **Ironbridge Gorge Museum** (tel: 01952 433522) spread over eight sites, skillfully brings it alive. Ironbridge is near Telford (map: *110C2*).

What to see The **Iron Bridge** itself was the world's earliest iron structure of its kind (built in 1779). Staff in period costume enhance the atmosphere of **Blists Hill Victorian Town▶▶▶** is the largest site, including a toll-house, period shops, a colliery and an inclined railroad that linked two canals. **Jackfield Tile Museum▶▶** is housed in a huge Victorian tile factory that had lain abandoned; today it has been reopened and tiles are put on display. The **Coalport China Museum▶▶** marks the original site of the Coalport china factory, based here from the 1790s until the 1920s; today there is a display of china as well as early brick beehive kilns. You have to wear a hard hat to enter the gloomy **Tar Tunnel▶**, where bitumen was once extracted. You can also visit the **Darby Houses**, where the ironmasters lived, the **Bedlam Furnaces** and the **Broseley Pipe Works**, which manufactured clay smoking pipes ("Broseleys"). At **Coalbrookdale Museum of Iron▶▶▶** you are in historic territory, the very spot where Darby sparked the industrialization of Britain.

History today: the daily round at Blists Hill

DON'T MISS
There is too much to see in a day in the gorge; if you have only a short time, concentrate on Blists Hill, the Iron Bridge, and Coalbrookdale. You can buy separate tickets for each site, or a "passport" that allows return visits on different occasions. Buses run between the sites.

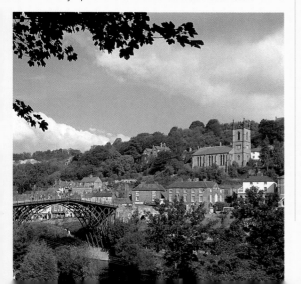

The Iron Bridge gives its name to the town of Ironbridge, which rises steeply from it

Ludlow Castle: the keep, seen from the Tudor stables

E.H., CADW, AND H.S.
Stokesay Castle is just one of hundreds of historic properties that are in the guardianship of the government organization English Heritage (E.H.). Its sister organizations are Cadw: Welsh Historic Monuments (for Wales, see page 167), Historic Scotland (H.S.; for Scotland), and Manx National Heritage (for the Isle of Man). Properties include prehistoric and Roman remains, medieval castles and abbeys, and working industrial monuments as well as some stately homes. Membership in any one of these groups provides half-price (free after first year's membership) admission to the historic sites protected by all four organizations. Overseas Visitors Passes are valid for seven or 14 days. For information tel: 020-7973 3434. Most properties open year-round. In this book, E.H., Cadw and H.S. denote staffed properties that charge entrance fees.

The Feathers, one of the finest examples of 17th-century half-timbering in Britain

▶▶▶ Ludlow   110C1
(tel: 01584 875053)

This is often acclaimed as England's most perfect country town—and it is easy to see why. On its hilltop site its streets spread elegantly out from the ancient butter cross and marketplace, on which is found the absorbing **museum** of local history. Just behind the market cross stands the cathedral-like **Church of St. Laurence▶▶**. Within its soaring interior, the patron saint's life and miracles are celebrated in the great east window, and there is a renowned set of 15th-century carved misericords. Poet A.E. Housman of *Shropshire Lad* fame (see page 130) is buried in the churchyard.

Broad Street is Ludlow's most celebrated thoroughfare, with its half-timbered Tudor buildings and 17th- to 19th-century brick facades combining happily along the gentle slope to a gateway at the bottom end. The **Feathers Hotel**, a riot of half-timbering, is the outstanding house of its period. **Ludlow Castle▶▶**, founded by Roger Montgomery, Earl of Shrewsbury, in 1085, was built to withstand both Welsh and Norman incursions; its long list of distinguished visitors includes Sir Philip Sidney, Edward IV, and Catherine of Aragon. A Norman chapel within the castle has an unusual circular nave. During the Ludlow Festival in June and July, outdoor performances of Shakespeare plays are held in the inner bailey.

Ludlow is splendidly situated for exploring the Welsh Marches, and the South Shropshire Hills (see page 130) are within close reach. **Stokesay Castle▶▶**, near Craven Arms, is an outstandingly well-preserved example of a 13th-century fortified manor house; it was designed with windows unusually large for those lawless times. The adjacent church dates mostly from the 17th century but has a Norman doorway.

▶▶ Malvern Hills   *110B2*
(tel: 01684 892289)

The jagged Malvern ridge rises between the low plains of Herefordshire and the Vale of Evesham. From a distance it looks like a mountain range; close up it reveals itself as a friendly upland stripe offering superb views from the easily accessible paths along its spine.

Its advantages as a defensive site were exploited by Iron Age man: Worcestershire Beacon (the highest point, 1,381 feet) and Herefordshire Beacon are both well-preserved hill forts. To the west there are views of **Eastnor Castle**, a 19th-century mock-medieval extravaganza designed by Robert Smirke and A. W. N. Pugin in the Gothic Revival style. In the distance are the hills of the Welsh Marches; to the east is the Cotswold escarpment.

Worcester▶ is famous as the home of Royal Worcester porcelain (factory tours Mon–Fri; tel: 01905 23221) and Worcestershire Sauce. It was an important center in the Civil War, as you can learn from the exhibition in the **Commandery** in Sidbury Road, Charles II's headquarters during the Battle of Worcester. The city is a mix of the sublime and the mundane: a fine **cathedral▶▶** (look in for the monuments, crypt, cloister garden, and marble pulpit), but insensitive post-war development that mars the center. The **county cricket ground**, stationed by the Severn with a magnificent view of the cathedral, is a classic place for trying to fathom the English summer game.

Just west of Worcester, **Lower Broadheath▶** was the birthplace on June 2, 1857, of composer Edward Elgar (see panel). The modest cottage commemorates his life with scores, photographs, and concert programs.

Malvern Wells and **Great Malvern▶** lie right under the Malvern Hills. Malvern Water put the area on the map as a spa after a Dr. Wall wrote in 1756 of the waters' medicinal value. Within a modest stone pavilion is St. Ann's Well, the original source. The priory church, the glory of Great Malvern, has fine 15th-century stained glass.

Southwest is **Ledbury▶**. The town's broad main street focuses on John Abel's 16th-century half-timbered market house. Pretty Church Lane leads to the church, with its "gold vane surveying half the shire," in the words of locally born John Masefield, former Poet Laureate.

A Royal Worcester vase

125

SIR EDWARD ELGAR (1857–1934)
Elgar's musical education was derived mainly from his experience as a violin player, as a singer at the church where his father was organist, and from browsing the scores in his father's music shop in Worcester. For a long time he felt the musical world was set against him, yet the fact that he was mainly self-taught probably gave him a freshness of vision and made him perhaps the greatest English composer since Henry Purcell.
Elgar's early works were recognized only locally, but his international reputation was assured when Richard Strauss acclaimed the ever-popular *Enigma Variations* (1899). *The Dream of Gerontius* (1900) enjoyed success in the Three Choirs Festival (see panel, page 117) in 1902. The *First Symphony* (1908) and the *Pomp and Circumstance Marches* (1901–1930) won widespread popularity.

Worcester's spectacular Guildhall, dated 1722

CHRIST CHURCH COLLEGE

Tom Quad, the main quadrangle, is so called because of Tom Tower, designed by Sir Christopher Wren and named after the bell, Great Tom, which strikes the hour. Ever since 1682, at 9:05 PM it has rung 101 times, commemorating the original number of students; this signaled the time for students to be back in college. The 16th-century college hall has portraits of some of the college's distinguished former members, including William Gladstone, Lewis Carroll, John Ruskin, and W.H. Auden.

OXFORD VERSUS CAMBRIDGE

The two universities maintain an ancient rivalry, most obviously displayed in the University Boat Race, rowed on the Thames in west London every spring, and in the Varsity rugby match, played at Twickenham in the fall.

"OXBRIDGE" SUBTLETIES

Oxford and Cambridge universities are referred to jointly as "Oxbridge."
● When steering a "punt," a shallow boat, on the river in Oxford, you stand inside the boat; in Cambridge you stand on its platform.
● Only at Oxford does formal academic dress feature a mortar board as well as a gown.
● In Cambridge, colleges have courtyards, in Oxford they are known as quadrangles (or quads).
● At Cambridge, students' academic work is charted by directors of studies; at Oxford the terminology is tutors.
● There are more colleges at Oxford, and they mostly all have fewer students than their Cambridge counterparts.

▶▶▶ Oxford
111A3

(tel: 01865 726871)

What you'll first notice about this, the home of one of the great universities of the world (founded about 1200), is its stunning heritage of historic buildings, the number of students swarming around, and the coexistence of a busy city with large swaths of greenery along the Cherwell and Thames (or Isis) of Christ Church Meadow. As with Cambridge, there is no single campus in Oxford: the colleges are set in cloistered seclusion behind high walls; most are open to visitors in the afternoon.

Most notable among the university buildings are the **Sheldonian Theatre**, built in 1664 as a ceremonial assembly hall, and the **Radcliffe Camera**, a domed building, now a reading room for the **Bodleian Library**, which contains well over 5½ million volumes. The Bodleian is one of five "copyright" libraries in the United Kingdom, entitled to receive a copy of every book published in the country. The view from the tower of **St. Mary the Virgin**, the university church on the High Street, extends over the city.

Christ Church▶▶, founded as Cardinal College by Cardinal Wolsey in 1525, is the largest college, has the biggest quadrangle, and its chapel (which predates the college) is England's smallest cathedral; the college picture gallery contains works by Dürer and Michelangelo. **Magdalen College▶▶** (pronounced "mawdlin") has its own deer park. **All Souls College** has a highly scholarly reputation and admits only graduate students, while **St. John's College** is the wealthiest of all, and has luscious gardens. **New College▶** (founded 1379) has a splendid chapel with a statue of Lazarus by Jacob Epstein. Also seek out **Oriel▶**, **Merton▶▶**, **Queen's▶** and **Keble▶** colleges, the latter a relative newcomer whose ornamental red-brick buildings are Victorian masterpieces.

Of Oxford's museums, the outstanding attraction is the **Ashmolean▶▶▶**, a treasure-house of art and antiquities whose exhibits include a 9th-century brooch made for King Alfred. The city's history, both town and gown, is illustrated in the **Museum of Oxford**, St. Aldates, while a livelier, less traditional approach is provided by the **Oxford Story**, Broad Street, where you sit at moving desks on a voyage through the city's past.

OXFORD

Walk

Start from Magdalen Bridge, pass **Magdalen College▶▶** and turn right into Queen's Lane, which weaves past

Despite its name, New College was founded in 1379

Magdalen Bridge to the Botanic Garden

St. Edmund's Hall▶ (founded 1220) and **New College▶** (1379). Just before the Bridge of Sighs (which spans the street), take an alley on the right, passing the Turf Tavern, an old pub with an appealing courtyard. Turn left along Holywell Street and continue past the **Sheldonian Theatre**, with its array of sculpted heads of Roman emperors, and along **Broad Street** to the **Martyrs' Memorial**, where three bishops were burned for their Protestant beliefs in the 1550s. Diagonally opposite is the **Ashmolean Museum▶▶**. Double back along Broad Street and turn right down Turl Street to the **Radcliffe Camera** and **Bodleian Library**. Cross the High Street, taking Oriel Street on its south side to enter **Christ Church▶▶** by the gate near the college's picture gallery (if closed, continue along Merton Street to the start of the walk), crossing Tom Quad and leaving by the turnstile at the south side of the college to follow Broad Walk along **Christ Church Meadow**. The **Botanic Garden▶** is the oldest of its kind in the country.

127

There are few pleasanter ways to explore Britain's scenery, wildlife, and history than an easygoing voyage along the inland waterways. The slow, unhurried pace of a narrowboat gives a chance for once to take a long look at things. Canals run through towns as well as the countryside, and supply unexpected perspectives. Spectacular flights of locks, aqueducts, tunnels and bridges, warehouses and workshops, pleasant pubs and inns are the legacy of a time when the canal system seemed to hold the future of Britain's transportation system.

WATERWAYS VACATIONS
Britain's canals are now used primarily for leisure—boating trips, horse-drawn barge trips, fishing, towpath walks. For information about vacations, contact: Customer Services, British Waterways, Willow Grange, Church Road, Watford, Hertfordshire WD1 3QA (tel: 01923 201120).

CANAL ART
During the 19th century a rich tradition of canal art developed. Boat owners covered the boats and their interiors and utensils with a riot of roses and castles, daisies and marigolds in simple patterns and vivid primary colors—a popular art form similar to the one which developed in the same period in traveling fairs.

Some 2,000 miles of navigable inland waterways have been described as the British tourist industry's best-kept secret. From prehistoric times down to the 18th century, travel by river was generally faster, safer, and more comfortable than travel by road. Rivers like the Severn, the Thames, and the Trent bustled with boats carrying goods and people, and towns along their banks prospered as inland ports.

The Canal Age dawns The trouble with rivers is that they do not always go where you want them to, they silt up, water levels vary, and shallows block navigation, as do periodic floods. Attempts to control and improve rivers were made from early times, and artificial cuts were made to shorten routes, straighten bends, and evade shallows. The Canal Age in the 18th and 19th centuries brought much more radical action. A network of artificial rivers was constructed to mesh with the natural waterways and create an efficient system covering much of the country. The canals were the principal arteries of the first stage of the Industrial Revolution.

The first canal of this period was begun in Lancashire in the 1750s to link St. Helens with the Mersey, but much more excitement arose in the 1760s when the **Duke of Bridgewater** ordered the construction of a canal to be built to carry coal mined on his estates at Worsley a distance of 7½ miles into Manchester. The duke's engineer was an illiterate genius from Derbyshire named **James Brindley**. The Bridgewater Canal was soon extended to the Mersey, linking Manchester with Liverpool. (The Manchester end is now part of the Castlefield urban heritage area.)

Not only did the duke's canal halve the price of coal in Manchester, but the spectacle of canal boats crossing the River Irwell at Barton on an aqueduct, above the barges on the river, fired the public imagination. A bold plan was swiftly hatched to build a canal joining the Trent and the Mersey—Josiah Wedgwood, the great china-maker, was one of its most eager promoters—from which other canals would run to the Thames and the Severn. This would link Britain's four most important rivers and provide an inland waterway connection between London, Birmingham, Hull, Liverpool, and Bristol. Brindley was the engineer for the Trent and Mersey, which was completed in 1777, five years after his death, and the other components of the plan soon followed.

The heyday The success of the early ventures set off "canal mania," a frenzy that had people flocking to meetings all over the country to invest in new waterways. It reached its peak in 1793, when Parliament passed 24 canal construction acts in that single year. One politician of the time said he hoped his grandchildren would be born with webbed feet, since no dry land would be left in England for them to walk on.

A total of 170 miles of canal in 1770 grew to 1,600 miles by the end of the century and 4,250 miles in the 1850s as armies of "navvies" (navigators)—tough, brawling, hard-drinking laborers, the terror of peaceful folk—drove the new waterways across country on giant embankments and through cuttings and tunnels. The earliest tunnels had no towpaths and the boats had to be "legged" through by the crew, lying on their backs or sides, walking along the brickwork.

The canals' brief heyday was ended by the railroads from the 1830s on, and the development of car travel almost finished them off. Even so, some 4 million tons of goods are still carried on the waterways every year, though they are used far more today for recreation. Some waterways have been revived: Millennium projects include restoring both the Rochdale Canal from Manchester to Halifax, and the Huddersfield Narrow Canal through the country's longest canal tunnel.

NARROWBOATS IN THE SKY
Among the most spectacular engineering feats of the canal engineers were flights of locks and aqueducts. The most famous staircase of locks is probably the Bingley Five Rise on the Leeds and Liverpool Canal, which climbs 60 ft. The most sensational of aqueducts is the Pontcysyllte near Llangollen in North Wales, designed by the great engineer Thomas Telford in the 1790s. The canal is carried across the aqueduct for 335 yds. in an iron trough almost 12 ft. wide, with an iron towpath set above it. Boats still go across, and visitors can also walk across on the towpath.

129

The Rochdale Canal at Hebden Bridge: boats were once pulled by horses plodding along the towpath

Shrewsbury Castle: rebuilt in the 13th century, but has Norman origins

Decorative quatrefoils in the Square, Shrewsbury

▶ Shrewsbury   110C1
(tel: 01743 350761)

The town has a natural defensive site, within a tight loop of the meandering River Severn, with a castle to guard the land-linked neck of land. Shrewsbury's collection of Tudor half-timbering and red-brick Georgian, reminders of prosperity brought by the wool trade, is remarkable. Look, for example, at **Owen's Mansion** and **Ireland's Mansion** (both near the arcaded old market hall), and **Council House Court**: the half-timbering includes decorative cable-molding and quatrefoils.

Finds from the Roman city of Wroxeter (Uriconium), a short way out of town, are displayed in **Rowley's House Museum**. Robert, Lord Clive (of India) was the local M.P. in the 1760s; you can visit his house (**Clive House**). **Bear Steps**, a tiny alley, looks medieval, with a hall founded in 1389 as a guild for wool merchants. **Shrewsbury Quest**, on Abbey Foregate, is a hands-on re-creation of monastic life, where you can try out the crafts and chores of medieval monks. The Benedictine **abbey** has Norman features and a statue of Edward III on its tower. Street names can bemuse. Butcher Row is self-explanatory (although the butchers are not in evidence) and Grope Lane suggests a variety of possibilities, but Wyle Cop, where Henry VII had a house, may baffle you—it means "hill top." The meaning of Dog Pole is uncertain: perhaps a low gate or "ducken poll" where one had to stoop to get through.

The **Shropshire Hills▶▶** are south of Shrewsbury, the heartland of the territory immortalized in A.E. Housman's 1896 collection of poems, *A Shropshire Lad*. **Church Stretton** is the starting point of the **Long Mynd** area, a massif of bracken- and bilberry-clad hills deeply cut by valleys such as Ashes Hollow and Carding Mill Valley (parking available in the latter); these and nearby Caer Caradoc, itself best reached by walking from Hope Bowdler, offer magnificent walking. The **Stiperstones** are a series of quartzite rocks atop a breezy ridge close to **Snailbeach**, a village with many relics of a lead-mining industry that flourished in the 18th and 19th centuries.

►► Stratford-upon-Avon
(tel: 01789 293127)

111B3

Long since celebrated as the birthplace and deathplace of William Shakespeare, Stratford-upon-Avon is swamped with visitors. The Shakespeare connection looms large at every turn; the souvenir shops are stocked with miniature ceramic models of Anne Hathaway's cottage, there is a shopping mall christened Bard's Walk. For devotees of the Bard the town is a must; but be warned, some find it a disappointment. The attractions can be divided into three categories: the historic Shakespeare sites, the town itself, and the ancillary attractions tacked on for visitors who wonder why they have come here. The town is agreeable enough, with half-timbered buildings and a pleasant boating scene on the Avon; look in Holy Trinity Church for a famous memorial to Shakespeare, quill pen in hand.

An open-topped bus tours the sites at 15-minute intervals (board at any point on its route). The places in town can be easily reached on foot, but the bus is handy if you want to take in Anne Hathaway's Cottage and Mary Arden's House; a ticket (valid for one day only) allows its holder cut-price entry to Shakespeare properties. You can get around them all in one full day if you start early.

I know a bank whereon
   the wild thyme blows.
Where oxlips and the nod-
   ding violet grows
Quite over-canopied with
   luscious woodbine,
With sweet musk-roses,
   and with eglantine:
There sleeps Titania some
   time of the night,
Lull'd in these flowers
   with dances and delight;
And there the snake
   throws her enamell'd
   skin,
Weed wide enough to
   wrap a fairy in.
—William Shakespeare,
A Midsummer Night's Dream

131

Britain's most hallowed literary shrine: Shakespeare's Birthplace

Foremost among the sites maintained by the Shakespeare Birthplace Trust is obviously **Shakespeare's Birthplace**►► itself. Entrance is through a visitor center and the cottage's garden. Inside, an auction notice describes the property ("a truly heart-stirring relic") when it came up for sale in 1847 and was purchased, for the sum of £3,000, as a national memorial. A miscellanea of Shakespearean bits and pieces make up the exhibits. Shakespeare's daughter Susanna and her husband Dr. Hall lived at **Hall's Croft►**, a rather grander house, now furnished with Tudor trappings and home to an exhibition about medicine in Shakespeare's day and the career of Dr. Hall.

Shakespeare died in New Place, a house adjacent to **Nash's House►**; New Place is no longer, but an Elizabethan-style knot garden marks the site, and Nash's House itself displays Tudor furniture and exhibits relating to Stratford's past. Shakespeare was baptized and buried at **Holy Trinity Church**.

A NATIONAL TREASURE
Before the auction in 1847, Shakespeare's Birthplace had been in the keeping of two widowed ladies, who had made a good thing out of showing such relics as "the identical lantern with which Friar Laurence discovered Romeo and Juliet at the tomb." The house was a ruinous mess but, spurred by the approaching tricentennial in 1864 of Shakespeare's birth and a rumor that a wealthy American planned to ship the house across the Atlantic, the people of Stratford determined to buy the property. The place was cleaned up, judicious restoration was done, and a shilling (5 pence) was charged for admission. The town can never have regretted its investment.

Shall I compare thee to a
  summer's day?
Thou art more lovely and
  more temperate:
Rough winds do shake the
  darling buds of May,
And summer's lease hath
  all too short a date: ...

But thy eternal summer
  shall not fade,
Nor lose possession of
  that fair thou ow'st
Nor shall death brag thou
  wander'st in his shade,
When in eternal lines to
  time thou grow'st ...
—William Shakespeare,
Sonnet XVIII

Out of town at the village of Shottery, **Anne Hathaway's Cottage►** was the home of Shakespeare's wife Anne before her marriage; it is a picturesque thatched timber building that reaches the bursting point at peak times (you may have to line up to get in). Nevertheless the old-world atmosphere has been kept intact, thanks to the Trust's foresight in purchasing the cottage back in 1892. Less hectic, but an equally good example of domestic Tudor architecture (minus the thatch), is **Mary Arden's House►**, the farmhouse childhood home of Shakespeare's mother, at the village of Wilmcote. This has been set up as a farm and countryside museum, with falconry flying demonstrations, rare farm breeds, and exhibits evoking rural life in the last century.

Shakespeare productions are performed at the **Royal Shakespeare Theatre** by the Royal Shakespeare Company (01789 205301); **Behind the Scenes with the RSC►** exhibits over 1,000 props and costumes used for past performances. The company has a London base at the Barbican (see page 46). There is a fascinating **backstage tour►►** of the Royal Shakespeare and Swan theaters.

Cox's Yard tells the story of Stratford from medieval times to the present, using audiovisuals and tableaux, and has its own micro-brewery, while the **Butterfly Farm and Jungle Safari** re-creates a jungle environment as a setting for some 1,000 exotic butterfly species. Stratford is home to the **Teddy Bear Museum**.

The Royal Shakespeare Theatre, one of the venues used by the Royal Shakespeare Company

►► Waddesdon Manor   111A4
(tel: 01296 651282)

Ferdinand de Rothschild had this French Renaissance-style château built in the Buckinghamshire countryside in the 1870s and 1880s, with no expense spared. It is breathtaking in its opulence—the contents as much as the house itself. Harkening back to the golden days of collecting, the treasures include clocks, Sèvres porcelain, lace, and paintings by Rubens, Gainsborough, and others. Within the grounds are two fountains and an aviary. Waddesdon, in the care of the National Trust, is the grandest of a trio of local Rothschild mansions (*Open* to the public): the others are **Mentmore Towers►** and **Ascott►** (N.T.).

►► Warwick

(tel: 01926 492212)

111B3

Warwick Castle rises sheer from the River Avon

Warwick is a pleasant country town with a magnificent castle, one of Britain's most visited stately homes. Indeed, on weekends and at vacation periods your visit may be spoiled by the crowds. The center of the town was rebuilt after a fire in 1694; a walk around **High Street** and **Northgate Street** takes you past some of the finest buildings, including Court House and Landor House. The **County Museum** (*Admission free*) in the market square is a good place for children, with displays including natural history, a model of old Warwick, and the historic Sheldon tapestry map of Warwickshire; its **Doll Museum**, on a separate site, displays antique toys and games. Two of Warwick's medieval **gateways** survive, complete with chapels. Westgate Chapel forms part of **Leycester's Hospital►**, a tottering half-timbered range enclosing a pretty courtyard; since 1571, the building has been used as a hospice for retired soldiers, and part of the interior houses the Queen's Own Hussars regimental museum. Pre-fire features of the collegiate **Church of St. Mary►** include the fan-vaulted Beauchamp Chapel, with a collection of Warwick tombs, and a Norman crypt.

Warwick Castle►► looks its very best from Castle Bridge, where the 14th-century walls are reflected in the waters of the Avon. There is a walk along the ramparts and, inside, a tour of the palatial mansion takes you from the grim austerity of the original dungeons to the gloomy but sumptuous opulence of rooms later adapted for comfortable living. There are wax figures of a royal weekend party and the Kingmaker Exhibition (with the sounds, sights and smells of the castle getting ready for battle). In the grounds are a re-created Victorian rose garden, the formal Peacock Gardens, and an expanse of open parkland, landscaped by Capability Brown.

KENILWORTH CASTLE
On the western edge of Kenilworth, this huge sandstone castle is the site for events featuring medieval pageantry, drama, and music. The castle was built as a fortress in Norman times but was much adapted by the Earl of Leicester, Queen Elizabeth's favorite, whose neglected wife Amy Robsart died nearby in mysterious circumstances (it was never discovered whether her fall down stairs was murder, accident, or suicide). The Virgin Queen was compelled by the resulting controversy to distance herself from Leicester, whom she eventually had executed for treason.

▶▶▶ REGION HIGHLIGHTS

Audley End House *page 143*

Blickling Hall *page 142*

Cambridge *pages 138–139*

Ely *page 140*

Hatfield House *page 146*

Lincoln *page 141*

North Norfolk coast
page 142

Norwich *page 143*

Southwold and area
page 146

Stamford *page 147*

Woburn Abbey *page 147*

The River Ant near How Hill: typical of the waterscapes of the Norfolk Broads

"On a still day, the light can have the delicate outlines of a Japanese picture. On a stormy day, even in summer, the grey sea batters itself against the shelf [of pebbles], dragging the shingle down with a scrunching, grating, slithering sound. To anyone born on the Suffolk coast, this sound has always meant home."
—Imogen Holst, *Britten*, in the "Great Composers" series (1966)

EASTERN ENGLAND This region extends from the northern edge of London to the brink of Humberside. There are no uplands: the rural landscape is flat or gently undulating agricultural country, with only the Lincolnshire Wolds, Bedfordshire's Dunstable Downs, and Leicestershire's Charnwood Forest rising to any appreciable height. Fields are often prairie-like in scale. Although much of the landscape is uninspiring, the region does have rewarding corners.

EAST ANGLIA The most consistently picturesque area of eastern England is East Anglia, the collective term for **Norfolk**, **Suffolk**, northern **Essex**, and eastern **Cambridgeshire**: here, above all, the prosperity brought about by the medieval wool trade left a noble legacy of church architecture and villages and towns of handsome half-timbered and plaster-fronted cottages. A specialty of the countryside immortalized by the paintings of Constable on the Essex/Suffolk border is pastel-colored plasterwork ornately decorated with relief patterns known as "pargeting." In **Norfolk**, flint walls and Dutch gable ends, reflecting former trading links with the Low Countries, are a common sight. Windmills are ubiquitous, the skies are vast, and the light effects subtle.

Scenically, the coast is the most appealing part: south Essex is drably developed around the Thames Estuary, but east of Ipswich **Suffolk** has lots of interest for the walker and naturalist, although the presence of Sizewell nuclear power station is unfortunate. The **Norfolk Broads** is an excellent place to rent a sail-it-yourself boat. More solitary beauty is abundant along the unspoiled north Norfolk coast. North of Cambridge lie the **Fens**, a vast expanse of fertile, flat, black-soil farmland, formerly beneath water but drained by cuts and sluices; much of that landscape transformation was begun by the Dutch engineer Cornelius Vermuyden in the 17th century. Wicken Fen near Ely gives an idea of what the Fens were like before this great agricultural upgrading.

THE INLAND SHIRES There are various pockets of interest inland. **Hertfordshire** has some fine country houses and oases of rural charm such as Ayot St. Lawrence and Benington, but Hertford, Hemel Hempstead, and others are commuter satellites. **Bedfordshire** has grand houses such as Luton Hoo and Woburn Abbey, but the former hat-making center of Luton and Bedford itself are uninteresting. Northampton is famed for shoemaking, and the best of the gentle **Northamptonshire** countryside includes Rockingham Forest and the ironstone villages of Badby and Everdon, while there is an appealing canal scene and canal museum at Stoke Bruerne. Milton Keynes is the newest of Britain's new towns. **Althorp** is the seat of the Spencer family; Diana, Princess of Wales, is buried on a lake island, and visitors can pay their respects at a shrine; the house and grounds open in July and August (booking essential; tel: 01604 592020). **Leicestershire** is endowed with some large country estates and rolling countryside on its eastern side, but farther west many of its towns belong to the industrial east Midlands; Leicester, the county town, is an industrial center, though it does have an excavated Roman site within the Jewry Wall Museum and all the museums are free, making it a good place for day visits. Belvoir Castle, home of the Duke of Rutland, is one of the grandest 19th-century statements of wealth and social prominence. **Nottinghamshire** is the county of Robin Hood, although what is left of Sherwood Forest is inevitably smaller and tamer than in the famous outlaw's day; the great country estates known as the Dukeries include Newstead Abbey and others, while Clumber Park is a popular strolling ground. The writer D. H. Lawrence lived at Eastwood, in the Nottinghamshire coalfield, and his house is open as a museum. Nottingham itself is no great beauty but has an attractive lace market and an excellent crop of museums.

CAMBRIDGE AND THE CATHEDRAL CITIES Visitors come above all to the university city of **Cambridge**, whose colleges and river combine in perfect composition. Alumni include Oliver Cromwell, John Milton, Isaac Newton, Lord Byron, and Charles Darwin. **Ely**, **Norwich**, **Peterborough**, **St. Albans**, **Southwell**, and **Lincoln** each have splendid cathedrals, abbeys, or minsters. Of these places, Norwich and Lincoln are less well known, because of their relative isolation, than many of England's other great cathedral cities and deserve a longer look.

137

St. Albans Abbey and the parkland containing remains of the Roman city of Verulamium

▶▶▶ Cambridge   134B3
(tel: 01223 322640)

The home of one of the world's oldest and greatest universities (founded in 1284) is a city ideal for wandering. It is a place of tranquility, students on bicycles, and riverside beauty, as well as a bustling market town. You can go into many colleges, but respect "Private" notices; some close to visitors April through June. The Tourist Information Center, Wheeler Street, offers guided tours.

The university comprises about 30 colleges scattered around the city, of which 16 have medieval origins. **King's College** has the most famous building; its **chapel**▶▶▶, a symphony of fan-vaulting and magnificent stained glass, is regarded as the finest example of the Perpendicular (15th-century Gothic) style. Nearby **Clare College**▶ is a formal composition, like a Renaissance palace. The grand Palladian **Senate House** is used for formal functions, including graduation ceremonies. **Trinity College**▶▶ has the largest courtyard in Oxford or Cambridge, and Christopher Wren's famous library (*Open* to the public) in Nevile Court. **St. John's College**▶▶ has two Tudor courts; beyond them the Bridge of Sighs leads into 19th-century Gothic New Court. More modest in scale is **Queens' College**▶, with its half-timbered courtyard and painted hall.

The Mathematical Bridge is a wooden structure originally built without any bolts—until engineers dismantled it and were unable to reassemble it as it was!

Behind Trinity and King's, the River Cam slices through a delectable swath of greenery, fringed by neat gardens and lawns; this area is known as The Backs. Punts (boats originally designed for gathering reeds for thatching) can be rented near Silver Street Bridge. Walk south through riverside meadows for 2 miles to Grantchester, or head north from Magdalene Street Bridge to watch college rowing crews training.

The **Fitzwilliam Museum**▶▶▶ (*Admission free*) is a major collection of art, medieval manuscripts, armor, and more. The **Cambridge and County Folk Museum**▶ is packed with local memorabilia, and **Kettle's Yard**▶ is an idiosyncratic private house and modern art gallery.

THE COLLEGIATE SYSTEM

Colleges are the life and soul of the University of Cambridge, just as they are at Oxford (see page 126). The colleges are where most students live, eat, and have their supervisions (in which small groups of students discuss their work with teachers). Lectures, examinations, and societies are organized on a university basis, but there are comparatively few "university" buildings as such.

EXCURSIONS FROM CAMBRIDGE

Wimpole Hall (N.T.) is Cambridgeshire's grandest house, a formal Georgian composition. It has restored Victorian stables and a large park with lots of walks. Rare breeds of domestic animals and two centuries of farm machinery can be seen at adjacent Home Farm.
Anglesey Abbey (N.T.), built around 1600, has impressive grounds laid out this century.
Duxford Air Museum, part of the London-based Imperial War Museum, claims to hold Europe's largest collection of historic military aircraft; it also includes the American Air Museum in Britain. There are hourly buses from Cambridge.

The classical grandeur of the Fitzwilliam Museum

Walk

The colleges, river, and streets

With the **Church of Great St. Mary's** (fine view from **tower▶**) on your left, follow King's Parade (which becomes Trumpington Street). On the right is **King's College** with its **chapel▶▶▶**. Pass **Corpus Christi** (its Old Court is hidden at the back) and **Pembroke** (chapel by Wren); farther on are

Peterhouse (founded 1284, the oldest college) and the **Fitzwilliam Museum▶▶▶**. Enter Little St. Mary's Lane, turn right by the river (you can rent a punt). Pass Mill Inn, cross Silver Street Bridge to pass **Queens' College▶**. Take a path on right across grass for views from **the Backs**. Garret Hostel Lane leads over river to Trinity Lane. Turn left past **Trinity Hall▶**. Enter **Trinity▶▶** and **St. John's▶▶** colleges from Trinity Street; at river, take walkway on right to a footbridge by the **Lock** and turn right across Jesus Green to Portugal Street. Return past the **Round Church▶** and **Sidney Sussex College** in Sidney Street.

GRIME'S GRAVES
A major center of England's neolithic flint industry occupies a site in Thetford Warren, the conifer forest on the low-lying sandy tracts of the Breckland (east of Ely). Over 400 shafts have been discovered; neolithic men climbed down these shafts to work in cramped tunnels, chipping away the flint for use in tools and weapons. One shaft is open to the public.

For centuries, Ely was dependent on the Ouse as a waterway

WICKEN FEN
Britain's oldest nature reserve, located south of Ely and now owned by the National Trust, gives an idea of what the fens were like before they were drained. Villagers left the fen undrained to preserve its supply of reeds for thatching; it is in parts wooded, wetland, and meadow, with waterways enclosing the site. A nature trail takes you past a re-erected pumping mill, some bog oaks (logs submerged for thousands of years under the fen and recently unearthed), and the birdwatchers' blind.

▶▶ Ely 134C3
(tel: 01353 662062)

The little town is dwarfed by its great cathedral, occupying a slightly elevated site that lets it dominate the pancake-flat Fenland plain for far around. The region is still called the Isle of Ely—a reminder of the days when the town was more or less an island in the undrained marsh. There is surprisingly little to see in town, but the **cathedral▶▶▶** ranks among the greats.

Part of the building shows Norman work, including the west front and tower, but restoration was soon needed: in 1250 the east end was rebuilt in Purbeck marble. In 1321 Alan of Walsingham supervised the building of the Lady Chapel; when the central tower collapsed the next year he created the wonderful octagonal lantern, lodged on eight oak pillars, that graces the building today (divine intervention must have prevented a further collapse: the structure has little to support it). Attached to the cathedral are a stained-glass museum and a brass-rubbing center. Around the precincts are the houses of the King's School, an eminent "public" school founded by Henry VIII.

▶ King's Lynn 134D3
(tel: 01553 763044)

Once a member of the Hanseatic League (a powerful commercial association of towns in northern Germany formed in the 14th century), King's Lynn still has a continental look in its darkened red-brick buildings. It traded with northern Europe for many centuries and its docks and industrial area are still very much functional. St. George's Guildhall (1420) is the oldest guildhall in England, and has a splendid beamed roof; this and twin-towered St. Margaret's Church (Norman, with fine memorial brasses) make a visit to the town worthwhile. Lifestyles of yesteryear are evoked within **True's Yard**, where a pair of fisherman's cottages house a museum.

The villages of **Castle Rising** and **Castle Acre▶**, respectively 4 miles north and 13 miles east of King's Lynn, both have an impressive Norman castle. West of Castle Acre, the priory church of a Cluniac foundation survives almost intact. Castle Rising has jousting contests in summer.

Fenland churches▶▶ Among the finest of these are **Walpole St. Peter**, with superb benches, font, and pulpit, and **Walsoken**, a Norman church with a magnificent roof and a 16th-century painting of the *Judgment of Solomon*.

Lincoln Cathedral: one of the great masterpieces of Gothic architecture

►►► Lincoln 134E2
(tel: 01522 763044)

The massive towers of Lincoln's superb cathedral soar high from a hilltop site. The cathedral, castle, museums, and historic streets provide plenty of attractions for a full-day visit. However, outside the small historic core much of the city is quite undistinguished.

The **cathedral►►►**, one of England's finest, was largely rebuilt in the 13th and 14th centuries after an earthquake in 1185 destroyed an earlier structure. Highlights are the elaborate west facade, the carved choir stalls, and the stained-glass rose windows known as the Dean's Eye and the Bishop's Eye. High up, the Lincolnshire Imp carving steals the show; the story goes that he got too close to the angels and was turned to stone for his sins. Steps lead up the central tower to a viewing spot.

Minster Yard, the cathedral close, has Georgian and medieval houses. Near the cathedral's east end, the **Bishop's Old Palace** dates from the 12th to 15th centuries. **Steep Hill** lives up to its name, climbing from the River Witham, past the Jew's House, inhabited from Norman times and so named because of a Jewish community that once existed there, and continuing beyond the cathedral as **Bailgate**. The street is spanned by Newport Arch, a Roman gateway into the city. Opposite the cathedral's west facade, **Exchequergate** leads to **Lincoln Castle►** which dates from Norman times and has thick walls, gateways, towers, and a 19th-century prisoners' chapel.

► Norfolk Broads 135C5
(tel: 01603 610734)

Ever popular with boat enthusiasts and birdwatchers, the Broads is an area of fertile fens, waterways and reedy lakes (called "broads") formed from peat excavations. Windmills, erected to pump water to drain the farmland and now mostly defunct, proliferate. The broads are difficult to see except from a boat; one of the best waterside walks is in the vicinity of Horsey, where the pumping mill is open to the public. The National Trust owns the broad of Horsey Mere; marsh harriers, bitterns, and otters make up part of the population. Other strolls include the banks of the rivers Bure, Thurne, and Yare.

MUSEUMS IN LINCOLN
Lincoln's indoor attractions include the Museum of Lincolnshire Life, with a sizeable collection of horse-drawn vehicles, and domestic and agricultural bygones; the Incredibly Fantastic Old Toy Show, with old toys and pier amusements and the Usher Gallery, which exhibits applied arts, including a collection of watches, memorabilia relating to poet Lord Tennyson (born at Somersby in the Lincolnshire Wolds), and paintings by Lincolnshire artist Peter de Wint.

SPALDING
A major bulb-growing center in the Fens, Spalding hosts the Flower Parade (usually first Sat. in May, but may be earlier for 2000; check with the tourist office, tel: 01775 725468). It's one of the great free shows of eastern England, where often as many as three million tulips are used to decorate the floats in a procession accompanied by bands and general bonhomie. During the same weekend, many churches in the surrounding South Holland area have spectacular flower festivals.

The virtue and the joy of this little-explored corner of English coast is its isolation. The area also has a tremendous sense of place and history, and lots to interest the naturalist. Dutch gables, flint walls, huge medieval "wool" churches, and weather-beaten coastal villages supply the manmade elements—salt marshes (Europe's largest expanse), vast sandy beaches, prolific birdlife, and dramatic skyscapes are among the natural attractions.

NORFOLK HOUSES
Blickling Hall (N.T.) is a lovely red-brick 17th-century house, famed for the Jacobean plasterwork in its Long Gallery. **Holkham Hall** is a neat Palladian mansion built for Thomas Coke, 18th-century agricultural pioneer. **Felbrigg** (N.T.), a tall-chimneyed, 17th-century house in a wooded park, has Georgian furnishings and a fine 18th-century library. **Houghton Hall** exudes Palladian elegance and was the seat of Sir Robert Walpole, the first English prime minister. **Sandringham** (*Open* only when the Royals are not in residence; park and drives always open) was built in the 19th century as a country home for the Prince of Wales, the future Edward VII.

A shrimping boat at Wells-next-the-Sea

THE VILLAGES Cromer, famed for its crabs, and **Sheringham** are demure Edwardian resorts atop crumbly cliffs; from the latter a private steam railroad heads towards Holt. Inland lies Norfolk's highest land (heathy rises rather than full-fledged hills). **Cley▶** has an often-photographed windmill (*Open* periodically). While **Blakeney** is a yachting center, where mast-stays flap in the wind and a gravelly bank leads to Blakeney Point (still building up westward). Inland, **Binham▶** has a superb 13th-century priory church beside the ruins of an 11th-century Benedictine priory.

Wells-next-the-Sea produces 80 percent of English whelks (edible marine snails); the attractive port looks out over wide salt marshes. A walk westward brings you to **Holkham Gap**, where Corsican pines stabilize the dunes, flanking an immense beach. Another steam railroad connects Wells with **Little Walsingham▶**, a pilgrimage center for 900 years with both Roman Catholic and (incense-filled) Anglican shrines to Our Lady of Walsingham. It's fascinating even to non-pilgrims.

The "Seven Burnhams" are a scattering of hamlets and villages all named with the prefix Burnham. **Burnham Overy Staithe▶** broods over salt marshes with a fetching harbor scene—close by are a tower windmill and pretty watermill. **Burnham Thorpe** is famed as Admiral Lord Nelson's birthplace—every other pub hereabouts seems to be called the Nelson or the Hero. The nation's greatest sailor died on board H.M.S. *Victory* (see page 104) after defeating the French and Spanish at Trafalgar in 1805; he was buried in St. Paul's Cathedral in London, but there are memorials in Burnham Thorpe Church. **Burnham Market** is an attractive village set around a spacious green. **Hunstanton** is a quiet resort beside chalk cliffs, with its **Sea Life Centre** tunnel-style aquarium.

THE WILDLIFE Among the best places for observing Norfolk's wildlife are the reserves at **Holme-next-the-Sea**, at **Cley**, a site with reedbeds and shallow lagoons, and **Blakeney Point**, reached by boat from Morston or by a long coastal walk over sand and rocky beach from Blakeney. The coast supports a huge population of waders, with wood and curlew sandpipers in summer; great tern colonies exist at Scolt Head island, common and gray seals breed here, and there are sizeable numbers of fall migrants and wintering birds.

142

►►► Norwich   135C4
(tel: 01603 666071)

Tucked away in the northeast corner of East Anglia, Norwich is less touristy than most other great cathedral cities in England. It is the major commercial center for the region and a university city, too, which gives it a workaday bustle. For the visitor there is enough to fill a weekend, and you can escape to the Norfolk Broads for peace and space (see page 141). The marketplace (one of England's grandest), antiques showrooms, and specialty shops (including the Colman's Mustard shop) make for fascinating browsing, and there is a fair range of theaters. The medieval center has a mix of good streets—the finest being **Elm Hill**, **Bridewell Alley**, and Colegate—a number of ancient buildings (head for the **Guildhall** and **Pull's Ferry**), and a multitude of medieval churches, notably **St. Peter Mancroft** (Perpendicular) and **St. Peter Hungate**, which has a fine hammerbeam roof, a museum of church art, and a brass-rubbing center.

Top of the sights is the **cathedral**►► (founded 1096), surrounded by a close of houses and boasting remarkable detailing in the roof-bosses, misericords, glass, and stone vaulting; the Norman cloister is the largest in the country. More prominent is the **castle**►; guided tours take you around the Norman keep, battlements, and dungeons.

Pull's Ferry, a 15th-century watergate on the Wensum River at Norwich

► Saffron Walden   134B3
(tel: 01799 510444)

From medieval times until the 18th century this was a center for the saffron crocus industry. The legacy of its wealth is a knot of historic streets around the largest parish church in Essex, which is in the Perpendicular Gothic style and has notable carvings, roofs, and brasses. The former Sun Inn on Church Street is outstanding among many examples of the East Anglian craft of pargeting (decorative external plasterwork). On the Common is an enigmatic turf maze.

Just west of the town is **Audley End House**►►. Although only a fraction of its original size, it represents Jacobean architecture on its grandest scale. Vanbrugh and Robert Adam were responsible for the early 18th-century alterations; Capability Brown landscaped the park.

MUSEUMS IN NORWICH
Bridewell Museum, Bridewell Alley, shows the trades and industries of Norwich over two centuries, in a former prison. **Castle Museum**, Castle Meadow, displays a celebrated collection of paintings by the Norwich school; ceramics (including hundreds of teapots), archeology, and natural history (Norfolk's last pair of great bustards are here, in stuffed form). **Sainsbury Centre for Visual Arts**, University of East Anglia campus (western edge of the city), has an outstanding art collection, innovatively displayed in a striking building by Sir Norman Foster. On King Street, **Dragon Hall** is a medieval merchant's hall with a fine roof and vaulted undercroft. In Oak Street, **Inspire** is a hands-on science center in a former church.

143

AROUND SAFFRON WALDEN
The area's pretty villages make for excellent touring by car or bike, with quiet back-roads through gently rolling farmland. To the west are **Clavering**, with its cozy Cricketers Inn and village green, and **Brent Pelham**, where thatched cottages overlook the old stocks and whipping post. To the south, **Newport's** main street displays many examples of pargetting (ornamental plasterwork).

That national asset, the British countryside, is adored for its infinite variety. Yet the landscapes of Thomas Hardy and John Constable have already been transformed in the name of progress. In recent years public attitudes have become more preservationist, but is it too late?

THE NATIONAL PARKS
Apart from the Peak, the other National Parks are: the **Lake District**, the **Yorkshire Dales**, **Northumberland**, and the **North York Moors** (in northern England); **Snowdonia**, the **Pembrokeshire Coast**, and the **Brecon Beacons** (in Wales); **Exmoor** and **Dartmoor** (in the West Country). The New Forest and the Broads have a similar status to National Parks. There are also Areas of Outstanding Beauty such as the Lincolnshire Wolds and the Forest of Bowland, which have strict planning controls. Scotland has National Scenic Areas, such as Wester Ross.

144

THE SHAPING OF THE LANDSCAPE The countryside is made by a combination of human and natural activity. Patches of the primeval tree cover that once cloaked much of the country exist here and there, but slash-and-burn led to a legacy of barren moorland, while farming produced a patchwork of hedge-lined fields, and wealthy landowners created great estates and hunting grounds. Yet so embedded in Britain's national culture is the landscape that this unique blend of elements has become "nature" in the public imagination. No value can be placed on landscape beauty, but the populace tends to expect it to be available for them to enjoy.

THE THREATS AND THE SAVIORS The delicate eco-systems that have thrived for centuries in Britain's varied landscape have suffered greatly in the past half century, with agricultural mass-production, road-building, urban development, and other changes in land use. Since 1945, the British countryside has lost 40 percent of its heathlands, 80 percent of its chalk downland pastures and 95 percent of its herb-rich hay meadows. Fortunately the countryside is so prominent in the national conscience that there has been abundant support for saving what remains, from local campaigns to government environmental policies and conservationist bodies like the National Trust.

Britain's footpaths need a constant watch to insure that they are in usable condition

SAVING THE LAKES
Early in the 19th century, poet William Wordsworth was anxious about the development of the Lake District and expressed his wish that it should be deemed "a sort of national property, in which every man has a right and interest who has an eye to perceive and a heart to enjoy." The children's author Beatrix Potter was another who loved the area, and used revenue from her books to acquire local farms and estates, which she donated to the National Trust.

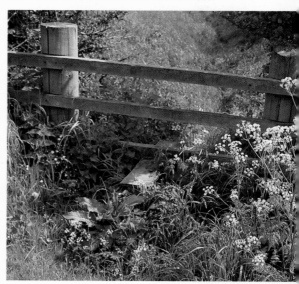

NATIONAL PARKS AND PUBLIC ACCESS The major catalyst in the formation of National Parks in England and Wales was in 1932, when hikers (or "ramblers" as they called themselves) mounted a mass trespass against the denial of public access to the hills of the Peak District. Fights broke out with landowners' gamekeepers, who jealously guarded the privately owned moorlands; six ramblers were arrested and five received prison sentences. This event brought the issues of access to the fore, and after World War II the Peak became Britain's first such designated area—seen as both valuable and vulnerable for its proximity to industrial cities.

The National Parks that were created in the 1950s (see sidebar) had several aims, including provision of access and facilities for the public, preserving the landscape, protecting wildlife and buildings, and maintaining established farming use. However, walkers do not have total freedom of access (although the law may soon allow the "right to roam" in open country), and the national parks differ from their counterparts in the U.S.A. and most other countries in that the land is privately owned.

At the same time a unique system of registering public rights of way over private land was set up—giving anyone the right to walk on some 140,000 miles of paths and bridleways in England and Wales—all now shown on Ordnance Survey maps.

HELPING HANDS The National Trust, a charitable body (see sidebar page 102) has since 1895 acquired large areas of coast, downland, upland and forest, which it has the statutory power to declare inalienable (making it impossible ever to be sold) for public enjoyment in perpetuity. In this way large areas of coastal Devon and Cornwall's magnificent coastal cliffs have been saved for the nation, and access guaranteed. There is free access on foot to all the Trust's countryside sites.

Some of Britain's most valuable wildlife sites are protected as **National Nature Reserves**. On the South Downs in Sussex, for example, many of the hillsides that attracted a wealth of wildlife have been ploughed up and agriculturally "improved" since the 1940s; however, a few pockets have been preserved as nature reserves, such as Mount Caburn (near Lewes), with its rare orchids and butterflies, and Lullington Heath (near Alfriston), with its unusual mixture of acid and chalky soils, giving rise to a diverse flora. **The Royal Society for the Protection of Birds** (R.S.P.B.) is the principal body concerned with wild birds and their environments in the U.K. and has 120 reserves, many—among them Minsmere in Suffolk—with hides for birdwatchers. For information contact the R.S.P.B. at The Lodge, Sandy, Bedfordshire SG19 2DL, tel: 01767 680551 (website: www.rspb.org.uk).

Additionally, numerous specialist bodies play a role in safeguarding wildlife. Based at **Slimbridge** on the Severn Estuary in Gloucestershire, the **Wildfowl and Wetlands Trust** is dedicated to the protection of wetland sites—with a huge population of geese, swans and ducks on site—and has wildfowl collections at seven other centers in the U.K. Meanwhile the **Tamar Otter Park** at North Petherwin in Cornwall breeds otters with the aim of re-introducing this once-familiar animal to England's rivers.

145

Walberswick, a scattered hamlet, abuts reedbeds, mud flats, and heath, a habitat for bearded tits, reed warblers, bitterns, water rails, and marshland plants. Much of the former port of Dunwich has disappeared beneath the sea; Dunwich and Westleton heaths are nearby, and Minsmere is a freshwater lake owned by the Royal Society for the Protection of Birds (over 280 bird species have been recorded locally, including bearded tits, nightjars, woodpeckers, and nightingales). Access to Minsmere Reserve is tightly controlled, but birdwatchers' blinds are open to the public.

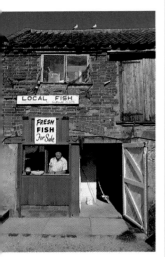

Southwold: choose from today's catch at the harbor

▶ St. Albans 134A2
(tel: 01727 864511)

Less than 20 miles from London, St. Albans has preserved its provincial character surprisingly well. Its **abbey church▶** is a medieval foundation built on the site where Alban, the first British martyr, was executed in the 4th century. Its brick-and-flint architecture dates from the 11th century and has been added to in every century since. The Roman city of **Verulamium▶** lies in a nearby park; excavations include a semicircular amphitheater, part of the city walls, foundations of houses, and a temple. Site finds are well displayed in the Verulamium Museum.

The Gardens of the Rose▶, the Royal National Rose Society's home at Chiswell Green, southwest of St. Albans, have some 30,000 bushes, at their best in July. Five miles east of St. Albans, **Hatfield House▶▶** has been in the same family since it was built for Robert Cecil in 1611. It has state rooms and knot and scented gardens.

▶ Southwell 134D1
(tel: 01636 678962)

The medieval minster in this small Nottinghamshire town is not England's best-known, but the chapter house (begun in 1292) boasts some of the country's most breathtakingly intricate carving: a celebration of Sherwood Forest's foliage in stone, featuring oak, maple, and vine and ivy leaves. Two of the three Norman towers were rebuilt after a fire in 1711, but the nave, crossing, and transept display characteristic Norman simplicity.

▶▶ Southwold 135C5
(tel: 01502 724729)

An old-fashioned coastal town, Southwold is a center for exploring the best of Suffolk's coast. The former home town of essayist and novelist George Orwell, it was rebuilt after a fire in 1659 around a charming series of greens edged by flint, brick, and color-washed cottages. The great Perpendicular church has a superb interior, a lighthouse gleams behind the Sole Bay Inn, and the town museum and Sailors' Reading Room have displays on maritime life. Just south of town, the River Blyth has an attractive boating scene. Around Southwold lie numerous marshlands, some unspoiled low-lying coast, and heathy grassland—the traditional sandlings, or sheepwalks, on which Suffolk's economy depended in the wool-prosperous Middle Ages—making it an area of interest for naturalists.

Southward 16 miles, **Aldeburgh▶** is a small coastal town, the birthplace of George Crabbe, an 18th-century poet. His poem *The Borough* was adapted by Benjamin Britten for his opera *Peter Grimes*, a brilliant evocation of life on this coast, which premièred in 1945. Britten (1913–1976) is buried in the churchyard of St. Peter and St. Paul; a memorial window was designed by John Piper. Britten cofounded Aldeburgh's esteemed June music festival, which is centered on The Maltings at Snape.

Just north of Aldeburgh is **Thorpeness▶**, a resort village planned in the early 20th century as a weatherboarded and half-timbered "olde-English" haven. Beside the Meare, the village's artificial lake, is a former grain windmill, moved here to pump water to the adjacent tall former water tower, known as the House in the Clouds.

►► Stamford 134C2
(tel: 01780 755611)

An oasis of mellow, Cotswold-like limestone buildings, Stamford was the first landmarked area designated in England. Its clutch of medieval churches includes **St. Martin's**, a complete Perpendicular church with a notable 16th-century alabaster monument to Lord Burghley. Of Stamford's inns **The George** is the most conspicuous, with its "gallows" inn-sign spanning the street. Look for two good examples of almshouses, 15th-century **Browne's Hospital** and Elizabethan **Lord Burghley's Hospital**.

Capability Brown's landscaped park at **Burghley House►►** laps the brink of Stamford. The palatial mansion was built by one William Cecil, chief minister to Elizabeth I. The Elizabethan exterior belies an interior refurbished 100 years later, full of baroque flourishes, including a dazzling array of Italian plasterwork and painted ceilings by Verrio and Laguerre in the "Heaven" and "Hell" rooms, magnificent porcelain, paintings by Veronese and Gainsborough, and notable portraits. **Rutland Water►**, to the west, is a huge reservoir and major recreation area. Farther afield, 14 miles southeast of Stamford, **Peterborough** is sprawling and industrial but worth a visit for its Norman **cathedral►►** that boasts a superb painted wooden ceiling—Europe's largest. Some 3 miles from the town is **Flag Fen►** (see sidebar).

►► Woburn Abbey 134B2
(tel: 01525 290666)

Britain's largest animal safari park forms part of the grounds of this stately home, the seat of the Russells, the Dukes of Bedford, since 1550. Despite its abbey origins—a Cistercian foundation prior to the Reformation—the house is an 18th-century Palladian composition set in a deer park. Within is the finest set of Canaletto paintings to be found anywhere. You can feel the family connection with the house (which claims to be the birthplace of afternoon tea), with portraits and possessions spanning many centuries.

FLAG FEN
Discovered in the wetlands of the fens in 1982, the remarkable Flag Fen Bronze Age Monument is the only site of its era where archeological excavations are open to the public. A huge line of posts, some 0.6 miles in length, and wooden platforms have been discovered; the purpose of the site is believed to be ritualistic. There are reconstructed Bronze Age and Iron Age houses, a museum and guided tours.

147

A windmill stands among the tranquil marshes flanking the Blyth Estuary near Southwold

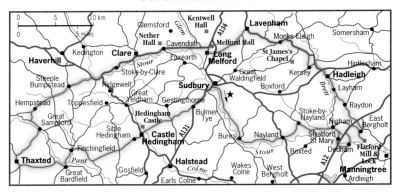

CONSTABLE COUNTRY

Drive

Constable country

As pretty as a picture: the candy colors of local plasterwork, the village greens, and the great medieval churches, paid for by the prosperous wool trade, have changed little since Constable's day. The countryside is mild and agreeable if unspectacular: it is the towns and villages—well endowed with tearooms, and craft and antiques shops—that have most appeal (approx. 90 miles).

Start at **Sudbury** (tel: 01787 881320), where Thomas Gainsborough's birthplace is now a museum. The route follows the River Stour, along the

Gainsborough's House, Sudbury

B1508 to **Bures**, then eastward through **Stoke-by-Nayland▶**, where the church tower (a familiar feature in Constable's paintings) presides over the Maltings and Guildhall.

Dedham▶ has an attractively broad main street and the building of Constable's school survives; the artist Alfred Munnings lived here, and his works are displayed in his former house. Near **East Bergholt**, Constable's birthplace, is **Flatford Mill▶** (also reached by a pretty 1¼-mile river path or by boats rented in Dedham); Willy Lott's Cottage by the millpond is still recognizable as the setting for Constable's painting *The Haywain*.

Turn northwest along the B1070 through **Hadleigh▶**, a handsome town by the River Brett with a fine church and half-timbered Guildhall. Detour through **Kersey▶**, a charming village of one street, and join the A1141 to **Lavenham▶▶**, with its resplendent half-timbering, a huddle of inns, and an outstanding church. Westward, **Long Melford▶** has antiques shops, a magnificent church, and two fine stately homes adjacent.

The A1092 heads past **Cavendish**, a confection of pink rendering and thatch around the green, and **Clare**, with its marketplace and flint-built church noted for its woodcarving. Seek out the church, windmill, and Recorders' House at **Thaxted▶▶**.

Eastward lies **Finchingfield▶** with a delightful green and a windmill. **Castle Hedingham▶▶** has a mighty Norman keep.

The landscape of East Anglia has always held a special fascination for painters. Gainsborough and Constable both came from Suffolk, and Gainsborough's birthplace in Sudbury is now a museum. Constable was born at East Bergholt, and pictures such as The Haywain *and* Flatford Mill *made the winding valley of the Stour "Constable country" even during the painter's own lifetime.*

While Constable and Gainsborough are the two biggest names (see page 38), many other distinguished artists recorded the East Anglian scene. Philip Wilson Steer painted the Suffolk coast in the 1880s. **Sir Alfred Munnings** painted equestrian scenes and his house at Dedham is now a museum. **John Nash**, a major

landscape artist, lived and worked in Essex for years before his death in 1977.

THE NORWICH SCHOOL Norwich's Castle Museum has a splendid collection of paintings by the Norwich School of painters, which began in 1803. Its chief figures were **John Crome** and **John Sell Cotman**. Crome was much more successful, to the anguished jealousy of Cotman, who is now regarded as the greater painter, admired for his ability to impose simple and satisfying patterns on the natural scene. The work of the Norwich School echoes the Dutch school of landscape painting. They responded to a similar setting—a flat landscape studded by windmills and grazed by cattle beneath a sky of towering cloudscapes.

The wealth and the comparatively isolated position of Norwich in the early 19th century meant that most of its painters were known only locally. The local gentry wanted representations of the scenes they knew—the tranquil Norfolk landscape, picturesquely dilapidated cottages, ruined towers and crumbling abbeys, cattle and sheep, river and coastal views. The Norwich School painted the rural scene as it was in the last days before the Industrial Revolution changed the face of Britain.

Above: from
Wood scene *by John Crome, 1810*

Fishing boats off Yarmouth *by John Sell Cotman*

149

EAST ANGLIAN ART ON SHOW
In addition to Gainsborough's house in Sudbury, there are notable collections of works by East Anglian artists at the Castle Museum and the Sainsbury Centre, both in Norwich, the Fitzwilliam Museum in Cambridge, and at the Tate and the National Gallery in London—the latter has Constable's *The Haywain*.

"How much real delight have I had with the study of Landscape this summer. Either I am myself much improved in 'the Art of seeing Nature' (which Sir Joshua Reynolds calls painting) or Nature has unveiled her beauties to me with a less fastidious hand—perhaps there may be something of both so we will divide these fine compliments between us..."
—John Constable, to his future wife (1812)

150

Carmel Head
Amlwch
Holyhead Bay
ISLE OF ANGLESEY
Holyhead
Holy Island
Llangefni
Beaumar
Menai Bridg
Llanfair P
Bang
Plas Newydd
Newborough
Caernarfo
Caernarfon Bay
Llanberis
(1085m Snowdon)
Penygroes
Beddgelert

E

Nefyn
Porthmadog
Lleyn Peninsula
Pwllheli
Harlech
Aberdaron
Abersoch
Bardsey
Barmout

D

Cardigan Bay

Tywyn
Aberdyfi

Aberystwyth

C

Aberaeron
New Quay
CEREDIGION
Templ
Bar
Aberporth
Lampeter
Cardigan
Dinas Head
Nevern
Strumble Head
Pembrokeshire Coast
National Park
Fishguard
Newcastle Emlyn
Teifi
Mynydd Preseli
St David's Head
PEMBROKESHIRE
St David's
Solva
CARMARTHENSHIRE
C
Ramsey St Non's Chapel
Carmarthen
Towy
St Brides Bay
Haverfordwest
Skomer
Pembrokeshire Coast
National Park
Narberth
St Clears
Pontyberem
Marloes
Milford Haven
Kidwelly
Burry Pontardul
Port
Llanelli
Dale
Skokholm
Pembroke Dock
Carew Castle
Saundersfoot
Gorseinon
SWANSE
Pembroke
Tenby
Carmarthen Bay
Kitts
Bosherston
Manorbier
Caldey
Llanrhidian
Llanmadog
St Govan's Chapel
Gower
Rhossili
Oxwich
Worms Head
Culver Hole

B

A

★ Walk start point

0   10   20   30   40   50 km
0   10   20   30 miles

1   2

Wales

▶▶▶ **REGION HIGHLIGHTS**

Beaumaris *page 154*

Brecon Beacons National Park *page 155*

Elan Valley *page 159*

Pembrokeshire Coast National Park *pages 165–166*

Plas Newydd *page 164*

Powis Castle *page 166*

Snowdonia National Park *page 167–170*

Welsh Folk Museum *page 157*

Wye Valley *page 171*

Traditional Armenian dancing at the Llangollen Eisteddfod

THE WELSH LANGUAGE
Visitors to Wales will not need to speak Welsh, but the language—one of Europe's oldest—is in evidence everywhere; on signposts, official notices, on T.V. and radio, and in place names. It is, however, useful to pick up the pronunciation to make it clear what town or village you are talking about. Many places begin with *Llan* (meaning church), the *ll* pronounced as a soft ch followed by an *l* sound—put the side of your tongue against your teeth and blow. Other useful rules are: *u* as in wh**ee**l; *y* as in t**i**n or t**u**rn; *f* as in **v**an; *ff* as in **f**un; *th* as in **th**ought; *dd* as in **th**en; *ch* as in lo**ch**; *au* as in m**i**d; and *w* as in l**oo**k. So Fforest Fawr is pronounced *forest vowr*, Llanwrtyd as *chlanuhrtid*; and Caersws as *kairsooce*.

WALES Constitutionally Wales is closer to England than is Scotland; there is no separate legal system, and the two principalities have been unified since 1535. Yet the Welsh are proudly independent in culture and outlook; the Welsh language is very much alive (much more so than Gaelic in Scotland) and is taught in schools. Welsh is the first language of many, particularly in North and West Wales; signs ("dim parcio/no parking," "croeso i Gymru/welcome to Wales") are predominantly bilingual; roughly one in five of its inhabitants is a Welsh speaker. Plaid Cymru, the Welsh Nationalist Party, has sent members to Parliament since 1966, and devolution—restoration of some powers to the local Welsh government—is a current talking point. (In September 1997, the Welsh people voted by a narrow margin to establish a Welsh Assembly in Cardiff, which came into existence in 1999. There are strong traditions of choral singing and of Nonconformism (that is, the Protestant denominations such as Baptist that have broken away from the Established Church), virtually every village having at least one chapel. The Welsh love of music, literature, and art manifests itself in the numerous *eisteddfods* (festivals), in which music, poetry, drama, and fine arts feature. Welsh domestic architecture on the other hand is humble—typically sturdy stone-built farmsteads and houses beneath slate roofs; the railroad age added red and yellow brick facades. Grand houses are few, but there are plenty of medieval castles to visit. Wales also prides itself on its educational system; it has the highest teacher/pupil ratios in the U.K.

SOUTH WALES For all its proximity to central and northwest England, Wales is strikingly remote. Cross into South or Mid Wales from the English border and the hills rise immediately. The southern borderland (the border country often being termed as the Marches) is defined precisely by the gorge of the **Lower Wye**, whose scenic reaches are punctuated by features such as Tintern

Abbey, Chepstow Castle, and Symonds Yat rock. Criss-crossing the English border from the South Wales coast to its northern one, the exhilarating and extremely hilly 177-mile **Offa's Dyke** Path roughly follows the line of a 9th-century boundary dike built by Offa, King of Mercia. Farther into South Wales lie the coalfields and the dying industrial heartlands of the **valleys**, which though hardly picturesque have their own fascination. **Cardiff**, the Welsh capital, is the administrative and cultural capital. The coast becomes increasingly seductive as you proceed westward; Nash Point near Llantwit Major on the Vale of Glamorgan coast displays extraordinary candy-striped rocks, while the **Gower Peninsula**, on the back doorstep of the industrial city of Swansea, has magnificent bays and cliffs. **Pembrokeshire**, too distant for mere day-trips, is a favorite destination for seaside vacations without the host of commercialized trappings found in so many of the English resorts.

MID WALES This nebulous term is applied to a relatively unknown region, sparsely populated except by sheep, which are encountered everywhere (one-quarter of the E.U.'s sheep population is here). The **Brecon Beacons National Park** offers the grandest scenery, with its best-known tracts on its eastern side—the Black Mountains, the Brecon Beacons, and the secondhand bookshop town of Hay-on-Wye. Farther west, the **Cambrian Mountains** are scarcely inhabited and largely impenetrable by car, except by a handful of spectacularly lonely mountain roads laid along routes used by drovers taking sheep to market in the pre-automobile era. Aberystwyth is the principal coastal town of Ceredigian (or Cardigan), whose shoreline, though not as scenic as Pembrokeshire, does have a few pleasant places, such as Llangranog, New Quay, and Aberaeron.

NORTH WALES Along the north coast stretches a line of resorts, largely undistinguished with the notable exception of Llandudno. But more significantly, North Wales contains the **Snowdonia National Park**; here are the highest mountains in England and Wales, and a good range of attractions, including castles, mines, and steam trains. Nevertheless, this can be a frustrating area for motorists: roads are often sunk down in the valleys and the scenery slips by quickly; but there are outstanding walks at varying levels of difficulty, from easy forest strolls to tough scrambles up challenging scree-covered mountain slopes.

RECOMMENDED SMALL TOWNS
Carmarthenshire: Llandeilo.
Conwy: Conwy.
Monmouthshire: Chepstow, Monmouth.
Pembrokeshire: St. David's.
Powys: Hay-on-Wye, Llandrindod Wells, Llanidloes, Montgomery, Presteigne.
CASTLES
Caernarfon, Caerphilly, Conwy, Harlech.
COASTAL TOWNS
Llandudno, Tenby.
WALKING AREAS
Brecon Beacons National Park, Gower, Offa's Dyke Path, Pembrokeshire Coast National Park, Snowdonia National Park, Lower Wye Valley. (See Walks, page 158.)
INDUSTRIAL INTEREST
Snowdonia National Park, the South Wales mining valleys
SCENIC DRIVES
Mid Wales: Elan Valley, Beulah to Tregaron, Llanidloes via Dylife to Machynlleth, Rhayader to Aberystwyth.
Brecon Beacons National Park: Gospel Pass (Hay-on-Wye to Llanthony).
Snowdonia National Park: see Drive, page 170.

153

Rounding up sheep the Welsh way—but sheep dogs normally do the precision work

Anglesey Sea Zoo: all-weather fun

THE DRUIDS OF ANGLESEY
The religious leaders of the Celts were the Druids, and Anglesey was famed far and wide as a druidic center. Tacitus, the Roman historian writing in the 1st century AD, speaks of Anglesey as the place where youths aspiring to the priesthood were sent to be schooled in philosophy, religion, and poetry. In more sinister mode, he also speaks of human blood being smeared on the Druids' altars and human entrails being used for prophesies.

Rugged cliffs embrace Porth Dafarch, on Anglesey's Holy Island peninsula, a popular beach for divers and canoeists

▶ **Anglesey, Isle of**   150E2
(tel: 01407 762622)

Wales' largest island is flat and fertile, and it is its shores that provide most of its attractions to visitors. Good beaches include **Newborough Warren**, which offers distant views of Snowdonia, and **Amlwch Bay**.

Pioneering neolithic man built an amazing number of chamber tombs on Anglesey, the most notable being Bryn celli ddu and Barcloddiad y Gawres. The island's geographical position en route to Ireland and its gold and copper inevitably attracted the Celts too; a great hoard of Iron Age chariot fittings and weapons was found at Llyn Cerrig Bach. In medieval times, when the island's farmland provided valuable supplies for granaries in England, Anglesey was held by the English. Edward I built a stronghold in the 1290s at **Beaumaris▶▶**; the castle (Cadw) was never attacked and the moated shell survives to this day. The town's former prison houses a museum where you can find ghoulish delights such as the treadmill, the condemned cell, and the route to the scaffold.

Between Anglesey and the mainland is the Menai Strait, spanned by Thomas Telford's suspension bridge, the longest such structure in the world when it was built (1826) and one of the engineer's greatest achievements. Overlooking the strait is **Plas Newydd▶** (N.T.), the Pagets' 18th- and 19th-century family home; it has a *trompe l'oeil* mural in the dining room, painted by Rex Whistler in the 1930s. **Holy Island**, attached to Anglesey by a ½-mile causeway, is good for birdwatching and, although the industrial port of Holyhead is disappointing, there are good walks on Holyhead Mountain, the island's highest point, which has the remains of a Roman watchtower and traces of 3rd- and 4th-century hut circles. Ferries leave from Holyhead for Dublin in Ireland.

▶▶ Brecon Beacons National Park   151B3
(tel: 01874 624437)

The park is an east–west upland of four distinct areas, the Black Mountains, Fforest Fawr, the Brecon Beacons themselves, and the Black Mountain. It is less rugged than Snowdonia but has some fine views and excellent walks.

The eastern flanks comprise the **Black Mountains**, a series of ridges enclosing deep sheep-grazed valleys. Drive up from **Hay-on-Wye▶**, a small town crowded around its castle and a mecca of secondhand bookshops. Above Hay the **Gospel Pass▶▶** is perhaps the most scenic drive in the park, with easy access to the summit of Hay Bluff. The road dips into a valley, past the ruins of 13th-century **Llanthony Abbey▶**. Up an obscure side valley **Patrishow Church▶** boasts a rare musicians' gallery and an eerie mural of a skeleton bearing a shovel, scythe, and hourglass. Farther west, the A479 skirts the massif between the attractive towns of **Crickhowell** and **Talgarth** before passing through **Tretower▶**, with its fortified medieval manor (Cadw) by the ruin of an earlier castle.

The **Brecon Beacons** are really a sandstone ridge culminating in Pen y Fan (2,906 feet), the highest point in Wales outside Snowdonia. The graceful M shape of the twin summits is seen from far around. To the south is the little **Brecon Mountain Railway**. **Brecon** itself is an amiable market town with a small cathedral and the **Brecknock Museum**. Out of town, the **Brecon Beacons Mountain Centre** is the main national park information outlet.

Predominantly grassy upland, **Fforest Fawr** includes, near Pont Nedd Fechan, the superlative "**waterfall country**"▶▶ of the wooded Nedd, Hepste, and Mellte gorges (see Walks, page 158). **Dan-yr-ogof Caves▶** nearby are part of Britain's largest known cave system; one has a re-creation of a Bronze Age dwelling, another presents a history of caving in a sound-and-light show.

To the west, the **Black Mountain** is an expanse of moors and forests dominated by the craggy ridge of **Carmarthen Fan**. Much of it is for the serious walker only, but **Carreg Cennen Castle▶▶** (Cadw), a majestically placed ruin in a valley close to Llandeilo, merits a detour.

The national park includes the highest land in South Wales

155

LOVE SPOONS
Throughout rural Wales during the 17th, 18th, and 19th centuries, young men would spend many long, dark evenings carving ornamental wooden "love spoons." These would be presented as tokens to the girls or women they courted; if accepted, it was a sign that courtship would lead to marriage. They are still produced as souvenirs; the Brecknock Museum in Brecon and the Welsh Folk Museum at St. Fagans (see page 157) have fine collections of this genre of folk art.

The industrial valleys of South Wales present a startling transition from the lonely wilds of the Brecon Beacons to the north. Here, stretching from Pontypool in the east (close to the English border) toward Llanelli in the west, is one of the most strongly characterized industrial regions in the whole of Britain.

156

"NYE" AND THE N.H.S.
Aneurin Bevan, or Nye as he was fondly called, was born the son of a miner in 1897. As a boy he was himself a miner and had early trade union experience in the South Wales Miners Federation. In 1929 he was elected M.P. for Ebbw Vale and held the seat until he died in 1960. One of parliament's greatest orators, he has gone down in history as the minister who in 1948 introduced the National Health Service, providing the people of Britain with a comprehensive medical, dental, and welfare service funded largely by general taxation.

An old pit head

How green was my valley Between narrow fingers of rising ridges extend the valleys—running deep and roughly north to south, each grooved with long rows of houses built in the heyday of the areas' industrial prosperity.

Toward the end of the 18th century, the Industrial Revolution heralded a new dawn; peasants from rural areas migrated en masse into the Valleys as ironmasters established works at Aberdare, Dowlais, Hirwaun, and Merthyr Tydfil. In 1804 Richard Trevithick gave birth to the age of rail with his steam railroad from Merthyr to Abercynon. The Merthyr ironworks supplied cannon for the British forces in the Napoleonic wars and track for railroads across the globe.

Coal, choirs, and rugby Later, iron production ceased and the Valleys specialized in coal extraction; the coalfield witnessed a great influx of new population. Work was hard and often dangerous, but community life brought its rewards—passions for rugby and choral singing; the Valleys choirs still carry away the honors at the International Eisteddfod (see panels, pages 160 and 163). Numerous leading socialists were born and bred here, including Aneurin Bevan, a miner's son who was to be the instigator of the National Health Service (see panel), and Neil Kinnock, former leader of the Labour Party.

Facing the future At the height of the Valleys' industrialization, people joked disbelievingly that it would have once been possible for a monkey to have swung from tree to tree along the Rhondda Valley. Now the smoke has gone with closure of the collieries as seams are largely exhausted, and greenery is returning: evergreen plantations cloak the upper slopes. Tower Colliery at Hirwaun, the last of the nationally owned pits, has been privatized; open-cast mining continues, but only two deep mines and eleven open-cast mines operate in Wales, providing employment for merely a few hundred people. Unemployment overall is running high, and many houses stand empty. Service industries are alive however, and the area has awakened to its tourist potential. At Pontypool there is Torfaen Museum, which includes the Valley Inheritance Museum, chronicling the story of a typical mining valley, and organizes tours of the blast furnaces and casting sheds of the nearby 18th-century Blaenavon Ironworks. The major heritage museum is the Big Pit Mining Museum in Blaenavon, where former miners, well-stocked with anecdotes, show visitors the pit-head showers, winding machine, and the depths of the mine.

▶▶ Cardiff

(tel: 02920 227281)

151A4

Although it is located in the industrial heartland of Wales, Cardiff is a surprisingly clean and livable place. Despite its status as Welsh capital and as home of Welsh rugby union and of the (much-acclaimed) Welsh National Opera, Cardiff is not a particularly Welsh city. Bute Park cuts a swath by the banks of the Taff, close to the civic center, a gleaming complex in Portland stone begun in the 1890s. **Cardiff Castle▶▶** dates from Norman times but had money poured into it in the 1860s and onward by the fabulously wealthy 2nd Marquess of Bute (who built the city's docks and made Cardiff the world's prime coal port); the result was a mock-medieval fantasy of Ludwig II proportions, designed by William Burges.

Cardiff has a fine array of **museums▶▶**. At the wideranging **National Museum of Wales**, collections include paintings by French Impressionists as well as silver, ceramics, fossils, dinosaur skeletons, and shells, while the Millennium Stadium has a **Rugby Experience** museum. Cardiff Bay, where the harbor and docklands are being newly developed, now has numerous attractions: a three-dimensional model of the bay can be seen in the futuristic **Cardiff Bay Visitor Centre**; and **Techniquest** is one of the largest hands-on science centers in the country, a "won-

157

A locomotive on show at the Welsh Industrial and Maritime Museum; other galleries display trams, shipping, cars, and industrial engines

derland of science and technology" for all age and experience levels. The Welsh Assembly is also based here.

The medieval **Llandaff Cathedral▶** is dominated by the figure of "Christ in Majesty" by Jacob Epstein, an impressive creation in concrete. The **Welsh Folk Museum▶▶▶** at nearby **St. Fagans** has a collection of rural dwellings from all over Wales, including a farmhouse, a terrace from the mining valleys, a Unitarian chapel, and a Working Men's Institute.

North of Cardiff, double-moated **Caerphilly Castle▶▶** (Cadw), dating from the 13th and 14th centuries, is the largest castle in England and Wales after Windsor. South of Abergavenny, **Big Pit Mining Museum, Blaenavon▶▶**, is the best attraction in the industrial Valleys, capturing the atmosphere of a working mine (see opposite page).

Walks

Dinas Island, 150B1
Pembrokeshire Coast
National Park, Pembrokeshire

Off the A487 east of Fishguard; parking lot near Sailors' Safety Inn. The "island" is in fact a peninsula, ideal for an exhilarating circular walk of 1 to 1½ hours along the clifftop path, passing Dinas Head, the highest point, and Needle Rock, with its large birdlife population. A well-walked public footpath cuts across the narrow neck of land to complete the circuit.

158

Llyn Idwal, Snowdonia 150E2
National Park, Gwynned

Parking lot by Idwal Cottage Youth Hostel on the A5. The nature trail around Llyn (lake) Idwal gives straight-forward access to supremely dramatic scenery, passing the crags of the Devil's Kitchen beneath Glyder Fawr (1½ hours). The slopes support rare flora, including alpine species, and the area is an officially designated National Nature Reserve. Trail leaflet available on site.

Moel Famau, 151E4
Denbighshire

Parking lot and picnic site on the B5429 between Llanbedr-Dyffryn-Clwyd and Llandyrnog. The walk up

from the road to the partly collapsed Jubilee Tower gives views westward to Snowdonia and eastward to the Peak District. Start from the picnic site and walk through the forest (following the blue or red markers); return along the open ridge to drop down to the road, then turn left to the starting point. (1½ hours)

The Nedd, Hepste, and 151B3
Mellte Waterfalls, Brecon
Beacons National Park, Powys

Parking lot at Pontneddfechan, east of Glyn Neath. These mighty waterfalls crash their way along wooded gorges in the southern fringes of the national park. The Hepste and Mellte falls can be reached by a woodland path from Craig y Ddinas parking lot at the east end of Pontneddfechan or from Porth yr Ogof to the north; the highlight is here Sgwd yr Ira, where you can walk behind the curtain of the fall. (1 to 2 hours)

Symonds Yat, Lower 151B4
Wye Valley, Herefordshire border

Parking lot at end of the B4432, north of Coleford. This renowned scenic overlook over the Wye gives access to one of the prettiest parts of the gorge. Descend to the west, past a refreshment stand and on a marked path to the riverside Saracen's Head Inn, where a chain ferry takes you across. Turn left on the far bank to the wire suspension bridge (it will bounce as you cross); return along the old railroad track on the east bank. (1½ hours)

▶▶ Elan Valley and the Cambrian Mountains   151C3

(tel: 01970 612125)

One of the best places for spotting the rare red kite (a huge bird of prey identifiable by its forked tail), the **Elan Valley** is a chain of reservoirs which graces the great unpopulated wilds of the Cambrian Mountains. The lakes supply water to Birmingham, and both the dams and Elan village, built for the reservoir workers, are in characteristically solid Edwardian style. The Elan Valley Visitor Centre in Elan village has details of walks; the trackbed of an old railroad used in the construction of the reservoirs is a good route for lakeside strolls.

An exciting **mountain road▶▶** climbs the Cambrian range, leaving Rhayader for the Elan Valley and continuing past abandoned lead and zinc mines to **Devil's Bridge▶**, where three bridges, stacked one upon the other, span a gorge. Tiny steam trains run along the scenic narrow-gauge **Vale of Rheidol Railway▶** from here to **Aberystwyth**, the main seaside resort for Cardigan Bay. A crescent of bay-windowed Victorian guest houses on the seafront overlook a rocky beach, which is hemmed in by the bulky bluff of Constitution Hill from where you can see Snowdonia and the Preseli Hills. A cliff railroad makes an effortless ascent to the top, and a camera obscura enhances the panorama on sunny days.

▶▶ Erddig   151D4

(tel: 01978 355314)

Although not a particularly distinguished house architecturally, Erddig (N.T.), 2 miles south of Wrexham, is an excellent introduction to life "below stairs" in a country mansion. The National Trust rescued the house when mining subsidence threatened the structure; all the service buildings and most of the contents had survived intact, and it is now preserved as a fascinating picture of the workings of a country estate in the 18th and 19th centuries.

The Yorke family, which lived here from 1733 to 1973, treated its servants kindly, and as a visitor you see the house somewhat through a servant's eyes, entering not by the main door but through the servants' quarters.

Pennygarreg Reservoir Dam, Elan Valley

159

DOLAUCOTHI GOLD MINES
Remotely sited near Pumsaint, just off the A482 southeast of Lampeter, the mines (N.T.) were periodically worked from Roman times up to the 20th century. Some of the 1930s machinery is still in place and, equipped with helmets and miners' lamps, visitors tour the mine tunnels and pan for gold. During July and August get there as early as possible or book ahead (tel: 01558 650359).

Far left: the family bicycle collection at Erddig

Look at any vacation brochure or tourist poster for Wales and you are likely to come across the same well-worn images: male voice choirs; young girls playing the harp in Welsh hats; mist-shrouded mountains and lakes; and rugged mining valleys. Like all clichés, they convey only a superficial picture. The reality is far more vital: a combination of reverence for the past and passionate concern for the future. One element links all the strands of politics and culture: a fervent sense of Welsh identity.

THE NATIONAL EISTEDDFOD

Welsh-language culture is seen at its most robust at an eisteddfod. All over the country, local eisteddfodau (literally "sittings") are set up in schools and chapels, where singers, dancers, musicians, actors, artists, and writers of all ages compete to reach the next level in the categories of Awdl (a complex, ancient form of Welsh poetry) and Pryddest (free verse). The nationwide contest culminates, in the first week of August, in the National Eisteddfod, presided over by the Gorsedd of Bards in their druidic robes.

DYLAN THOMAS AND LAUGHARNE

One of Wales's cultural giants, Dylan Thomas (1914–1953) penned *A Child's Christmas in Wales* as well as the autobiographical short stories of *Portrait of the Artist as a Young Dog* (1940). Born in Swansea, he worked as a newspaper reporter, and from 1938 he stayed and eventually settled in the village of Laugharne (northwest of Swansea). The boathouse which he made his haven and the adjacent shed in which he wrote (and drank heavily) now form a museum, with photographs and furniture on display. He is buried in the churchyard.

Dylan Thomas summed up the eccentricity and claustrophobia of small-town Welsh life in his play *Under Milk Wood.* The action is set in Llareggub, a mythical fishing community whose name read backwards is the rude phrase "bugger all." One of its residents, the Reverend Eli Jenkins, captures the emotional exuberance of Welsh culture with his cry "Praise the Lord! We are a musical nation!" Music and poetry have an influence which is recognized and nurtured in Wales. The famous male-voice choirs, some of which now perform and record all over the world, are still rooted in the close-knit mining communities of South Wales and the farming and slate-mining areas of the north; and the Eisteddfod (presided over by Bards chosen for their contributions to Welsh life), a well-known celebration of Welsh culture, is an important focus for the 500,000 or so Welsh-speakers in Wales (see panel).

The Welsh language The survival of this ancient Celtic language—one of Europe's oldest—does much to explain the defensive pride of the Welsh. Banned from use in official channels by Henry VIII, one of the Welsh Tudor dynasty, the language lived on in the home and in the arts. Fluency in English became essential for anyone wishing to get ahead in life, and many parents with ambitions for their children favored and encouraged its use. But Welsh continued to be the language of worship, and as Nonconformist chapels (especially Baptist and Methodist denominations) sprang up in the wake of religious revival, it survived as the linchpin of many communities.

Political issues With new generations came new attitudes, and the 20th century saw a battle to reestablish Welsh education. Plaid Cymru, the Welsh Nationalist Party (which now has four M.P.s in Westminster), began in the 1920s calling for a return to the agrarian, Welsh-speaking way of life—a call not welcomed by the struggling industrial communities of South Wales, where socialism still has a firm hold.

In the 1960s and 70s, nationalism took a more radical turn, as young members of Cymdeithas yr Iaith Gymraeg (the Welsh Language Society) kept the "language issue" in the headlines with acts such as painting out anglicized place-names on road signs. In recent years the language has enjoyed a revival—it's now included in the statutory school curriculum, a Welsh T.V. channel has been established, and a lively pop culture has developed, willing to absorb the dreaded Anglo-American influence. Today you will hear Welsh spoken by both children and their elders in much of North and West Wales particularly, and Welsh is taught at schools.

The current hot political issue in Wales is the influx of English people and the decline of traditional Welsh communities. For example, English "incomers" living on the northern Lleyn peninsula have been issued with threats and deadlines for leaving the country, but the intermittent arson attacks on such buildings seem to have ceased. Most Welsh people are quick to condemn these acts, which veil the very real fears of communities whose younger generations are leaving in search of work, while cottages are sold at unaffordable prices to absent landlords and stand empty for half the year, turning once vibrant areas into sad and ghostly places.

Conflict in the field For a glimpse of the whole Welsh nation at its sentimental and raucous best, try to get hold of a ticket for one of the international rugby matches at the Millennium Stadium in winter—preferably Wales vs. England, when rivalry is strong and emotions are high. Hearing a stadium full of fans singing the Welsh anthem before watching their national game can bring a lump to the throat—whatever the final score might be.

Part of the Eisteddfod ceremony: a handmaiden makes her offering to the crown bard

THE "WELSH NOT"
In 1847 education commissioners visited schools in Wales. There they heard children using their native Welsh language, which they attacked as immoral and backward. A campaign to stamp out the use of Welsh was rigorously pursued—often by the Welsh themselves. Pupils overheard slipping into the language were forced to wear wooden boards around their necks bearing the words "Welsh Not." The commission's report, bound between blue covers, was never really forgiven and has passed into Welsh history as the Treason of the Blue Books.

Like southern Pembrokeshire, the Gower has been a "little England beyond Wales," with a long history of English-speaking. In the 12th century the Normans held the Gower and built a chain of castles, of which remains exist at Oxwich, Oystermouth, Pennard, Penrice, and Weobley.

▶▶ Gower Peninsula 150A2
(tel: 01792 468321)

The Gower Peninsula stretches out west of Swansea. The residential and industrial outskirts of that city abruptly give way to green countryside, and a coast that, on its southern seaboard, is the rival of Pembrokeshire (see pages 165–166). It has great limestone cliffs and superb sandy beaches, followed for their length by a coastal path, while the north seaboard is low-lying and marshy.

The western tip is the best part of all: here **Rhossili Down**, a moorland ridge with views of the entire peninsula, dips to a seemingly endless beach; westward stretches **Worms Head**, a high-tide island accessible on foot by those courageous enough. Nearby, **Mewslade Bay** shows rock strata tilted and folded. Farther east are more good beaches at **Oxwich Bay** and at tiny **Brandy Cove**. Gower oddities include **Llanrhidian village**, with a mysteriously carved leper stone in the church and a village green dominated by a pair of gigantic stones.

▶ Llandrindod Wells 151C3
(tel: 01597 822600)

A rare instance of a spa town whose traditions are still alive. A few years ago Llandrindod's Victorian pump-room was semiderelict; today it stands proudly in restored state, and you can sample the rusty-tasting waters spurting from a nearby fountain. Grand red-brick terraces and spa hotels, ornate wrought-iron arcades and balconies, and spacious tree-lined streets suggest something larger than a town of under 5,000 in the heart of Mid Wales sheep country.

Cefnllys▶ is an Iron Age hill fort situated above the River Ithon beside a lone church and the (now robust) Shaky Bridge. There is a nature trail along the river. The **Beulah to Abergwesyn road▶▶**, an old drovers' road to the southwest of the town, takes a spectacular course over the wilderness of the Cambrian Mountains.

Toward New Radnor, the quaintly named waterfall **Water-Break-Its-Neck▶** is to be found north of the A44 in Radnor Forest, a lonely massif of rounded hills and steep-sided valleys. **Old Radnor Church▶** is possibly the finest parish church in Wales, with a medieval screen, Britain's oldest organ case, and a font hewn from a prehistoric monolith. Little has changed for 200 years in the border town of **Presteigne▶**, which has another impressive

Llandrindod Wells, Builth Wells, Llangammarch Wells, and Llanwrtyd Wells are the spa towns of Mid Wales. Back in 1732, Rev. Theophilus Evans tried the highly sulphurous waters and thus found a cure for his skin ailment. Chalybeate and saline springs were discovered close by, and the area became known as a place for taking the waters. A Mrs. Jenkins found a sulphur source in 1736 at Llandrindod, and by the 1830s Llangammarch was offering barium chloride as a remedy for heart conditions.

Llandrindod Wells: its hotels recall its heyday as a spa

church. In Broad Street the **Judge's Lodging**►► adjoins the former (criminal) assize court, which are the subject of a lively museum, with an audio tour taking you round the house where circuit judges used to stay.

►► Llangollen, Vale of   150D4
(tel: 01978 860828)

This deep valley, hemmed in by natural terraces of limestone crags, is a landmark on the A5. From it the A542 rises up the hairpin bends of the **Horseshoe Pass**, engineered by Thomas Telford. **Llangollen** itself, site of the international musical *eisteddfod* (see panel), is of little intrinsic interest but is a busy tourist center, a convenient base for a number of attractions. On the valley floor stand the picturesque ruins of **Valle Crucis Abbey**► (Cadw), a Cistercian foundation of 1201; notable features are the Early English west facade and the vaulted 14th-century chapter house. A wooden roof installed in St. Gollen's in Llangollen is said to have been taken from here. On the edge of Llangollen, horse-drawn barge trips operate along the **Llangollen Canal**; the canal's proudest moment occurs farther east as it crosses 126 feet above the valley on the Pontcysyllte Aqueduct, built by Telford in 1805. Steam train lovers should visit the **Llangollen Railway Society**. Above town is the so-called **Panorama Walk**, really a small road. Even better views, extending toward the Berwyn Hills, are to be had by making the steep climb up to the spectacularly placed ruins of **Castell Dinas Bran**►►, built about 1236.

The view from Castell Dinas Bran, looking toward the limestone buttresses that tower above the Vale of Llangollen

THE LLANGOLLEN INTERNATIONAL EISTEDDFOD
Established in 1947, this *eisteddfod* (see panel, page 160) has become a major international musical competition, now attracting competitors from some 30 countries. The hugely popular event takes place in the first week of July. During this time, informal performances by groups of musicians and dancers take place on the Dee Bridge.

Wind turbine at the Centre for Alternative Technology

THE CENTRE FOR ALTER-NATIVE TECHNOLOGY
The center was established in 1974 as a place for promoting envi-ronmentally friendly technologies. A water-pow-ered cliffside train whisks you up to the site entrance, and a trail takes you around an informative exhibition that includes an energy-efficient house, ecologically oriented gar-dens, and displays of solar heating and other alternative energy sources. Although obviously an idealized setup, the center is a great place for talking to people (several workers live on site) and learning how to cut your energy bills, improve your garden, and give a greener tinge to your lifestyle. Plenty of appeal for children includ-ing the Strawbale Performance Space.

Right: Pistyll Rhayader, Wales' most spectacular waterfall

Just south of town, **Plas Newydd**▶▶ (N.T.) is a remark-able mock-Tudor inspiration, home for half a century starting in 1780 to eccentric recluses Lady Eleanor Butler and Miss Sarah Ponsonby, the "Ladies of Llangollen." They transformed a cottage into this remarkable half-tim-bered house, where they entertained a distinguished number of guests, including Sir Walter Scott and the Duke of Wellington. The house is whimsical in the extreme and full of personal touches.

Pistyll Rhayader▶, Wales's tallest waterfall, is at the head of a remote valley south of Llangollen. The fall has been engineered to give the water a twist as it tumbles, but the effect is pleasing. There is easy access by road.

Machynlleth   *151C3*
(tel: 01654 702401)

A market town centered on a clocktower (of a design that seems to be mandatory for Welsh towns), Machynlleth is comfortably set in the peaceful hills south of the Snowdonia National Park. It is an uneventful place in a pleasant kind of way. The town's hinterland is partly inhabited by a significant hippie population. Topping the bill of local attractions is the excellent **Centre for Alternative Technology**▶ (see panel).

The road to Dylife▶ is a scenic drive that runs over the shoulder of Plynlimon, a boggy upland from which rise the Wye and the Severn, the two great rivers of Wales. At **Dylife** a stream plummets into a gorge via Ffrwd Fawr, a splendid waterfall. A scenic overlook at a curve in the road takes in Cader Idris, the major summit in southern Snowdonia. It is worth carrying on past **Llyn Clywedog reservoir** to the unspoiled town of **Llanidloes**▶.

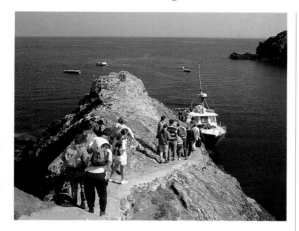

*A boat trip leaves
Martin's Haven for
Skomer Island*

ISLAND HOPS
Skokholm and Skomer are
major bird sanctuaries,
supporting the largest
concentration of Manx
shearwaters in Britain.
Puffins abound on
Skomer, and Skokholm
has a population of storm
petrels. Boat trips start
from Martin's Haven.
Ramsey Island has lots of
gray seals, which can be
seen off the mainland too,
and cliff-nesting birds
including choughs; boat
trips begin from St.
Justinian. Caldey Island,
reached by boat from
Tenby, is home to a
community of
Cistercian monks.

165

▶▶▶ Pembrokeshire Coast   *150B1*
National Park
(tel: 01437 720392)

As its name implies, the national park is largely confined
to a coastal strip. Here are magnificent cliffs, sandy coves
(many excellent for swimming if you can bear the chilly
water), complex natural harbors, and a diversity of
wildlife which ranks on a par with the best of Cornwall.
The south and north parts of the park are strikingly different: a wave-cut platform, now raised high above sea
level, leaves the southern cliffs mostly level-topped, while
farther north the scene is more exciting, with assertive
bluffs, soaring headlands, and dramatic variations in
height. Southern Pembrokeshire was for a long time a "little England beyond Wales," owned by the English, who
left a legacy of English place-names and Norman castles
for keeping watch over the unruly Welsh. Regrettably, the
army's foothold on the south coast in the vicinity of
Castlemartin means restricted access. Walking is the main
draw of the north, which is less populated and consequently less busy in season. Scenic drives are few—the
roads generally keep too far inland; a better bet is to take
in some of the coastal path, which snakes around the intricate seaboard for some 180 miles. A car will, however, get
you into the wilds of the Preseli Hills (see page 166).

TOWNS AND VILLAGES Most famous is undoubtedly **St.
David's ▶▶▶**. Scarcely more than a large village of craft
shops, galleries, and cafés, it keeps its great Norman
cathedral half-hidden in a valley, alongside the considerable ruins of a 14th-century bishop's palace (Cadw).
Allegedly, relics of St. David, patron saint of Wales, lie
beneath the altar. Of the coastal towns, **Tenby ▶▶** is perhaps the most appealing, with its maze of narrow streets, a
harbor surrounded by tiers of color-washed Georgian
and Tudor merchants' houses, a castle up the hill, and a
five-arched gate in the town wall. It is very pretty—and it
suffers badly for that in summer, with bumper-to-bumper
traffic. **Pembroke ▶** is less important than its name suggests, a one-street market town completely dominated by
an exceptional Norman castle, which has a 75-foot tower,
and tunnels to explore. **Fishguard** is split in two by the lie

*St. David's Cathedral:
39 steps (or "Articles")
lead down to its door*

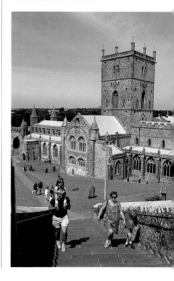

THE PRESELI HILLS
The national park also encompasses the Preseli Hills (or Mynydd Preseli), a tract of remote upland near Fishguard that is scattered with the burial mounds and hill forts of early settlers. It was from here that the bluestone rocks were transported to Wiltshire for the construction of Stonehenge (see page 84), a feat that has baffled archeologists. The rocks may have been moved by raft (this is technically feasible), but more plausible perhaps is the theory that they were naturally moved closer to Stonehenge by glaciers during the last ice age, possibly as far as the Somerset Mendips.

166

of the land, with the lower town crowded around the harbor and the upper town grouped around sloping streets. Ferries depart from nearby Goodwick to Rosslare in Ireland (99 mins by catamaran). The village of **Solva**▶ is a boating center and one-time port prettily set at the end of a narrow, steep-sided bay.

THE BEST OF THE COAST In the south, the indented headlands and bays around **Dale** and **Milford Haven** (itself an industrial port adjacent to oil refineries, but worth seeing for its natural harbor site) have constantly changing views, while **Wooltack Point**▶▶ near Marloes has views across to Skomer and Skokholm islands. At **Bosherston** a series of **lily ponds**▶ makes a popular walk which can be tacked onto a visit to a fine beach. On the margins of some luscious estuary landscape east of Milford Haven is **Carew Castle**, adjacent to a tide mill and a superb 11th-century Celtic cross. Perched among Pembrokeshire's cliffs are three primitive hermitage chapels, **St. Govan's**, just west of St. Govan's Head, **St. Justinian's**, and **St. Non's** (both near St. David's). **St. David's Head**▶▶ and **Strumble Head**▶ have rugged grandeur; it is sometimes possible to see the Wicklow Mountains in Ireland from these. Among the most popular swimming beaches are **St. Bride's Bay**, **Tenby**, **Saundersfoot**, and **Whitesands Bay**, but there are numerous smaller ones offering greater privacy.

▶▶ Powis Castle   151D4
(tel: 01938 557018)
A great border stronghold, owned by the Herbert family from 1587 to 1952, Powis (N.T.) stands just outside Welshpool. It is memorable for its superb gardens (terraced in the 18th century), its architectural diversity through centuries of changes, and its lavish state apartments.
    Montgomery▶ is more English than Welsh in character: the tiny town center focuses on a gracious square with an 18th-century town hall and an assemblage of red-brick Elizabethan facades. The castle mound above town was the stronghold of Roger de Montgomery, who in the 13th century launched assaults on the Welsh.

THE WELSHPOOL AND LLANFAIR LIGHT RAILWAY
The privately operated steam train operates along 8 miles of track between Welshpool and Llanfair Caereinion. Its chief distinguishing features are the narrow 30-inch gauge, and the antique wooden cars from the Zillertal in Austria and 1961 carriages from Sierra Leone.

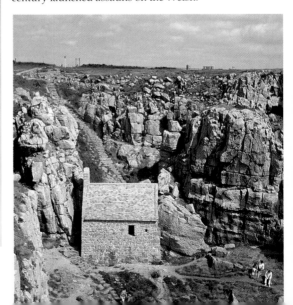

Tiny St. Govan's Chapel, tucked into the cliffs, can be reached on foot by taking the coastal path from Bosherston Lily Ponds

▶▶▶ Snowdonia National Park   *151D3*
(tel: 01690 710426)

Snowdonia is unsurpassed among the national parks of England and Wales for the wild drama of its scenery. Ideal for walking, rock-climbing, and horseback riding, it has a fair offering of scenic drives, although these tend to be confined to valley routes and are limited in scope.

The main mountain group is quite compact, centered on Snowdon, the highest point in England and Wales. Perhaps the hallmark of Snowdonia is the individuality of each of the main summits: each has its distinctive shape, and visitors soon find their personal favorites. Snowdonia's coast is disappointing, ribboned as it is by main roads and with no cliffs to speak of. Sightseeing interest, on the other hand, is particularly rich, with a host of nostalgic railroads, old mines, and castles built by Edward I in the 13th century to control the Welsh.

THE MAIN CENTERS In northern Snowdonia **Betws-y-coed** (pronounced Bettus-ee coe-ed) is a touristy village of Victorian hotels and craft shops. It has grand scenery on its doorstep and walks along the Llugwy River and the Swallow Falls, and a series of attractive reservoirs close by to the west; the big mountains keep hidden, however. Also central and with a touch more charm, the Victorian mountain resort village of **Beddgelert▶** lies close to the Aberglaslyn Gorge, Moel Hebog, and Snowdon. A much-publicized but probably bogus attraction here is Gelert's Grave, Gelert being the noble 13th-century Prince Llywelyn's dog. A tour can be taken around **Sygun Copper Mine▶▶**, which has formations of stalactites and stalagmites. Bala gets busy in high season; Wales' largest lake adjoins it, but the scenery is not quite so stupendous.

Of the resorts on the north coast **Llandudno▶** is by far the most attractive. It's one of Britain's best-preserved Victorian coastal towns, with its elegant curving bay, its pier, Punch and Judy shows on the sands, and a mountain tram up to Great Ormes Head. **Conwy▶▶▶**, also on the coast but a historic walled town, is the most rewarding town for casual wandering, with a splendid castle (Cadw), an elegant suspension bridge designed by Thomas Telford (N.T.), and a house that claims to be Britain's smallest. **Caernarfon▶▶▶**, too, boasts a great castle and is a place everyone should try to visit (although for some it may be too far out to serve as a base). **Harlech▶▶** straddles a slope above marshland, one of the few portions of this coast not to be followed by a main road; good beaches lie to the south. The castle is the spectacular attraction.

Mountains of slate scraps surround **Blaenau Ffestiniog**, at the heart of the Snowdonia slate industry. It is not pretty but has curiosity value and is in the center; it is establishing itself as a tourist town now that the **Llechwedd Slate Caverns▶▶** have been opened to the public . At **Llanberis** is the **Welsh Slate Museum▶** and a branch of the National Museum of Wales, **Dinorwic Discovery▶** which offers trips to the "Electric Mountain," underground hydroelectric storage station. There are also tours at the active Ffestiniog Power Station near Blaenau Ffestiniog.

Dolgellau▶, the only town inside the national park, is a place of gray-stone houses and narrow streets; life revolves around its marketplace. It makes a good base for

167

GREAT LITTLE TRAINS OF SNOWDONIA
The **Snowdon Mountain Railway** climbs 3,280 ft. from Llanberis to the summit. Many people walk back down. **Ffestiniog Railway**, built for the slate industry and now one of the most scenic of all Britain's private railroads, runs from Porthmadog to Blaenau Ffestiniog, while the **Talyllyn Railway** runs inland from Tywyn to Nant Gwernol. **Bala Lake** and **Llanberis Lake** railroads run alongside the lakes from which they take their names. The shorter **Welsh Highland Railway** starts from Porthmadog.

CADW MEMBERSHIP
Most of the great castles of Wales—including Conwy, Caernarfon, Harlech, Beaumaris, and Dolbadarn—and other ancient monuments are in the care of Cadw, the Welsh Historic Monuments Commission. Cadw (tel: 01222 500200) offers 3-day, weekly, and annual passes for its properties.

MOUNTAIN SAFETY
Beware! The Snowdon Mountains may not compete in height with the Alps or the Rockies, but they are full of dangers and have claimed many lives. Be sure to be appropriately dressed and equipped; check the weather forecast, take a good map, compass, and provisions, and tackle only those walks well within your abilities. Leave a note with your hotel of where you are going and when you intend to return.

Classic postglacial scenery: the towering form of Y Garn, seen across Llyn (Lake) Ogwen

touring southern Snowdonia, and it has some excellent easier walks on its doorstep, including Cregennan Lakes at the foot of Cader Idris, the old railroad track along the magnificent Mawddach Estuary, and the Precipice Walk (hair-raising for those with young children) above the Mawddach Gorge. Farther west, near the coastal resort of Barmouth, the railroad bridge across the Mawddach includes a footpath that makes a highly memorable walk in its own right.

THE MAJOR PEAKS The king of them all, **Snowdon** (Yr Wddfa in Welsh) rises high and majestic to 3,560 feet, five ridges (known collectively as Eryri, "abode of eagles") radiating from its central pyramid. Not surprisingly, it is the most popular mountain ascent, not just because it is the highest but also because of the views both on the way up and from the top. Paths approach from all directions, or you can cheat and use the Snowdon Mountain Railway (see page 167); the route from Llanberis, parallel to the railroad, is the easiest but least interesting path, while the Horseshoe Route (along knife-edge ridges) is the most enthralling and demanding, definitely not for the inexperienced. The first half of the Miners' Track from Pen y Pass (see page 170) takes you into the wilds, rising past lakes and abandoned copper mines to a splendid corrie beneath the summit and main ascent—this initial stage provides an unchallenging way of sampling a great mountain route.

Almost as high as Snowdon and just as spectacular are **Glyder Fawr** (3,277 feet) and **Glyder Fach** (3,261 feet), two peaks on a great ridge with rock pinnacles and precipitous drops; the **Carneddau group** and (lower but with good views) **Moel Siabod** (2,861 feet). The southern giant is **Cader Idris** (2,930 feet), a complex sprawling mass with some reassuringly gentle slopes but huge panoramas.

Caernarfon Castle, where the monarch invests the eldest royal son with the title of Prince of Wales

HOUSES, CASTLES, AND GARDENS Penrhyn Castle►► (N.T.) is an imposing mock-Norman structure built by slate magnate Lord Penrhyn in the mid-19th century; architect Thomas Hopper gave it battlements and turrets, and a grandiose interior which epitomizes high living of the period. Genuine castles abound in Snowdonia. Most famous of all is **Caernarfon Castle►►►** (Cadw), begun in 1283 after Edward I's conquest of Wales. It was the setting in 1969 for the investiture of the Prince of Wales; his investiture robes are on show here, together with a display of the dynasty of the Welsh princes. **Harlech Castle►►** (Cadw), also founded in 1283, has a fine site above the coast; although seemingly impregnable it was taken by Owain Glyndwr in 1404. **Conwy Castle►►►** (Cadw), another of Edward I's foundations, is sited in the town wall; it has 21 semicircular towers and overlooks a castellated suspension bridge, one of some 1,200 bridges designed by Thomas Telford between 1792 and his death in 1834. Less substantial, but set among the hills, are the castles of **Dolwyddelan►** (Cadw, near Blaenau Ffestiniog) and **Castell y Bere►** (Cadw, near Abergynolwyn).

Bodnant Gardens►► (N.T.), near Llanrwst, rates among Britain's finest horticultural creations. Try to visit **Portmeirion►►**, an Italianate *trompe l'oeil* fantasy village created in the 20th century by Clough Williams-Ellis to show that a scenic site could be developed and retain its beauty. It has often been used as a film set; the cult T.V. series *The Prisoner* was made here.

The Canal Terrace, Bodnant Gardens

SNOWDONIA NATIONAL PARK

Snowdonia National Park

A circuit of the grandest uplands in Wales (approx. 65 miles).

Start at **Betws-y-coed** and take the A5 past the entrance to the spectacular **Swallow Falls▶** to Capel Curig. Continue past Llyn (lake) Ogwen; from the parking lot at its far end, a short path leads to **Llyn Idwal▶▶**, beneath the vast crags of the Devil's Kitchen (see Walks, page 158). Beyond the mining town of **Bethesda** take the B4409, then the A4086 past **Llanberis**, base station for the **Snowdon Mountain Railway▶**. At the top of the **Llanberis Pass**, the Miners' Track and Pyg Track leave for an exciting ascent of **Snowdon**. Continue on the A498 past **Beddgelert▶** and along the **Pass of Aberglaslyn**. Take the B4410 and A496 to **Blaenau Ffestiniog**, passing **Ffestiniog Power Station▶**, and **Llechwedd Slate Caverns▶▶**. **Dolwyddelan Castle▶**, farther up the valley (A470), is supposedly the birthplace of Prince Llywelyn the Great.

SONS OF MONMOUTH
Henry V was born in Monmouth Castle, of which nothing now remains, in 1387. Before the Battle of Agincourt he gained the nickname Harry of Monmouth. The central plaza is named Agincourt Square in his honor. Charles Rolls was a pioneer of early aviation, engineering, and motoring who was a partner in Rolls-Royce. In 1910 he became the first Briton to die in a flying accident. His statue outside the town hall holds aloft a model airplane, and the town museum has a section devoted to his life.

▶▶ **Wye Valley**   151B4
(tel: 01600 713899)
The River Wye defines the English/Welsh border for its glorious finale as it enters a sandstone gorge whose slopes are cloaked with woodlands that display breathtaking colors in the fall. Once the gorge was a hive of industrial activity, the trees supplying charcoal for iron-smelting; brass was invented here in 1568. The valley established a name for itself during the late 18th-century Romantic movement, whose poets sought a deeper appreciation of the beauties of nature. **Ross-on-Wye**, though not in the gorge proper, has a mock-Gothic town wall built in the 1830s at the time of this "picturesque discovery." Its arcaded market house is two centuries older. **Symonds Yat▶**, a rock reached by a stairway, overlooks a bend of the Wye; paths lead steeply down to the river, which is crossed by chain ferry (see Walks on page 158). **Goodrich Castle▶** (E.H.) is an impressive 12th-century sandstone bulk, intact until a Parliamentary siege in the Civil War.

The Monnow flows into the Wye at **Monmouth▶**, the Monnow spanned by a medieval bridge with a fortified gateway. The **Nelson Museum** is a collection devoted to Nelson, including his letters and sword. Above the town, a rustic folly commemorating admirals of the Napoleonic wars caps **Kymin Hill▶**, a good place for views. Turner painted and Wordsworth revered the ruins of **Tintern Abbey▶▶** (Cadw), an ancient Cistercian foundation set on the valley floor. It is roofless, but standing to its original height, and with exquisite tracery in its east window.

Chepstow has a formidable Norman **castle▶▶** (Cadw) with keep and mighty outer wall. The main street rises up to a gateway in the Port Walls, the town wall. Above the east bank, **Wintour's Leap** is a quarried cliff face by the road with a dizzy drop to the river, while the **Wynd Cliff▶**, on the west bank, offers a wider view.

One of the world's first iron bridges—the Regency Bridge over the Wye, at Chepstow

171

NORTHUMBERLAND
Kielder Water
Northumberland National Park
Hadrian's Wall

Newbiggin-by-the-Sea
Morpeth
Cramlington
Blyth
Whitley Bay
Ponteland
Newcastle upon Tyne
Gateshead
Sunderland
Washington
Seaham
Easington
Peterlee
Hartlepool

Dumfries
Gretna Green
Glencaple
Caerlaverock Castle
Nith Estuary
Bowness-on-Solway
Silloth
Carlisle
Wetheral
Low Crosby
Haltwhistle
Hexham
Corbridge
Stanley
Consett
Castleside
Lanchester
Chester-le-Street
Durham
Castleside

A74(M)
Wigton
Thursby
Caldbeck
Alston
Melmerby
Wearhead
Stanhope
Crook
Bishop Auckland
Spennymoor
Sedgefield
Newton Aycliffe
Middlesbrough
Darlington
Stockton-on-Tees
Stokesley

CUMBRIA
Aspatria
Bothel
931m Skiddaw
Greystoke
M6 Penrith
893m Cross Fell
DURHAM
Wear
Middleton-in-Teesdale
Appleby-in-Westmorland
Barnard Castle
Bowes
Reeth
Scotch Corner
Richmond
Catterick
Northallerton
Thirsk

Maryport
Cockermouth
Keswick
Workington
Whitehaven
Cleator Moor
Egremont
Buttermere
Patterdale
Pooley Bridge
Shap
Grange
Settle Carlisle Railway
Kirkby Stephen
Brough
Leyburn
Bedale

Lake District National Park
978m Scafell Pike
Grasmere
Ambleside
Windermere
Gosforth
Hawkshead
Muncaster Mill
Coniston
Ravenglass
Broughton-in-Furness
Bootle
Newby Bridge
Kendal
Sedbergh
Dent
Tebay
Hawes
Thwaite
Aysgarth
Masham
NORTH YORKSHIRE

Millom
Ulverston
Levens Hall
Kirkby Lonsdale
Arnside
Yorkshire Dales National Park
693m Pen-y-Ghent
Buckden
Horse Head
2414 Great Whernside
Ripon
Easingwold
Boroughbridge

Barrow-in-Furness
Dalton-in-Furness
Grange-over-Sands
Carnforth
Ingleton
Settle
Grassington
Knaresborough

Isle of Walney
Morecambe
Heysham
Lancaster
Malham
Bolton Abbey
Blubberhouses
Harrogate
York

Irish Sea
Bowland Forest
Slaidburn
Gisburn
Hellifield
Skipton
Wharfe
Pannal
Wetherby

Fleetwood
Cleveleys
Thornton
Longridge
Barnoldswick
Otley
Keighley
Bingley
Harewood House
A1(M)

Blackpool
Kirkham
M55
LANCASHIRE
Ribble
Clitheroe
Whalley
Colne
Nelson
Shipley
Bradford
LEEDS

Lytham St Anne's
Preston
Leyland
M65
Accrington
Burnley
Halifax
Garforth
WEST YORKSHIRE
M62

Southport
Eccleston
M6
Chorley
Blackburn
Darwen
Todmorden
Rochdale
Brighouse
Huddersfield
Dewsbury
Wakefield
Pontefract
Hemsworth

Formby
Ormskirk
M61
Wigan
Bolton
Bury
M66
M62
Middleton
Oldham
Holmfirth
Penistone
Barnsley
A1(M)

Crosby
Skelmersdale
Kirkby
St Helens
Salford
MANCHESTER
Stretford
Chapeltown
PEAK
Holmfirth
Doncaster

Bootle
LIVERPOOL
Birkenhead
Port Sunlight
M57
Warrington
Sale
Stockport
Cheadle
Glossop
Rotherham
SHEFFIELD
Maltby
Worksop

Prestatyn
Rhyl
Ellesmere Port
Widnes
Runcorn
Altrincham
Tatton Park
Quarry Bank Mill
Lyme Park
DERBYSHIRE
Buxton
Tideswell
Dronfield
Chesterfield
Warsop

St Asaph
Denbigh
Flint
M56
Helsby
Middlewich
Holmes Chapel
Bakewell
Chatsworth
Haddon Hall
Hardwick Hall
M1

FLINTSHIRE
555m Moel Famau
Chester
Winsford
Little Moreton Hall
Congleton
Biddulph
Arbor Low
Youlgreave
Tissington
Matlock
Matlock Bath
Cromford
Sutton in Ashfield

DENBIGHSHIRE
Ruthin
Cerrigydrudion
Gresford
Crewe
Nantwich
Kidsgrove
Dove Dale
Alton Towers

Horseshoe Pass
Ruabon
Erddig
WREXHAM
Wrexham
Newcastle-under-Lyme
STOKE-ON-TRENT
Cheadle
Eleanor
Hucknall
NOTTINGHAM

Llangollen
Plas Newydd
Chirk
Whitchurch
Audlem
Woore
DERBY

Bala
Ellesmere
Wem
Market Drayton
Hodnet
STAFFORDSHIRE
Stone
Uttoxeter
Tutbury
Castle Donington
Long Eaton

ISLE OF MAN
Point of Ayre
Andreas
Ramsey
Nessdiffe
Newport
Shawbury
Gnosall
Stafford
Burton upon Trent
Loughborough

Ballaugh
Kirk Michael
Laxey
621m Snaefell
Shrewsbury
Rugeley
Cannock
Lichfield
Ashby-de-la-Zouch
Coalville
Ostock

Peel
St John's
Tynwald Hill
Douglas
Telford
M54
M6
M42
Tamworth
LEICESTER

Port Erin
Castletown
Calf of Man
Broseley
Ironbridge Gorge
WOLVERHAMPTON
Walsall
West Bromwich
M69
Hinckley
Nuneaton

Bridgnorth
Dudley
BIRMINGHAM
M6
SHROPSHIRE

NORTHWEST ENGLAND This strip covers the region from the industrial northern Midlands to the Scottish border. The most hallowed feature is doubtless the **Lake District**, within the northerly county of Cumbria.

LAKE DISTRICT DELIGHTS Here the lakes, high fells (mountains), pastures, and woodlands offer constantly changing vistas of peerless scenic beauty. It is all at a perfect scale for exploration on foot, as equally suited for those wanting a gentle saunter with the mountains as a backdrop as for aspiring rock-climbers. Another option available is to take a boat trip on the lake. Roads and parking lots get annoyingly busy in peak periods, but out of season driving is a delight. Public transportation is also feasible (Ambleside and Keswick would make good bases), though it restricts what can be visited. The Lake District scores highly for quantity and quality of accommodations, for the range of sights suitable for those all-too-frequent rainy days, and for the scope of other outdoor activities, which include sailing, mountain biking, horseback riding, and angling (swimming in the lakes is discouraged because of undercurrents). As a general rule, the western Lake District has more in the way of spectacle and wildness, while the east is milder, more crowded, and has more indoor sights.

THE REST OF CUMBRIA Outside the Lake District, the rest of Cumbria offers a long and not especially beautiful coastline, but an interesting one: along it are the early industrial town of Whitehaven, well worth a visit; St. Bees Head (ideal for birdwatching); and the free visitor center at Sellafield nuclear reprocessing plant, set up to woo support for the nuclear industry. Northern Cumbria is fairly flat, but it has nice views across the Solway Firth to southern Scotland and the historic city of Carlisle. Southern Cumbria is fringed by the great expanse of Morecambe Bay, an important site for wading birds and the setting for Britain's fastest incoming tides; tourist offices have details of guided walks over the bay (follow routes precisely to avoid the quicksands).

LANCASHIRE, MERSEYSIDE, AND GREATER MANCHESTER The more built-up parts of Morecambe Bay lie within **Lancashire**—Blackpool, Morecambe, and Southport were developed as resorts to serve the cotton-mill towns that

Below (left): Dove Dale, the best-known limestone valley in the Peak District, deserves time to be savored in full

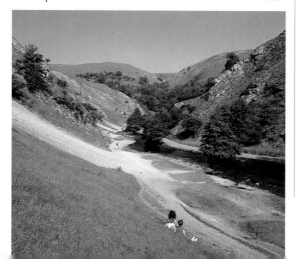

RECOMMENDED HISTORIC TOWNS AND CITIES
Cheshire: Chester.
Derbyshire: Buxton.
Cumbria: Carlisle, Cockermouth, Kendal, Kirkby Lonsdale, Whitehaven.
SCENERY
Lake District, Peak District, Isle of Man, Forest of Bowland, Morecambe Bay (north side).
TRAIN RIDES
Settle to Carlisle; Arnside to Ulverston; Barrow-in-Furness to Whitehaven; Ravenglass to Boot (narrow gauge).

174

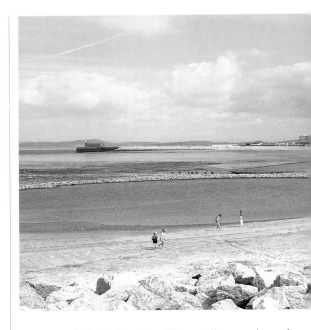

View across Morecambe Bay

▶▶▶ **REGION HIGHLIGHTS**

Chester *page 177*
The Lake District *page 178–181*
Little Moreton Hall *pages 189*
Liverpool *page 182*
Peak National Park *page 186–187*
Quarry Bank Mill *pages 189*
Stoke-on-Trent Potteries *page 189*

sprang up in the 19th century. Those mill towns changed the face of the county and heralded a major phase in the industrialization of Great Britain. The mills have closed or changed to other uses, but these urban landscapes, immortalized by the paintings of L.S. Lowry (see panel, page 183), still exist, the straight lines of millworkers' row houses being their dominant feature: Burnley and Accrington are examples. Manchester and Liverpool were the great cities created by this expansion; today Manchester is more prosperous, but Liverpool wins on museums and atmosphere. The Forest of Bowland in northern Lancashire is, despite its name, a tract of high, open country; access is limited but there are exhilarating views.

CHESHIRE, DERBYSHIRE, AND STAFFORDSHIRE
Cheshire extends from the Welsh border to the brink of the Peak National Park; between lies a fertile plain, pockmarked by tiny lakes and ponds called meres. Black and white half-timbering and red brick are predominant building materials, seen to best advantage in Chester, remarkable for its intact city walls. Cheshire, Staffordshire, Derbyshire and South Yorkshire share the **Peak District**, a very accessible and popular national park; although it cannot match the Lake District for scenery, it has limestone dales, austere gritstone moors, caverns, the contrasting houses of Chatsworth and Haddon Hall, and some charming villages, many of which indulge in the ancient annual custom of "well dressing". Other houses in **Derbyshire** include Calke Abbey and Hardwick Hall. Although undistinguished visually, Derby has a number of good museums; Derby porcelain is on display at the Derby Museum and at Royal Crown Derby, and an 18th-century silk mill houses the Industrial Museum. Stoke-on-Trent (**Staffordshire**) is the china-making capital.

Walks

Arnside Knott, Cumbria *172D2*

Parking lot by seafront at Arnside.
The wooded limestone hill is laced
with paths to its summit, where a view
opens out over the southern Lake
District and Morecambe Bay, one of
Europe's most important sites for
waterbirds of the wader family. The
quickest way up is southward through
the village, on residential roads that
give way to paths. (1 hour)

Buttermere, Lake *172E1*
District National Park, Cumbria

Parking lot at Buttermere village.
A well-traveled path leads to
Buttermere. The path which runs
around the lake is straightforward and
level, but is graced with a fine mountain backdrop. The path weaves out of
forest, through a section of tunnel,
and along the water's edge (1½
hours). Optional add-ons include
the ascent of Haystacks, the jagged,
dark-topped fell to the south.

Grasmere and *172D1*
Rydal Water, Lake District
National Park, Cumbria

Parking lots at Grasmere village. Seek
out the path along the south side of
these two lakes: walk past Grasmere
Church on your right, take the left
fork of the road to reach the lakeside
path, which leaves the road near a
boathouse. After a short wooded
section, climb up to the level path
along Loughrigg Terrace on your right
for grandstand views of Wordsworth's
valley. Either continue on around
Rydal Water or head back by dropping
through woods, over a bridge and the
A591 to take a minor road to
Wordsworth's Dove Cottage at
the edge of Grasmere village.
(1½ hours)

Monsal Dale and *172B3*
Chee Dale, Peak
National Park, Derbyshire

*Parking lots at Miller's Dale (old sta-
tion).* Turn left along the railroad track

(Monsal Trail) to enter Miller's Dale;
the trail swings away from the train
track as it passes through a tunnel.
You pass the Wye's old textile mills,
rejoin the train tracks and cross
Monsal viaduct (2½ hours). In the
other direction from the parking lot,
the trail soon leaves the railroad track
for an exciting stepping-stone route
along the Wye as it enters a gorge
beneath Chee Tor, a popular haunt of
rock climbers. (2 hours)

Ullswater, Lake District *172D1*
National Park, Cumbria

Parking lot at Glenridding. Begin this
walk by taking the lake steamer from
Glenridding across to Howtown, and
then follow the well-traveled lakeside
path back (allow approximately
4 hours); it undulates delightfully and
ducks in and out of woods with sudden vistas. An optional add-on is to
climb Hallin Fell, close by Howtown,
by a path up its southern side.

175

*A Lake District scene between Rydal
Water and Grasmere*

Blackpool: roller-coaster by night

THE ISLE OF MAN
Ruled by Queen Elizabeth II but not part of the U.K. (it has its own parliament), the Isle of Man has a certain curiosity value. Its residents are called Manx, as is its almost extinct Celtic language. Manx cats are naturally tailless. Located in the Irish Sea, the island does not enjoy the greatest climate and its resorts are somewhat faded. Fish-and-chips is the rule, *haute cuisine* the exception. Yet to some the isle's charms are irresistible: its coastline, particularly in the south around the fishing port of Peel and the folk museum village of Port Erin, is of high, unspoiled cliffs, while inland the hills rise dramatically. A splendid legacy of historic railroads has been preserved, and the T. T. Races, an annual motorcycle event since 1907, draws large crowds. Reach the island by ferry from Liverpool, Heysham, or Fleetwood, or by air.

The Citadel, a prominent landmark at the center of Carlisle

Blackpool   172C1
(tel: 01253 478222)

In Victorian times, Blackpool was the traditional day-out treat for millworkers in the Lancashire cotton towns; it is still the liveliest coastal resort in the North, offering fairground fun, nightlife, pleasure gardens, and views of Morecambe Bay and the Lakeland fells from Blackpool Tower. Trams travel up the seafront to Fleetwood, giving the best view of the Illuminations (September to November). The beach has had a bad record for pollution.

► Carlisle   172E1
(tel: 01228 512444)

Cumbria's largest town has recently spruced itself up as a regional shopping center. This does not rank among the great cathedral cities, but there is enough here for an absorbing half-day in the compact historic center.

For centuries, Carlisle was plagued by border skirmishes, and the **castle►►**(E.H.), dating from 1092, was much attacked and rebuilt (the view from its walls is stomach-churning). The keep is 12th-century; inside, the story of the Border Regiment is told with uniforms and weapons. Don't miss the graffiti carved by captives in the prison.

The castle is to be linked to the old city by a foot tunnel and bridge in 2000, in a scheme extending **Tullie House►►**, an outstanding city museum. Also in the center are some good Georgian and earlier streets, and the medieval **cathedral►**, one of Britain's smallest, notable above all for its east window with its 14th-century glass. Also worth a brief look is the **Guildhall**, a striking timber-framed survival dating back to 1407.

The scenic **Settle–Carlisle line►►**, part of the nation's railroad network, was saved in recent years by a volunteer-led campaign. From Settle, in the Yorkshire Dales, the route crosses the high Pennines in spectacular fashion, over the Ribblehead Viaduct in the shadow of Whernside and along the Eden Valley. Special steam trains sometimes run on the route. By far the most dramatic landscape is between Settle and Appleby-in-Westmorland, which has a fine castle.

▶▶▶ Chester   172B1
(tel: 01244 402111)

Founded as the Roman city of Deva, Chester was a major port until the River Dee silted up in medieval times. Its fortunes then slumped until a revival in the 18th century. Today, it has plenty to show for these three periods.

Foremost is the **city wall▶▶▶**, one of the finest in the country, which provides a fascinating 2-mile walk, raised above street level for much of the way. A number of its gateways are still in place and Roman masonry can be seen, although much of the wall is medieval. A superb set of Roman tombstones are exhibited at the **Grosvenor Museum▶** (*Admission free*). By **Newgate**, on the east side, part of the **Roman amphitheater** (Britain's largest) can be seen near a park , but more evocative is the **Dewa Roman Experience▶▶**, where Roman streets are reconstructed with sounds and smells, and there is a hands-on section and artifacts found in the city.

Of medieval Chester, the most famous feature is **The Rows**, which has an upper tier of shops with its own walkway above street level. Nobody quite knows why it developed this way, but today it is a thriving shopping area. The central streets harbor a pleasing mix of half-timbered Tudor, red-brick Georgian, and exuberantly elaborate 19th-century fake black-and-white buildings. Chester's Victoriana also includes a Gothic-style **town hall**, where the Council Chamber and Assembly Rooms are open to the public, on Northgate Street. The red sandstone **cathedral▶▶** was restored in the 19th century, but its superbly carved 14th-century choir stalls are unaltered. Many of the abbey buildings survived the Reformation in the 16th century, including the chapter house and cloisters.

Chester Zoo▶▶ is 3 miles north up the A41. Animals roam in enclosures that simulate natural environments.

177

A WALK ALONG CHESTER'S WALLS: PART 1
From Grosvenor Bridge (the largest single span in the world when erected in 1832), take a counterclockwise tour of the walls, crossing Bridgegate with its pleasant boating scene a little east (boat rentals available). The walls now turn north, past Newgate and the Roman amphitheater, over Eastgate with its ornamental clock of 1897.

A WALK ALONG CHESTER'S WALLS: PART 2
Skirt the cathedral precincts (Abbey Square); the northeast tower is known as the King Charles Tower since that king watched from here the defeat of his army by the Parliamentarians on Rowton Heath in 1645. By Northgate the drop on the canal side plummets spectacularly; on the south side is the Bluecoat Hospital (1717) and the sideless Bridge of Sighs, which condemned felons had to cross on their way to prison. From the Water Tower (1322) are views of the Welsh hills. The west side of the walls (where you must follow the road) has less of interest.

View towards Chester Cross from the city's east gate

The Lake District National Park—Lakeland, the English Lakes, or just the Lakes, call it what you will—is a microcosm of breathtaking variety and scenic perfection. Its character wavers between windswept mountainous upland and dry-stone-walled, lowland pastures. It is outstanding for outdoor pursuits, particularly walking, climbing, and sailing, but the climate can be fickle: benign-looking summer days have a habit of clouding over suddenly. Fortunately the area has plenty of indoor attractions, especially for those on a literary pilgrimage.

LITERARY LAKELAND
Wordsworth was born in Cockermouth in 1770, and a happy childhood there was to influence his poetry in later life. His favorite home was Dove Cottage, in Grasmere, where he lived from 1799 to 1808. He loved the place deeply and wrote about the area; aptly, he is buried in Grasmere churchyard.

The Wordsworths were the center of a group of friends, among them poet Samuel Taylor Coleridge. Tennyson reputedly wrote *Idylls of the King* at Mirehouse, near Keswick; later, poet Matthew Arnold and critic John Ruskin both lived here.

Beatrix Potter wrote and illustrated her children's stories at Hill Top in Near Sawrey. Arthur Ransome set his *Swallows and Amazons* in the Lakes.

LAKELAND GEOGRAPHY
The district is formed out of a huge volcanic dome, pushed out from within the earth, subsequently overlain with rocks and sculpted by glaciers into valleys and corries. The Skiddaw Slates, found in northwest Lakeland, make up green slopes, while the volcanic Borrowdale rocks include rugged fells. Limestone predominates in the eastern tracts.

THE NORTH AND WEST Keswick▶, the major center for the northern lakes, is a gray-slate Victorian town, full of walkers, tourists, bed-and-breakfast signs, and outdoor sports shops. Here are traditional **Keswick Museum** (with its "piano" of Cumberland slates), a unique pencil museum and the Cars of the Stars collection. Just east is the prehistoric **Castlerigg Stone Circle▶**. **Derwent Water▶▶▶** is breathtakingly beautiful; a boat service circuits the lake.

Borrowdale appealed to early discoverers of the "picturesque"; Castle Crag is a good vantage point. The main road heading over **Honister Pass** skirts **Buttermere▶▶▶**, magnificently located and looking like a miniature Scottish loch. **Cockermouth▶**, outside the park, is a likeable market town of colorwashed row houses and odd corners.

North of Keswick, the fells flatten and the crowds disappear, but the moors have a quiet beauty of their own. **Hesket Newmarket**, with its green and its old market cross, is the prettiest village hereabouts. Southeast of Keswick, **Thirlmere▶**, a lake enlarged into a reservoir, is the most popular starting point for walks up Helvellyn (3,117 feet). The lake of **Ullswater▶▶▶** twists its way south from Pooley Bridge, the scenery getting better all the time; a steamer plies the length of the lake. By the A592, **Aira Force▶▶** is a popular waterfall, tumbling into a shady chasm at the side of Gowbarrow Park, the hill where Wordsworth saw that host of golden daffodils. East of Ullswater, **Askham▶** is a trim village of stone cottages.

The Lake District's western tracts are less accessible and are a great place to get away from it all. **Wast Water▶▶▶** is one of the great sights, looking to the heights of Great Gable, and Scafell Pike is the highest peak in England at 3,207 feet. **Eskdale▶** is mellow and broad; the narrow-gauge Ravenglass and Eskdale Railway runs along the valley to the tiny village of Boot with its restored grain mill. At the dale's east end, the **Hardknott Pass▶▶▶** is the great scenic drive of Lakeland, rather like taking your car for a fell walk; the Isle of Man may be visible from the remains of a Roman fort at the top. Drivers can continue along **Wrynose Pass** or into the **Duddon Valley (Dunnerdale)**.

THE SOUTH AND EAST Windermere, England's longest lake, has wooded shores sprinkled with villas built by 19th-century industrialists; steamers ply the length of the lake, and from Lakeside at the southern end (near the Aquarium of the Lakes) a steam train runs to Haverthwaite. **Bowness-on-Solway** is a tourist trap, clogged with traffic in summer; **Windermere town**, away from the lake, is railroad-age suburbia. **Ambleside**, at the lake's northern end, is more attractive, particularly up the hill. The **Armitt Library and Museum** includes natural history watercolors by Beatrix Potter and Lakeland photos by Herbert Bell. On Windermere's shores are a number of gardens (**Holehird▶**, **Stagshaw▶**, and **Graythwaite▶**), the **Brockhole National Park Visitor Centre▶** and the **Windermere Steamboat Museum▶**.

West of Windermere, the landscape rolls gently, thickly cloaked in trees; in **Grizedale Forest** woodland paths are enhanced by modern sculptures. **Stott Park Bobbin Mill▶**(E.H.) demonstrates the process of bobbin making. Visit the pretty village of **Hawkshead▶ ▶** out of season—or wait in line for the parking lot and join the crowds in its quaint little streets; it has craft shops, tearooms, a Beatrix Potter gallery, and Wordsworth's former school. Just out of the village, **Tarn Hows▶** is a pretty, if too-visited, pair of tarns artificially merged into one as a landscape feature. Above the village of Coniston, beneath the Old Man of Coniston, are spectacular relics of its bygone copper-mining industry. Glide silently over **Coniston Water** on the National Trust's antique steam yacht, *Gondola*▶ ▶.

North of Ambleside, the A591 enters more mountainous terrain; **Grasmere▶ ▶** and its surroundings are immortalized by the works of Wordsworth (see panel, page 178). Westward loom the craggy **Langdale Pikes**.

Farther south, **Cartmel▶ ▶** is a handsome village, less overrun than Hawkshead, with a fine priory church and a pretty square. **Kendal▶** (just outside the national park) deserves special mention for its Art Gallery and **Museum of Lakeland Life and Industry▶ ▶**.

Far left: the Windermere Steamboat Museum

Bliss was it in that dawn
  to be alive,
But to be young was   -
  very heaven.
—*The Prelude*, William Wordsworth (1770–1850).

KNOW YOUR LAKELAND TERMS
Small lakes are called *tarns*, mountains are always *fells* (from the Nordic *fjaell*), streams are known as *becks*, spotted black-faced sheep are *Herdwicks*, white-faced ones are *Swaledales*, loose stones created by freeze-thaw weathering are termed scree. *Force* means waterfall. Bassenthwaite Lake is the only lake in Lakeland termed as such: all the others are *meres* or *waters*. "Lake Windermere" is a useful term to avoid confusion with the town of Windermere, but Lake District purists will shudder if they hear you say it!

179

Grasmere, beloved of William Wordsworth

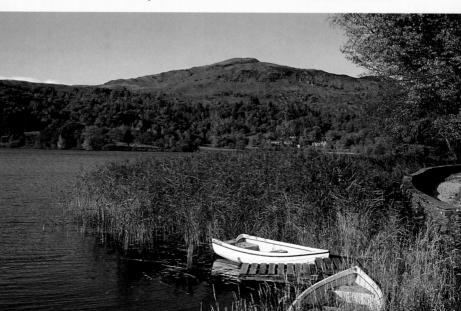

Drive

The Lakes

The best of the Lakes (approx. 80 miles), taking in Wordsworth's Grasmere, spectacular high passes, and the less-visited western areas.

From **Keswick** (tel: 017687 72645) the route heads south along the A591 past **Thirlmere►**, beneath the shadow of Helvellyn, and past the Wordsworths' former houses, Dove Cottage at **Grasmere►►** and Rydal Mount, **Rydal**. Turning west at the resort town of **Ambleside**, you soon enter **Langdale**, passing beneath the impressive forms of Langdale Fells, whose slopes were once home to a neolithic axe factory. A minor road loops around the end of the dale, above Blea Tarn, to turn right onto the **Wrynose Pass**. This leads to the magnificent **Hardknott Pass►►►**, passing the substantial remains of a Roman fort on the right after the summit; drop into **Eskdale**, with glimpses of its narrow-gauge railroad. Fork right to **Santon Bridge** (from where you can detour to majestic **Wast Water►►►**) and continue to **Gosforth**, with its renowned **Celtic cross►** in the churchyard. Take the A595 to **Calder Bridge**, then fork right to **Ennerdale Bridge** via a high-level road with views of the coast and **Sellafield nuclear reprocessing plant** (its visitor center is now a major draw). Beyond **Lamplugh** bear right and right again on minor roads to **Loweswater** and the B5289, where you turn right for a superb finale past **Buttermere►►►**, up the **Honister Pass**, along Borrowdale and beside **Derwent Water►►►**.

❏ Houses open to the public:
Brantwood, east side of Coniston Water: home of critic/artist John Ruskin.
Dalemain, near Penrith: Norman pele tower, Elizabethan rooms, priest's hole.
Dove Cottage, Grasmere: Wordsworth's home during his most productive period.
Hill Top (N.T.), near Sawrey: Beatrix Potter's farmhouse.
Holker Hall, near Cartmel: flamboyant Victorian house in Elizabethan style.
Levens Hall, near Levens: Elizabethan manor, gardens. Superb topiary.

THE LAKE DISTRICT

❏ Houses open to the public (continued):
Mirehouse, near Keswick: manuscripts of Tennyson, Wordsworth, etc.
Muncaster Castle, Eskdale: built around pele tower; bear menagerie, owls, etc.
Rydal Mount, Rydal: Wordsworth's last house; grander than Dove Cottage.
Sizergh Castle (N.T.), near Levens: Elizabethan paneling, carvings; gardens.
Townend (N.T.), Troutbeck: traditional Cumbrian farmhouse.
Wordsworth House (N.T.), Cockermouth: birthplace of William Wordsworth. ❏

In the rejuvenated docklands

MUSEUMS AND GALLERIES IN ALBERT DOCK
(The Eight Pass covers entrance fees for eight Merseyside museums and galleries for 12 months.)
Beatles Story The Fab Four, who immortalized Penny Lane and the Cavern Club, are the focus for this sight-and-sound experience of the music of the 1960s.
Merseyside Maritime Museum An ambitious museum tracing the history of the port: pier-master's house, pilotage building, boat hall, ship-building, and an display on European emigrants.

182

Museum of Liverpool Life Social history: culture, making a living, voting and much more.
Tate Gallery (*Admission free*) A branch of the great London establishment; modern art.

OTHER MUSEUMS AND GALLERIES IN LIVERPOOL
Conservation Centre, Whitechapel. Shows how all types of objects (including textiles, paint-ings and stuffed animals) are conserved.
Liverpool Football Club Visitors Centre, Anfield Road: trophies, memora-bilia, videos, and a look into the playing fields.
Liverpool Museum and Planetarium, William Brown Street: science and natural history.
Speke Hall (N.T.) Fine half-timbered house, dat-ing from 1490. Minibuses from here to **20 Forthlin Road** (N.T.; no cars allowed; booking essential on 0151-486 4006), the 1950s house where Paul McCartney lived and where the Beatles rehearsed.
Walker Art Gallery, William Brown Street: among Britain's finest provincial art galleries.

▶▶ **Liverpool**   *172B1*
(tel: 0151/709-3631)
Industrial activity on the River Mersey (Merseyside) has declined and the city's population is less than it was in the early 1900s; out of the center, run-down streetscapes are testimony to some of the worst urban problem areas in Britain. Yet despite the long economic slump, Liverpool has an strong sense of place, recalling its 19th-century hey-day as England's second greatest port. After the silting up of Chester's port, Liverpool took over; it flourished in the late 18th century in its trade with the West Indies.

The ocean-going liners of the 19th and early 20th cen-turies have gone—to get a hint of what it was like to arrive by sea, you should take the **ferry** to Birkenhead and back. The **Royal Liver Building** (1911) and **Cunard Building** (1917) stand sentinel by the Mersey waterfront. Architecture in the city displays a legacy of wealth and civic pride, at its best around **Dale Street**, **Water Street**, and **William Brown Street**, and around classical **St. George's Hall** (1854). Now revamped, **Albert Dock**▶▶ (1846) has shops, cafés, and a branch of the Tate Gallery in the rejuvenated warehouses.

At either end of the plum-brick Georgian townhouses of **Hope Street** stand the city's cathedrals. The **Anglican cathedral**▶▶, the largest of its denomination in the world, is a mightily proportioned Gothic edifice, built between 1906 and 1980 to the design of 21-year-old Giles Gilbert Scott. To make the most of its hillside setting, the conventional east–west orientation was not used. An ele-vator, followed by a flight of more than a hundred steps, will take you to the top of the tower for a superb view. By contrast, the **Metropolitan Roman Catholic Cathedral of Christ the King**▶ is a squat, tent-like affair set beneath a pinnacled lantern. This design by Frederick Gibberd was adopted after it became apparent that the original plan of Sir Edwin Lutyens was too costly. Of Lutyens's vast build-ing, the foundation stone (1933) and the crypt exist.

▶ Manchester

172B2

(tel: 0161/234-3157)

Manchester was the great commercial center for the Lancashire cotton industry. It has suffered some dreary post-war development, but there are several glimpses of 19th-century grandeur and enjoyable museums. The **town hall▶** is a Gothic creation with a marble interior by Alfred Waterhouse that fills one side of Albert Square. Just north of this are the classical **Royal Exchange**, with its lunar-module-style theater (live theater); **Barton Arcade**, a Victorian shopping arcade of iron and glass; and at the city's heart the cathedral (originally a medieval church).

Farther south around **Peter Street** imposing buildings include the Athenaeum (1837), the Theatre Royal (1845), and the Free Trade Hall (1856); just behind, in the former Central Station, is the modern G-Mex exhibition center. On Deansgate is the Gothic Revival **Rylands Library**, with its richly ornamental facade, while just off **St. John Street** is the finest Georgian street in the city. The **City Art Gallery▶** in Deansgate re-opens in 2001.

The revived area of Castlefield includes a reconstruction of a Roman fort that once stood here. The canal basin, where the Bridgewater and Rochdale canals meet, has atmosphere; the walk along the Rochdale Canal passes Victorian warehouses. The outstanding **Museum of Science and Industry▶▶** occupies the world's oldest passenger train station; displays include stationary steam

183

Trams have made a comeback on the city's streets

L.S. LOWRY (1887–1976) Manchester-born Laurence Stephen Lowry studied art in Manchester and Salford, and around 1916 developed an interest in painting the bleak landscapes of industrial Lancashire mill towns. The naïve style of his matchstick figures has been much copied, but at the time his choice of subject was quite apart from the mainstream; many of his works had touches of darkness and satire, and an element of the grotesque. A selection of his work is on display at the gallery in the Lowry, a waterfront complex in Salford (opening April 2000) which will be linked by footbridge to the new Imperial War Museum for the North (opening 2002).

engines and a hands-on science center. A major draw to the city is the **Granada Studios tour▶▶**, with exhibitions on TV and movies, including the set used in the TV soap opera *Coronation Street*. The **Gallery of English Costume▶▶** in Platt Hall exhibits 400 years of fashion.

Soccer fans should head for **Old Trafford** to see the Manchester United Museum and for the tour. The **Millennium Quarter** project (completion 2001) includes a cathedral center, a city park and the Urbis cultural center.

The largest cities in Britian were once its great manufacturing, engineering, and trading hubs. Their centers are packed with historical interest and cultural attractions. Yet with the demise of their original industries, many of their inner areas have become run-down, presenting policy challenges for governments since 1945. Many of the problems are now being tackled anew.

"The peculiar character of these streets, and the close resemblance each one bears to its neighbour, by no means tends to decrease the bewilderment in which the un-experienced wayfarer through 'the Dials' finds himself involved. He traverses streets of dirty, straggling houses, with now and then an unexpected court composed of buildings as ill-proportioned and deformed as the half-naked children that wallow in the kennels. Brokers' shops, which would seem to have been established by humane individuals as refuges for destitute bugs ...are its cheerful accompaniments."
—Description of Seven Dials, London, from *Sketches by Boz* (1850) by Charles Dickens

184

For many centuries, a town was virtually all center. With its houses and churches, shops and inns huddled tightly together, the typical town was snugly protected from the outside world by its surrounding wall. The Industrial Revolution caused towns to swell out over the neighboring countryside and many became cities, their centers transformed by grandiose public buildings endowed by proud and philanthropic local entrepreneurs.

Community spirit Despite this vast expansion, the areas around the city's core still enjoyed a strong sense of identity: people lived near their work and often close to their extended families. The tiny back-to-back houses sheltered large families who shared a water tap and latrine at the end of the terrace with neighbors, but community spirit was strong even in the most overcrowded streets.

No-go areas With the decline of heavy industry and the migration outward toward the suburbs, some of these inner-city areas became deprived pockets of high unemployment and poor housing, isolated from the country's trend of increasing affluence. A wave of riots in the summer of 1981—in Brixton, Toxteth, and Bristol—led to them being portrayed by the media as "no-go areas" and caused the government to look urgently at making inner-city areas better places in which to live, work, and do business.

Upwardly mobile Birmingham Visitors to industrial cities some 20 years ago would have seen much dereliction round the centers, but there have been some massive changes for the better. Long considered England's unglamorous second city, Birmingham has witnessed a remarkable renaissance, has become a major convention

Narrow boats in Birmingham's Gas Street Basin

destination—boosted by its geographical centrality—and now takes its heritage seriously. The Jewellery Quarter is once again flourishing after the recession-hit 1980s, and visitors flock in great numbers to such attractions as Cadbury World at the headquarters of one of the foremost chocolate manufacturers. Neglected canals have been cleaned up, new cobbles laid, towpaths signposted and the waterfront developed with pubs, eateries, smart shops and gleaming offices. Much of the city center is now traffic-free. And there's even earnest talk of demolishing the much-hated Bullring, a massive 1960s brutalist building adjoining New Street Station and housing a labyrinthine shopping center and market.

Manchester's Millennium Quarter Manchester is an example of revitalization for the third millennium, funded by the Millennium Commission (set up to assist public projects with revenues from the National Lottery). In 1996 a huge terrorist bomb devastated the Arndale Centre, Manchester's vast and drab-looking shopping center. Fortunately there were no fatalities, and this event provided the catalyst for upgrading this area and its surroundings. The medieval town center around the cathedral has been a neglected backwater since World War I; the scheme, due for completion in 2001, will link this area to the south with a City Park—providing much-needed greenery—and a traffic-free street will be created giving a vista of the cathedral from the main part of the city center. Meanwhile Manchester will gain a cathedral visitor center and a new cultural attraction called Urbis. The Arndale Centre itself will be totally refurbished. Even the long-buried medieval bridge that originally served Manchester will be excavated and visible to all once again.

Prosperity and pride Environmental pressure on the countryside and congestion on the roads has further led to a revival in the inner cities. In London, the once-neglected warehouse districts around London Bridge, for instance, have become distinctly yuppified, while previously unfashionable Hackney has become the city's major artists' community. The Docklands area virtually died after the end of London as a port, but has been rebuilt with futuristic office blocks and waterside housing, much of it extremely desirable real estate.

It is in the inner cities' smartly refurbished buildings, new concert halls, swathes of parkland and new architecture that future visitors should become aware of a reviving sense of civic pride.

Demonstrating a new spirit of enterprise: Manchester's MetroLink trams

THE SECOND BLITZ
Prince Charles once remarked that far more damage had been inflicted on London by developers after World War II than the entire might of Hitler's *Luftwaffe* had achieved during it. The same, unfortunately, is true of many other British cities and towns, devastated by a postwar alliance of urban planners, and architects, but the emergence of civic societies and the designation of conservation areas has saved many centers in the past 30 years. There is increasing recognition of heritage; even Victorian warehouses that might have been torn down in the 1970s are now being carefully preserved.

London's Docklands: the redevelopment made use of the waterside

Monsal Dale: the old viaduct now carries the 8½-mile Monsal Trail, one of the most popular walks in the Peak

On the High Peak Trail

▶▶ Peak National Park   172B3
(tel: 01629 813227)

Britain's first national park, created in 1951, is encircled by large industrial cities. Though there are no major peaks as such—the district is essentially one of rolling hillscapes—the feeling of escape is exhilarating. The Peak forms the southern part of the Pennine chain, which forms the backbone of northern England.

THE WHITE PEAK Most of the southern park comprises the limestone landscapes of the White Peak, where rivers cut deep-grooved gorges, or "dales," beneath a plateau of stone-walled farmland. Most spectacular of all are **Dove Dale**▶▶ and its continuation, **Beresford Dale** (despite the crowds), **Monsal Dale**▶▶ (with its famous viaduct), the **Manifold Valley**▶ just below Wetton, and wooded **Lathkill Dale**▶ near Youlgreave. Rewarding villages include **Winster, Alstonefield, Tideswell, Ilam, Ashford in the Water**, and **Eyam**▶, whose villagers were ravaged by the plague in 1665 when, following their vicar's lead, they confined themselves to their village after an infected box of cloth arrived from London. **Tissington**▶ has perhaps the loveliest of all Peak village streets, with wide grassy borders and a Jacobean hall. Equally absorbing is **Cromford**▶, an industrial village where Richard Arkwright set up the world's first water-powered cotton mill in 1771 (now a museum). The Peak's finest prehistoric monument is **Arbor Low**▶, south of Monyash, a 2,000-year-old stone circle. **Castleton**▶▶ is the nub of the Peak's caving district (see panel): north of the village, a ridge ends at Mam Tor, known as "Shivering Mountain" because of frequent landslips; Cave Dale looks up to the Norman keep of Peveril Castle, holding its head high above the village.

The national park boundary excludes all the local towns except for **Bakewell**, home of Bakewell puddings (made of almond, jam and puff pastry). The center is ruined by traffic, but it is more pleasant up the hill around the church and the delightful Old House Museum of relics of the past. Out of town are the Peak's two great houses.

Haddon Hall►► is a wonderfully preserved medieval house with a paneled gallery, a chapel, and walled garden; palatial **Chatsworth House**►►, home of the dukes of Devonshire, has a breathtaking collection of art and furniture. Its grounds were landscaped by Capability Brown and Joseph Paxton (see page 17).

Buxton►►, an elegant former spa, is the *de facto* Peak capital. Its classically inspired 18th-century Crescent, an Opera House, pavilion gardens, and town hall all contribute to the distinguished air. An excellent town museum features a Wonders of the Peak exhibition. **Matlock Bath**, a former spa, occupies an extraordinary site in the Derwent Gorge. Cable cars make it easy to explore the **Heights of Abraham**, a park with woodland walks, views, and caves. Nearby at Crich is the wonderful **National Tramway Museum**►►, which offers tram rides and a host of exhibits related to this mode of transportation. **Wirksworth**► is a characterful old town amid limestone quarries; the church has a superb 8th-century lead carved coffin lid known as the Wirksworth Stone.

THE DARK PEAK Millstone grit is the underlying rock in the northern Peak. The moors and grassland really are dark; the scenery is bleaker and more rugged. Millstones, for grinding grain, were once a major industry—workings litter abandoned quarries and the stone disks now stand on plinths to mark the national park boundary. The one-street village of **Edale** lies below the massive peat bog plateau of Kinder Scout, the highest terrain in the Peak (2,087 feet).

CAVES
Of the five limestone caverns near Castleton that are open to the public, Treak Cliff has some fine stalactites and displays of Blue John (a crystalline fluorspar, worked into jewelry and souvenirs, and sold locally), Speedwell Cavern features an underground boat trip along a tunnel that forms part of an old lead mine, and Bagshawe Cavern near Bradwell may appeal to those wanting to try adventure caving. Peak Cavern on the edge of Castleton has a magnificent entrance and is the largest cave in England. Blue John Cavern has Blue John but no stalactites. On the edge of Buxton, Poole's Cavern has the finest formations.

187

The A57 heads over the **Snake Pass**, giving a good picture of the austerity of the northern moors, while the **Derwent Reservoirs**► near Hope are the most attractive of many manmade lakes. Old cotton-mill towns have a 19th-century workaday character: **New Mills** is one of the most rewarding, with a gorge beneath the Torrs Aerial Walkway. **Lyme Park**► (N.T.) has a Palladian hall with Grinling Gibbons woodcarving; its park has gentle walks. The gritstone edges such as **Stanage Edge** provide dramatic level tops, with easy paths and challenging rock climbs.

"Bakewell pudding" started life at the White Horse Inn, when a cook attempting to make a strawberry tart put the jam in first and poured the egg mixture on top

LEAD MINING
Lead mining was big in the White Peak until the last century—the Manifold Valley and Lathkill Dale have traces of past mining activity, Magpie Mine near Sheldon being the most conspicuous relic. Many villages expanded for the purpose; today these stone-built settlements are surprisingly rural and merge into the scenery along with their agricultural neighbors. At Matlock Bath an excellent mining museum lies close to the reopened Temple Mine, which non-claustrophobics may like to walk around.

This most famous of factory workers' villages looked forward to a new age of cities: of greenery, clean air, and sanitation. It was conceived as a place in which, in the words of its founder, the inhabitants "will be able to know more about the science of life than they can in a back slum, and in which they will learn that there is more in life than the mere going to and returning from work, and looking forward to Saturday night to draw their wages."

VILLAGE TRAIL
The Port Sunlight Heritage Centre tells the story of Port Sunlight, and a village trail leads visitors around the garden village, taking in the Lady Lever Art Gallery. Set up by Lever after the death of his wife, the gallery contains a surprising wealth of art, including pre-Raphaelite paintings and Wedgwood ceramics.

188

Fair deals for the workers Port Sunlight was in fact one of several 19th-century innovations in the Wirral (the peninsula between the River Mersey and Liverpool on one side and the River Dee and Wales on the other). In 1842 Joseph Paxton's Birkenhead Park had been Britain's first public park, and in 1853 Prices Patent Candle Company had created Bromborough Pool Village for its workers.

The soap king The industrialist William Hesketh Lever, the first Viscount Leverhulme, was a Liberal Member of Parliament and philanthropist with an interest in the arts and landscape design. He co-owned a soap factory in Warrington; the success of Sunlight Soap spiraled and in 1887 he came to the Wirral to set up a new factory. He acquired Thornton Manor and transformed Thornton Hough into a mock-Tudor village for his estate workers.

A vision of the future The factory village of Port Sunlight was to be a haven of peace and cleanliness. Cottages were built to a high standard in half-timbered Tudor and bricky Queen Anne and Elizabethan styles (no two groups of cottages are the same); gardens and parks were liberally provided. The village's visionary design was a predecessor of the garden cities of Ebenezer Howard, which in turn influenced the growth of the garden suburb and of the first "New Towns."

►► Quarry Bank Mill   172B2
(tel: 01625 527468)

The centerpiece of Styal Country Park—a swath of green on the fringes of Manchester—is this water-powered cotton mill, built in 1784 and now maintained by the National Trust. It gives an excellent idea of the working of a weaving mill, complete with the deafening clatter of the looms. Exhibits explain cotton processing, the working conditions of the time, and the role of the mill owners as factory pioneers. Spinning and weaving demonstrations take place. Visitors can also see living conditions of the 1830s inside the Apprentice House. An 1840 beam engine is in steam in the **Steam Power Galleries**.

►► Stoke-on-Trent (The Potteries)   172B2
(tel: 01782 284600)

Stoke is a conurbation of six towns—Burslem, Fenton, Hanley, Longton, Stoke, and Tunstall—but only locals can tell where one ends and the next begins. At first glance the industrial and residential sprawl is unappetizing; but this is the heart of pottery country, and anyone interested in the craft should certainly make a visit.

The **Gladstone Pottery Museum**►►► is a preserved 19th-century pottery with massive bottle-shaped brick kilns (once a common feature of Stoke-on-Trent, now all but vanished). It has pottery demonstrations, informative displays, and fine ceramics ranging from high-class ornaments to Victorian lavatories. The **Etruria Industrial Museum**► features the last steam-powered potter's mill in Britain (where bone and flint were crushed to supply the potteries; the engines are usually in steam the first weekend of the month, Apr–Dec). **The Potteries Museum and Art Gallery**►► has a fine collection of Staffordshire pottery. Also open to the public and each with museums are the visitor centers for **Spode**►►, **Royal Doulton**►► and **Wedgwood**►►.

Huddled around a courtyard and built in the 15th and 16th centuries, **Little Moreton Hall**►► (N.T.), 9 miles north of Stoke-on-Trent, is the best example of the half-timbered "vernacular," with a wainscoted gallery, great hall, chapel, and knot garden.

About 15 miles east of Stoke-on-Trent is **Alton Towers**. Here the extensive parkland surrounding the ruined home of the Earl of Shrewsbury is today full of the sounds of Britain's most famous amusement park.

VISITING THE POTTERIES
The Wedgwood Express bus links most main sites and Stoke rail station. Aim to see the **Gladstone Pottery Museum** (tel: 01782-319232) and some of Stoke's many bargain-price factory shops. Then visit one of the potteries (book ahead for factory tours, available Mon–Fri). The main ones (with visitor centers/craft demonstrations year-round) are **Wedgwood**, famous for its Jasper Ware, (tel: 01782 204141); **Spode**, specializing in blue and white bone china and still on its original 1770 site (tel: 01782 744011); and **Royal Doulton** (tel: 01782 292434), famous for its intricate figurines. There is also a visitor center at Etruria and the Ceramica center opens in 2000. Tourist office, tel: 01782 236000.

189

Duns Chirnside **Berwick-upon-Tweed**
Greenlaw Swinton Northumberland
Gordon Coldstream Coast
Kelso Ford Lowick Holy Island
St Boswells Town **Lindisfarne**
E Yetholm Wooler Bamburgh Farne Islands
Jedburgh **Castle**
Denholm Seahouses
Cheviot Hills 816m
The Cheviot Embleton
Alwinton Rothbury **Dunstanburgh** Craster
Cragside **Castle**
House **Alnwick** Almouth
Longframlington Warkworth
NORTHUMBERLAND Amble
Otterburn
Kielder Newbiggin-
Water West Kirkwhelpington Ashington by-the-Sea
Woodburn Morpeth Bedlington
Northumberland Wansbeck **Blyth**
National Belsay Cramlington **TYNE**
Park Ponteland **Whitley Bay**
Housesteads Hadrian's Wall Chollerford **Longbenton** **Tynemouth**
Birdoswald Chesters Fort **Gosforth** **South Shields**
D **Fort** Corbridge Ryton **Newcastle upon Tyne**
Vindolanda Tyne **Jarrow**
Haltwhistle Hexham **Whickham** **Gateshead**
Stanley **Beamish** **Washington** **Sunderland**
Derwent Chester- **Houghton**
Reservoir **Consett** le-Street Seaham
Lanchester le-Spring
Castleside **Durham** Thornley Easington
Alston Crook A1(M) **Peterlee**
CUMBRIA Wearhead Stanhope Spennymoor Trimdon
Melmerby 893m Sedgefield **Hartlepool**
Cow Green Wear **Bishop** Billingham **Redcar**
Temple Cross Reservoir High Force **Auckland** **Middlesbrough**
Sowerby Fell Middleton-in- **Newton** **Stockton-**
Teesdale Eggleston **Aycliffe** **on-Tees** Skelton
Appleby-in- Barnard **Darlington** Guisborough
Westmorland Castle Piercebridge Tees Great
C Warcop Bowes Stokesley Ayton
Brough Scotch Great
Settle- Kirkby Corner Smeaton Mount Grace
Carlisle Stephen Richmond Priory
Railway Thwaite Reeth Hipswell Catterick Ellerbeck Osmotherly
Tebay Leyburn Bedale Northallerton **Rievaulx** Hutton-
Kirkby Hawes Swale **Abbey** le-Hole
Lonsdale Dent 736m Aysgarth Ure **Jervaulx** Thirsk Helmsley
Whernside **Yorkshire Dales** **Abbey** Sutton **Byland**
National Park Masham Bank **Abbey**
Ingleton 693m Buckden Coxwold
Pen-y-Ghent 728m Great **NORTH YORKSHIRE** Easingwold
Arncliffe Whernside Studley
B **Malham** Kettlewell Pateley Royal **Ripon**
Tarn Grassington Bridge **Fountains** Boroughbridge
Settle **Brimham** **Abbey** Strensall
Bowland Malham Burnsall **Rocks** Ripley Knaresborough
Forest Hellifield **Stump** A1(M)
Slaidburn Bolton **Cross** Blubberhouses **Harrogate** **York**
Gisburn Abbey **Caverns** Wetherby
Skipton Middleton Pateley Knaresborough
LANCASHIRE Barnoldswick Otley Harewood Tadcaster
Clitheroe Colne Yeadon House A1(M)
Longridge Whalley **Keighley** Wharfe Harewood Selby
Ribble **Nelson** Haworth **Bingley** Yeadon Tadcaster
Burnley Cullingworth **Shipley** **LEEDS**
M65 **Bradford** **WEST** Garforth
M6 **Accrington** Hebden Halifax **YORKSHIRE** **Castleford**
Blackburn Bridge Todmorden **Dewsbury**
Darwen Rawtenstall Brighouse **Wakefield** **Pontefract**
Chorley Rochdale **Huddersfield** Hemsworth Askern
Ramsbottom M62 Meltham M1 Hatfield
Horwich M66 Bury Holmfirth **Barnsley** A1(M)
A **Bolton** **Middleton** **Oldham** Penistone **Doncaster** M18
Wigan **GREATER** Ashton-under-Lyne **SOUTH** Thorne
MANCHESTER Chapeltown Conisbrough Park
Salford **MANCHESTER** Peak **Rotherham** YORKSHIRE
M6 Stretford Glossop District Maltby
Warrington Sale Stockport New National **SHEFFIELD**
Altrincham Quarry **Cheadle** Mills Park M1
Park Mill Castleton Edale Worksop
1 **Wilmslow** Chapel- Hathersage Dronfield 2
Knutsford le-Frith

NORTHEAST ENGLAND This region includes most of the **Pennines**, the chain of hills that forms the backbone of upland England, from the Peak District in the south to the Scottish borders in the north. It also encompasses **Yorkshire**, the largest county in Britain, divided into North, West, and South for administrative purposes. It has a reputation for friendliness, with the finest of Britain's medieval cities in York itself and a magnificent heritage of abbey ruins and ecclesiastical architecture.

INDUSTRIAL YORKSHIRE The industrial parts of **West Yorkshire** should not be overlooked. The moorland and the scenically sited, 19th-century stone-built mill towns around Calderdale have a strong and unique personality; you can explore canals and hills and the adjacent Brontë country at Haworth. Industrial heritage is the big theme here. Leeds recalls its mill days in the Armley Mills

★ Walk start point

0 10 20 30 40 50 km
0   10   20   30 miles

▶▶▶ REGION HIGHLIGHTS

Beverley *page 194*
Castle Howard *page 195*
Durham *page 196*
Fountains Abbey *page 197*
Hadrian's Wall *page 201*
National Museum of Photography, Film and Television *page 194*
Northumberland Coast *pages 199–200*
North York Moors National Park *pages 202–203*
York *pages 204–206*
Yorkshire Dales National Park *pages 207–209*

The Swaledale tup, the Yorkshire Dales National Park emblem

192

RECOMMENDED HISTORIC TOWNS AND CITIES
County Durham: Barnard Castle, Durham.
East Riding of Yorkshire: Beverley.
North Yorkshire: Harrogate, Helmsley, Knaresborough, Middleham, Richmond, Ripon, Scarborough, York. Northumberland: Alnwick, Hexham.
Tyne and Wear: Newcastle-upon-Tyne.
INDUSTRIAL HERITAGE
Abbeydale Industrial Hamlet, Beamish, Bradford, Halifax, Hebden Bridge, Hull, Saltaire.
SCENERY
North York Moors, Northumberland, South Pennines (Calderdale and Haworth areas), Yorkshire Dales.
COASTAL TOWNS AND VILLAGES
North Yorkshire: Robin Hood's Bay, Runswick Bay, Staithes, Whitby.
Northumberland: Bamburgh, Berwick-upon-Tweed.
HISTORIC SITES AND REMAINS
Fountains Abbey, Hadrian's Wall, Holy Island, Rievaulx Abbey.

Museum, and is home to the magnificent Royal Armouries Museum. Bradford is still fairly impressive for its vibrant museums. At Sheffield, in **South Yorkshire**, Abbeydale Industrial Hamlet is a fitting tribute to the city's steel manufacturing days. The Earth Centre (due for completion 2001) near Doncaster is a £100 million Millennium project looking at environmental issues.

THE DALES, THE MOORS, AND THE VALE OF YORK The **Yorkshire Dales** are for lovers of the great outdoors—an excellent area for car touring, walking, and caving. East of the Pennines in the **Vale of York** are York itself, the spa town of Harrogate, and the enchanting ruins of Fountains Abbey. Southeast Yorkshire is less visited: the flat agricultural scenery may be humdrum, but Selby and Beverley (the latter in the **East Riding of Yorkshire**) each have splendid churches; Hull has a range of sights, including the Town Docks Museum, which celebrates its nautical past; a huge suspension bridge spans the Humber. The **North York Moors** are detached from the Pennine chain and have quite a different character. The coast, with its high cliffs and fishing villages, is a joy. Farther south along the coast are the scalloped chalk cliffs of **Flamborough Head** and the narrow spit of **Spurn Head**.

COUNTY DURHAM, TYNE AND WEAR, NORTHUMBER-LAND The **Pennine** landscape becomes bleaker and more lonesome as one proceeds toward Scotland, through Teesdale, in **County Durham**, and the Cheviot Hills, in Northumberland. Elsewhere much of County Durham has an industrial face and, like Middlesbrough (in North Yorkshire), is economically depressed. The open-air museum at Beamish is a splendid re-creation of an early 20th-century industrial village, while Durham has a great Norman cathedral. **Tyne and Wear** incorporates a conurbation centered on Newcastle-upon-Tyne; locals here are nicknamed Geordies and are known for their quickfire humor and guttural accent. On its back doorstep, **Northumberland**, in total contrast, has wide open spaces, the great Roman structure of Hadrian's Wall, and a long and quiet coastline.

Walks

Hadrian's Wall,   190D1
Northumberland National Park
Nearly all the interest is along the wall itself, with its host of Roman features. There is not much reason to go far afield. Simply walking along the wall is a great experience, with views from the ridge of the Great Whin Sill across lonely Northumberland. For a sample, start at Housesteads Fort and walk west, past Craig Lough to Twice Brewed youth hostel and back (2½ hours). In summer you can use the bus service along the B6318 to take you back.

Holy Island,   190E2
Northumberland
Use main parking lot in village (note tide times). The island's best circular walk is three-quarters coastal, all of it level. Follow Sandham Lane north (turn left and left again out of the car park), turn right beyond the dunes and follow the coast around, past Emanuel Head, where an obelisk looks along the coast into Scotland. Then pass Lindisfarne Castle to finish by Lindisfarne Priory in the village. (1½ hours)

Ingleton Waterfalls,   190B1
Yorkshire Dales National Park
Parking lot by main entrance to falls. Also known as Ingleton Glen, this

Lindisfarne Castle, Holy Island

splendid gorge is well worth the entrance fee. A circular trail takes in a series of falls of considerable individuality; the most dramatic are the first two , Pecka Fall and Thornton Force. Beyond lies a handily placed refreshment stand, then the path leads into more open country with views of surrounding hills before a finale along the Doe Gorge (2 hours). A booklet available locally explains the geology.

Runswick Bay and   191C3
Staithes, North York
Moors National Park
Park just above Runswick Bay village. This walk along the clifftops (part of the Cleveland Way) links two captivating coastal villages. From Runswick Bay village, walk up the road; at the top follow the Cleveland Way as it branches off on the right, soon reaching the clifftop for an easy walk past Port Mulgrave and reaching Staithes harbor. Return the same way. (2½ hours)

Upper Swaledale,   190C1
Yorkshire Dales National Park
Roadside parking, Muker village. This walk from Muker enjoys a magnificent steep-sided section of the dale. Walk into the village and find a path out of its north end that leads to a bridge over the Swale; continue north up the dale for 1¾ miles to the next bridge (close by Keld). Cross and turn left on the Pennine Way (fork left soon for a short detour to Kisdon Force waterfall). The Way rises slightly, offering fine views. Finally leave it for a farm track that drops to Muker. (2½ hours)

MISERICORDS

The folding seats in the choirstalls of many cathedrals and major churches have a carved under-bracket known as a misericord. When the seats were turned up, the misericords made ledges for the monks to rest on during the long periods of standing in their services. Frequently carved in fanciful designs, the misericords were deliberately made so narrow that there was no chance of dozing off.

Open-top omnibus: Beamish

SALTAIRE

This famous example of a "factory village" dates from the 1850s, when Titus Salt, an enlightened industrialist of liberal views and temperance ideals, decided to house his workforce in this garden village of parks and spacious streets, free from Bradford's smog. The place has scarcely changed, though the houses are now mostly privately owned. The mill itself is used for a variety of purposes. Paintings by native son artist David Hockney are on display in the 1853 gallery, and there is a museum of harmoniums and reed organs. Other sections released for commercial use.

▶▶ Beamish: North of England Open Air Museum   190D2
(tel: 01207 231811)

Life in northern England in the early 1900s is re-created in meticulous detail at this ambitious museum. It is divided into five sections: the colliery village, the town with its shops and houses, the manor house, the railroad, and the farm. Costumed actors play roles within the museum.

▶▶ Beverley   191B3
(tel: 01482 867430)

Beverley has pleasing Georgian brickwork, the North Bar (the only survivor of five town gates), a Saturday market, and, above all, two gems of church architecture. Begun in Norman times, the **Minster▶▶** is famed for its Gothic stone-carving, its 68 misericords (see panel) made by the Ripon school of woodcarvers, and its fine-towered west front. **St. Mary's Church▶** has a 15th-century west facade and a paneled chancel ceiling depicting early kings, all cloaked and crowned against a gold background.

▶ Bradford   190A2
(tel: 01274 753678)

A patchily impressive Victorian city (knocked about by postwar planning), Bradford is the fruit of the textile-mill age; the Gothic Revival **town hall** and the spectacular tombs of **Undercliffe Cemetery▶** are monuments of past achievement. The entertaining **National Museum of Photography, Film, and Television▶▶▶** *(Admission free)* has put Bradford on the map: here you can see yourself read the news and watch a Victorian magic lantern show or 1950s TV advertisements. The museum *(closed* Mondays except public holidays) is attached to an IMAX theater (reservations tel: 01274 203395). The **Colour Museum▶** explores the use of color chemistry, and the **Bradford Industrial Museum▶**

with rebuilt back-to-back houses, has a tour through the world of textile production. Recommended visits (easy by rail) are **Saltaire▶▶** and **Leeds▶▶** (see sidebars).

▶▶ Calderdale
190A1
(tel: 01422 368725)

A former textile valley in the heart of the Pennines, Calderdale is rich with local color. Sturdy rows of stone cottages and the geometry of stone-walled fields stripe the sides of the valley. The largest settlement, **Halifax▶**, is unjustifiably ignored by many visitors; in fact it is the best-preserved of West Yorkshire's industrial towns, with the splendid galleried **Piece Hall▶▶**, the former cloth market built around a courtyard (now home to specialty shops), and handsome stone buildings. The town hall was designed by Charles Barry (one of the architects of the Houses of Parliament in London). **Calderdale Industrial Museum** covers the stories of mining and textiles. **Eureka!** on Discovery Road, is a hands-on museum for children.

Hebden Bridge▶, near the site of the last clog mill in England, is magnificently set at the meeting of two valleys, its gray houses rising row by row up the hillside. From the original Hepton Bridge a cobbled path rises steeply to the hilltop village of **Heptonstall▶▶**, a fascinating place with cobbled streets, a ruined church, and the world's oldest Methodist chapel in continuous use (since 1764). The village was a busy hand-looming center until eclipsed by the mills in Hebden Bridge.

▶▶▶ Castle Howard
191B3
(tel: 01653 648333)

In the gentle Howardian Hills, this early 18th-century house stands surrounded by a park adorned with ornamental lakes, a colonnaded mausoleum, and a "temple" designed by Vanbrugh. He is commonly attributed with the design of the house, yet he was then a man of no architectural experience; it seems extremely likely that his clerk of works, architect Nicholas Hawksmoor, lent a helping hand. The house has portraits by Holbein, statues, tapestries, porcelain, furniture, and a costume collection. It was also the setting for the T.V. dramatization of *Brideshead Revisited*.

LEEDS
Graced with 19th-century shopping arcades, Britain's oldest music hall (the City Varieties) and a majestic town hall, this industrial city has a rejuvenated Waterfront area, where the **Royal Armouries Museum** is home to a superb collection of arms and armor (previously housed in the Tower of London), with jousting demonstrations given outside. The **Thackray Medical Museum** presents a social history of medical care (the sections on early surgery are not for the faint-hearted). The city was a world leader in the cloth trade in the 19th century, and the **Armley Mills Museum** chronicles its textile industry. For information, tel: 0113-242 5242.

195

The handsome mill at Saltaire, pre-eminent in its day

CATHEDRAL FIRSTS

Durham Cathedral represents the highest achievement of the Norman style. In addition to the characteristic use of rounded arches, the building has what are thought to be the earliest transverse Gothic-style pointed arches in English architecture: since the cathedral was largely built during a single period, this really shows a transition between the two building techniques. The sense of scale is created by the hitherto unprecedented use of rib-vaulting, which creates greater space between load-bearing columns.

Durham Cathedral stands high above the Wear

ST. CUTHBERT

The Chapel of the Nine Altars in the cathedral contains the relics of St. Cuthbert, brought here by Lindisfarne monks who escaped from Holy Island (see page 199) when Danish raiders arrived in 875. Cuthbert was a shepherd boy from the Lammermuir Hills who decided to dedicate his life to God, living on Holy Island and later the Farne Islands. He remained a lover of all animals.

▶▶▶ Durham   190C2
(tel: 0191/384-3720)

Few places in Britain can rival the drama of Durham's setting, its majestic cathedral soaring high over sandstone cliffs and woodlands ribboning the tight curve of the River Wear. The historic center is compact and largely traffic-free. **Durham Heritage Centre** in St. Mary le Bow Church chronicles the city's history.

The nave, chancel, and transepts of the **cathedral▶▶▶** were built over a single period (1070–1140). The sense of balanced might and soaring space is enthralling—it's Britain's finest Norman church architecture. In the cathedral precincts is College Green, the most complete example of a Benedictine monastery in England. Durham was until 1836 a "palatinate," enjoying royal rights and ruled by prince bishops, who were thus lay and religious leaders.

The main entrance to the cathedral is via **Palace Green**, where other buildings belong to the **university**, England's third oldest. The **castle▶▶** (*Guided tours*), erected to serve as the palace of the prince bishops for almost 800 years, dates from the 1070s. The university rebuilt the octagonal keep in 1840 but several early features survive, including the Great Hall (1284) and the Black Staircase (1662). For the best views, follow the **riverside path▶▶**, cross over **Prebends Bridge**, beside weirs and old mills (one houses an **archeological museum**), up to **South Street**. To the north, **Crook Hall and Garden▶** is a 14th-century manor house with attractive gardens. In the university the **Oriental Museum▶**, Elvet Hill, is a treasure house of exotica, including Egyptian mummies and jade.

▶▶▶ Fountains Abbey and Studley Royal *190B2*
(tel: 01765 604625)

Fountains Abbey

In medieval times, **Fountains Abbey** (N.T.) had grange farms and lands across much of northern England and was a major wool producer. Its former prosperity is evident in what are regarded as Britain's greatest abbey ruins.

Founded for 12 Benedictine monks who later changed to Cistercian rule, the abbey still has a 12th-century nave and transepts, a tower completed shortly before the Dissolution, and buildings where the monks lived and worked. The **Studley Royal** estate has an 18th-century park with follies, deer park, and vistas of the abbey. St. Mary's Church is mock-medieval, with painted roof and walls of Egyptian alabaster.

Ripon▶ is an appealing town with a cathedral notable for its west front, misericords and Saxon crypt. Since 886 the nightwatch horn has been blown in the square at 9 PM to guard the town in darkness.

▶▶ Harewood House *190B2*
(tel: 0113-288 6331)

The seat of the Earls of Harewood is a stately composition, completed in 1771, with an impressive list of credits: interiors and furniture by Robert Adam, exterior by John Carr, murals by Angelica Kauffman, gardens by Charles Barry, and parkland by Capability Brown. Painted ceilings, porcelain, and intricate plasterwork further grace the building, and there is an aviary of exotic birds.

▶ Haworth *190B1*
(tel: 01535 642329)

The Brontë Parsonage Museum (see page 198) and the walk to the Brontë Waterfalls and Top Withins justify a literary pilgrimage to this extremely popular Pennine village. The village is a stop on the **Keighley and Worth Valley Railway▶**, which steams from Keighley to Oxenhope.

RIPON'S SAINT
St. Wilfred was the abbot of the monastery of Ripon in the 7th century and later became Bishop of York. On the Saturday before the first Monday in August, a procession with floats is headed by a man dressed as St. Wilfred, complete with miter and crook, riding a horse; the dean greets him at the west door and a service of thanksgiving follows.

Charlotte (1816–1855), Emily (1818–1848), and Anne (1820–1849) Brontë were the daughters of an Irish clergyman. The Brontës' lives were constantly beset by ill health and unfortunate circumstance. Charlotte had an unhappy love affair in Brussels, Emily had no close friends, and Anne had a tendency toward religious melancholy. Meanwhile, their brother Bramwell, disillusioned with his attempts to be a writer and artist, took to drink and opium.

"My sister Emily loved the moors. Flowers brighter than the rose bloomed in the blackest heath for her; out of a sullen hollow in a livid hillside her mind would make an Eden. She found in the bleak solitude many and dear delights; and not the least and best loved was—liberty."
—Charlotte Brontë (1816–1855)

Haworth's cobbled main street is today lined with gift shops

THE BRONTE NAME
The family name was originally Brunty or Prunty but the form Brontë was adopted after Lord Nelson was given the title Duke of Brontë by the King of Naples after the Battle of the Nile in 1798.

The Brontës lived in the bleak parsonage (now a museum) in Haworth, overlooking a graveyard that polluted the water supply, severely reducing villagers' life expectancy. The girls consequently escaped into fantasy worlds. It was Charlotte's determination that got the Brontës into print, after she had chanced upon some secret poetry of Emily's and had been convinced of its worth; the three contributed works to a volume published in 1846 under the pen names of Acton (Anne), Currer (Charlotte), and Ellis (Emily) Bell; the sales were dismal (two books in the first month), but with Charlotte's drive, the sisters each submitted novels. Emily's *Wuthering Heights*, probably set in the now-ruined farmhouse of Top Withins, and Anne's *Agnes Grey* were published in 1847. Charlotte failed to get *The Professor* published, but the constructive comments of one publisher gave her encouragement: she completed *Jane Eyre* soon after and it won immediate acclaim—Thackeray read it in a single sitting.

Hard times But the sisters had to spend much time nursing their brother Bramwell, and the money from the books went to paying off his debts; after his death in September 1848, Emily contracted tuberculosis ("consumption") and died three months later. Anne too fell ill and died the next year at Scarborough, after writing *The Tenant of Wildfell Hall*.

Charlotte was brought to London as a literary celebrity; here she made friends with the successful novelist Mrs. Gaskell, who later wrote a biography of Charlotte. Meanwhile, Charlotte worked on *Villette*, based on her time in Brussels, and married Arthur Bell Nicholls, their curate, after two years of strong opposition from her father. She died nine months later in pregnancy.

IN MEMORY OF
EMILY JANE BRONTË
WHO DIED DEC. 19TH 1848,
AGED 30 YEARS.
AND OF
CHARLOTTE BRONTË
APRIL 21ST 1816
MARCH 31ST 1855

►► Northumberland Coast　　　*190E2*
(tel: 0191/375-3000)

England's northeasternmost seaboard is low-lying and virtually unspoiled, characterized by expansive beaches, profuse birdlife, quiet resorts with golf courses and sands, and wind-haunted castle ruins.

Berwick-upon-Tweed►► changed hands 13 times between England and Scotland during the period 1100–1510. The Tweed, a salmon river which runs just south beneath a trio of bridges (including 17th-century Berwick Bridge with its 15 arches), would seem a natural border, but the town has been English since 1482. An excellent walk follows the 16th-century walls, the best-preserved fortification of its date in Britain, which encircle the town; you'll pass the restored quay, Berwick Barracks of 1717 (E.H.; Britain's oldest purpose-built barracks; with an exhibition re-creating the life of British infantryman; plus a regimental museum and part of the Burrell art collection), and a church built in 1652.

199

Holy Island►►, accessible by car at low tide (the times are given) via a causeway, is excellent for walks (see page 193) and has great historic interest as the cradle of Christianity in England (see panel). Lindisfarne Castle, lone by the shore, was converted in the 1900s by architect Sir Edwin Lutyens and is open to the public. **Bamburgh►** close by has a Norman castle, revamped in the 18th and 19th centuries, with porcelain and armor collections. The Grace Darling Museum pays tribute to the woman who helped rescue nine shipwrecked marines in a gale in 1838. **Dunstanburgh Castle►** is an eerie ruin, the largest of the Northumbrian coastal strongholds, begun in 1313. It is an easy walk along the coast from the port of **Craster**, which has a workaday harbor and kipper smokeries. Inland lies **Alnwick►**, a dignified stone-built market town and a pleasant base for exploring the area. **Alnwick Castle►** dates from Norman times, but has a sumptuous Renaissance-style interior, fine Meissen china, and paintings by Reynolds and Titian; the

The Farne Islands

HOLY ISLAND
In 635, at the request of the king of Northumbria, a missionary landed here from the Scottish island of Iona. St. Aidan founded the Lindisfarne Priory on what is today known as Holy Island, and from this spot Christianity spread across northern England. Lindisfarne became a Benedictine monastery in 1082. A museum tells the story. *The Lindisfarne Gospels*, an illuminated manuscript of *ca*700, is now in the British Library.

LINDISFARNE NATURE RESERVE
Home to wildfowl and waders, a major site for wigeon, and the only British wintering ground for pale-bellied Brent geese, the nature reserve includes mud flats and dunes around Holy Island, and the farther-flung Farne Islands. The latter are an important habitat for seals and seabirds; April through September (inclusive) cruises depart from Seahouses (N.T. information center, tel: 01665 721099)—it is an exciting boat ride that offers really close encounters with the surprisingly tame wild birds.

Man-made beauty: the huge Kielder Water amid the conifers of Kielder Forest

Victorian architect Salvin was responsible for much of the building, and a century earlier Capability Brown had landscaped the parkland. Adjacent Hulne Park is open for walks on weekends; there is a Carmelite priory and an 18th-century folly tower. At the mouth of the River Coquet, **Warkworth▶** has a medieval castle and a 14th-century hermitage chapel (both E.H.) gouged out of the cliffs, with the hermit's living quarters still intact (walk along the river and take a ferry across).

In complete contrast, **Newcastle-upon-Tyne▶** is a sprawling industrial conurbation, definitely not pretty at first sight, but with plenty of atmosphere. Its six great river bridges include Robert Stephenson's double-decker road and rail bridge of the 1840s. A cluster of medieval quayside buildings, the 17th-century guildhall, and the castle are preindustrial survivals, while Grey Street and Eldon Square are fine examples of early 19th-century townscaping. Newcastle's big three museums are the **Laing Art Gallery** (*Admission free*), the region's premier art collection; **Discovery Museum** (*Admission free*), with interactive science, plus costumes, displays on Tyneside inventors, the 100-foot vessel *Turbinia* and a hands-on social history of the city; and the **Hancock Museum**, with natural history, a Living Planet environmental gallery and Egyptian artifacts.

▶▶ Northumberland National Park   190D1
(tel: 01434 220616)

Because of its remote location and lack of facilities, this is one of the least visited national parks. Villages are modest and scattered, the grassy hills are quiet and strikingly empty—even at the height of summer you often have only Cheviot sheep for company. It's a great place for solitary walks, although the variety is not immense. Vast Kielder Forest spreads its seemingly endless evergreen plantations, home to red squirrels and deer, over western Northumberland. Kielder Water and the forest trails offer

The Roman ruins of Housesteads Fort, on Hadrian's Wall

a retreat from the elements, and there is a 12-mile forest drive. You can also rent the boats and canoes that are available here.

The **Cheviot Hills** reach to the Scottish border. The best of the walks involve treks along solitary sheep-drovers' roads, now quiet grassy tracks, to the ridge which forms the border, taking in the summits of Windy Gyle (2,031 feet) and The Cheviot (2,677 feet). The scenic drives tend to be of the there-and-back variety; notable among these is the road along **Coquetdale** from Rothbury, past the craggy Simonside Hills, to Alwinton and beyond. **Rothbury** itself is an attractive sandstone town with a sloping green and a spacious main street; **Cragside▶** (N.T.) on the edge of the town was built by the 19th-century architect Norman Shaw and was the first house in the world to be lit by hydroelectric power. The wooded grounds here are laced with trails and have lakes, a formal garden, and a fine show of rhododendrons. **Chillingham Castle** has for more than 700 years been home to Wild White cattle, a breed that was kept by ancient Britons. **Ford** is a model estate village for Ford Castle and has craft workshops.

The southern part of the national park holds the finest surviving stretch of **Hadrian's Wall▶▶▶**(E.H.), the largest Roman monument in Britain (see panel). Of its 74-mile length, remains can be seen along 10 miles, the best sections being between points north of Haltwhistle and Hexham. Walkers may like to make use of a summer bus service which runs along the main road parallel to the wall. Housesteads Fort, which still has a hospital and latrines, and Chesters, a cavalry fort, are particularly well preserved. At Vindolanda Fort a section of wall is reconstructed as it would have been at the time of the Roman occupation, while at Corbridge are the remains of the garrison town of Corstopitum and a museum of finds. Also try to take in Birdoswald Fort, over the border in Cumbria, and the national park information center at Once Brewed. **Hexham▶** makes an attractive base. It has a superb abbey church; both its crypt and bishop's throne are Saxon—before destruction by Danish marauders in 875 it was the largest church in northern Europe. Local history features at the Border History Museum (in an old prison).

HADRIAN'S WALL
This great fortification at the northernmost point of the Roman empire was planned in AD 122 by Emperor Hadrian from Newcastle to the Solway Firth on the Cumbrian coast. The natural feature of the Great Whin Sill, a ridge of hard rock, made an ideal base for the construction for much of its length. To the north lay wilderness and the Picts, and it still feels primevally wild on the wall today. Structures known as mile-castles were placed at intervals of Roman miles; the Vallum, or southern rampart, was below the wall and is visible in places. Seventeen forts, housing 13,000 infantry-men and 5,500 cavalrymen, were connected by a military road. The best preserved is Housesteads (N.T.). At Wallsend (just east of Newcastle-upon-Tyne) a museum and reconstructed bath house stand beside the remains of Segedunum Fort.

MORE NORTH YORKSHIRE PRIORIES AND ABBEYS

Byland Abbey, near Coxwold, had the largest priory church in England—the shattered rose window gives a scant idea of its glory. Mount Grace Priory, near the attractive village of Osmotherley, was a Carthusian house; the lifestyle was austere, with vows of silence and prison-like confinement; one cell has been reconstructed. Guisborough Priory, an Augustinian foundation at the edge of Guisborough in Cleveland, is now largely razed but retains a huge east window. The substantial ruins of Whitby Abbey overlook the sea; an inscription on a stone cross commemorates the Creation Hymn, the first poem in the English language, penned by Caedmon, an Anglo-Saxon herdsman.

The ruins of Rievaulx (pronounced "reevo") Abbey, desolate and still in sheltered Ryedale

RIEVAULX ABBEY

Before Henry VIII started his Dissolution of the monasteries in 1536, there were more monasteries in Yorkshire than in any other county in England. In North Yorkshire Rievaulx Abbey is the undoubted star. Founded in 1131, it became very prosperous, rich in sheep, and by the 1160s there were 140 monks and 500 lay brothers. By the Dissolution numbers had dropped to 22. The ruins occupy a site of remote beauty in Ryedale.

►► North York Moors National Park *191C3*
(tel: 01751 473791)

This distinctive massif, tucked into Yorkshire's northeast corner, is England's largest tract of heather moor, a plateau dotted with ancient stone crosses and interrupted by contrasting green dales (valleys) scattered with red-roofed, yellow-stone farms and hamlets. The most dramatic scenery is at the point where the high terrain dips abruptly to the plain, as well as the sublime stretch of coast, absorbing villages, beaches, and walks along the east coast's highest cliffs. This variety of moods is perhaps the key to the area's enduring appeal.

THE MOORS AND DALES Farndale, celebrated for its wild daffodils, and **Rosedale**, once an ironstone-mining center, typify the contrasts of moorland plateau and lush vales. **Helmsley►** is a small market town with craftshops, bookstores, and a handsome market square; close by are the east tower of the Norman castle and Duncombe Park, a revamped Palladian mansion memorable for its fine classical entrance hall and paneled saloon, and for its grass terrace complete with temples.

The village street of **Coxwold►** is without blemish, all trim grass-edged lanes and stone cottages; Laurence Sterne lived and wrote *The Life and Times of Tristram Shandy* at what is now known as Shandy Hall (house open). Lonely St. Gregory's Minster in **Kirkdale** has a remarkably preserved Anglo-Saxon sundial from 1060. **Hutton-le-Hole►►**, with its sloping, sheep-nibbled green, is home to the Ryedale Folk Museum, where rural buildings have been rebuilt to give an insight into the life of yesteryear. **Lastingham Church►** is built over a remarkable Norman crypt, and the touristy village of **Thornton-le-Dale►** has some pretty corners by its brook.

The area's major tourist attraction, the **North Yorkshire Moors Railway►►** (journey takes about an hour), runs from Pickering to Grosmont along pristine dale scenery.

Enthusiasts reopened this line as the North Yorkshire Moors Railway in 1973; it had closed eight years earlier

Pickering▶ itself is a bustling market town with a lively local museum and the remains of a Norman castle (E.H.); look around the church for the set of 15th-century murals, one of the most complete in all of England. **Goathland** has a long green and sheep are everywhere; from the Mallyan Spout Hotel a path drops down to **Mallyan Spout**, a waterfall, while south of the village you can walk along a section of Roman road, **Wade's Causeway**▶. At **Grosmont** you can peer into the locomotive shed or take a train into **Eskdale**.

Much of the eastern moors is dominated by commercial forestry, including **Dalby Forest**, laid out with trails, picnic sites, and a drive; it abuts **Bridestones Nature Reserve**, where mushroom-shaped rocks are clustered on the moor. The western and northern escarpments, followed by the long-distance **Cleveland Way** footpath, offer grandstand views towards the Pennines and over industrial Teesside respectively; **Sutton Bank**▶, by the A170, is an inland cliff with a dizzying view across the Vale of York to the Pennines; at its southern end is the White Horse, a 314-foot-tall hill carving created by local schoolchildren and their teacher in 1857.

ALONG THE COAST A footpath (the end of the Cleveland Way) follows the coast continuously; roads reach the coast in only a few places. **Staithes**▶▶ is an authentic-looking fishing village, not too prettified; **Runswick Bay**▶ is smaller and neater, picturesquely huddled beneath the cliff. **Whitby**▶▶ was once a famous whaling center, hence the whalebone arch above town from which you can look across to the ruined abbey and St. Mary's Church. The town has expanded as a resort but has kept its character in a maze of old streets around the harbor; a few shops still specialize in Whitby jet ornaments. The densely stocked Whitby Museum displays some impressive local fossils. A beach extends north to Sandsend.

Red-roofed **Robin Hood's Bay**▶▶, one of the most famous of all English fishing villages, clings to steep slopes that drop to the shore, where low tide reveals tide pools and fossils; tales of smuggling haunt the quaint hodgepodge of lanes. **Scarborough**▶, just outside the Park, is both a Regency spa and a Victorian resort with sandy bays. It is an exhilarating blend of brashness and gentility. Wood End Museum displays natural history and has a section on the ultraliterary Sitwell family, which used to live in this house. Naval battles are reenacted in miniature in Peasholm Park on North Bay.

CAPTAIN JAMES COOK
The great explorer was born in 1728 at Marton (now part of Middlesborough, Cleveland), where a museum charts his life and travels. The site of the Cooks' house at Great Ayton is marked by an obelisk, and the school James attended is a modest museum. After being a shop apprentice in Staithes, he was apprenticed to a Quaker ship-owner in Whitby (the house where he lived with his master is a museum of Cook's life). From 1768 onward he undertook his voyages of discovery to New Zealand, the east coast of Australia and the Pacific Isles. He was killed by natives in Hawaii in 1799.

203

The Laurel Inn, Robin Hood's Bay

York Minster, one of the wonders of Gothic architecture, as seen from the north corner of the city wall

THREATS FROM BELOW AND ABOVE
In the 1960s York Minster's lantern tower was threatened with imminent collapse. Only a major project, with supports erected between 1967 and 1972, saved the day; the undercroft exhibition gives a view of this repair operation. In 1984 the Minster was struck by lightning and was badly damaged by the fire that ensued. Some people interpreted this as an act of God after the Bishop of Durham, one of the Church of England's less traditional bishops, had made outspoken remarks that revealed his doubts about the literal truth of the Virgin Birth.

▶▶▶ **York** 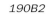 *190B2*
(tel: 01904 320557)

York is England's unrivaled showpiece cathedral city: nowhere else has such a concentration of medieval and other historic treasures. There are far more museums than can be visited in a single day (see page 206): the Castle Museum, the National Railway Museum, and the Jorvik Viking Centre are the top three. Around every corner are examples of buildings of every period, including medieval churches and time-warp streets like the Shambles, with its overhanging upper floors. Shoppers, sightseers, and street performers throng the center; much of it is pedestrianized and a pleasure to explore on foot. York prospered as a center of the wool trade in medieval times, when it was second only to London in importance.

THE CITY WALL▶▶▶ The Romans built the original defensive wall around the settlement of Eboracum, at the confluence of the rivers Ouse and Foss; in Viking times the city was known as Jorvik, later corrupted to "York." Today's wall is largely medieval. It can be followed along its top for much of its 2¾-mile length and provides a splendid city overview (see Walk, page 205); west of the river, the wall skirts a largely railroad-age residential area. The wall's gateways are known as bars; on Micklegate Bar during the Wars of the Roses, the heads of enemies would be exhibited on spikes.

THE MINSTER▶▶▶ Built 1220–1475, this is the largest medieval cathedral in Great Britain and the city's crowning glory. Its magnificent glass dates from 1150—look for the depictions of Genesis and Revelation in the east window, as well as the "Five Sisters" windows within a quintet of lancets. Look too for the rich interior of the chapter house, the painted roof of the nave, the carved rood screen, the undercroft display, and the Treasury.

YORK

Walk

City highlights

Outside **Castle Museum►►►**, face **Clifford's Tower►**, turn left to take a path to the near side of the tower; beyond Ouse Bridge view the city from the north riverbank; recross by Lendal Bridge. Enter the **Museum Gardens**, pass fragments of medieval **St. Leonard's Hospital**; **Multangular Tower**, a Roman relic beside a section of Roman wall; and the ruins of **St. Mary's Abbey**. The **Yorkshire Museum►►** is also in this park.

Find a gate into Marygate and go to **Bootham Bar**; join the walkway along the top of the wall, with superb views of the Minster. Leave the wall at Monk Bar; the **Treasurer's House►** (N.T.) is filled with 17th- and 18th-century décor, while **St. William's College** has an exhibition on the **Minster**. Skirt the **Minster►►►** to its main entrance. Pass **St. Michael-le-Belfrey Church** (fine 15th- and 16th-century glass), detour to Stonegate for its shopfronts; go on along Low Petergate, detour left to Goodramgate for **Holy Trinity Church►**. Find **The Shambles►►** York's most famous street. From Fossgate visit the **Merchant Adventurers' Hall►►**; beyond Coppergate are the **Jorvik Viking Centre►►►**, **Fairfax House►**, and the **York Story**.

205

206

The Shambles, originally a street of butcher shops

York's museums

For those arriving by train, First Stop York vouchers are available from stations and tourist offices (except summer), giving half-price admission to most attractions.

A.R.C.► St. Saviourgate: hands-on archeology for all; learn how to sort and label real Roman finds, and weave on a reproduction Viking warp-weighted loom.

Bar Convent Blossom Street: still a convent, but housing a museum on early Christianity in northern England.

Castle Museum► ► ► Eye of York: this alone justifies a visit to York. Collections include a full-scale cobbled street of shops, re-creations of domestic interiors over the centuries, and a working water mill by the river.

City Art Gallery Exhibition Square: includes nudes by local artist William Etty.

Clifford's Tower► ► Tower Street: a neat 14th-century quatrefoil castle on a Norman site, with a good view from the top. Scene in 1190 of the mass suicide of 1,250 Jews to escape slaughter by their Christian debtors.

Fairfax House► Castlegate: a Georgian town house showing life in the mid-1700s: furniture, clocks, and paintings, mostly from Joseph Terry, a Quaker candy magnate.

Guildhall St. Helen's Square: a painstaking re-creation of the original 15th-century building, destroyed in an air raid.

Jorvik Viking Centre► ► ► Coppergate: entertaining and realistic time-travel journey into 10th-century Viking York. Go early or late when the lines are shorter.

Merchant Adventurers' Hall► ► Fossgate: the most impressive half-timbered building in the city; the 14th-century hall of a city merchants' guild, still in use.

National Railway Museum► ► Leeman Road: Britain's finest selection of historic locomotives and cars (including the royal car used by Queen Victoria). Timetabled working demonstrations.

Richard III Museum Monk Bar: the medieval monarch on trial—guilty or not guilty?

York Dungeon Clifford Street: a chilling glimpse into a world of punishment and death.

The York Story Castlegate: a model of the city illustrates York's long history.

Yorkshire Museum► ► Museum Gardens: collection of treasures and finds: Roman, Saxon, Viking and medieval, including a Viking ship and the Middleham Jewel.

The Castle Museum's re-created cobbled street, Kirkgate, takes its name from Dr. John Kirk, who started the museum with his collection of everyday miscellanea

Drive

This tour (approx. 55 miles) takes in waterfalls, Castle Bolton, unspoiled dales, and lonely moors.

From the busy little town of **Hawes** at the heart of Wensleydale, take the

The Yorkshire Dales (see also pages 208–209)

A684 Sedbergh road, turning off very soon for an unclassifed road leading to Kettlewell. Here you'll enter the northern end of **Wharfedale** at **Hubberholme** (with its charming church). The B6160 leads over into Bishopdale and **West Burton▶**, with its long village green. Proceed past the **Aysgarth Falls**, taking the road rising up to the formidable fortress of **Castle Bolton▶▶**.

Beyond this, the road rises onto Redmire Moor; pause to admire the views at the top and drop down into **Swaledale** at **Grinton**. The odd castellated structure on the right as you descend is a former shooting lodge and now a youth hostel.

Grinton Church, grandiosely dubbed "Cathedral of the Dales," is worth a short pause, while **Reeth▶**, with its inns ranged around a sloping green, makes a good halfway stopping point.

The route goes along bleak **Arkengarthdale**, rising to the incredibly remote **Tan Hill Inn**, England's highest pub, near the meeting of Cumbria, North Yorkshire, and County Durham.

Re-enter **Swaledale** at **Keld**; beyond **Thwaite** the road to Hawes is known as the **Buttertubs Pass**, so-called because of the natural limestone "sinks" into which farmers used to place their butter to keep it cool on long journeys.

Grassington, in Wharfedale

NIDDERDALE AND TEESDALE

Although outside the national park, Nidderdale's scenery matches the best of the Dales; but access is limited by grouse shooting (season: Aug 12–Dec 10) and reservoirs. How Stean Gorge has small cliffs; near Pateley Bridge (fine folk museum) are Brimham Rocks, a weird, naturally sculpted landscape of tors. Stump Cross Caverns are a tour-it-yourself show cave. North of the park, within County Durham, lies Teesdale in the midst of the wildest and emptiest tracts of the Pennines. High Force is the mightiest waterfall in England. With its harsh climate and unusual soils, the official nature reserve harbors Arctic and alpine species, including the rare Teesdale violet.

▶▶▶ Yorkshire Dales National Park   *190B1*
(tel: 01756 752774)

The great Pennine mass that forms the backbone of England has its proudest moments here, in the limestone dales and gritstone moors of the Yorkshire Dales National Park, where villages and field walls are almost universally gray stone. Spend a few days in the area and you will see the subtle differences between one dale and another.

WHARFEDALE This is a long dale, with several moods. Around **Bolton Abbey**▶, all is pastel-shaded and gentle, graced by the ruined Augustinian priory and the functioning priory church; upriver the Wharfe swirls through a chasm in Strid Wood. **Burnsall**, with its old bridge and green, and **Arncliffe** are two idyllic villages; **Grassington** is larger and busier, with a range of shops and places to eat around its central square. Looming over the dale is **Kilnsey Crag**, England's largest overhang, quite a challenge for rock climbers. Like many Dales places, **Buckden** and **Kettlewell** grew up around the lead-mining industry; relics litter the moors. Tiny **Hubberholme** has a gem of a church, with a rare musicians' gallery of 1558.

AIREDALE England's most famous limestone scenery is concentrated in the area around **Malham**▶▶▶, where the subterranean River Aire reappears at the base of Malham Cove, a great inland cliff topped by limestone pavements. A short walk away, formidable Gordale Scar waterfall impressed the early Romantics. Other local walks include to Janet's Foss waterfall and Malham Tarn, with its rich plant and bird life. Downstream lies **Skipton**, a market town with a rewarding castle restored by the indefatigable Lady Anne Clifford after Civil War damage; a steam railroad heads into Wharfedale.

SWALEDALE Stone barns, abandoned lead mines (notably in Gunnerside Gill), and Swaledale sheep are features of the landscape along with the fast-flowing Swale itself. **Reeth**▶, ranged around a spacious green, is a charming large village. Enchanting **Richmond**▶▶▶ crowns a hilltop site, its mighty Norman **castle**▶▶(E.H.) staring down to the Swale and over the marketplace. There are

A traditional landscape: Swaledale has 750 stone barns and numerous drystone walls

BARNARD CASTLE
Just beyond the park's northeastern boundary, in County Durham is the town of Barnard Castle, whose namesake castle (E.H.) perches above the Tees. The Bowes Museum here, built in opulent French château style, houses a splendid collection of fine arts.

209

two museums (the Richmondshire Museum and the Green Howards regimental museum) and the streets are full of interest, but there is nothing self-conscious here. The **Georgian Theatre Royal** ▶▶ (1788), the oldest in its original form in England, is concealed by a barnlike exterior; it is open for tours. Walk by the Swale, through Hudswell Woods or to the ruins of **Easby Abbey** (E.H.).

WENSLEYDALE The cheese-making heritage is illustrated by the rural relics in the folk museum in **Hawes** and shops sell the crumbly Wensleydale cheese. This town is conveniently located, but villages such as **Askrigg**, **Bainbridge**, and **West Burton**▶ have more appeal; **Middleham**▶▶ has a pretty central square (around which stable hands parade horses from nearby racing stables) and a 12th-century castle (E.H.), former home of Richard III. Of the dale's many waterfalls, **Aysgarth Falls** are the best known; close at hand are a museum of antique carriages and Aysgarth Church, with its superb screen brought from **Jervaulx Abbey**▶, whose ruins can be seen farther east. **Hardraw Force**▶, the tallest waterfall in the country, is reached through the pub at Hardraw. **Castle Bolton**▶▶ is an impregnable-looking bulk, little altered since the 14th century; here Mary, Queen of Scots was imprisoned between 1568–1569. **Masham**▶ has an attractive heart around its large cobbled marketplace.

RIBBLESDALE AND DENTDALE Settle is a likable market town, if a bit noisy with quarry traffic; the train ride to Carlisle gives great views (see page 176). The "Three Peaks"—**Whernside** (2,414 feet), **Ingleborough** (2,372 feet), and **Pen-y-ghent** (2,277 feet)—are nearby; a popular challenge walk, often started from Horton-in-Ribblesdale, takes in all three. Ingleborough is dotted with potholes and caves, including **Ingleborough**▶ and **White Scar**▶ caverns (both are open to the public), and Gaping Gill, big enough to hold London's St. Paul's. Ingleton is the base for walks into **Ingleton Glen**▶▶ (see page 193). Dentdale, in Cumbria, lies below Whernside; don't miss **Dent**▶▶ with its cobbled streets, the epitome of the rural Pennines.

Limestone pavement above Malham Cove

Southern Scotland

Braemar
Linn O'Dee
Balmoral Castle
1154m Lochnagar
Deeside & Lochnagar
Strachan
Stonehaven
Fettercairn
Inverbervie
Laurencekirk
Johnshaven
North Esk
Clova
Spittal of Glenshee
Kirkmichael
ANGUS
Edzell Castle
Brechin
Aberlemno
Montrose
South Esk
Bridge of Cally
Kirriemuir
Friockheim
Inverkeilor
Alyth
Forfar
Blairgowrie
unkeld
Isla
Glamis
Glamis Castle
Birnam
Coupar Angus
Arbroath
Caputh
Stanley
Muirhead
Dundee
Carnoustie
Balbeggie
Scone Palace
Monifieth
Perth
Newport-on-Tay
M90
Glencarse
Firth of Tay
ridge
Earn
Elcho Castle
Newburgh
Leuchars
Auchtermuchty
St Andrews
Craigtoun
Fife Ness
M90
Falkland Palace
Ceres
FIFE
Crail
Ladybank
Kinross
Pittenweem
Anstruther
Cupar
umbling
Bridge
Loch Leven
Glenrothes
Elie
Earlsferry
Buckhaven
Cowdenbeath
Leven
Dunfermline
Kirkcaldy
Burntisland
Firth of Forth
North Berwick
opetoun
House
Inverkeithing
Gullane
Dunbar
South Queensferry
M9
EDINBURGH
Dalmeny
Haddington
East Linton
Cockburnspath
oxburn
Livingston
Musselburgh
Dalkeith
EAST LOTHIAN
St Abb's Head
St Abbs
18
Loanhead
Bonnyrigg
Gifford
Grantshouse
Eyemouth
West Linton
Penicuik
Newtongrange
Chirnside
Berwick-upon-Tweed
MIDLOTHIAN
Lammermuir Hills
Duns
Dolphinton
Eddleston
Lauder
Greenlaw
Swinton
Peebles
Dolphinton
Eildon & Leaderfoot
Gordon
Coldstream
Lowick
Biggar
Traquair House
Galashiels
Kelso
Tweed
Ford
Drumelzier
Tweeddale
Abbotsford House
Melrose
ppe
Tweedsmuir
Selkirk
St Boswells
Town Yetholm
Wooler
Grey Mare's Tail
BORDERS (SCOTTISH)
Jedburgh
Cheviot Hills
816m
The Cheviot
Moffat
Hawick
Denholm
Beattock
Teviothead
Alwinton
Rothbury
A74(M)
Eskdalemuir
Hermitage
NORTHUMBERLAND
Coquet
Otterburn
Liddel
Kielder Water
ochmaben
Langholm
Border
Forest Park
West Woodburn
Lockerbie
Northumberland National Park
Kirkwhelpington
Housesteads Fort
Hadrian's Wall
Chollerford
aerlaverock
Castle
Gretna Green
Birdoswald Fort
Vindolanda
Tyne
Chesters Fort
Bowness-on-Solway
Annan
Brampton
Haltwhistle
Hexham
Corbridge
illoth
Carlisle
Crosby
Wetheral
Derwent Reservoir
Wigton
Thursby
Eden
Alston
Castleside
Aspatria
CUMBRIA
Lazonby
Melmerby
Wearhead
Stanhope
Maryport
Bothel
Caldbeck
Langwathby
893m
Cross Fell
DURHAM
ockermouth
Bassenthwaite
931m
Skiddaw
Greystoke
Penrith
Cow Green Reservoir
High Force
4
M5
M6
5

The miniature Highland scenery of the Trossachs: Loch Arklet

RECOMMENDED CITIES Edinburgh, Glasgow.

INLAND TOWNS AND VILLAGES
Scottish Borders: Peebles.
Stirling: Stirling.

COASTAL TOWNS/VILLAGES
Angus: Arbroath, Montrose.
Fife: Anstruther, Crail, Culross, St. Andrews.

GREAT HOUSES
Angus: Glamis
Argyll and Bute: Hill House
Dumfries and Galloway: Culzean, Drumlanrig.
Perth and Kinross: Scone.
Scottish Borders: Abbotsford, Bowhill, Mellerstain, Traquair.
West Lothian: Hopetoun.

Castles
Argyll and Bute: Bothwell, Rothesay (Bute).
City of Edinburgh: Edinburgh.
Dumfries and Galloway: Caerlaverock.
Fife: Kellie, St. Andrews.
Stirling: Doune, Stirling.
West Lothian: Linlithgow. Craignethan.

RUINED ABBEYS AND CATHEDRALS
Dumfries and Galloway: Sweetheart.
Fife: St. Andrews.
Scottish Borders: Dryburgh, Jedburgh, Melrose.
Angus: Arbroath.

ROYAL PALACES
Stirling: Stirling.
Fife: Falkland.
West Lothian Linlithgow.

Gardens
Dumfries and Galloway: Castle Kennedy, Threave.
City of Edinburgh: Edinburgh Royal Botanic Garden.

THE SCOTTISH NATION Scotland is now part of the U.K., but has a long history as an independent state. After having fought hard to maintain its sovereignty, Scotland surrendered its independence in an act of Parliamentary Union with England and Wales in 1707. Scotland's parliament was abolished, and since then it has been ruled from London by a British parliament in the House of Commons. However, it was allowed to keep its church, legal and educational systems distinctive and separate. In 1997, the Scots voted to have their own parliament once again. The first elections for the Scottish Parliament were held in 1999, and a new Parliament building is being erected near the Royal Mile in Edinburgh; however, Scotland still retains Members of Parliament representing its views in Westminster.

THE LAY OF THE LAND Southern Scotland is composed of the Central Lowlands and the Southern Uplands, a wide band of hills that stretches from coast to coast. In the west this latter, wild area is known as **Dumfries and Galloway** while the eastern part is known as the **(Scottish) Borders**, though in fact both parts have acted since time immemorial as a war-torn border country, a self-governing shield between England and Scotland. The Lowlands occupy a rift valley, comprising the westward flowing River Clyde and the long eastern intrusion of the Firth of Forth. This is the heart of Scotland, studded with ancient Christian sanctuaries, sturdy medieval burghs, royal palaces, baronial seats, thickly populated manufacturing towns, and its great rival cities of Glasgow and Edinburgh. The Central Lowlands, encompassing **Argyll and Bute**; **West**, **mid-** and **East Lothian**; **Stirling**; **Fife**, and part of the **Perth and Kinross**, and **Angus** regions, are by no means uniformly low-lying. The handsome capital city of **Edinburgh** is perched among volcanic hills, Glasgow—Scotland's most populous city—is overlooked by the Campsie Fells, Dundee is fringed by the Sidlaw Hills, and the Kingdom of Fife is given a

TAMDHU
SINGLE MALT SCOTCH WHISKY
YEARS **10** OLD
PRODUCT OF SCOTLAND 100% SCOTCH WHISKY
DISTILLED AT
TAMDHU DISTILLERY

backbone by the Ochil Hills. The northern frontier of the Lowlands is the Highland Boundary Fault, which divides the island of Arran in half, continues northeast through Helensburgh to Loch Lomond and skirts through old market towns such as Crieff and Dunkeld to reach Stonehaven on the east coast.

THE HERITAGE Most of the great prehistoric monuments of Scotland are found in the north, but there are good collections of Pictish and early Christian carved stones to be seen in Angus and St. Andrews. Viking invasions in the 9th century destroyed much of the evidence of Celtic Christianity except for the distinctive round towers at Brechin in Angus, and Abernethy in Perth and Kinross. Dunfermline Abbey and the famous Norman church in Leuchars, near St. Andrews in Fife, are good examples of the Romanesque influence, which came to Scotland in the late 11th century. This was followed by the Gothic period, well represented by the ruined Border abbeys as well as the surviving cathedrals of Dunblane and Glasgow.

The 15th century is the most distinctively Scottish period: the simpler collegiate church developed then, with battlemented towers and stone-slabbed roofs and spires. This period also saw the birth of the tower house with its thick, vertical stone walls, a concept gradually enriched by combining towers into L, T, and Z plans; the roofs budded a playful array of corner turrets, crow-stepped gable ends, and balconies. The neat burghs, or market towns, are dominated by a broad high street, typically with a mercat cross and the Tolbooth, which served as both jail and town hall. The 16th-century royal palaces at Linlithgow, Falkirk, and Stirling reveal the influence of the Renaissance, but it was not before the more peaceful politics of the late 17th century that Scotland produced a truly classical style. Sir William Bruce ushered in this period, but it was dominated by two generations of the Adam family (William and sons—Robert, James and John), who gave the term Adamesque to their Palladian vision of 18th-century Britain. Mellerstain, Culzean, and Charlotte Square in the New Town of Edinburgh are among the family's great works.

In the early 19th century the Romantic movement encouraged a return to a native Scottish spirit, leading to the Gothic-Baronial style of the high Victorian era, which still dominates the land.

By contrast the unrivalled modernist architect Charles Rennie Mackintosh created an idiosyncratic version of Art Nouveau in such buildings as Hill House and the Glasgow School of Art, among many others.

O Caledonia! stern and wild,
Meet nurse for a poetic child!
Land of brown heath and shaggy wood,
Land of the mountain and the flood,
Land of my sires! what mortal hand
Can e'er untie the filial band
That knits me to thy rugged strand?
—Sir Walter Scott, The Lay of the Last Minstrel (1805)

▶▶▶ **REGION HIGHLIGHTS**

The (Scottish) Borders pages 217, and 218–219

Caerlaverock Castle page 221

Culross pages 226–227

Culzean Castle page 216

Edinburgh pages 223–225

Glasgow pages 228–229

New Lanark page 220

St. Andrews page 230

Stirling Castle page 231

Threave Castle and Gardens page 221

SCOTS GLOSSARY
Some of the Gaelic and local terms you might come across:
Broch Circular stone defensive tower
Burn Stream
Ceilidh Impromptu gathering with singing and story-telling
Cist Ancient coffin made of slabs or a hollow tree
Croft Small farm, often tenanted
Glen Valley
Law Isolated hill
Linn Waterfall
Machair Coarse grass beside the sea, often used for grazing
Mull Promontory

Walks

Callander Crags, Stirling *210D3*

Parking lot on west side of Callander.
A marked path from Tulipan Crescent,
by the tennis courts, leads into
woods. A steep climb is rewarded by
splendid views of the Trossachs from
the top of the Crags, which form the
edge of an abrupt escarpment.
(1½ hours)

Culzean Country Park, *210B2*
South Ayrshire

Parking lot by Culzean Castle. The
park is laced with trails; a detailed
map is available on site. Aim to visit
the castle, Happy Valley (with its
exotic trees), the walled garden, and
Swan Pond. Maidens village to the
south is an alternative starting point,
where you can walk along the shore to
the estate gates. (1 to 2 hours)

Grey Mare's Tail, *211B4*
Dumfries and Galloway

*Parking lot by A708 between Selkirk
and Moffat.* A fine waterfall, visible
from the road, but worth taking either
of the marked trails for close-up
views. The longer trail climbs to the
top of the fall and heads for lonely
Loch Skeen. (1 to 2½ hours)

*St. Abb's Head: the view of the cliffs at
White Heugh, where guillemot and kitti-
wake may be seen*

New Lanark, *210C3*
South Lanarkshire

Parking lot in New Lanark. This
remarkable "model" village is the
starting point for walks along the
Clyde Gorge, with its dramatic waterfalls. Walk south, parallel with the
river, through the village, then fork
right onto a track and right again onto
a path above the river. Cross the river
at a sluice bridge and turn right for further views to ruined Corra Castle.
Return the same way. (2 hours)

St. Abb's Head, *211C5*
(Scottish) Borders

*Parking lot by nature reserve visitor
center just west of St. Abb's village.* A
short path leads toward the village,
then turns north parallel with the
coast for bracing cliff views to the
lighthouse at St. Abb's Head, where
there are nesting sites for 50,000
birds, including puffins. Either return
along the cliffs or take the easier lighthouse access road, with spectacular
views of the coast. (1 hour)

▶ **Angus**   *211E5*

(tel: 01382 434664)

The county of Angus extends westward from the North Sea across prosperous farmland (renowned for its black cattle) to the Grampians. The best scenery is to be found in the "Braes of Angus"—beautiful glens such as Glen Isla, Glen Prosen, Glen Clova, and Glen Esk—and on the rocky coast between **Montrose▶** and **Arbroath▶**. Montrose is a delightful summer resort whose Flemish-style architecture reflects centuries of trading with the Low Countries. **Montrose Basin**, the adjacent brackish tidal inlet, is the haunt of thousands of birds, including oystercatchers, curlews and pink-footed geese; there is a wildlife center on the A934. The fishing and market town of Arbroath, too, has something of a resort air in the summer. Its most famous monument is the 12th-century, red-stone abbey—a picturesque ruin which is surrounded by tombstones.

Inland and north of Arbroath by 14 miles is **Brechin**, a red-stone market town on the banks of the South Esk River. Standing proud beside the small cathedral is Scotland's finest **round tower▶** (H.S.). Only three such tall, slender towers are known outside Ireland; they date from the 10th century and were used as the refuge and watchtower of the independent monasteries of the Celtic Church. At **Aberlemno**, 5 miles southwest along the back road to Forfar, are some fine carved Pictish stones.

Due north of Brechin is **Edzell▶ ▶**. The ruins of its castle are handsome enough, but it is the Pleasance, the walled garden laid out by the scholar Sir David Lindsay in 1604, that makes the place exceptional.

In the fertile Vale of Strathmore, a little southwest of Forfar, is **Glamis Castle▶ ▶** (as in Shakespeare's *Macbeth*), its brooding bulk standing quiet and solemn in the spacious acres of its deer park. Near the castle, a row of stone-roofed cottages houses the **Angus Folk Museum ▶** (N.T.S.) of reconstructed interiors and domestic bygones.

▶▶ **Arran**   *210C1–C2*

(tel: 01292 288688)

The largest of the Clyde Islands, Arran is a traditional vacation island, easily and quickly reached from Glasgow by train and ferry. Sheltered by the Kintyre Peninsula, it enjoys unusually warm weather and has dramatic mountains (Goat Fell rises to 2,867 feet), deep valleys, and sandy and rocky bays. As you approach the island on the ferry from Ardrossan, **Brodick Castle▶** (N.T.S.), an ancient stronghold of the Stuarts and from 1503 the Hamilton family, dominates the shoreline. Its gardens include one of the finest rhododendron collections in Scotland. Arran is studded with prehistoric stones and is a paradise both for hill-walkers and birdwatchers, and for geologists, who come by the busload because virtually every rock type is represented on the island.

North lies the flatter, fertile island of **Bute**. Another important Clyde resort, the capital town of Rothesay is reached by ferry from Wemyss Bay. Ruined Rothesay Castle, like Arran's, was once the property of the Stuart kings. Cromwell destroyed it in the 17th century. Following a minor road to the south of the island and then a footpath across a field, you can walk among the ruins of St. Blane's monastery with views of the Firth of Clyde.

215

Brodick Castle and Garden, Isle of Arran

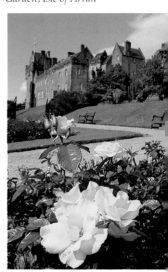

ROBERT BURNS
Often described as
Scotland's ploughman
poet, Robert Burns
(1759–1796) was well
educated for his time.
Though his amorous
exploits have gained
notoriety, his contribution
to literature was through
poetry that shrewdly
observes the foibles of his
fellow men. He also wrote
numerous sentimental,
lyrical, and narrative
pieces and was an avid
"improver" of Scottish
traditional songs. A major
theme running through
his work was a belief in
the universal brotherhood
of man.

MORE BURNS SITES
Near the birthplace and
Burns Museum in Alloway
are the Brig o'Doon and
17th-century Alloway Kirk;
both feature in Burns's
poem *Tam o'Shanter*, and
Burns was baptized in the
Kirk itself. The imposing
Burns Monument was
erected in 1823 and
bears figures (added five
years later) of Tam
o'Shanter and his
drinking companion,
Souter Johnny.

*Culzean Castle, Robert
Adam's elegant creation*

▶ **Ayr** 210B2

(tel: 01292 288688)

Admirers of Scotland's national poet, Robert Burns, will
need no encouragement to visit his birthplace at **Allo-
way▶** on the southern outskirts of the coastal resort of
Ayr. Burns was one of the few European poets to rival
Shakespeare for wit and vigor. Burns spent his first
seven years at the humble cottage next to what is
now the Burns Museum. Close by, the **Tam o'Shanter
Experience** is an audiovisual show recounting his famous
poem. To the south is the Burns Monument of 1823.

High on a clifftop 12 miles down the coast road from
Ayr, **Culzean Castle▶▶▶** (N.T.S.), built 1772–1790 and
the ancient seat of the Kennedys, hides behind its battlemented exterior a supremely elegant classical interior
by Scottish architect Robert Adam, one of his finest
Scottish creations. The celebrated oval staircase rises
through three tiers of columns to an exceptional second-
floor salon. Culzean Country Park, with its walled
summer garden, woodland walks, lake, and camellia
greenhouses, is the most popular of the National Trust for
Scotland's properties. Laid out on the dunes a little south
of Culzean is the famous **Turnberry Golf Course**.

THE (SCOTTISH) BORDERS

Drive

The (Scottish) Borders towns, abbeys, and houses to visit

A 100-mile tour of the best of the (Scottish) Borders towns, abbeys, and uplands. See also pages 218–219.

Start from **Peebles** and take the A72 east, following the Tweed, to **Traquair House**▶ ▶ outside Innerleithen. Continue along the A72 (passing the Scottish Museum of Woollen Textiles in Walkerburn) to reach Galashiels. Here, look for the turning to Walter Scott's house, **Abbotsford**▶. From Abbotsford join the A72, but turn off into **Melrose** for the ruined **abbey**▶ ▶. Head back onto the A72 then the A68 for St. Boswells and **Dryburgh Abbey**▶ ▶. Detour north on the B6356 to Scott's View. Take the B6404 for a look at **Smailholm Tower** on your way north to **Mellerstain House**▶ ▶. From here cross to **Hume Castle** and join the B6364 to Kelso to see its ruined abbey and, to the west of town, **Floors Castle**▶ ▶.

Follow the A698 south along the Teviot Valley to **Jedburgh** with its ruined **abbey**▶ ▶, Jail Museum, and Mary, Queen of Scots House. You can detour south of the town to Ferniehirst Castle Centre and the Capon Tree. From Jedburgh take the A68 north to St. Boswells and turn west onto the A699 to **Bowhill House**, west of Selkirk.

Follow Yarrow Water upstream, along the A708, turning north at Mountbenger onto the B709 for the lonely crossing of Deuchar Law to Traquair House. From here a small road on the south bank of the Tweed passes **Kailzie Gardens**, near Cardrona, on the return to Peebles.

Dryburgh Abbey, founded in 1150

217

Young Walter Scott, in Smailholm Tower

218

THE EILDON HILLS AND WALTER SCOTT

Legend has it that these pink hills that rise prominently out of the valley near Melrose were cleft in three one night by the 13th-century wizard Michael Scott (Michele Scot in Dante's *Inferno*), to settle a dispute with the devil (the wizard's spellbook is said to be buried in Melrose Abbey). Geologists insist they are the relics of old volcanoes. Either way, they make excellent walking territory for those staying in Melrose and were a favorite of Sir Walter Scott. Visit Scott's View, beside the B6356 north of St. Boswells, for the view of them he so enjoyed.

▶▶ The (Scottish) Borders   211B4
(tel: 01750 20054)

As famous for its salmon as for its tweed, the (Scottish) Borders is a land scarred by centuries of turbulence. Fought over since the days of the Romans, it has many sites that bear silent testimony to this past—tower houses built to ward off border raiders, skeletons of abbeys vengefully destroyed by England's Henry VIII. It is also Sir Walter Scott country, the countryside that inspired Scotland's most celebrated novelist. There is nowhere else quite like it in Scotland—no big mountains but lonely, rounded hills, good for bracing moorland walks, and a pleasant coast. Even in the vacation season, there are no tourist jams.

The town of **Jedburgh**▶▶ is best known for its **abbey**▶ and anyone planning to visit the four great Borders abbeys—Jedburgh, Dryburgh, Melrose, and Kelso—should visit the Abbey visitor center here, which admirably explains their role. Jedburgh Abbey holds the record for border raids—destroyed and rebuilt eight times in its 400-year working life. Its finest features are the two late Norman doorways and the excellent tracery window in the north transept. Also in the town are Mary, Queen of Scots House, which tells the story of the queen who stayed here in 1556, and the Castle Jail Museum.

Selkirk is a tweed-manufacturing town and a good base. **Bowhill House**▶ is 4 miles west, set in the high ground between two tributaries of the Tweed. Its many magnificent works of art include the last Leonardo da Vinci in private hands in Britain. The house is surrounded by beautiful grounds.

Just outside Innerleithen, is **Traquair House**▶▶, one of Scotland's oldest inhabited houses, dating from about 1,000 years ago, although most of the structure is 17th century. Its forbidding outline is softened by the pale harling of its walls, but it remains dark and chilly inside. In the gardens is an excellent maze that children will love. The house includes an 18th-century brewery, which brews the excellent Traquair House beers. **Peebles**, a pleasant town set on the River Tweed, was the home of the writer John Buchan (1875–1940), most famous for his tales of spy-hunter Richard Hannay.

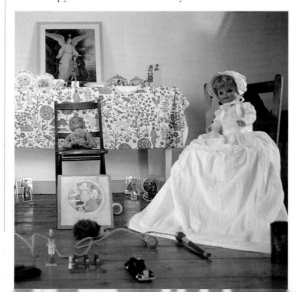

Children's playthings on display in Traquair House

Between Galashiels and Melrose is **Abbotsford►**, the imposing turreted mansion that the great novelist Sir Walter Scott built himself on the banks of the Tweed. It is still inhabited by his descendants and houses his extraordinary collection of assorted Scottish curiosities.

Melrose is an appealing town. Close by the compact main square stands **Melrose Abbey► ►**, its remains being the finest example of the golden age of Scottish ecclesiastical architecture. Its soft pink stone is warm, forgiving, and kind, and a magical atmosphere pervades the site. Robert the Bruce's heart is said to be buried here. From the town there are delightful walks up to the Eildon Hills (see panel, page 218) and along the River Tweed.

Dryburgh Abbey► ►, set peacefully in an exquisite bend of the graceful River Tweed near St. Boswells, is the most moving of the four Borders abbeys. Large sections stand astonishingly well preserved, especially the cloisters. If you walk nowhere else, walk here; it's the best way to enjoy the peace and tranquility of Scotland's most serene ruin. Leave your car and cross the Tweed by the footbridge.

A little way northeast is **Smailholm Tower►**, a classic pele tower (see panel). **Mellerstain House► ►** is found 6 miles northwest of Kelso. This breathtaking Georgian house, built by William and Robert Adam in the mid-18th

century (see panel page 51), is the perfect example of the Adams' skill in combining stateliness with domestic ease and comfort. Inside, the large, wide, light rooms, in their pale Adam colors, are as perfect as the day they were finished. A museum contains a wonderful portrait of Bonnie Prince Charlie disguised as Flora MacDonald's Irish maid, Betty Burke (see page 246).

Kelso is a proud town, but the abbey ruins are the least captivating of the Borders' abbeys, the square tower resembling a fortress. To the west of Kelso stands **Floors Castle► ►**, its William Adam and William Playfair exterior one of the stateliest of all the Border palaces. On a sunny day its pinnacled facade gleams above its terraced riverside grounds. Only the hall retains its original Adam interior, but in the state rooms are many treasures. The 19th-century Gothick bird room is a popular curiosity.

The coast at **St. Abb's Head►** (see Walks, page 214) is a prime site for naturalists and birdwatchers.

PELE TOWERS
The word "pele" or "peel" is derived from the Latin *palus* or palisade and was the name given to the tower houses built around the Scotland-England border against the raiding enemy. Smailholm Tower, near St. Boswells, is a well-preserved example from the 16th century. Then it housed a continuous day and night watch; now it stands square and stern and stark on a moorland crag, overhanging a sullen pool. The 15th-century tower house at Cranshaws in the Lammermuir Hills features in Scott's *The Bride of Lammermuir*.

219

Founded in the 12th century, Jedburgh Abbey was used as a place of worship until 1875

TWEED MAKING
For countless centuries Borderers have made tweed, a practical, hard-wearing woolen cloth that was formerly known as "Galashiels Grey." In the 1820s Sir Walter Scott brought the material to the attention of fashionable London society by making a sensational appearance in black-and-white checked trousers, and later tweed enjoyed the patronage of Queen Victoria and Prince Albert. The styles and colors have become more sophisticated, and today many spinners, weavers, designers and tapestry makers work in the Borders. In Galashiels, the **Scottish College of Textiles** is a renowned center, while the **Lochcarron of Scotland Cashmere and Wool Centre** (open for tours) is the producer of the world's largest range of wool worsted tartans.

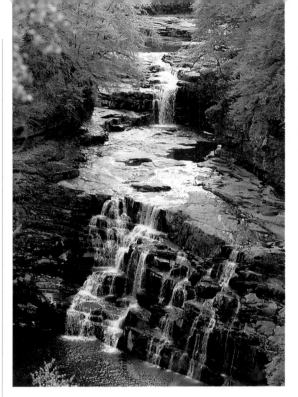

The Falls of Clyde run through a gorge just below New Lanark

THE COVENANTERS
The Covenanters were a leading faction of Scottish society in the 17th century that supported a Presbyterian system of church government. The National Covenant was signed in 1638 and the bishops, appointed by the Crown, were abolished the same year. Under the leadership of Archibald Campbell, 8th Earl of Argyll, the Covenanters successfully opposed an army sent north by Charles I. This campaign, known as the First Bishops War, led directly into the greater engagement of the Civil War. Sir Walter Scott's novel *Old Mortality* tells the story of the Lowland Covenanters and the extremes to which their religious fervor led them.

MARY, QUEEN OF SCOTS' LOVER
James Hepburn, Earl of Bothwell, is one of history's more exciting characters. He was the lover of Mary, Queen of Scots, the possible father of James VI, and certainly the murderer of Darnley, the queen's second husband, whose body was found strangled outside the bombed-out house of Kirk O'Field. He then divorced his wife and rushed the queen out to a secret marriage at Dunbar Castle in 1567. Hounded by their enemies, the lovers were, however, forced to part, and Bothwell was eventually imprisoned in the Danish Castle of Dragsholm, where he died insane.

▶ The Clyde Valley   210C3
(tel: 0141-204 4400)

Deep in the wooded Clyde Valley near Lanark (see Walks, page 214) is the 18th-century model mill town of **New Lanark▶▶**. It is linked with such key figures of the Industrial Revolution as the inventor Richard Arkwright and Robert Owen (1771–1858), the social reformer, who attempted through enlightened programs to create a cooperative industrial community here; Owen believed that such ideas would one day replace private ownership. His Nursery building, the Institute for the Formation of Character, the school, and apartments housing the workers have all been restored. You can take in a short introductory history "ride" in the award-winning visitor center before looking in at Robert Owen's House, the Millworker's House and the period-style village store.

Some 5 miles west of Lanark, **Craignethan Castle▶▶** is a fine example of a 16th-century stronghold. The most exciting feature is the caponier, a large vaulted gallery built onto the floor of the moat providing protection from artillery fire (though it nearly suffocated the defenders in smoke); this one is thought to be the earliest in Britain.

Bothwell▶▶, just southeast of Glasgow, boasts a pretty 14th-century church and a monument, by the bridge, that commemorates the defeat of the Covenanters (see panel) at the battle of 1679. However, the town is chiefly renowned for its 13th-century castle. Set high above the Clyde, its walls studded with round towers, it always held a strategic role. It was much damaged in the Wars of Independence of 1296–1330 against England.

► **Dumfries and Galloway** *210B3*
(tel: 01387 253862)

The western hills are wilder and more expansive than the better-known (Scottish) Borders District to the east. The character of the region is also more solemn, though it's enlivened by some interesting archeological sites, some haunting ruins, and some splendid castles. While much of the countryside inland is humdrum, the southern coast is a pleasant place to wander around, with an occasional surprising view of the English Lake District (best from the top of Criffel, south of Dumfries). The area is never crowded; some of the wildest parts of the Southern Uplands are in Galloway Forest Park (parts of which are tediously blanketed in evergreen plantations), and some of the Lowlands' most beautiful countryside is in the hills and valleys of the Rivers Nith, Annan, and Esk, to the north and east of the gray-stone town of Dumfries.

Standing beside the Solway Firth 9 miles south of Dumfries is **Caerlaverock Castle►►**. Its unusual triangular plan, its full moat, and the green serenity of its site make this, "the lark's nest" castle, one of the most memorable in the country. It has been much fought over, and the outer walls were beseiged by King Edward I in 1300 less than a decade after the foundations had been laid. The interior bears a very fine Renaissance facade added by the enlightened Lord Nithsdale, head of the Maxwell clan, in the 17th century. Not far away at Ruthwell is the particularly fine carved Anglo-Saxon **Ruthwell Cross►**. Over 16 feet high and dated to the 7th century, it is one of the most important monuments of the Dark Ages.

Threave Castle and Threave Gardens (N.T.S.)**►►**, a grim castle and a delightful garden, lie a few miles apart near Castle Douglas, 10 miles northeast of Kirkcudbright. Threave Castle was built by Archibald the Grim, who boasted how the awful gallows' knob that sticks out over the entrance "never wanted a tassel." Threave Castle was a 14th-century stronghold of the notorious Black Douglases, so called because of their merciless pillaging, and was besieged unsuccessfully by the royal forces of James II in 1455. South of the ruined castle is the Threave Wildfowl Refuge, where wintering birds include wild geese and teal.

CURLING
For at least 350 years this team game, played on ice, has been enjoyed all over Scotland. The curling stones are made from granite and have handles sunken into the top. The object is to slide the stones along the ice into a tee, the team with the most stones at the center of the tee being the winner. The best stones are reputed to be from Ailsa Craig, a 1,100-ft-high volcanic plug of a rock 10 miles off Girvan that persistently pops up into view as you drive around the Ayrshire coast.

221

On its island in the River Dee, Threave Castle speaks of a strife-ridden period in Scottish history

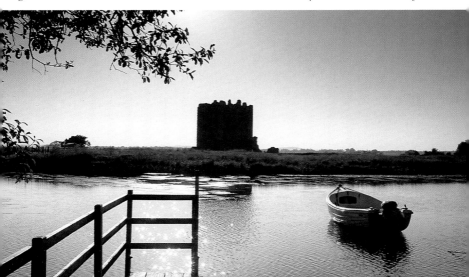

DULCE COR
The beautiful ruined red walls of Sweetheart Abbey, south of Dumfries on the A710, have a romantic tale to tell. The abbey was founded in 1273 by Lady Dervorgilla after her husband John Balliol was killed by Robert the Bruce (she also founded Balliol College, Oxford, in his honor). She kept her husband's embalmed heart close to her until her death at the age of 90. Both were then interred in the church, which became known as Dulce Cor ("sweet heart").

Drumlanrig Castle, ringed by forests and rolling hills

The nearby (but separately administered) Threave Gardens are where the National Trust for Scotland trains its budding young horticulturalists. Every type of terrain and condition they are likely to encounter is authentically re-created here, from rose to heather garden, from rock to wood; there are herbaceous borders, a walled garden, and fabulous glasshouses in which exotic flowers and fruits grow. In spring there is a display of some 200 different types of daffodil.

The town of **Kirkcudbright►** is set sweetly on the River Dee around MacLellan's Castle. With its typical pastel-painted housefronts, it has long been beloved of Scottish artists; E.A. Hornel was a member of the artists' colony founded here in the early years of this century. There are several art galleries in the town today. It is a tranquil place to spend a day wandering around. Visit the ancient tollbooth, with its curious and beautiful spire, or the Stewartry Museum with its many local antiquities and curios; a display explains the strange and ancient Scottish pastime of curling (see panel, page 221). In Gatehouse of Fleet, 8 miles northwest, is the **Mill on the Fleet►►**, a visitor center based on a restored 18th-century cotton mill that portrays the town's industrial past.

Whithorn, 18 miles south of Newton Stewart, is one of the oldest Christian centers in Britain; here, in 397, St. Ninian built the first Christian church in Scotland, although the present ruin dates from the 13th century. The Whithorn Museum (H.S.) has finds related to the saint.

The southwesternmost corner of this region is the strange spit of land known as the Rhinns of Galloway (from which there are views of the Mourne Mountains across the water in Northern Ireland). Here is the **Logan Botanic Garden►**, where plants from the temperate regions of the southern hemisphere thrive in a walled garden. **Castle Kennedy Gardens►**, near Stranraer, were laid out on a grand scale by the 18th-century Earl of Stair, with ruins, lakes, and wooded walks. It is at its most majestic when the rhododendrons and azaleas are in bloom in early summer.

In the northern part of Dumfries and Galloway, set beside the River Nith near Thornhill, is **Drumlanrig►►**. No building looks more solid or more imposingly rooted in Scotland than this pink 17th-century palace. Within its massive walls are the region's finest collections of Old Masters, including a Rembrandt, and exquisite French furniture of the 18th century. Rural craftsmen, with work for sale, operate in the grounds.

▶▶▶ Edinburgh   211C4
(tel: 0131-473 3800)

The capital of Scotland is an outstanding city. It is rich in open spaces, museums, beautiful buildings, and elegant streets, all lit by the clear Lothian light. The dark courts, cobbled streets, and steep steps of the medieval Old Town contrast with the gracious squares, circuses, and crescents of the Georgian New Town. It is at its most exhilarating during the International Festival and Fringe in August.

The Royal Mile▶▶ is the original and chief street of the city. At its western end lies the **castle▶▶**(H.S.), on the site of an ancient fortress and home to the Scottish Crown Jewels; at the other end are the Abbey and **Palace of Holyroodhouse▶**, the official Scottish residence of the Queen (open to the public when the Royal Family is not here). The Royal Mile is the heart of the Old Town; many of the city's most historic landmarks are on it, and there are numerous museums and houses to visit (see panel).

St. Giles' Cathedral▶, the High Kirk of Edinburgh, was originally built in the traditional shape of a cross, though later additions have given it an unusual square design. **Canongate Kirk▶** is a dignified example of a Presbyterian church, with typical white-painted walls and wooden box pews. **The Royal Museum of Scotland▶▶** on Chambers Street is a worldwide collection with decorative art and archeology galleries, a natural history section, a geology department, and (most popular with the young) technology galleries. Admission covers the adjacent **Museum of Scotland**, which concentrates on all things Scottish. In Holyrood Road, **The Dynamic Earth▶▶** (a funded Millennium project) uses state-of-the-art technology in a voyage of discovery around our planet. **The Grassmarket▶▶** is for many the pleasantest part of the Old Town, with its plentiful antique shops and bistros.

The Mound is a causeway between the Old and New Towns. There are views across to chilly **Calton Hill▶▶** where the **National Monument▶** stands, modeled on the Parthenon in Greece to commemorate the Scots who fell in the Napoleonic Wars. Though never completed, it's

Princes Street and Edinburgh Castle, dramatically perched on a volcanic crag, as seen from Calton Hill

THE ROYAL MILE
The Camera Obscura, near the castle in the Outlook Tower, gives a "living image" of the city projected via lenses (best on a bright day). Opposite, **The Scotch Whisky Heritage Centre** tells all there is to know about whisky. **Gladstone's Land** (N.T.S.), on the Lawnmarket, is a re-creation of a typical Old Town, six-story tenement house. **The Writers' Museum** contains memorabilia of Scottish writers, including Robert Burns, Sir Walter Scott, and Robert Louis Stevenson. **The People's Story** tells the story of ordinary folk from the 18th century on. **John Knox House** displays interesting artifacts from the life of this pivotal figure of the Scottish Reformation. Opposite is the absorbing **Museum of Childhood**. **Huntly House,** a striking 16th-century mansion, houses the city's excellent museum of its own history.

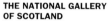

THE FORMER ROYAL YACHT *BRITANNIA*

The Queen's famous royal yacht, built in Clydebank near Glasgow and launched in 1953, is now a museum berthed at Leith, on the edge of Edinburgh. Britannia buses run by Guide Friday depart from Waverley Bridge, or you can take a less expensive city bus number 10 or 17 from the shop side of Princes Street. Leith has pleasant waterfront restaurants.

THE NATIONAL GALLERY OF SCOTLAND

The collection includes Rembrandt's self-portrait at the age of 51, Poussin's sequence of *The Seven Sacraments* (now set in a room whose details are taken from the pictures), Velasquez's *Old Woman Cooking Eggs*, El Greco's *Savior of the World*, and many works by Scotland's own painters. *The Reverend Robert Walker Skating on Duddingston Loch* by Sir Henry Raeburn (1756–1823) is one of Scotland's favorite paintings. An excellent cross-section of modern works are on show at the Scottish National Gallery of Modern Art in Belford Road, west of the New Town.

evidence of the 18th-century boast that Edinburgh had become the Athens of the North. Beside the Mound is the **National Gallery of Scotland▶▶▶**, a classical building housing the national art collection (see panel).

Princes Street▶ is the principal shopping street. Running along one side are Princes Street Gardens; the **Scott Monument** is the most striking, if endearingly excessive, landmark, covered with statuettes depicting characters from Sir Walter Scott's novels and poems; you can climb steps to the top.

On Queen Street, in the New Town, a distinctive red-brick Venetian palace houses the **Scottish National Portrait Gallery▶**. There is not one second-rate picture in the portrait gallery, and no shortage of famous subjects. Especially striking is the wonderful Allan Ramsay portrait of the great 18th-century Edinburgh philosopher David Hume. In 1791 Robert Adam was commissioned to design one superb square to enhance the quality of the New Town. Grand, spacious, and elegant, his **Charlotte Square▶** is the quintessence of the New Town. Number 7, the **Georgian House** (N.T.S.), has been restored as a typical Georgian New Town home, giving a glimpse of an interior of about 1800.

The **Royal Botanic Garden▶**, beyond the New Town, has superb tropical greenhouses. Good walks are to be had on **Arthur's Seat**, a volcanic hill in Holyrood Park, and along the **Water of Leith**, to the west of the New Town.

EDINBURGH

From the Castle to Charlotte Square

Start at the **Castle▶▶**, then enter the **Royal Mile▶▶** at Lawn Market to visit the **Scotch Whisky Heritage Centre▶**, **Camera Obscura▶**, and **Gladstone's Land▶** (N.T.S.). Continue along High Street past Parliament House, the Tron Kirk, **St. Giles Cathedral▶**, and the City Chambers. Go on past the **Museum of Childhood▶** and **John Knox House** along Canongate, to the **People's Story▶**, **Huntly House Museum**, and the **Canongate Kirk▶**, to **Holyrood Palace▶**.

Return up Holyrood Road and along the Cowgate to pass the University, the **Royal Museum of Scotland▶▶**,

Greyfriars Church▶ (and statue of the loyal little dog, Greyfriars Bobby) and then the **Grassmarket▶▶**. Turn up Victoria Street, left down Bank Street to **Lady Stair's House▶**, and then down The Mound to the **Scottish National Gallery▶▶▶** and the **Royal Scottish Academy** (catch the views toward the National Monument on Calton Hill). Turn right onto **Princes Street▶** to the **Scott Monument**, across and onto St. Andrew Square and Queen Street for the **Scottish National Portrait Gallery▶** and **Museum of Antiquities▶**.

Follow George Street as far as Frederick Street, turn left, then right on Rose Street, and continue to Robert Adam's **Charlotte Square▶** to visit the **Georgian House** (N.T.S.).

*The Cramond ferry
leaving the Dalmeny side
of the river*

226

END OF AN ERA
With the opening of the
Forth road bridge, the
villages that stand on
either side of the Firth—
known as North and South
Queensferry—lost the
ferry service that had
existed for some 900
years. Among the earliest
travelers here was Queen
Margaret, wife of Malcolm
Canmore, who used this
route in the 11th century
between her palace
and her abbey near
Dunfermline—hence the
name "queen's ferry."

THE FORTH BRIDGES
The Forth train bridge,
built between 1882 and
1889 and illuminated
since its centennial, still
wins the admiration of
young engineers. For most
of its life it was the
longest bridge in the
world. A little west is the
fabulous modern suspen-
sion road bridge (1964),
much lighter and a superb
feat of modern engineer-
ing. A visitor center at
South Queensferry
explains the structures.

▶▶ **The Firth of Forth**   211D4
(tel: 01334 474609 north of Forth; 0131-473 3800 south of Forth)
The Firth of Forth is a wide tidal inlet that bites deep into
the east coast of the country. From a first glance at a map
it appears to have almost severed Scotland into two. It has
functioned more as a trading canal than as a frontier
moat. The long tidal shores are dotted with merchant
towns whose markets and privileges are established in
ancient royal charters. The old local adage says that a
farm by the Forth is better than an earldom in the north—
expressing the realities of this land that formed the
heartland of the medieval kingdom of Scotland.

Four miles west of the Forth rail and road bridges is
Hopetoun House▶, the beautiful stately home of the
Marquis of Linlithgow. Begun in 1699 by Sir William Bruce
and completed by William Adam and his sons, it houses a
sumptuous collection of paintings, tapestries and furniture.
An equal distance east of the bridges, near South Queensferry, is **Dalmeny▶**, a large 19th-century house set in a fine
park. It's home to one of Britain's outstanding Rothschild
Mentmore collections of 17th-century French furniture,
tapestries, and Sèvres porcelain. Dalmeny can be reached
on foot along the estuary from Cramond, a lovely walk.
Cramond▶ is a pretty village of whitewashed cottages and
old mills at the mouth of the River Almond, on the outskirts
of Edinburgh. A little ferry takes you across to the Dalmeny
estates, and there are delightful walks up the riverbank.

Farther west, still on the southern side of the Firth,
Linlithgow Palace▶▶ stands above the town of Linlithgow. At the time of Mary, Queen of Scots' birth here in
1542 it was a magnificent structure, but a fire in 1746 left it
a ruin. Its enormous roofless red body survives, and there
is a fine octagonal fountain in the courtyard, a vast Great
Hall, and a swath of grass around the outer walls on
which to picnic.

Across the Firth, on the western edge of Fife, the small
coastal town of **Culross▶▶▶** (pronounced Coo-ross) is
set in an unpromising landscape of coal mines with a

distant view of the Grangemouth refinery. Persevere, however, for Culross is one of the jewels of the Scottish National Trust. This perfectly preserved example of an early 17th-century trading burgh made its way in the world by digging coal from under the Forth, smelting iron to be hammered out into girdles, and boiling up seawater to extract salt. The cobbled streets are lined with traditional corbeled houses, roofed with the distinctive terracotta pantiles of Fife. You can inspect three period interiors: start at the town's Tolbooth where free video shows on local history are shown alongside the jail chamber in the basement. Next door is the restored palace of Sir George Bruce, the local entrepreneurial landowner, with its painted ceilings, tiled kitchen, and paneled rooms. Bishop Leighton's Study, also carefully restored, is the traditional name for the tall corbeled town house that overlooks the Mercat Cross. From there a short walk up steep Kirk Street leads to the slight ruins of a Cistercian monastery standing immediately beside the old abbey chapel, which has functioned, with later additions, as the parish church since the Reformation.

Dunfermline Abbey▶▶ stands above the wooded glen of Pittencrieff Park in Dunfermline. The abbey was founded as a Benedictine house in the 11th century. Its tower and the eastern end were rebuilt in the 19th century to serve as a parish church, but the sturdy 12th-century nave with its solid pale stone columns, strong round arches, and the zigzag chevrons so characteristic of the Romanesque is more interesting. The visitor center has a good range of display material.

A more recent attraction at North Queensferry is **Deep Sea World**▶▶, an elaborate and innovative aquarium, with the world's largest viewing tunnel, as long as a soccer field. In summer, boat trips can be taken from South Queensferry, by the Forth bridges, to Inchcolm Island, to see the well-preserved abbey and a colony of seals.

See page 230 for more information on the fishing villages of the East Neuk of Fife.

Dunfermline Abbey, burial place of King Robert the Bruce

227

The Forth railway bridge, which needs continuous repainting on a four-year cycle

ROYAL TENNIS
The 16th-century Falkland Palace (N.T.S.), inland from Kirkcaldy, was a favorite hunting seat of the Scottish kings until James VI died in 1625. The royal tennis court was built in 1539 and is still in use. Sir Walter Scott used the palace as the setting for part of his novel *The Fair Maid of Perth*, which was made into an opera by Bizet.

GLASGOW SCIENCE CENTRE

Opening in spring 2001 as a major Millennium project funded by revenue from the National Lottery, this development on the south bank of the Clyde in the Govan area will have a range of hands-on activities. Exhibits will include virtual volleyball, animatronic figures, space, the human body, and the environment, including monitoring the Clyde.

FOR A DIFFERENT PERSPECTIVE

To see another side of Glasgow, visit The Barras, the extensive and world-famous weekend flea market. It was established 100 years ago and now has 800 covered stalls. With street musicians, cafés, and even a crèche, it makes for a lively visit, even if you don't find a bargain. The market is reached via London Road or Gallowgate in the East End (just north of the People's Palace).

The great shipbuilding yards on the Clyde were born in the 19th-century steam era when Clyde-built vessels acquired a high reputation worldwide

▶▶▶ **Glasgow**　　　　　　　　　　　　　　*210C3*
(tel: 0141-204 4400)

Glasgow's skyline of chimneys, factories, and high-rises offers a prospect of almost grotesque beauty. These outskirts are a reminder of Scotland's 19th-century industrial core, but the middle of Glasgow is today a place of captivating charm and a vibrant center. The city's merchant dynasties bequeathed it an extraordinary legacy of art and architecture—and most of the museums and galleries are free. The grid plan of the streets makes it easy to explore.

The city has three distinct areas: the original medieval center, the Merchant City, and the West End. The **cathedral▶**, a dark-hued, heavy Gothic glory begun in the 13th century, is one of the two surviving buildings of the medieval town, on the eastern side of the city. St. Mungo (or Kentigern) founded a missionary chapel here in the 6th century, around which the trading burgh of Glasgow later grew. Opposite the cathedral, the unique **St. Mungo's Museum▶** explores the religions of the world. On High Street, is **Provand's Lordship**, built in 1471 for a canon of the cathedral and now displaying period artifacts and furnishings; it is the city's oldest house.

The Merchant City district has its origins in the heyday of the "tobacco lords." Glasgow was well placed for trade with the New World, and the 18th century saw a period of glory as an international trading city. By the 19th century Glasgow was one of the world's greatest shipbuilding centers and, in an expression of bursting civic pride, money was poured into the Merchant City district to create some of the best Victorian streets in Britain, with some of the most innovative architecture of the day. The great rectangular **George Square▶** is the center of Glasgow today, flanked on one side by the splendidly overblown facade of the **City Chambers▶▶** (*Guided tours* of the marbled interior free, 10:30 AM, 2:30 PM), built 1883–1888. Immediately to the north is Queen Street Station; Central Station, with its even more impressive 19th-century interior, is just a few blocks west. **Trades House** with its Adam facade dates from 1791, while **Hutchesons' Hall** and **Stirling Library** are early 19th-century. Glasgow Green is one of many city parks and here is the **People's Palace▶**, an excellent museum devoted to the social history of Glasgow, and its huge Winter Gardens conservatory. Nearby is the old Templeton's carpet factory (1889), an amazing replica of the Doge's Palace in Venice.

In the leafy area of the West End, with its fine early 19th-century town houses around Glasgow University, is the **Kelvingrove Art Gallery and Museum▶▶**, an enormous Victorian red sandstone building in Kelvingrove Park. It holds works of art from neolithic weapons to Cubist paintings; there is a strong emphasis on 17th-century Dutch and Flemish works. In Kelvin Hall, opposite, is an exciting **Transport Museum▶▶**, with reconstructed Underground stations and shops, old trams, cars, and motorcycles. The **Hunterian Art Gallery▶▶** is renowned for its collection of works of James McNeill Whistler (1834–1903). Also strongly represented is 19th- and 20th-century Scottish art, including works of the Scottish colorists, the "Glasgow Boys," a group of painters who advocated realism in art instead of Victorian romanticism. The Mackintosh Wing is an elegant re-creation of the nearby house (now

The interior of the City Chambers

CHARLES RENNIE MACKINTOSH (1868–1928)
Mackintosh was prominent in the Arts and Crafts Movement and was the first Scottish architect since the 18th century to achieve international fame. While his stained glass and metalwork used the art nouveau motifs of intertwining tendrils, his buildings have a taut quality of geometric simplicity; his furniture design is typified by the tall, starkly simple ladder-chair. The Glasgow School of Art (1896–1909) is his masterpiece, designed when he was only 28; other notable buildings include Scotland Street School, the Willow Tea Rooms on Sauchiehall Street, and the Lighthouse (the former *Glasgow Herald* Building) in Mitchell Street—now a center of architecture and design including a Mackintosh Interpretation Centre. In Bellahouston Park, House for an Art Lover was built in 1996 using Mackintosh's plans of 1901. At Helensburgh, west of Glasgow, Hill House (N.T.S.) is an outstanding example of his domestic style.

Facade of the Glasgow School of Art

demolished) occupied and furnished by Glasgow architect Charles Rennie Mackintosh (see panel). Within the Botanic Gardens is a beautiful 19th-century glasshouse, **Kibble Palace►►**, where tree ferns grow amid white statuary.

The **Glasgow School of Art►►** (*Guided tours* Mon–Fri 11 AM and 2 PM, Sat 10:30 AM; no tours mid to end of June), in Renfrew Street, is the finest completed example of Mackintosh's vision. It houses a comprehensive collection of his paintings and his designs for furniture, metalwork, light fittings, and stained glass. **The Tenement House►►** (N.T.S.) on nearby Buccleuch Street is the ordinary city apartment of a Miss Agnes Toward, preserved as she left it in 1965, having changed virtually nothing in more than half a century. The simple dignity of her four-room apartment and belongings tell a visitor more about the realities of a Scottish life than two dozen ducal palaces.

A short drive out (or take a bus or train from Glasgow Central station; courtesy bus from Pollokshaws West rail station) is a fantastically light, glass-walled building, constructed in 1983 in the grounds of Pollock House. It houses the extraordinary art collection of shipping magnate Sir William Burrell. Though it's vast, the **Burrell Collection►►►** (*Admission free*) is one that you will want to visit and revisit. Everything is of the best, be it the Egyptian alabaster, the Chinese ceramics or jade, the Persian rugs, the tapestries, the medieval illuminated manuscripts, stained glass, or carved doorways.

St. Andrews, Scotland's first university town, seen from St. Rule's Tower

GOLF IN ST ANDREWS
To many St. Andrews is synonymous with golf, a sport that has been played there since the 15th century. In 1754 local dignitaries set up the Society of St. Andrews Golfers, which had the title Royal and Ancient ("R & A") conferred upon it in 1834. New courses have been added around the Old Course, where the 18th hole is named after the great Tom Morris. There are more than 500 courses in Scotland, and "round" and day tickets are available at most (including St. Andrews, except for the Old Course); discounted golf passes cover some areas. For a Golf Map of all the courses, contact the Scottish Tourist Board (see page 274).

▶▶▶ St. Andrews
(tel: 01334 472021)

211D4

Scotland's oldest university, its first golf course, and the ruins of its principal pre-Reformation cathedral mingle with the everyday business of an old Fife market town and summer resort. It was already a holy place for the southern Picts when a shrine to St. Andrew, patron saint of Scotland, was established on the eastern clifftops in the 8th century. Within a century St. Andrews had become the administrative center of Christianity in Scotland. The top of 12th-century St. Rule's church tower gives a bird's-eye view over the enormous ruined nave of the adjoining 14th-century **cathedral▶▶** and of the town's little harbor with its long pier, known as a mole. Westward along the coast are the ruins of the bishop's **castle▶** with its bottle dungeon, from which no one ever escaped, and 16th-century mine and counter mine (a defensive tunnel). Below the Martyrs' Memorial, the handsome **Royal and Ancient Club House** (home of the ruling body for golf the world over) overlooks the oldest course in the world and the British Golf Museum. Nearby a Sea Life Centre stands by the long West Sands. On the three converging streets that comprise the "auld grey toun" are lesser but impressive buildings such as the university's 15th- and 16th-century colleges and the West Port gate, all among town houses and secret "wynds," or alleyways.

The East Neuk A road south leads to **Anstruther▶**, one of several pretty old fishing villages dotted along the southern coast of Fife's East Neuk. Here is the Scottish Fisheries Museum and an aquarium. There are boat trips in summer to the Isle of May. Fishermen's cottages in **Crail▶▶** are now home to artists and vacationers. To see a fishing fleet in action go to the harbor at **Pittenweem▶**. Flemish gables reflect former trading links with the Low Countries. Inland is **Kellie Castle▶▶** (N.T.S.), a good example of the 16th-century round tower houses typical of the Lowlands; another is **Scotstarvit Tower▶** (N.T.S.), near Ceres. Also in the vicinity is the **Hill of Tarvit Mansion-house** (N.T.S.), rebuilt by Sir Robert Lorimer in 1906 to house the art collection of a jute magnate; there are paintings by Raeburn and Ramsay, fine furniture, Chinese porcelain, and an Edwardian laundry evocative of life "downstairs."

►► Stirling 210D3
(tel: 01786 479901)

Stirling Castle►► stands in a strategically commanding position on a volcanic crag, the symbolic key to Scotland, at the geographical and historical center of the country. Nearby, the **Old Town Gaol**, St. John's Street, recaptures the feel of prison life, with the actor-guide playing the role of both guard and prisoner.

On the other side of town, the **Bannockburn Heritage Centre** tells the story of the most famous battle in Scottish history (see panel). Midway between them on the banks of the Forth are the restored Gothic ruins of **Cambuskenneth Abbey**. Walk up to the old town to see the **Church of Holy Rood** where in 1543 Mary, Queen of Scots was crowned at the age of nine months. The **Guildhall**, the shell of **Mar's Wark**—built in 1570 as the town house of the 1st Earl of Mar, Regent of Scotland—as well as **Argyll's Lodging**, are all notable buildings in this vicinity (all *open*). Within the gray castle walls are 18th-century artillery batteries, gardens, a royal chapel, and the Renaissance palace of the Stewart kings. Also here is the Argyll and Sutherland Highlanders regimental museum.

The **Wallace Monument**►►, on the northeastern edge of the town, commemorates Scotland's first freedom fighter, William Wallace; Wallace rose from obscurity to lead the national resistance to the advancing English king, Edward I, winning a victory at the Battle of Stirling in 1297.

Dunblane► is a small residential town beside the meandering River Allan. Although its name is now indelibly associated with the 1996 massacre, when a gunman opened fire on children at school, Dunblane does have one of Scotland's finer Gothic cathedrals. The tower is 12th-century, but the splendid interior, one long soaring 207-foot nave, is mid-13th century. The town is also a good base for touring the Ochil Hills to the east. At the foot of the Ochils near Dollar, 10 miles east of Stirling, **Castle Campbell**► (N.T.S.), built at the end of the 15th century, stands perched on a huge crag. Do take the short trail around its base through Dollar Glen, part of it hewn out of rock, over catwalks and past cascades and drippy ferns. A little west of Dunblane, **Doune** is worth a visit for a fine 14th-century royal **fortress**► and motor museum.

ROBERT THE BRUCE
The Battle of Bannockburn was one of the most decisive in Scottish history. For several years Robert the Bruce (1274–1329) had been successfully waging a guerilla war against the English—and those of the Scottish nobility whom he had alienated. In 1314 he was forced into a pitched battle over the vital control of Stirling Castle; with a mere 5,000 men but great cunning, he destroyed an English force of some 20,000. Stirling surrendered and Edward II fled to Dunbar; Scotland later won independence for 400 years, and Bruce was acknowledged as king of Scotland.

231

Castle Campbell towers above the Burn of Sorrow and the Burn of Care

TROSSACHS WALKS

The area's most energetic hikes are the main peaks such as Ben Ledi, Ben Lomond, and Ben Venue, but numerous lesser summits have fine views, among them Ben An (climb up from the Trossachs Hotel north of Loch Achray on the A821) and Conic Hill, near the southeast corner of Loch Lomond. For lower-level walks try the forest around David Marshal Lodge near Aberfoyle, where there is an old tramway to explore, or the wooded glen north of Rob Roy's Grave at Balquhidder. (See also Walks on page 214.)

ROB ROY MACGREGOR

Robert MacGregor, known for his red hair as Rob Roy (Red Robert), was a colorful and free-booting cattle thief whose exploits frequently involved robbing the rich for the benefit of the poor. He was forced to become an outlaw in about 1712, but having successfully outwitted all attempts to bring him under control, he gradually returned to living openly among his own people. In 1725 he was given a formal pardon. The full story of this Scottish folk hero is told at the Rob Roy and Trossachs Visitor Centre in Callander.

▶▶ The Trossachs   210D2

(tel: 01786 475019)

The Trossachs is an area of rugged hills, tumbling streams, and picturesque lochs. It may lack the drama of the true Highlands, but its accessibility from central Scotland has made it popular. Strictly speaking, the Trossachs is a narrow strip of country between **Loch Katrine** and **Loch Achray**, but in effect it's considered to stretch west from the busy town of **Callander** to the shores of Loch Lomond, with the somewhat commercialized **Aberfoyle** as its heart. Undeniably beautiful, it is also one of the most visited areas in Scotland, and in high summer there are just too many buses and tourists here for those who prefer more lonesome parts.

The area became fashionable with the 18th-century Romantics in their cult of the picturesque—it was wild, but not too wild, and it was also easy to reach. Sir Walter Scott also helped to popularize the area, using the Trossachs as the setting for his poem *Lady of the Lake* and his novel *Rob Roy*. For this was the territory of Rob Roy's Clan Gregor, a near-criminal band touched by a spirit of romantic lawlessness (see panel). The Trossachs was also the favorite sketching ground of the Glasgow Boys (see page 228).

The 23-mile-long **Loch Lomond▶**, Scotland's largest inland loch (in terms of surface area), stretches from the suburbs of Glasgow to the fringes of the Highlands. It is surrounded by a dramatic variety of empty hills, rocky shores, and wooded farmland, but because it's the nearest Highland loch to the Clydeside conurbation, traffic along the road up its western shore is sometimes so busy that it is hard to enjoy its beauty.

There are several pleasant summer **boat trips** (but get there early to avoid lines): along the length of Loch Katrine on the S.S. *Walter Scott*; on Loch Lomond from Balloch, Ardlui, and Tarbet, on the western shore, and from Balmaha or the Inversnaid Hotel pier on the quieter eastern shore; a more modest excursion goes out to the ruins of **Inchmahome Priory** (H.S.) on an island in the Lake of Menteith. Activities such as "pony trekking" (riding), cycling, fishing, and golfing are available. Walkers can choose between numerous forest trails or hill walks. The area's scenic drives can be combined with short walks from the road, to beauty spots such as the Falls of Leny, off the A84 northwest of Callander, and the Trossachs viewpoint at the top of the A821 north of Aberfoyle.

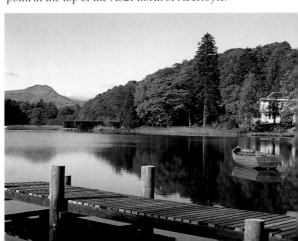

Still waters: Loch Ard

The Highland clans in their 15th-century hey-day formed a tribal system strong enough to threaten the authority of the Stewart monarchs. The aftermath of the last Jacobite rebellion of 1745 brought about the final dismantling of their distinctive way of life. However, the dress and tartan of the Highlands of former times then became fashionable—and the scene was set for the once outlawed cloth of a tribal minority to become the most potent symbol for the whole of Scotland.

Life beyond the Highland Line In Gaelic the word "clann" means family. By the 13th century, clans had evolved into self-governing tribal units at whose head was a chief or "father" to whom lesser chieftains and ordinary clansmen gave allegiance. The clan, at least in earlier times, counted its wealth in cattle. Consequently, cattle-raiding was common, as were territorial disputes. However, not all of the clan's preoccupations were warlike. The more powerful chiefs kept extensive retinues, an important member being the clan bard, who was official record keeper as well as composer. By the 18th century, better communications meant that the clans came more into contact with southern or Saxon—hence "sasunnach"—ways. Some chiefs even sent their children to school in the Lowlands and developed a taste for fine wines or fashionable clothes. Thus the system was already in decline before the shock of Culloden (see page 246).

The dress of the clans The idea of a "clan tartan" was essentially a marketing device of 19th-century textile manufacturers. Tartan was banned after Culloden, though the Highland regiments of the British army were still permitted to wear it. Later, the fashion industry used the military as a source of inspiration and tartan became very fashionable. Then the visit of King George IV to Scotland in 1822 created an excuse for the new landowners and clan chiefs of Scotland to act the part and dress up in tartan costumes. The cloth has remained popular ever since, creating its own mythology and conventions.

HOW TO RECOGNIZE A FELLOW CLANSMAN
Contemporary evidence from the Battle of Culloden indicates a wide variety of tartans worn even by members of the same clan. The government forces were identifiable by the red or yellow tied badges on their bonnets, while the Jacobites had their famous "white cockades," inspired by the wild white rose said to have been plucked by Bonnie Prince Charlie as a symbol for the campaign. In fact, the British army was the first to define uniform tartans in the 18th century.

THE BLACK WATCH
One of General Wade's ways of policing the Highlands (see page 244) was to recruit local Highlanders. Six independent companies first enlisted in 1725 and from these was formed the 43rd, later the 42nd or Black Watch Regiment. By creating fighting units of this type, the martial spirit of the Highlands was harnessed for Britain's imperial wars of the 19th century.

NORTHERN SCOTLAND The **Highlands and Islands**, with their awesome mountain and coastal scenery, have contributed much of what is now considered typical of Scotland. Malt whisky, bagpipes, tartans, clans, kilts, and Highland flings were all distinctive aspects of Highland culture that today are considered essentially Scottish. This would have amazed any 17th-century Scot, for one of the key facts of Scottish history was the marked division between the northern Highlands and the main body of Scotland. The Highlands and the Lowlands were as different as night and day, and they held each other in mutual scorn.

The water of life—pure single malt Scotch whisky

236

RECOMMENDED COASTAL TOWNS
Argyll and Bute: Inveraray, Oban.
Highland: Portree (Skye), Dornoch, Ullapool.
Orkney: Stromness.
COASTAL FEATURES
Highland: Cape Wrath, Handa Island, Stacks of Duncansby.
Orkney: Old Man of Hoy.
CASTLES
Aberdeenshire: Crathes.
Argyll and Bute: Duart (Mull), Kilchurn.
Highland: Dunvegan (Skye), Eilean Donan.
PALATIAL INTERIORS
Aberdeenshire: Haddo.
Argyll and Bute: Inveraray.
Highland: Cawdor.
Perth and Kinross: Blair.
MOUNTAIN WALKING
Cairngorms, Cuillins (Skye), Fort William area, Glen Coe, Torridon.
PREHISTORIC MONUMENTS
Orkney and Shetland: Maes Howe, Ring of Brogar, Skara Brae, Jarlshof, Mousa Broch.
Western Isles: Callanish Circle (Lewis).
ISLAND ESCAPES
Argyll and Bute: Jura.
Highland: Raasay, Rum.
Western Isles: Barra.
CHRISTIAN ARCHITECTURE
Aberdeenshire: St. Machars Aberdeen,
Argyll and Bute: Iona.
Moray: Elgin Cathedral.
Orkney: St. Magnus Kirkwall.
GARDENS
Aberdeenshire: Crathes.
Argyll and Bute: Crarae.
Highland: Inverewe.

THE GREAT DIVIDE Though they might have traded cattle for grain at market towns, Highlanders and Lowlanders otherwise kept their distance. The Highlanders were Gaelic-speaking with a highly developed oral culture of bards, oaths, and undying loyalty to kinship groups; the Lowlanders were English-speaking, literate, and fond of lawsuits. The Highlanders were seminomads who counted their wealth in cattle and avoided towns, whereas the Lowlanders were firmly rooted in the farms and well-established towns that were evenly scattered over the coastal plains.The Highland Boundary Fault, running from southwest straight across to northeast Scotland, was not merely a geological divide: it was a linguistic, social, military, legal, and economic boundary.

A WAR-TORN TERRITORY Though the Highlands brought limited rewards back to the central government in Edinburgh, they provided a vital resource in times of danger. The mountain valleys could be relied upon to produce hardened troops for any military adventure that offered loot. The region also served as a bulwark against foreign conquest, most graphically in the 14th century when the English occupied the Lowland towns for a generation but could make no effective headway into the Highlands. Even after the Act of Union between England and Scotland in 1707, the Highlands continued to supply manpower for Britain's imperial adventures, and to this day there is a tradition of military service.

Jacobite rebellions broke out in 1715 and 1719 as part of a long history of dissidence, but this time the south responded differently. General Wade was commissioned to build and design a string of strategic forts and fortified barracks for the military occupation of the Highlands, all linked by roads and elegant bridges. Several examples survive in the old county of Inverness-shire, in what is now known as the **Highland** region. The Jacobite rising led by Bonnie Prince Charlie in 1745 (see page 246) had catastrophic effects, for the Hanoverian victory at Culloden Moor near **Inverness** was followed by the deliberate destruction of the military basis of Highland society. The legal powers of the clan chiefs were destroyed, the kilt and weapons were forbidden, and a series of ruthless judicial commissions brought the gallows to every glen. This was followed, a generation later, by an economic crisis resulting in the Clearances—wholesale eviction of the tenant farmers to make space for sheep pastures (often run by English-speaking farmers from the Lowlands), particularly in **Sutherland** and the **Black Isle**, the **West Highlands**, and the **Western Isles**. Today, the shells of single-story cottages are the desolate reminders of more populous times.

THE HERITAGE The primitive stone castles of the Highland chiefs decayed into romantic ruin while the turf and stone round huts of the tenant crofters were reduced to lumps in the pasture. They were replaced by neat stone farmhouses, crisp neoclassical manses for the influential clergy, and the light plain halls of their Presbyterian churches. Ironically, at the same time as the Highland crofters were being packed off in emigrant boats, the fashion for all things Highland got into full swing, intensified by Queen Victoria's patronage of **Deeside**. In the late 19th century a series of enormous and exclusive sporting estates were created for the summer recreation of Britain's wealthy, notably in **Angus, Perth and Kinross, Moray, Aberdeenshire, Sutherland** and **Wester Ross**. A series of wonderfully excessive Gothic Baronial lodges, hotels, and palaces still are the dominant architectural note of the Highlands, softened by modern bungalows and the older, stone-built dormer-windowed houses still seen all over the Highlands and Islands. The influx of English speakers helped make the Gaelic tongue obsolete, and, though its use is still widespread in the crofting population of the **Western Isles**, Gaelic is now rarely heard on the mainland.

▶▶▶ REGION HIGHLIGHTS

Blair Castle page 253
Deeside pages 240–241
Iona page 247
Inveraray page 248
Lochaber
pages 244–245
Orkney and Shetland ancient sites
pages 250–251
Scone Palace
pages 252
Skye pages 254–255
Torridon area page 258
The Western Isles
pages 260–261

237

Quoth God to the Highlander,
"What will you do now?"
"I will down to the Lowland, Lord,
And there steal a cow."
—Anonymous

"HAD'S A DH'FHÀSAS FLÙR AIR MACHAIR MAIRIDH CLIÙ NA H-AINNIR CHAOIMH. THE PRESERVER OF PRINCE CHARLES EDWARD STUART WILL BE MENTIONED IN HISTORY, AND IF COURAGE AND FIDELITY BE VIRTUES, MENTIONED WITH HONOUR"
JOHNSON

Walks

Beinn Lora, Argyll and Bute
234B2

Forestry Commission parking lot just south of Benderloch village (north of Oban). Beinn Lora is a 1,010-foot-high hill with magnificent views of Loch Linnhe. Follow a path through the forest; follow signs and eventually skirt an area of boggy pools; the summit then comes into view. Return the same way. (2½ hours)

Findlater Castle, Aberdeenshire
235D4

From Cullen harbor follow the shore-level road eastward; this dwindles to a coastal path. On a clear day the Caithness and Sutherland coastline can be seen across the Firth. Walk onto the 15th-century ruins of Findlater Castle, perched high on the cliff. Then return the same way. (2½ to 4 hours)

Duncansby Head, Highland
235E4

Parking lot at Duncansby Head lighthouse. From the northeastern-most tip of the British mainland a fine coastal path heads south to the Stacks of Duncansby, a trio of natural pillars cut off from the mainland by erosion from the sea. Return the same way. (1½ hours)

Glen Nevis, Highland
234B3

Parking lot at end of road in Glen Nevis, southeast of Fort William. There is a waterfall by the parking lot. The path leads into a splendid gorge before entering more open terrain, passing further waterfalls and reaching ruins at Steall. Return the same way. (2 hours)

Kenmore, Perth and Kinross
235B4

Start in Kenmore village square (east end of Loch Tay). Take the road northwest, cross the River Tay, then immediately take a riverside path on the right; a little later, turn right on a road, then left on a rising forest track, which soon levels out; 45 minutes' walking leads to a well-marked vantage point for views over the loch and over Taymouth Castle; return to the last track junction you reach and then turn right downhill to Kenmore. (2½ hours)

The stacks at Duncansby Head

▶▶ Aberdeen

(tel: 01224 632727)

In the tropical hot houses of Duthie Park

The "Granite City" is the third largest in Scotland, but although the oil boom years of the 1970s gave rise to handsome new buildings on the waterfront and huge oil-rig vessels in the harbor, the town has managed to retain its Georgian roots and its 19th-century dignity. A major port, it has long been a bustling center of commerce, and the grand sweep of Union Street reflects the city's rich history. Elegant floral displays soften the imposing Victorian buildings and the silver granite squares and terraces.

St. Machar's Cathedral▶ was founded in 1131; the main part was built in the mid-15th century. It dominates the part of the city known as **Old Aberdeen**, a calm haven of cobbled streets and houses that date from 1500. In this area too is **King's College**, founded 1500–1505 and part of the university, as well as the Cruickshank Botanic Gardens and Seaton Park. Farther out, the **Brig o'Balgownie** across the River Don is the oldest medieval bridge in Scotland.

Central Aberdeen is more formal, with straight rows of granite town houses and spacious streets. Its numerous university buildings, markets, and museums are dotted on and around Broad Street and Union Street. The **Tolbooth**, on the corner of Broad Street, is the town jail, built in 1627, and open to the public. On Ship Row, the **Maritime Museum▶▶** brings the city's relationship with the North Sea to the fore, with absorbing exhibits on fishing, shipbuilding, and the oil industry; it also includes Provost Ross's House of 1593. **Provost Skene's House** has changing exhibits and period furnishings, while **Satrosphere** is a hands-on science and technology center. The **city library**, **St. Mark's Church**, and **His Majesty's Theatre** are known collectively as "Education, Salvation, and Damnation." The **Art Gallery and Museum▶** has works by Romney, Reynolds, James McBey, Augustus John, and Scottish impressionist William McTaggart among others. The **Duthie Park Winter Gardens** are the largest glassed gardens in Europe, a tropical paradise.

Haddo House▶ (N.T.S.) is a half-hour's drive north, near Pitmedden, a handsome house designed by William Adam in 1731 and relatively unchanged. On Viewfield Road, the **Gordon Highlanders Museum** pays tribute to what Churchill called "the finest regiment in the world."

NORTH SEA FLIER
Cruden Bay, north of Aberdeen, witnessed the takeoff of the first flight across the North Sea back in 1914, when solo pilot Tryggve Gran flew 300 miles to Stavanger in Norway. But with the advent of World War I, his achievement went almost unnoticed. There is a monument to Gran close to the sinister ruin of Slains Castle, which Bram Stoker saw on a visit in 1895, inspiring him to write *Dracula*.

THE BUCHAN COAST
Aberdeen is the gateway to some of the country's most pristine coastline. Northward to Cruden Bay and on to the busy fishing ports of Peterhead (the biggest whitefish port in Western Europe) and Fraserburgh stretch glorious miles of untouched sandy beaches. Along the north-facing coast of this far corner of Scotland little fishing villages such as Pennan and Gardenstown, west of Rosehearty, hide under spectacular cliffs.

HIGHLAND GAMES

Athletes compete at these traditional Highland gatherings, held all over Scotland in summer. Venues include Inverness, Stirling and Callander, with the most famous being the **Royal Highland Gathering** in Braemar (September), usually attended by the Royal Family. Events include throwing the hammer, hill races, putting the stone and tossing the caber (a long wooden pole). Braemar's caber weighs in at 132 pounds, claims to be the longest at 19¾ ft., and has been thrown successfully—i.e. absolutely straight and from end to end—fewer than five times. There are also bagpipe and dancing competitions. Tradition has it that the games originated in martial contests held by King Malcolm Canmore back in the 11th century, to find the toughest men to fight the Normans. The tradition was revived in the 19th century.

The River Dee near Braemar

MALT WHISKY

Single malts, as distinct from blended whiskies, have their origins in more than a hundred distilleries, whose white-washed buildings and barley-drying kilns are a component of the Highlands landscape. Many offer guided tours, and in Speyside is the signposted Malt Whisky Trail, a road touring route. Malt whisky varies greatly in taste; in Islay, for example, the peat burned for drying out the barley gives a highly distinctive flavor. For an overview of the whisky industry, visit the Scotch Whisky Heritage Centre in Edinburgh's Royal Mile.

▶▶▶ Deeside   235C4
(tel: 01224 632727)

The River Dee drains the eastern slopes of the Cairngorms and flows almost 80 miles east to Aberdeen and the North Sea, passing on its way through a classic Scottish landscape of blue hills and heather moors, woods of larch, juniper, and birch, rocky riverbeds and rippling waters.

The village of **Braemar**, 1,083 feet up and circled by layers of hills, is at the heart of the most beautiful stretch of the Dee and a popular summer vacation area. Braemar is famous for its round-towered, L-plan castle, which was built as a hunting lodge by the 2nd Earl of Mar in 1628 and buffeted by the Jacobites in 1689, as well as for the Braemar Gathering held on the first Saturday in September. The Royal Family usually pays a visit to these Highland Games (see panel), which may account for the crowds of around 50,000 people. Robert Louis Stevenson wrote *Treasure Island* while staying in Braemar in 1881. To the west of the village, at the head of the valley just beyond Inverey, is the **Linn o'Dee▶**, where the river waters cascade down into a series of rocky pools. The minor road from Braemar to this beauty spot, often reproduced in Victorian engravings and contemporary postcards, is an attractive drive. From the road, you can set off for some beautiful walks in the Mar Forest and the foothills of Ben Macdhui (4,301 feet).

Balmoral Castle, some 9 miles east of Braemar, was bought by Queen Victoria and her husband Prince Albert in 1852. The old castle was too small, and today's mansion, typically Scottish Baronial in style, was commissioned by Prince Albert. The Royal Family still spends vacations here; the grounds and exhibitions are open to the public May 1 through July 31. The peak of Lochnagar (3,786 feet), which towers over Balmoral, was featured in Prince Charles's first book, *The Old Man of Lochnagar*, an illustrated children's story written to amuse his younger brothers. Across the main road is the granite Crathie Church, attended by members of the Royal Family when staying in Balmoral. Queen Victoria's favorite dram was Lochnagar malt whiskey; the Royal Lochnagar Distillery today has a visitor center and shop and offers visitors a tour of the distillery.

Continuing east along the banks of the boulder-strewn Dee, the A93 passes through the granite village of **Ballater**, built at the end of the 18th century to accommodate visitors taking the spa waters of nearby Pannanich Wells. With its hotels and guest houses, it makes a good base for walking around on the hills of Craigendarroch, Craig Coillich, and Glen Muick.

The main road stays close to the river, pausing at **Aboyne**, a town neatly planned around a large level green where the Highland Gathering takes place in September. The valley then opens out to **Banchory**, where the Water of Feugh joins the Dee from the Forest of Birse. Watch the salmon leaping up the rapids from the Bridge of Feugh. Like most of these Deeside resorts, Banchory has a golf course.

North from Banchory about 15 miles, near Kemnay, **Castle Fraser▶** (N.T.S.) is a massive Z-plan castle. It is an excellent example of the Scottish baronial style, notable for its turrets.

East along the Dee from Banchory, **Crathes Castle▶▶** (N.T.S.) is a celebrated L-shaped tower house dating to 1553, one of the finest Jacobean houses in the country. Inside, the Room of the Nine Nobles, the Room of the Muses, and the Room of the Green Lady are renowned for their remarkable, highly decorative ceilings. The ghost of the Green Lady, carrying a baby and, of course, dressed in green, is thought to haunt certain rooms. The grounds too are special, a labyrinth of color enclosed within the dark green walls of a 300-year-old yew hedge. Don't look at the map, just be lured on by the skilfully contrived arches, avenues, and enticing prospects.

About 6 miles down the glen, in the midst of a surviving section of the Caledonian Forest called the Old Wood of Drum, stands **Drum Castle▶** (N.T.S.). A cold, solid 13th-century keep, thick-walled and 66 feet high, adjoins a crowstepped gabled Jacobean mansion. It houses a collection of portraits, silver, and furniture and has fine grounds with a café and adventure playground.

RAISING THE OLD PRETENDER'S STANDARD
Only the Highland chiefs were able to raise the men needed to fight the cause of Britain's exiled Stuart king. When George of Hanover became king of Britain in 1714, it was in Braemar, on the spot where the Invercauld Arms Hotel now stands, that the 6th Earl of Mar raised the standard in 1715 to launch the Jacobite Rising, proclaiming the Old Pretender, James VIII and III as king.

The alleged appearances of this supposedly dinosaur-like beast lend a hypnotic lure to the loch. The Loch Ness Monster Exhibition at Drumnadrochit has photographs of "Nessie," together with scientific explanations and demonstrations of the latest techniques being used to solve the mystery.

DOLPHIN CRUISES
Dolphin Ecosse run boat trips from Cromarty into Moray Firth to see bottlenose dolphins (all year, weather allowing), and harbor porpoises and, in summer, minke whales (for reservations, call 01381 600323).

Loch Ness, seen near Drumnadrochit, lies in the Great Glen Fault, which runs across the Highlands

Inverness 234C3
(tel: 01436 234353)

Now as ever the Capital of the Highlands, Inverness has a strategic position at the head of the Great Glen. Its often violent history has left it with few historic buildings. The Museum and Art Gallery have good, original collections.

Less than 6 miles out of town, the vast depressing Drummossie moor, renamed **Culloden**, witnessed the last battle fought on British soil, on April 18, 1746. This was the last gasp of Prince Charles Edward Stuart's attempt to gain the throne from George II (see page 246). There is a good **visitor center** (N.T.S.) that tells the story of that rainy day in which a thousand of Bonnie Prince Charlie's Highlanders met their deaths. A mile south lie the prehistoric **Clava Cairns** and standing stones. **Cawdor Castle►**, a little to the east, was built by the Thanes of Cawdor in the 14th century. The original keep remains and inside are Jacobean rooms. At the entrance to the Inverness and Beauly Firth sits **Fort George►**, built between 1748–1769 in demonstration of the government's intent to keep the Jacobites at bay.

The largest loch in Scotland in terms of volume of water, **Loch Ness**'s reputation relies more on the "Nessie" legend (see panel) than its beauty. Good views can be had from **Urquhart Castle** (H.S.), its ruins set on a rocky cliff.

Visit **Beauly►**(H.S.) for the remains of its 13th-century priory and for Campbells, a good tweed, tartan, and woolen shop. **Strathpeffer** is a Victorian spa town with several old hotels; walk from here to the Rogie Falls. The **Black Isle►** is in fact a broad, fertile peninsula whose shores are the haunt of wading birds. In Cromarty look at the old port, the lighthouse, and **Cromarty Courthouse►** where you can tour the cells and courtroom. In **Rosemarkie** see the Pictish stone in the churchyard and Groam House Museum. In nearby **Fortrose** visit the Gothic cathedral ruins (H.S.).

LOCH NESS AND THE BLACK ISLE

Drive

Loch Ness and the Black Isle

A 130-mile tour through varied mountain and coastal landscape.

Leave Inverness on the A9 southeast, turn onto the B9006 to see **Culloden battlefield** and visitor center (N.T.S.) and nearby **Clava Cairns** prehistoric stones. Continue to **Cawdor Castle▶**, scene of the murder of Duncan in Shakespeare's *Macbeth*.

Turn back and take the narrow B9006 to **Fort George▶** with its regimental museum of the Queen's Own Highlanders. Follow the east coast of the **Moray Firth** into Inverness and out again on the A82 along the northern shore of **Loch Ness** to ruined **Urquhart Castle** and the Nessie Exhibition in **Drumnadrochit**.

From here take the road back north over the hills to the remains of **Beauly Priory** (H.S.). At Muir of Ord take the A832 northwest to reach **Strathpeffer**. Head east to **Dingwall** and follow the Black Isle shore to reach the old seaport of **Cromarty**. Go south along the A832 to the charming little resorts of **Rosemarkie** and nearby **Fortrose**. Continue southwest to rejoin the A9 and cross over Moray Firth on the Kessock suspension bridge (1982) back into Inverness.

A sgian dubh (Gaelic dagger) in Inverness Museum and Art Gallery

Ben Nevis and Carn Mor Dearg

The Caledonian Canal

▶▶▶ Lochaber 234C3
(tel: 01997 421160)

This is the region once known as the West Highlands, an area of archetypal highland landscape—bleak moorlands set against soft valley meadows and the long reach of still lochs. It is the land of the Camerons and the Macdonnels, clans that provided the core support for the '45 Rebellion (see page 246) and that, a year later, dumped the Jacobite treasure into Loch Arkaig rather than see it in the hands of the Hanoverians.

At the southern end of Loch Ness (see page 242) the little town of **Fort Augustus** sits around the Caledonian Canal, a splendid waterway, with several staircase locks, designed by Thomas Telford. By linking the lochs of the Great Glen the canal joins Fort William at Loch Linnhe with Inverness on the Moray Firth. Fort Augustus has long since lost the fort built by General Wade (see panel).

The resort and aluminum-smelting town of **Fort William** stands in the shadow of **Ben Nevis▶**, Britain's highest mountain at 4,406 feet. It is not the best in the Highlands for walking, but if you do wish to climb it, allow five hours to get to the top and three hours to pick your way back down (it looks deceptively small because it lacks a definitive peak). It is of course essential to be properly equipped and take all safety precautions. Low-level walks with superb views of the mountains include Glen Nevis (see Walks, page 238), the towpath of the Caledonian Canal (notably Neptune's Staircase, a flight of locks north of Fort William), and Glen Leven (east of Kinlochleven), which threads its way up to the vast Blackwater Reservoir. Fort William is a modern, commercialized place, but makes a convenient base. Its story began in 1655 when General Monk built an earthwork fort here. This was later replaced by General Wade's stone construction in the reign of William III, which was pulled down in the 19th century. The West Highland Museum on Cameron Square provides a good introduction to the region and its natural history.

South from Fort William the main road passes through **Glen Coe▶▶**, the scene, in the early hours of February 13, 1692, of Scotland's most infamous massacre. Acting under government orders, members of the Campbell militia

Fishing boats in Mallaig harbor: the catch, mainly large shrimp, is auctioned on the quay

THE WEST HIGHLAND LINE
The railroad that runs from Glasgow to Mallaig justly claims to be Britain's most scenic route. The construction of the line between Fort William and Mallaig in particular involved some major feats of engineering, with gradients of up to 1 in 48, several rock cuttings, and dramatic bridges, viaducts, and tunnels. Some services are steam-hauled.

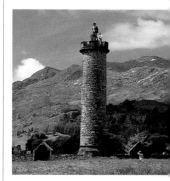

The monument to the '45 at Glenfinnan

THE WEST HIGHLAND WAY
This 95-mile long-distance footpath starts from Milngavie, just north of Glasgow, and heads north of the eastern side of Loch Lomond, passing Rannoch Moor, Glen Coe, Lochaber, and Ben Nevis to reach Fort William. As you get farther north, the scenery is more and more magnificent. It is never really steep, but be prepared for plenty of up-and-down sections.

who were billeted on members of the MacDonald clan, turned on their hosts—breaking the strict code of hospitality that existed between clans—and indiscriminately massacred them. An act, so the government thought, that would dissuade anyone from harboring doubts about the legitimacy of Queen Mary on the throne instead of her brother James VII (James II to the English). There is a visitor center near the foot of the glen.

West of Fort William, at the head of Loch Shiel, the **Glenfinnan Monument▶** (N.T.S.) marks the spot where the Young Pretender, Prince Charles Edward (see page 246), raised his standard on August 19, 1745, and launched the campaign to see his father recognized as rightful king.

The songwriter's "Road to the Isles" from Fort William leads to **Arisaig and Mallaig▶▶** past the coral sandy beaches that featured in the movie *Local Hero.* Inland are the dark waters of Loch Morar, the deepest freshwater stretch of water in Britain, with its own lesser-known monster, Morag. On the wooded islands in the loch, the Jesuits maintained a secret seminary to keep the Roman Catholic faith alive. The busy fishing port of Mallaig is the departure point for ferries to the Inner Isles of Eigg, Muck, Rhum, Canna, Soay, and Armadale on Skye (see pages 254–255). All the islands are easy day-trips; only the Skye boat takes cars.

To the south is the untamed **Ardnamurchan Peninsula**, whose far point is the westernmost part of the British mainland. Isolated on a tide-washed island in Loch Moidart stands the empty keep of **Castle Tioram▶**, last used by the MacDonald chief of Clan Ranald, who burned it after the 1715 uprising failed, rather than let the Campbells take possession. A short walk from the hotel in the village of Kilchoan, **Castle Mingary▶** stands in one of the most impressive locations on the peninsula's southern shore, looking across the Sound of Mull to Tobermory.

The small Highland village of **Lochaline▶**, where ferries depart for Mull, sits on the picturesque Morvern Peninsula overlooking the tidal inlet of Loch Aline. The strong square keep of 14th-century Ardtornish Castle was one of the chief bases of the Lord of the Isles (see panel, page 254).

Seen by contemporary opponents as a political and military threat to 18th-century Britain's stability, the Jacobites and their hopeless quest to restore a Catholic monarch to the British throne was soon turned into a romantic lost cause. At its head was the most romantic figure of all: Italian-born Prince Charles Edward Louis Philip Casimir Stuart, know variously as the Young Pretender, the Young Chevalier, and, most familiarly, Bonnie Prince Charlie. He was in Scotland for only 14 months.

"Charles was the candle who lighted the bonfire, but they [his Highland supporters] were the timber that filled a dark sky with their splendid ardour."
—Eric Linklater, in *The Prince in the Heather*

246

Charles set off from St. Nazaire on his escapade with the blessing of a French government eager to see Britain de-stabilized. When the handsome young man landed on the island of Eriskay in the Western Isles, the local MacDonald chief told him to go home. Charles rather romantically replied that he had "come home" and, undaunted, went on to raise his standard at Glenfinnan in August 1745.

A persuasive personality The fatal charm of the Stuarts managed to persuade about one-sixth of the estimated 30,000 fighting men in the Highlands of Scotland to take up arms in his cause. The campaign met with early successes but was finally halted on Culloden Moor in April 1746. There the Jacobites were blown away by the superior artillery of the British army. Charles went into hiding, and the government forces (which comprised a number of Scottish regiments) went on to commit numerous atrocities in its efforts to destroy the Highland way of life. This policy was implemented by a far-off government in Westminster, which perceived the Highlands as a hotbed of potential Jacobites, where clan chiefs were able to call on what were, in effect, private armies.

The romance of a lost cause From these bare facts sprang the legend of an irresistibly handsome young man on a lost cause. With the real threat out of the way, the Jacobites were soon reinterpreted in song and story. Bonnie Prince Charlie became the figurehead of Jacobite mythology and has been seen on shortbread boxes ever since. Flora MacDonald—whose dealings with the Prince covered only a few days and who had to be persuaded to have anything to do with the business at all—was quickly elevated to a romantic heroine. The notion

OVER THE SEA TO SKYE
"Carry the lad born to be King over the sea to Skye" is perhaps the best-known line from the corpus of Jacobite songs, and alludes to the perilous voyage from Benbecula to Skye which Charles took while disguised as Betty Burke, Flora MacDonald's maid. *The Skye Boat Song*, however, is a 19th-century fake: its famous lyrics date from 1884 and most of the melody from 1879.

that the Prince was never betrayed by a sympathetic Scottish people is a still current tale. In reality his supporters had to keep him well out of the way. But none of this matters. With Bonnie Prince Charlie, the romance is all.

▶▶ Mull

(tel: 01688 302182)

The beautiful "isle-of-the-cool-high-bends," 24 miles long and 26 miles wide, has many aspects—fierce rocky cliffs, sheltered sandy beaches, quiet fishing coves, bleak moors, lone gray castles, and lofty mountains—but is dominated by treeless green terraces of grazing land skillfully managed by crofts and small farms. Mull is served by ferries from Oban, Lochaline and, in summer, Kilchoan.

Duart Castle, perched above the Sound of Mull 3 miles from Craignure, has its origins in the 13th century. It has been restored as the summer home of the chief of Clan Maclean. **Torosay Castle**, just outside Craignure, is a 19th-century baronial building (designed by David Bryce) with grounds laid out by Sir Robert Lorimer. A narrow-gauge railroad runs between the castle and Craignure .

Tobermory▶, named after a holy well dedicated to Our Lady, is the island's main town, its arc of brightly painted houses encircling a bay popular with sailboat owners.

The Holy Island of **Iona▶▶▶**, the "Cradle of Christianity," is served by ferry from Fionnphort on the

ANCIENT BURIAL PLACE OF KINGS
St. Oran's Cemetery on Iona is the oldest Christian cemetery in Scotland. Here are buried 48 Scottish kings, including Kenneth MacAlpin, who first united the Scots and Picts in 843, and Duncan, murdered by Macbeth in 1040. Eight Norwegian kings also have graves here, a reflection of the several hundred years of Norse occupation of Scotland from the 9th century on.

A prehistoric standing stone on the Ross of Mull

western tip of the Ross of Mull or by boat excursions from Oban via Mull. No cars are allowed on the island, but all sights can be easily reached on foot. In 563 St. Columba and 12 companions landed here from Ireland and established a monastery as a base for numerous missionary journeys among the pagan Picts. It became the mother-house of the Celtic church in Scotland and England. This era of great spiritual and creative achievement ended, however, with the Norse raid of 803, which killed 68 monks and persuaded those left alive to return to Ireland. Nothing of their monastery remains, but an astonishing collection of early Christian stone carvings recalls this heroic period. Apart from St. Oran's Chapel of 1080, the existing abbey buildings all date from the second foundation in the early 13th century, when a Benedictine monastery and nunnery were established. In the 20th century, the abbey buildings were restored and are now the home of the Iona Community. The island's sense of peace is a source of spiritual refreshment for many visitors.

FINGAL'S CAVE, STAFFA
The cathedral-like cave that inspired Felix Mendelssohn's *Hebrides Overture* is one of several on this tiny uninhabited island north of Iona. Smooth columns of black basalt, the result of volcanic action, rise out of the sea in what is known in Gaelic as "An Uamh Ehinn" (the musical cave), because of the echoing sounds that the sea makes within it. Boat trips leave from Oban throughout summer.

► Oban and Argyll   234B2
(tel: 01786 475019)

Oban is a popular family resort, accessible by bus and train from Glasgow. The harbor bustles with fishing vessels and ferries for the islands of Mull, Coll, Tiree, Colonsay, and the Western Isles. Stroll along the seafront, browse in the woolen mills, then head for Dunollie Castle where the Lords of Lorne used to preside. McCaig's Tower, an unfinished 19th-century folly modeled on Rome's Colosseum and built to give work to unemployed masons, overlooks the town with fine views across to the Inner Hebrides. Oban is not known for reliable weather, but there are a number of indoor attractions to enjoy when it rains, such as a glass factory, pottery, toy and model display, and the distillery, best known for its 12-year-old malt whisky. Just east of the town is the Oban Rare Breeds Farm Park. The road north passes the 13th-century MacDougall fortress of **Dunstaffnage** on its way to the Sea Life Centre on the shore of Loch Creran.

Just north of the village of Taynuilt is the **Bonawe Iron Furnace►**. Here you can see the restored remains of a charcoal furnace, founded in 1753, which used local wood for iron smelting. The village of Lochawe sits at the head of Loch Awe, the longest loch in Scotland, famous for its fishing. In summer the steamer *Lady Rowena* threads through the romantic burial islands of the MacNaughtons on Innis Fraoch and the MacArthurs on Innishail. The gaunt ruins of Kilchurn Castle, the original fortress home of the Campbells of Breadalbane, stands at the head of Kinloch Awe.

Inveraray►►, at the head of Loch Fyne, is a supremely elegant 18th-century town noted for its bridges, fishing harbor, gibbet pier, judges' lodgings, and central double church. Its chief attraction is the jail, with its tableaus of jailers and wretched inmates. **Inveraray Castle►►**, home of the Campbell Dukes of Argyll, is a heavy gray-stone castellated mansion, but it has delightful 18th-century interiors and is stuffed with Highland weapons, portraits, and memorabilia. Walk through the grounds to the stone folly tower on the summit of Duniquaich for a panoramic view over the area.

THE CRINAN CANAL
In 1793 work started on the construction of this short 9-mile canal that would link Loch Fyne with the Sound of Jura, saving ships the long, hazardous journey around the Mull of Kintyre. The chief engineer, Scotsman John Rennie, met with financial and engineering problems (Thomas Telford was also called upon for his expertise) and it was never a commercial success. However, it passes via 15 locks through a beautiful landscape of wooded mountains, and its basin at Crinan is now popular with yachtsmen.

A "Cal Mac" ferry arrives in Oban from the islands

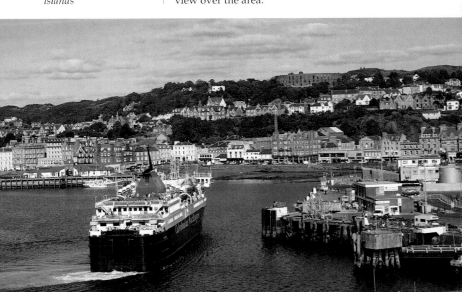

Crinan▶ is a tiny place at the western end of the Crinan Canal (see panel), its handful of houses and a hotel overlooking the yachting activity in the old basin. The village of **Kilmartin▶ ▶** is surrounded by prehistoric sites, including the Nether Largie Linear Cemetery—an alignment of Bronze Age burial mounds, including one you can climb into by ladder—and the Temple Wood stone circles; in the churchyard is a collection of medieval carved stones, and in the church itself a Celtic cross. **Dunadd Fort** may have been the capital of the early Scots kingdom of Dalriada. On its rocky top are carved a footprint and a boar.

Across the Sound of Jura lies **Jura▶**, the rugged, barely populated island, home of red deer, where George Orwell wrote *1984*. Next door is the lovely, peaty isle of **Islay▶ ▶** (ferries from Kennacraig on the Kintyre Peninsula), where no fewer than six distilleries operate. Islay's sights include the superb 9th-century Kidalton Cross and the local history museum at Port Charlotte.

A carved stone at Kilmartin

249

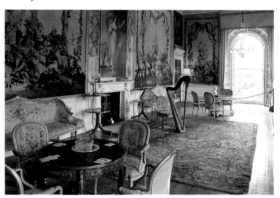

The dazzling interior décor of Inveraray Castle

Drive

Oban and Argyll (see yellow route on map, page 234)

This tour takes in the beautiful Loch Etive, the dramatic Pass of Brander, and the shores of Loch Fyne, with its fine Inveraray Castle. Return through an area studded with prehistoric remains on a road past many sea lochs with views of the Inner Hebridean islands (about 100 miles). There is an optional detour of about 40 miles down the Knapdale Peninsula.

Leave **Oban▶** going north on the A85 to pass Connel Bridge. Continue to Taynuilt for **Bonawe Iron Furnace▶** and then on the A85 through a narrow treeless defile, the Pass of Brander, to **Lochawe**. Take the A819 south to **Inveraray▶ ▶** with its splendid **castle▶ ▶** and then turn south on the A83, skirting the shores of Loch Fyne and passing Auchindrain open-air museum and Crarae Glen woodland gardens. Reach the market town of **Lochgilphead** and turn north up the A816. A detour may be taken on the B841 to **Crinan▶** at the end of the Crinan Canal and then south to Castle Sween and **Kilmory Knap** for its medieval carved stones.

Continue north on the A816 to **Dunadd Fort** and **Kilmartin▶ ▶**, center for some absorbing prehistoric sites. Pass **Carnasserie Castle** at the west end of Loch Awe and, twisting in and out of view of the Firth of Lorne, return to Oban.

WILDLIFE

Both island groups are renowned for their seabird colonies, which are among the most important in the world. On Shetland, visit the Island of Noss, accessible by small ferry (weather permitting). Here and at Hermaness on the north of Unst you get wonderful views of puffins, gannets, guillemots, razorbills, and many more species. As you explore the island, watch out for great skuas, arctic skuas, and whimbrels, which nest on the moorland. On Orkney, visit Yesnaby Cliffs on Mainland, both for their seabirds and for the rare and miniature Scottish primrose.

The relentless pounding of waves at Yesnaby, Orkney, creates a precarious pillar of rock, now detached from the mainland

▶▶ Orkney and Shetland   235A5/E5

(tel: 01856 872856, Orkney; 01595 693434, Shetland)

These two northern archipelagos have such a different cultural atmosphere from the rest of Scotland that many visitors feel they have arrived in another country. For 600 years they were under Norse rule, and even when this domination officially ended, in the 15th century, it was another 200 years before the Scottish throne became strong enough to exert any real authority over these remote islands. Both groups of islands are astonishingly bleak and treeless and initially seem almost featureless, but both have splendid cliff and sea loch scenery and rare birdlife. Despite boasting what is arguably the finest collection of prehistoric sites in Britain, they receive comparatively few visitors.

ORKNEY ISLANDS In Kirkwall on Mainland the unaltered pre-Reformation **Cathedral of St. Magnus▶▶** stands in proud dominance over the town. It was begun in the 12th century, and the massive round pillars and arches of the arcades date from this time. In one of the pillars two skeletons were discovered early this century, one of which may be St. Magnus himself. In the cathedral precincts are the ruins of the Bishop's Palace and Earl's Palace and **Orkney Museum**, a 16th-century town house turned into a museum of Orkney. Around the precincts wind streets of crowstepped gabled houses, brightly painted.

Skara Brae▶▶▶, also on Mainland, is an entire neolithic settlement that lay perfectly preserved in sand dunes for 4,000 years until a storm first uncovered a corner of it in 1850. Inside the houses are beds, hearths, dressers, closets, even fish tanks. The inhabitants left pots, jewelry, clothes, and tools, which are displayed in the museum. **The Ring of Brodgar▶▶** (H.S.) is a wide circle of stones. When first constructed it was surely one of the most magnificent stone circles ever built by neolithic man. The scale is quite breathtaking, and although only some of the stones remain, the original majesty is well preserved. Many of the stones reach a height of 14¾ feet. Nearby, **Maes Howe▶▶** is the finest chambered cairn, or burial chamber, in Europe, both for size and preservation. It was built around 2700 BC and so had been standing for at least a century before the first circle was marked out at Stonehenge in Wiltshire. It remained intact for nearly

4,000 years until the Vikings plundered it; their rude Norse inscriptions can still be seen on the walls.

A more modern curiosity is the **Italian Chapel►** at Lamb Holm, created from Nissen huts and scrap materials in 1943 by Italian prisoners of war who were building the Churchill Barriers in the bay of Scapa Flow. **The Pier Arts Centre►** is a delightful little gallery in the ferry port of Stromness. It has the best collection of modern British art in the north of Scotland. The masterpieces of Ben Nicholson and Barbara Hepworth admirably complement the island's ancient remains.

The famous **Old Man of Hoy► ►** is an enormous stack of rock rearing a tremendous 443 feet out of the sea off the island of Hoy. Like most of Orkney's cliff scenery, it is best seen from a boat (or the ferry from Scrabster, or you can walk the 2-mile path from Rackwick).

SHETLAND ISLANDS These are the most northerly part of Great Britain (Shetland is about 60 miles north of Orkney), and the beauty of midsummer nights when there is little or no darkness has to be seen to be believed. The main industries are crofting, fishing, and knitting. The fine wool of the Shetland sheep is knitted in traditional, distinctive colors and patterns, often known as Fair Isle.

Some people travel to Shetland just to see **Mousa Broch► ► ►**, on a little island to the southeast of Mainland. The Iron Age fortress tower still stands over 39 feet high, all its distinctive features wonderfully preserved. Interestingly, when Shetland was covered with brochs (see panel), Mousa was acknowledged to be the smallest and least noble of them all. **Clickhimin►**, near Lerwick, is another well-preserved broch.

On the southernmost tip of Mainland is **Jarlshof► ► ►**, one of the most remarkable prehistoric sites in Europe. Impressive remains, standing several feet high, can be seen of the Bronze Age courtyard settlements, the Iron Age "wheelhouses" (see panel) that succeeded them, and the longhouses of the Viking settlers who came next. There is also a 16th-century laird's house, home of Earl of Orkney Patrick Stewart and linked with Walter Scott's novel *The Pirate*. The same earl, renowned for his cruelty, built **Scalloway Castle**. The **Shetland Museum** in Lerwick tells the islands' story.

BROCHS AND WHEELHOUSES

Brochs are round towers, shaped like modern cooling towers, that are found only in the north of Scotland, the Outer Hebrides, and Orkney and Shetland. Built by the Picts during the 1st and 2nd centuries bc as defensive structures, they have double stone walls, with an inner staircase giving access to upper galleries. In the middle was a courtyard. Wheelhouses were a specialty of prehistoric Scotland, round buildings with a thick outer wall and a slab or corbeled roof. A number of inner walls ran in from the outer wall to a central area, like spokes of a wheel, forming "rooms."

251

This Iron Age wheelhouse is part of Jarlshof's remarkable legacy of 3,000 years of settlement

Sinuous Loch Tay, one of Scotland's great salmon-fishing spots

THE STONE OF SCONE
Also known as the Stone of Destiny, this is believed to be a druidic talisman, consecrated by St. Columba at Iona, that was used in the investiture of the Dalriadic princes. It was brought here in the 9th century by Kenneth MacAlpin, the man who united Scotland after his defeat of the Picts at Scone. In 1296 it was removed by King Edward I of England and placed under the coronation chair in London's Westminster Abbey; in the 1950s it was sensationally stolen and mysteriously reappeared in Arbroath Abbey. In 1996, the government announced that the Stone was to be returned to Scotland after 700 years.

▶▶ Perth and Kinross 235B4
(tel: 01738 627958)

At the center of Scotland and rich in historical associations, Perth and Kinross (formerly Perthshire) is a county of contrasts. As you travel north the farmland of the south is transformed into the rounded heather-covered slopes of the Grampian Mountains. Cut through with great lochs, it is bound into one region by the waters of the Tay.

The town of **Perth▶** enjoys a pleasant position beside the River Tay. Despite its bridges, its Georgian terraces, and the Millais paintings in the **Perth Museum and Art Gallery**, and the distinctive watercolors of J.D. Fergusson in the **Fergusson Gallery**, it does not quite live up to the expectations set by its long history. On the north edge of town, the **Caithness Glass Factory** gives the chance to see glass-making in progress (it has a factory shop), while above the town, Kinnoull Hill is graced with two 18th-century follies, imitations of Rhenish castles. **Branklyn Garden▶** (N.T.S.) is a small but delightful collection of rhododendrons, shrubs, and alpines. Balhousie Castle houses the regimental museum of the Black Watch.

Located just 2 miles upriver from Perth is **Scone Palace▶▶▶**, one of Scotland's great treasure houses. Scone (pronounced "Skoon") was the coronation place of all the Scottish kings until the time of James I, the seat of Pictish government, and the site of the famous Stone of Scone (see panel). The present palace was built over the foundations of the ancient abbey by Wyatt at the onset of the fashion for Gothick in the first decade of the 19th century. Its state rooms display the treasures from England and France assembled by the Earls of Mansfield, but it is chiefly loved for its lived-in, family atmosphere.

Pitlochry▶ is a Highland resort town, in a beautiful setting of loch, river, mountain, and wood, created in the Victorian era when the railroad station and the Hydro, the large (and originally strictly teetotal) hotel, offered healthy walking breaks away from the smog and sin of the big cities. It boasts a respected Festival Theatre with a broad summer program. Local beauty spots include the Queen's View up Loch Tummel and Loch Rannoch, beneath volcano-shaped Schiehallion (3,490 feet). Just outside town is the site of the Battle of Killiecrankie (an early Jacobite victory) with its visitor center (N.T.S.).

To the north of Perth the attractive "Little Houses" of **Dunkeld▶** date from its rebuilding following a siege during the Jacobite rebellion of 1689, in which the vastly outnumbered Lowland Cameronians held out against the Highlanders; the nave of the ruined 14th-century cathedral was later restored to serve as the parish church.

To the northwest is **Blair Castle▶▶▶**, its white walls and turrets surrounded by the rugged beauty of the Atholl Hills. The province of Atholl has been ruled from this tower house since the 13th century. The castle is famous as the seat of the only duke to be permitted a private army, the 100-strong Atholl Highlanders, who are recruited from tenants and neighbors. They parade on the last Sunday of May; the tunics, worn with a distinctive white bow tie, enliven many a Highland Ball throughout the year. The castle has many rooms open to the public, packed with treasures, including some rare surviving examples of 17th-century Scottish furniture. In the model 18th-century village outside the castle gates there is a local folk museum. A 3-mile track leads to the gorge, bridges, and waterfall of Bruar.

Each loch in Scotland has its own marked character, but **Loch Tay▶▶**, overlooked to its north by the 3,983-foot summit of Ben Lawers, has a serenity which is totally out of keeping with the bloody clan feuds that went on around its shores. At its western end the village of **Killin** is noted for the **Falls of Dochart▶**. Between the village and Loch Tay are the ruins of Finlarig, the murderous stronghold of Black Duncan of the Cowl, who was the acquisitive chief of the local Campbells. His wealthy descendants built the elegant bridge and model village of **Kenmore▶** at the east end of the loch. The market town of **Aberfeldy**, 7 miles east, with its monumental Wade bridge (see panel, page 244), is a popular base for summer visitors. You can walk to such nearby attractions as **Castle Menzies▶**, a classic 16th-century Z-plan tower house; the old **Kirk of Weem** with its pair of Celtic crosses; and the **Birks of Aberfeldy▶**, a sylvan glen made famous by Burns's poem.

HIGHLAND GENEALOGY
Beware of trying to follow too closely the tangled web of Highland genealogies. Despite fearsome blood feuds, practically all the great chiefs and nobles were, and are, interrelated. This allowed any one family to keep a finger in a number of pies, which was the best way to survive the mercurial and murderous politics of Scotland. The Murrays are a fine example: during the '45 Rebellion John Murray, the 1st Duke of Atholl, remained a fervent Hanoverian while his son George was in command of the Jacobite army.

253

Above: Perth city's coat of arms, on a lamppost
Below: Queen Victoria's bedroom at Scone Palace

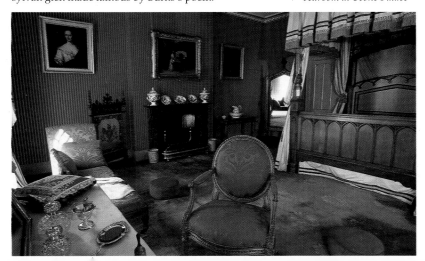

▶▶▶ Skye
(tel: 01478 612137)

234C2

The most startlingly magnificent of the Hebridean islands, Skye is also the closest to the mainland. Since 1995, Skye has been joined by a bridge from Kyle of Lochalsh to Kyleakin. It is an island of extremely irregular shape, a sort of smudged hand-print some 50 miles from end to end and varying from 4 to 25 miles in width. It consists of a central nexus—on which are **Portree**, the bustling capital (and hub of the island's bus network), and the Cuillin Hills; a number of long peninsular fingers stretch out from there, intersected by sea lochs. The landscape changes with disorienting ease from alpine peaks, to rolling farmland, bleak moorland, wooded valleys, coves of white coral sand, and cliffs dotted with secret caves.

Close to the ferry terminal at Armadale, the restored ruins of the 19th-century castellated mansion of Armadale now house the **Clan Donald Centre▶**. Displays and videos tell the story of the clan and its progenitor, Somerled, the first Lord of the Isles (see panel).

The central chain of mountain peaks, the **Cuillins▶▶**, their jagged silhouette seldom seen without at least a wisp of cloud, provides some of the most splendid scenery and demanding climbing in Britain. Rising to 3,310 feet, they enclose Loch Coruisk, a great pool of water locked in an amphitheater of crags of the blackest gabbro; it's a scene of overpowering desolation and grandeur. You can reach it by boat trip from Elgol, or in a full day's walk from Elgol or Sligachan (it's not a walk, however, for the faint-hearted). An easier option is to walk the 4 miles along the coast from Elgol to Loch na Creitheach on the Threshold of the Cuillins.

In Portree, the **Aros Heritage Centre▶** tells the island's story from the point of view of the ordinary people rather than the landowners. At Skeabost, a little way northwest of Portree, are the ruins of the tiny **Columban Chapel▶**, one of a number of the earliest Celtic churches known to have been built here.

Farther west, **Dunvegan Castle▶▶** has been home to the MacLeods of Skye since the 12th century. Striking a

254

LORDS OF THE ISLES
The lordship of the Isles was an independent state that controlled the islands and much of the west coast of Scotland in the medieval period. The founder was Somerled, the progenitor of clan MacDonald, who used the conflict between his Norse overlords and the Scots kings to establish a near-autonomous state in the 12th century. When Norse overlordship ended, the MacDonald chiefs agreed to accept the rule of Donald of Islay, as Lord of the Isles. James IV managed to annex the title in 1493 (one still borne by the heir apparent to the British throne).

The path to Moonen bay and cliffs

magnificent attitude on this remote shore of the island, it contains treasures sacred to the clan such as the fairy flag, which when waved has the power to save the clan. Legend says it will only work three times, and it's already been used twice, with miraculous results. In the churchyard at **Kilmuir** lie the remains of Flora MacDonald, Hebridean heroine of the '45 Rebellion (see panel, page 246), beneath an imposing Celtic cross. Nearby, the **Museum of Island Life** uses four thatched cottages to recreate aspects of the simple yet heroic self-sufficiency of the island's crofters.

North of Portree, the **Old Man of Storr▶** is another of the geological wonders of Skye—a precariously balanced rock needle. The scene of weird desolation is accentuated by the wind sobbing in the gullies. **The Quiraing▶ ▶ ▶** is one of the strangest and most fascinating hills in Scotland. Seldom seen without its raven guardians swirling around, it is a confused mass of cliffs, scree slopes, and towering pinnacles.

On a wind-blown promontory at the northern end of the Trotternish Peninsula stand the ruins of **Duntulm Castle▶**, a historically impressive fortress built by the MacDonalds of Sleat when they were battling with the MacLeods of Dunvegan for the control of this region (see panel, page 254).

From Sconser a little ferry journeys across to the tranquil island of **Raasay▶ ▶**. A track follows the island's long spine of hills to end at the silhouetted ruins of medieval Brochel Castle.

Across the Cuillin Sound south of Skye lie the **Small Isles**, Rum, Eigg, Muck, and Canna, served by ferries from Mallaig on the mainland and Armadale on Skye. Each has limited accommodations. **Rum▶ ▶** is the largest of the group and has a volcanic mountain cluster, the highest peak being Askival (2,657 feet). The haunt of red deer, wild goats, golden eagles, and sea eagles, the island is a national nature reserve and has nature trails and a hotel owned by Scottish Natural Heritage.

Skye style: old croft house, traditionally maintained with white-washed walls, a central doorway, and a roof of heather thatch

MIGHT IS RIGHT?
The 1882 Battle of the Braes was a half-heroic, half-comical affair. A group of bailiffs who were attempting to evict crofters from the coastal strip just south of Portree were beaten off by a fierce band of Hebridean house-wives armed with stone-weighted stockings. The English government, used to sending gunboats all over the world to force their way, promptly sent one up to Skye but backed down in the face of universal hostility. Instead they sent a Commission whose report paved the way for the enlightened Crofting Acts.

The valley of the River Spey near Newtonmore

▶ Spey Valley   235C4
(tel: 01997 421160)

One of the broad classifications of single-malt whiskys is the Speyside malts which take their name from the River Spey. It rises in the Monadliath (literally "the gray moors") and runs northeast, spreading through the wildlife-rich Insh Marshes with the Cairn-gorms as a spectacular backdrop. Beyond Grantown-on-Spey it reaches the whiskey-distilling area stretching all the way to the Moray coast. The typical Strathspey view features a pleasing mix of woods and farmlands backed by moorland slopes and, inevitably, a plume of white steam jetting up from yet another distillery tucked into the landscape. Visit Glenfiddich at Dufftown for a wide-ranging and entertaining interpretation of malt whisky, though there are plenty of other famous names, many of which have visitor centers, some on the marked **Malt Whisky Trail**.

The resort town of **Aviemore** is a rather unattractive creation of the 1960s but it's a popular base for hill walking in the **Cairngorm Mountains▶▶** in summer and skiing on them in winter. Cairn Gorm itself rises to 4,084 feet; take the ski lift (it operates all year round) for a wonderful view. Other activities might include a visit to the osprey reserve at Loch Garten, a ride on the Strathspey Steam Railway from Aviemore to Boat of Garten (good walks at either end), or a visit to the Landmark Highland Heritage visitor center. South along the A9 toward Kingussie is the Highland Wildlife Park.

Kingussie▶, pronounced "Kinusie," is a pleasing town of just one main street, with plenty of beautiful walks nearby. If you visit only one highland history museum in Scotland, visit the **Highland Folk Museum▶▶** here. It is divided into indoor and outdoor exhibitions and includes a "black house" from the Outer Hebridean island of Lewis, a corn mill, a salmon smokehouse, and fascinating exhibits from farming and domestic life. Close

GORDONSTOUN SCHOOL
The school, near Elgin, is famous nowadays as the establishment where the Queen's three sons were educated, but its buildings have had a local notoriety since the 17th century, when they served as the residence of Sir Robert Gordon. Known as the Warlock Laird, he laid out the school's famous round square so that his diabolic familiars could never corner him. His accomplice, the local minister, was not so lucky and was found one morning horribly shred by giant claws outside the kirk.

by, the **Highland Folk Park▶▶** demonstrates the life and work of crofters in the early 1900s and has a turfhouse township evoking the 18th century. On a natural escarpment the other side of the Spey and the A9 stands the gaunt roofless ruin of the **Ruthven Barracks**, a sister to the one in Glenelg (see page 258). They were built to police the main Highland trade routes after the 1715 rebellion was suppressed, but a generation later, in 1746, they were blown up by retreating Jacobites.

Elgin▶, the administrative center of Moray, is the largest town in the favored Laigh of Moray. (Laigh means a sheltered low-lying area and, in this case, refers to its position in the "rain shadow" of the Grampians.) Elgin's cathedral, "the lantern of the North," founded in 1224, was burned in 1390 by the villainous Wolf of Badenoch. Though subsequently rebuilt, it is now a picturesque ruin. Beside it, the **Biblical Gardens** claim to incorporate every plant mentioned in the Bible, with paths laid out in the form of the Cross. The local museum features a display on Britain's oldest dinosaurs, found nearby. East of the town is the attractive community of **Fochabers**, with plenty of antiques shops to attract browsers, as well as another absorbing folk museum. On the coast, the otherwise rather workaday town of **Buckie** is enhanced by an interpretation of the development of the northeast fishery, the Buckie Drifter. Summer boat trips from here provide the opportunity to watch bottle-nosed dolphins. At Macduff, the **Macduff Marine Aquarium▶** displays the sealife of northeast Scotland in Britain's largest indoor tank.

Pluscarden Abbey▶ lies in a fertile valley about 6 miles southwest of Elgin. Its atmosphere is potent, with Benedictine monks going to and fro amid the Gothic ruins. Originally founded by Alexander II in the early 13th century, the abbey was badly damaged by the endemic warfare of the region and fell into further decay after the Reformation. It was partly restored by the Marquis of Bute in the 19th century, and in 1943 was bestowed by his son on a Benedictine community from Prinknash in Gloucestershire. The monks moved in five years later and are now rebuilding it.

257

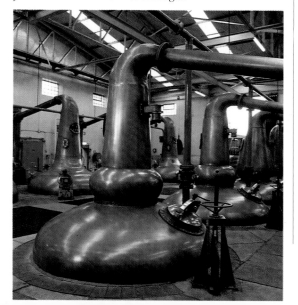

The copper stills at Glenfiddich Distillery; there are a total of eight distilleries on the Malt Whisky Trail

THE SPEYSIDE WAY
The 47-mile long-distance path starts at Spey Bay where the River Spey flows into the North Sea and offers fairly easy walking as far as Ballindalloch before tackling the more challenging section through the hills to Tomintoul. The countryside is varied and the path passes near several whisky distilleries.

THE SUTHERLAND CLEARANCES

Dominating the skyline around the village of Golspie is a statue of the 1st Duke of Sutherland. He is the infamous Leviathan of Wealth who between 1810 and 1820 evicted 15,000 of his tenants from their self-sufficient crofts in order to turn their small plots into profitable sheep pasture.

Eilean Donan Castle, a Mackenzie fortress, was rebuilt early in the 20th century by Colonel Macrae after he supposedly saw its original appearance in a dream

DORNOCH'S CLAIMS TO FAME

Besides having the third oldest golf links in the world, considered as far back as 1630 to be superior to those of St. Andrews, Dornoch also claims the best sunshine record in northern Scotland and the dubious distinction of being the last place in Scotland to burn a witch. The Witch's Stone by the 17th hole of the golf links commemorates the country's last judicial execution for witchcraft, in 1722.

►►► Sutherland, Caithness, and Wester Ross 234C2

(tel: 01997 421160)

The northernmost reach of mainland Scotland is often referred to as the last great wilderness of Europe. The eastern coast, a fertile strip backed by brown moorland, could not be in greater contrast to the green-gray mountains that overlook the sea lochs of the west coast of Ross.

In a remote and picturesque situation on the Sound of Sleat, **Glenelg►** was once on the main cattle-droving route to Skye. Here are found the two best-preserved brochs (see panel, page 251) in mainland Scotland, a handsome, ruined Hanoverian barrack block, and Sandaig Bay, site of Gavin Maxwell's otter refuge of "Camusfearna" so vividly described in *Ring of Bright Water*. In summer you can take a ferry across the surging Kylerhea tidal stream to Skye.

North, across Loch Duich, the stunning **Eilean Donan Castle►►** stands on an islet at the meeting of three lochs. On the northern shores of this peninsula are the stone-built houses and palm trees of the delightful coastal village of **Plockton►**. West of Lochcarron, the adventurous should take an exhilaratingly twisty road (certainly not one for more timid drivers) over **Bealach Na Ba (The Pass of the Cattle)►**. The glacier-scarred rocks on the summit of this pass offer a very fine view over Skye, especially at sunset. The road then leads down to the remote coastal village of **Applecross**. A carved Celtic cross beside the kirk marks the site of the once influential 7th-century monastery of St. Maelrubha.

Torridon►► lies at the end of one of Wester Ross's wildest glens. The road along the southern shores of Upper Loch Torridon offers magnificent views of Beinn Alligin (3,232 feet). A National Trust for Scotland countryside center in Torridon has a deer museum and an audio-visual presentation on local wildlife. Farther north, in one of the most beautiful corners of the west coast, lies the spectacular, world-famous **Inverewe Garden►►►** (N.T.S.), a collection of some 2,500 species of tender and hardy shrubs and trees which flourish in the warmth of the Gulf Stream.

The port of **Ullapool**, placed amidst breathtaking scenery, doubles as a resort. The A835 eastward heads down Loch Broom to the Falls of Measeach in the dizzying

Himalayan lilies and other exotic species flourish in Inverewe Garden, formerly a peaty wasteland

Corrieshalloch Gorge▶▶. To the north the same road passes **Knockan Cliff▶**, in the Inverpolly Nature Reserve, and sights Stac Pollaidh and Suilven, two of the most striking mountain shapes in Scotland.

In the far north, you can take a ferry and minibus from Durness to **Cape Wrath▶▶** to see some stupendous coastal scenery. Britain's highest mainland cliffs are nearby Clo Mor, east of Cape Wrath. Just outside Durness itself is the Smoo Cave, which is in fact three vast caves in the limestone cliffs, with a waterfall. A boat trip can be taken right into the second and third caves.

Few people who come this far north fail to visit Britain's most northeasterly point, **John O'Groats**, named after the Dutchman Jan de Groot (Dunnet Head, nearby, is actually the northernmost point). It's basically an untidy collection of tourist shacks, disappointing to many visitors. Persevere instead to nearby Duncansby Head (see Walks, page 238): the three dramatic offshore stacks rise to over 197 feet.

South of Wick, near the village of Lybster, are two impressive ancient relics, the **Hill O' Many Stones** and the **Grey Cairns of Camster▶▶**. The former is a curious and attractive arrangement of 22 rows of stones in a fan shape, the latter two excellently preserved neolithic burial chambers. If you don't mind the idea of crawling into someone's grave, you can enter one of the handsomest in the country, 197 feet long and 59 feet wide with separate chambers inside.

North of Dornoch the fairy-tale towers of **Dunrobin Castle▶▶** stand on a coastal escarpment, the former seat of the earls and dukes of Sutherland, the largest landowners in Britain. Despite its fanciful 19th-century exterior, it is an ancient fortress with a medieval keep as its core. The collection of paintings inside includes a Reynolds and two Canalettos. **Dornoch▶▶** is a secluded and ancient royal burgh, a pretty little sandstone town with miles of safe sandy beaches. The small cathedral of the Bishops of Caithness dates from the 12th century. The town is also renowned for its golf links.

(see Walks, page 238)

GENERATING POWER
Standing on the clifftops 10 miles west of Thurso, the giant golf-ball shape of Dounreay nuclear power station can be seen for miles around. Elsewhere the waters of Scotland's mountains and reservoirs are harnessed to produce electricity: the great pipes of the hydroelectric plant at Kinlochleven can be seen on the hillsides south of Fort William and those of the Tay-Tummel system around Glen Affric. The pumped storage plant at Ben Cruachan in Argyll has a visitor center.

WILDLIFE
The flow or marsh country of Caithness and Sutherland is a vast stretch of plantations. It is home during the summer months to greenshanks, dunlins, golden plovers, and other wading birds. Dunnet Bay, near Wick, is an excellent birdwatching spot in winter. Look for great northern divers, long-tailed ducks, and scoters. The flora of the Arctic species mingles with mountain species, almost at sea level. Handa Island, off Scourie, is another wonderful site for breeding seabirds. A private ferry often runs from Tarbert.

Scarista Bay, Harris, typifies the majestic remoteness of the Western Isles

A voice so thrilling ne'er
  was heard,
In spring time from the
  cuckoo-bird,
Breaking the silence of
  the seas
Amongst the farthest
  Hebrides.
—William Wordsworth,
The Solitary Reaper

THE LEWIS CHESSMEN
The chance discovery in
the 19th century of the
12th-century chessmen on
Lewis caused a storm of
controversy. Their artistry
was of a standard many
found hard to attribute to
the 12th century. Carved
from walrus ivory, they are
now divided between the
British Museum in London
and the Museum of
Antiquities in Edinburgh.
Replicas can be bought
on Lewis.

►►► The Western Isles 234D1
(tel: 01851 703088)

Sail west across the Minch and you reach the Western Isles, or Outer Hebrides. For the most part the eastern side of the archipelago is barren, rocky, and steep. Its west coast is all silver-white beaches, long and empty and backed by the "machair," fertile peaty grassland enriched by white shell-sand—an almost unique habitat that supports a rich wildlife. Between the two lie watery, peaty, and totally treeless moors.

The Western Isles change their religion with their latitude: strict Presbyterianism in Lewis, Harris, Berneray, and North Uist; Roman Catholicism in South Uist, Eriskay, and Barra; with Benbecula in between a mixture of the two. The difference is readily apparent: strict observation of the Sabbath in the northern islands means people go out only to attend church services (shops and bars are closed), whereas Sundays in the south are livelier and more relaxed. Even the houses on the southern islands have a brighter look, often with colored roofs and painted walls.

It is a perfect place to get away from it all. The people are exceptionally friendly and welcome visitors, but you will not find organized facilities. The few "sights" are mostly archeological; what visitors will remember is the empty beaches, the lochs, the hills, the wildlife, the pure quality of the light, and the way of life.

LEWIS AND HARRIS Lewis and Harris are in fact one island, linked to the mainland and Skye by ferries from Stornoway and Tarbert. The world-famous Harris tweed is still produced here. The stone circle of **Callanish**►►► is one of the most haunting and eloquent places in Britain (there is an exhibition in the nearby Visitor Center). An open-air temple of the Bronze Age that seems to have related particularly to the moon, it is tucked onto a broad peninsula on the west coast of Lewis that protrudes into the sheltered waters of Loch Roag. The inner circle of 13 stones surrounds a central 16-foot, 5-ton menhir. In the central cairn, remains of a human cremation were discovered when the 5-foot-high banks of peat were removed in 1860. At Arnol, the squat **Black House**► is now a museum (see panel, page 261); another museum evoking crofting life is found at nearby **Siabost**. To the west, Dun Carloway is one of the best brochs (Iron Age towers) in the Hebrides, dating from the 1st century BC and with walls rising to 20 feet; its interpretation center is open in summer. **Rodel Church►►**, a bold attractive cruciform dating from 1500, stands on the southern tip of Harris. The cold bleak interior preserves a number of carvings.

NORTH AND SOUTH UIST On the road south from Lochmaddy is the finest chambered cairn in the Hebrides, **Barpa Langass►**. A huge pile of stones sits on the side of the hill, Ben Langass; a little tunnel leads into the communal burial chamber built by Bronze Age Beaker people.

The northwest coast of North Uist has several beautiful coves and beaches; the one near Hosta is, on a clear day, the best place to see **St. Kilda**, the most remote of the Hebrides 45 miles out in the Atlantic. Nearby **Balranald R.S.P.B. Reserve►** harbors the rare corncrake and offers a nature trail across the flower- and bird-rich machair.

North Uist, Benbecula, and South Uist are linked by a causeway. At Milton a cairn stands on the site of the birthplace of Jacobite heroine Flora MacDonald (1722). At the island's southern tip a ferry goes to tiny **Eriskay**, celebrated in the Gaelic melody, the "Eriskay Love Lilt." It was here that Bonnie Prince Charlie first set foot in Scotland on his way from France.

Barra►► is a microcosm of all the Western Isles with its rocky coastline on the east, sandy bays, and machair on the west. Small-scale farming is still the main occupation and Gaelic is still spoken. Ferries connect Castlebay with South Uist and the mainland.

Harris wool, here being sold locally; the tweed is sold worldwide

261

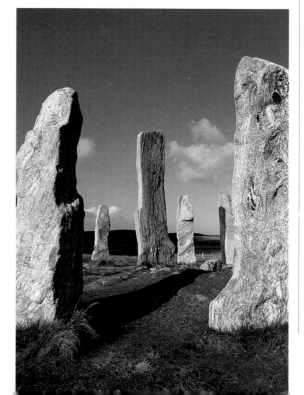

The standing stones at Callanish on the Isle of Lewis

CROFT HOUSES OLD AND NEW
The Arnol Black House on the west coast of Lewis is a traditional crofter's house that gives a fascinating insight into the way of life that was common only 20 years ago. Inside the thick stone walls a peat fire smolders in the middle of the floor, the smoke filtering out through the oat-straw thatch held down by stone-weighted strands of rope. Many of these old croft houses can still be seen, some left in ruin, some given new roofs. The modern houses that replace them are similarly low buildings, usually with dormer windows.

Mountains, lochs, and glens make a magnificent landscape but a harsh environment in which to live and work. Traditionally the Highlands supported a sophisticated, martial society with its own code of conduct and social responsibilities. This was willfully destroyed in the mid-18th century, and within a generation the infamous Clearances began, when the people were driven from the land.

PROPHET OF DOOM
The 17th-century poet Brahan Seer, born on Lewis in the Outer Hebrides, described how the glens would be emptied of their people by sheep, how the sheep would in turn be displaced by deer before the coming of the black rain that would clear all life from the land. The "black rain" has been widely identified with fallout from a nuclear war or a disaster at the Dounreay nuclear reactor. Too many of his prophecies have been fulfilled for his dark vision of the future of the Highlands not to cast a chill of apprehension.

Mass evictions and emigrations have left the landscape dotted with ruined crofters' houses

The rule of the Highland chieftain Up until the defeat of the Jacobite clans at Culloden Moor in 1746, the Highlands were divided into small communities by the dramatic landscape of mountains and sea lochs. It was primarily a cattle-breeding society that traded for grain grown in the Lowlands. The Highland cattle, small herds of sheep, goats, and chickens were highly mobile, and every community required a strongly motivated fighting force to protect its wealth from "lifting." This was the economic basis of the closely knit and intensely martial Highland clans. There was a long tradition of paternalistic care, but it was a feudal society for the simple reason that a hundred strong men in times of crisis were of much greater use than a money rent.

The changing tide After the Battle of Culloden, the victorious Hanoverian government, frightened by the partial success of the Highland army that rallied to Bonnie Prince Charlie, determined to control this militant society. They banned firearms, the martial kilt, and the strong legal powers of the clan chiefs—and they were undeniably thorough. Within a few years the Highlands were at peace and money rents began to replace feudal tenures. For a few glorious decades everything seemed rosy—the potato provided a new cheap staple crop for the poor, grain prices stayed down, and livestock prices soared. Capitalists built iron foundries, fishing harbors, piers, linen and woolen mills, partly financed by enormous profits made by gathering kelp. The population quickly doubled, but the plots of farming land became ever smaller.

The Clearances The end of the Napoleonic wars brought a violent depression with the total collapse of fish, cattle, and kelp prices and the near-extinction of rural industries. Only sheep brought in a handsome profit. Sheep farming, however, was incompatible with thousands of tenants packed into the glens and coastal strips, and many people began to be evicted from their land to make room for sheep paddocks. They were moved south to the slums of the industrial cities or packed off to Canada, Australia, New Zealand, and the U.S. Gladstone's Crofting Act of 1886 gave the surviving tenants a guaranteed claim on their smallholdings and allowed strong communities to survive in the Hebrides, but many big estates were turned over to deer hunting and grouse shooting. With forestry, fish farming, and tourism, these still play a major part in the Highlands' economy.

Travel Facts

Arriving and departing

By air London has five international airports. The largest is **Heathrow** (one of the largest in the world). **Airbuses** run to London Victoria, Heathrow Express trains to London Paddington (taking 15 minutes) and Underground trains (the cheapest option) take 45–60 minutes to central London. These services do not run all night.

The next largest airport, **Gatwick**, has a direct rail link to Victoria Station. **Luton** (north of London) has a bus link to Luton railroad station, and **Stansted** has trains to London Liverpool Street. **City Airport** is served by a shuttle bus from Liverpool Street and Canary Wharf, as well as overground trains. **Birmingham**, **Edinburgh**, **Glasgow**, **Leeds/ Bradford**, and **Manchester** also serve international flights.

By boat Numerous ports have cross-Channel services to the rest of Europe. Dover in Kent (71 miles from London) is the main cross-Channel port connecting with Belgium and France; if you get stuck here for the night, there are plenty of B.&B.s along the main roads.

By rail Trains via the Eurotunnel (Chunnel) run from Europe. Services from Brussels and Paris to London Waterloo take about 3 hours.

Camping

Campgrounds are abundant in Britain, ranging from small fields with just a single cold-water tap by way of facilities to large-scale grounds with showers and stores. Useful sources of information include the *Freedom* brochures published by the English Tourist Board (for a free copy tel: 01452 413041) and the list published by the Camping and Caravanning Club (Greenfields House, Westwood Way, Coventry CV4 8JH; tel: 024-766 94995). Tourist information centers can help with lists of local campgrounds. If you want to try camping in the wilds, be aware of all that the British climate can throw at you, and remember that even open moorland is owned by someone—try to ask permission first.

Children

Many hotels, particularly larger ones in big cities, provide babysitting services, and baby-listening devices are often available. Inquire when making your reservation about child discounts, and if there are any special facilities; British hotels are generally not too good about entertaining the youngest travelers—toy boxes, children's books, emergency medical supplies, and interesting children's meals are in short supply. Some establishments even operate a no-children rule.

Child **discounts** are offered for many admission fees. On the rail network, up to two children under five years of age may travel free with each fare-paying adult, while children of five and over and under 16 travel at half the full price. Anyone traveling by train with children should invest in a Family Railcard: up to four under-16-year-olds travel anywhere in the country

---

FOR TRAVEL DETAILS

London Heathrow,
  tel: 020-8759 4321
London Gatwick ,
  tel: 01293 535353
European Rail Travel Centre,
  Rail Europe, tel: 0990 848848
Eurostar, tel: 0345 881881

---

for £2, and up to two accompanying adults have a discount of 20 percent on most leisure fares.

Currently the law in **pubs** is that children under 14 are not allowed in the bar area. Some pubs allow accompanied children onto the premises (in the restaurant, for instance) and in the garden, but practice varies from one establishment to another. You have to be 18 years or over to buy or consume alcohol in a pub.

Theme parks and safari parks

These include Alton Towers (Staffordshire), Camelot Theme Park (Preston, Lancashire), Chessington's World of Adventures (Surrey), Knowsley Safari Park (Prescot, Merseyside), Legoland (Berkshire), Lightwater Valley (Ripon, North

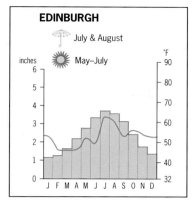

EDINBURGH

July & August

May–July

LONDON

July, August,
October & November

May–August

Climate and seasonal considerations

Britain is a temperate country—the weather is seldom extremely hot or extremely cold and there is no prolonged rainy or dry season. The British climate is a fascinatingly fickle beast: the seasons are distinctive but fuse into each other; brilliant mornings often cloud over as they proceed. No wonder the umbrella seems like part of the national costume. Be prepared for sudden changes in temperature.

The prevailing wind comes from the west, bringing most rain to western Britain; a rain-shadow effect causes eastern areas to have considerably lower rainfall. The south coast gets less rain than the far north, and the climate tends to get warmer the farther south you go. In mid-June it stays light until 10 pm (later in northern Scotland); but in winter it gets

265

LANCASTER

September–January

May–August

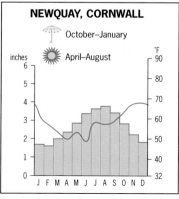

NEWQUAY, CORNWALL

October–January

April–August

Yorkshire), Lions of Longleat Safari Park (Warminster, Wiltshire), Thorpe Park (Chertsey, Surrey), West Midland Safari and Leisure Park (Bewdley, Herefordshire), and Woburn Wild Animal Kingdom and Leisure Park (Woburn, Bedfordshire). At Piccadilly Circus in London are Segaworld (futuristic rides and an IMAX theater) and the animatronic Rock Circus.

London, the South Coast (Devon, Dorset, and Sussex in particular), the North Yorkshire coast, and Cornwall are among the most appealing areas for families; older children may also enjoy the Lake District, Exmoor, Pembrokeshire, York, Edinburgh, as well as the Scottish Highlands.

The Family Holiday Guide *Children Welcome* lists many places to stay and visit for those traveling to Britain with children.

dark early, and the very far north stays gloomy all day.

Travel in spring and you could encounter blustery squalls or fragrant whiffs of nature reawakening in benign sunshine; May and June are excellent times to travel, with the long daylight hours and comparatively uncrowded roads and sights (except for three-day public holiday weekends). The colleges of Oxford and Cambridge are mostly closed in the weeks running up to examination time in late May and early June.

Schools' summer vacations make late July and all of August extremely busy in many areas, including national parks and coastal areas—Devon, Cornwall, the Lake District, the South Coast, the Scottish Highlands (also infested with midges over this period), and Snowdonia are among the most crowded regions. Some historic cities fill almost to capacity, York, Chester, and Canterbury among them. But other places are still quite manageable, including the Welsh borderlands, Eastern England, East Anglia, and the Scottish borders.

September can have fine late-summer weather; if you aren't traveling with school-age kids, this is a good time to visit.

Visitor numbers drop along with the temperature in October and November (the West Country stays reasonably mild), but Christmas is busier, with many hotels offering special Christmas break deals. Many attractions close in the off-peak season from October or November to

Easter (including most National Trust properties). Scottish winters get enough snow for skiing to be feasible in places, notably the Cairngorms.

Crime
Violent crime is still rare in Britain and city centers are mostly quite safe, but minor offenses against property have risen over recent years, particularly in some inner-city areas. Even in remote countryside, it is wise to be on guard against car theft, and keep all valuables locked out of sight. Be extra vigilant of your belongings at airports and major railroad stations: do not let them out of your sight. Because of the risk of terrorist bombs, unattended packages are likely to be removed.

Customs
Note the distinction between **duty-free** and **duty-paid** allowances. Duty-free goods (bought at duty-free shops in airports, ferry terminals on ferries, and on airplanes, even those in the E.U.) have had no duty paid on them and do not entitle you to the higher allowances now set for duty-paid goods bought in the E.U. Duty-free allowances have been abolished for travel within E.U. countries. The countries of the E.U. are Austria, Belgium, Denmark, Finland, France, Germany, Greece, Italy, Luxembourg, the Netherlands, Portugal, the Republic of Ireland, Spain (not the Canary Islands), Sweden and the United Kingdom (not the Channel Islands).

Visitors with disabilities
The English Tourist Board grades hotel, farmhouse, inn, and guest house accommodations according to suitability for visitors with disabilities from Category 3 (suitable for a wheelchair-user who is also able to walk short distances and up at least three steps) to Category 1 (accessible for a wheelchair-user traveling alone). You can get help finding suitable accommodations from the Holiday Care Service, 2nd Floor, Imperial Buildings, Victoria Road, Horley,

A clock in Chester commemorates Queen Victoria's diamond jubilee

DUTY-FREE ALLOWANCES

Duty-free allowances (for goods bought outside the E.U.) and duty-paid allowances for goods bought outside the E.U.

Cigarettes	200
or cigarillos	100
or cigars	50
or tobacco	250 g
Still table wine	2 liters
Spirits, strong liquor over 22% volume	1 liter
or fortified or sparkling wine	2 liters
Perfume	60 cc/ml
Toilet water	250 cc/ml
All other goods including gifts and souvenirs	£145 worth, for travelers from outside the E.U.; £75 for those coming from E.U. countries

Surrey RH6 7PZ, tel: 01293 774535 or Minicom (for hearing-impaired callers) 01293 776943, and from the Royal Association for Disability and Rehabilitation (R.A.D.A.R.), 12 City Forum, 250 City Road, London EC1V 8AF, tel: 020-7250 3222. R.A.D.A.R. annually publishes *Accessible Holidays in the British Isles: A Guide for Disabled People* as well as *Country Parks: A Guide for Disabled People*. The A.A. publishes *The Guide for the Disabled Traveller*, including restaurants and accommodations. Some hotel chains have bedrooms adapted for use by disabled people.

Toilets for wheelchair-users are provided in many museums and tourist sites; a booklet showing them is available from R.A.D.A.R.

Wheelchair-users planning train travel should first contact the rail network that they will be using—telephone numbers are in the *Yellow Pages*, or through directory enquiries (192)—so that arrangements can be made for boarding and seating. R.A.D.A.R. has addresses of local disability associations.

Driving

Driving in Britain can be a delightful way to see the country, or diabolically frustrating. In many remote country areas it is the only way of getting around; for village-to-village wandering (such as the Cotswolds, the Weald, and Constable Country), where local public transportation is limited, a car is essential. The huge network of narrow, crooked lanes (many very ancient indeed) is a particular feature. Rural tourist areas such as the Lake District and the Cornish coastal towns and villages can get so busy in summer that finding somewhere to park requires ingenuity; consider using local buses (if there are any) or finding a footpath. In big cities, finding your way can be difficult; in central London (where parking is something of an ordeal) avoid driving if possible and use public transportation or taxis.

Breaking down Car rental companies normally provide coverage with one of the major motoring organizations in Britain, the A.A. or the R.A.C. On

DUTY-PAID GUIDE LEVELS

Since July 1999 people traveling within the E.U. are no longer entitled to import duty-free goods—these are the guide levels for duty-paid goods bought in the E.U.

You can bring in any amount of goods, but beyond these guide limits you have to be able to show the items are for your own personal use (this includes gifts); if you are receiving any payment in return for these goods (including payment of your travel expenses) you will be liable for duty.

Cigarettes	800
Cigarillos	400
Cigars	200
Tobacco	1 kg
Spirits	10 liters
Beer	110 liters
Intermediate products (sherry, port, etc)	20 liters
Wine (of which not more than 60 liters to be sparkling wine)	90 liters

major highways, there are emergency telephones at the side of the hard shoulder every mile. Arrows on posts indicate the nearest telephone.

Car rental Large firms with numerous branches and desks at airports include Avis tel: 0990 900 500, Europcar tel: 020-8568 5606, and Hertz tel: 0990 996699. These may not be the cheapest; telephone around for the best deal. Most cars have a manual gearshift; if you prefer automatics, reserve one well in advance

Licenses (permits) Australian, Canadian, Irish, New Zealand, and American driving licenses or permits are acceptable. Holders of permits written in a foreign language should obtain an official translation from an embassy or recognized automobile association, or an international driving license. Car rental firms all require you to have held your license or permit for at least a year.

Motorways These freeways link most major cities; service areas (few and far between) are indicated well in advance. On some motorways, however, there are even fewer stopping places, e.g. the M25 (London's busy orbital route), the M11, and the M20.

Parking restrictions Never park on a double yellow line; parking on single yellow lines is generally permitted on Sundays and at other times as displayed. Wheel clamps are now used

Hiking is a national pastime

to combat illegal parking, and the fee/fine to release your car is hefty.

Traffic regulations Traffic drives on the left (it goes clockwise at traffic circles, which are common at intersections). Speed- limit and destination signs use miles. Speed limits are 70 mph for motorways and dual carriageways, 60 mph for other roads, and 30 mph in residential or commercial areas unless otherwise indicated. Front-seat passengers and drivers must wear seatbelts; rear-seat passengers must wear seatbelts if the vehicle has them. Drivers must be at least 17 years of age. Traffic cannot turn left at a red traffic light unless there is a green "filter" arrow.

Electricity
The current in Britain is 240 volts, alternating current. Plugs have three flat pins.

Embassies and consulates in London
Australia Australia House, Strand, WC2, tel: 020-7379 4334
Canada 1 Grosvenor Square, W1, tel: 020-73258 6600
Republic of Ireland 17 Grosvenor Place, SW1, tel: 020-7235 2171
New Zealand New Zealand House, Haymarket, SW1, tel: 020-7930 8422
U.S.A. 24 Grosvenor Square, W1, tel: 020-7499 9000

Health
Accident victims must be admitted through emergency rooms in hospitals. Local doctors (G.P.s) will see visitors; ask at your hotel or at a pharmacy for details. Under the National Health Service, visitors from countries which do not have a reciprocal agreement may find they are charged. If you take medication, make a note of medicines you use. A charge is made for dental treatment.

Hitchhiking
Hitchhiking is legal in Britain, but the occasional report of violent crime keeps many people from doing it. It is illegal to stand on the hard shoulder of motorways; however, hitchhikers may wait near traffic circles by motorway feeder roads.

Holidays

Schools' summer vacations generally last from late July to early September; the country virtually closes down from Christmas Day through to New Year's Day.

January 1 New Year's Day
January 2 New Year's Day (Scotland only)
Late March to early April Good Friday, followed three days later by Easter Monday
First Monday in May May Day Bank Holiday
Last Monday in May Spring Bank Holiday (Whitsun)
First Monday in August Bank Holiday (Scotland only)
Last Monday in August Bank Holiday (England and Wales only)
December 25 Christmas Day
December 26 Boxing Day

Insurance

Travel insurance should cover accident or illness, loss of valuables, injury or death while driving, and trip cancellation. You may be covered for personal items through your homeowner's insurance. Be sure to leave the original policy details at home and take only a photocopy on your travels. Shop around for the best buy: prices and what is covered vary enormously.

Language

Although there is nowhere in Britain where English is not understood, in certain parts it is very much the second language. Welsh is the main tongue in parts of Mid, West and North Wales, but less so in South Wales and the Welsh borders. Throughout Wales, road signs and the like are in both languages. Gaelic is spoken in a few parts of Scotland, notably the Hebrides.

The differences between American and British English can be the source of confusion (and amusement). A Briton thinks of a subway not as a mode of transportation but as a pedestrian passageway beneath the street, and "pants" is another word for "briefs." In America the Postal Service delivers the mail, whereas in Britain the Royal Mail delivers the post. Other examples are:

Beach umbrellas and windshields may be handy for a day at the sea

269

American	British
Bill	Bank note
Check (for food or drinks)	Bill
Crosswalk	Pedestrian crossing
Diaper	Nappy
Elevator	Lift
Freeway	Motorway
French fries	Chips
First/second floor	Ground/first floor
Garbage can	Dustbin
Gasoline	Petrol
Hood (of car)	Bonnet
Overpass	Flyover
Pants	Trousers
Panty hose	Tights
Restroom	Toilet/W.C./ loo
Sidewalk	Pavement
Subway	Underground/ Tube
Trunk (of car)	Boot
Two weeks	Fortnight
Windshield	Windscreen
Yard (of house)	Garden

Cultural diversity is often simplified into the notion of a land of two cultures, separated by a north/south divide. But to simplify accents this way would not be possible. In whatever area of the country you visit, you will come across marked regional accents; from Scouse in Liverpool to Brummie in Birmingham, from Geordie in Newcastle to Cockney in London.

Lost property

Items are often handed into police stations; they pass on information about lost items to other branches. Make sure your address in Britain is shown on all your valuables. For items lost on public transportation, contact the bus station, train station, or airport involved. The London Transport Lost Property Office is at 200 Baker Street, NW1 5RZ, tel: 020-7486 2496 (recorded message).

Maps

The Automobile Association (A.A.) publishes a comprehensive road atlas of Great Britain with a section on city and town plans. Britain has been mapped accurately by the Ordnance Survey (O.S.). If you intend to spend some time exploring a region, invest in the pink-covered O.S. Landranger maps, 1:50,000 scale (2 cm to the km): contours show relief, and footpaths are mapped. For hiking, the O.S. orange-covered Explorer maps (gradually replacing the green-covered Pathfinder series), 1:25,000 scale (4 cm to the km), showing field boundaries, are best; for some of the most popular walking areas (including many national parks) the yellow O.S. Outdoor Leisure and orange Explorer maps, both at 1:25,000 scale, are available instead. Most bookstores have local O.S. maps; the full range is sold at Stanfords Map and Travel Bookshop, 12–14 Long Acre, London WC2, tel: 020-7836 1321.

Media

Newspapers The style contrasts between the "quality" broadsheets (the *Independent*, *Guardian*, *Times*, *Financial Times*, and *Daily Telegraph*) and the more widely selling "popular" tabloids (the *Daily Mail*, *Daily Express*, *Sun*, *Mirror*, *Star*, and *Sport*). For London, the weekly *Time Out* gives the lowdown on eating places and entertainment. There are several regional dailies.

Television There are five channels: the government-funded BBC 1 and BBC 2, and the commercial channels ITV, Channel 4, and Channel 5. Many hotels now have cable and satellite T.V., giving access to foreign stations.

Radio There are five B.B.C. radio stations, Radio 1 (pop music), Radio 2 (light music), Radio 3 (classical music), Radio 4 (news, drama and general interest), and Radio 5 Live (sports and news). Classic F.M. broadcasts lighter classical music. Frequencies can be found in newspapers and the weekly *Radio Times* and *TV Times* magazines.

Money matters

Credit cards are accepted at nearly all gas pumps, most restaurants, and many stores. Traveler's checks are a safe way to carry money. Using your bank card or credit card to draw cash from ATM machines can get you more favorable exchange rates, but be sure to check the fees first—both your bank and the bank where you're making the withdrawal will charge you. The pound (£) is divided into 100 pence (or "p," pronounced "pee."). Denominations are 1p, 2p, 5p, 10p, 20p, 50p, £1 and £2 coins, then £5, £10, £20, and £50 notes. Banks in Scotland issue their own banknotes; they are legal currency throughout the U.K.

V.A.T. refunds Nationals of countries outside the E.U. may claim refunds for value-added tax (V.A.T.) on goods bought within the E.U.; ask for a form from the store when you make your purchase.

Tipping Generally, tip 10–15 percent in a restaurant if service has not already been added (if in doubt, ask whether service is included), or not at all if you think the meal and/or service was not up to par; total payment boxes on credit card slips are often left empty, leaving you to add a tip (remember to fill it in!). Taxi drivers expect 10 percent; with minicabs, which are ordered by phone, you are told a price before you travel, and drivers generally do not expect anything. Porters in luxury hotels will expect a £1 tip. Hairdressers and barbers can be tipped 10 percent.

Opening hours

Standard office hours are Monday to Friday, 9 to 5; stores generally stay open until 5:30 or 6, and operate 9 to

270

5:30 on Saturdays. In central London and certain other cities many stores are open until late in the evening on Thursdays. Banks are open Monday to Friday; most close at 4:30; some open on Saturday mornings.

Restaurants generally open for lunch from 12:00 to 2 PM, and for dinner 6 PM–10 PM, but practice varies; while you may be able to get lunch at 3 PM in one place, another may stop serving evening meals at 9 PM. Cafés usually operate from 9 AM to 5 PM.

Hours and dates when tourist attractions are open vary; many places close from the beginning of November through Easter, and are also closed on Sunday morning, plus all day on Monday or another weekday. Typical hours are 10 AM–5 PM, with last admission an hour before

A London "bobby" on the beat

closing. Check with the tourist office (phone numbers given for each entry) for opening times, particularly if you are making a special trip there.

Pubs may stay open from 11 to 11 seven days a week, but they often choose to close for the afternoons; on Sundays Scottish pubs open mostly from 12:30 to 2:30 and 6:30 to 11.

Organized tours
In London, sightseeing buses run by **London Pride** and the **Big Bus Company** take a number of routes

around the center, with commentary; for the price of a one-day ticket you can get on and off where you like; or you can save money by taking ordinary buses and using a Travelcard. The day tours can be a good way of seeing the sights, particularly for those with a crowded itinerary. Tour buses frequently circuit the sights of Oxford, Stratford-upon-Avon, Windsor, Bath, Cambridge, Edinburgh, and certain other historic centers.

In London special narrated **sightseeing buses** tour the center; the Original London Sightseeing Tour makes a 1½-hour round trip (join it at Piccadilly Circus, Victoria, or Baker Street), while the London Plus tour enables the user to get on and off at will over a two-day period. Tickets for both are available on the buses or at a discount rate from the Piccadilly Circus travel information center. Special-interest **walking tours** are given daily by Original London Walks (020-624 3978). Themes among the 300–350 walks each week include pubs, ghosts, the Beatles, and royalty, and there are trips to Salisbury and Stonehenge. Walks last about two hours, usually starting from a tube station; reservation is not necessary. From Westminster Pier several operators offer **Thames river cruises**, west to Hampton Court, Richmond and Kew, and east to Greenwich.

Pharmacies
Usually called chemists, these have a range of medicines you can buy without a doctor's prescription. Opening times vary; details of the chemist on call are posted in the windows.

Places of worship
Established churches in Britain are Protestant, but there are many Roman Catholic churches. In London, all major religions are represented. Denominational headquarters are **Westminster Abbey** (Church of England), Deans Yard, SW1, tel: 020-7222 5152, **Westminster Cathedral** (Roman Catholic), Victoria Street, SW1, tel: 020-7798 9055, **United Synagogue**, High Road, N12, tel: 020-8343 8989, **London Central Mosque**, 146 Park Road, NW8, tel: 020-7724 3363.

Mailboxes ("letterboxes") vary in size and shape but are always red

Police and traffic police
Telephone 999 for emergencies only; police stations are listed in the *Yellow Pages* under "Police." Traffic wardens (black and yellow uniforms) deal with everyday parking matters and sometimes direct traffic.

Post offices
Main post offices open from 9 to 5:30, Monday to Friday and 9 to 12:30 on Saturday. Many newsdealers sell stamps. Domestic letters bearing first-class stamps take a day less than those with second-class ones. First-class letter rate is the same as the rate for E.U. countries. Postcards and letters are charged at the same rate.

Public transportation
Air travel There are over 30 regional airports in England, Scotland, and Wales. British Airways tel: 0345 222111 and British Midland tel: 0345 554554 have networks of domestic flights, with discounts available; and domestic flights are also offered by Ryan Air tel: 0541 569569, and KLM UK tel: 0990 074074. There are bargain-price "no-frills" services run by Go (a subsiduary of BA) tel: 08456 054321, and EasyJet tel: 0870 600000.

Local buses Generally, services in rural areas are infrequent. The

exception is the Isle of Wight, where bus services are excellent.

Long-distance buses Known as coaches, these serve the towns the railroads don't; fares are lower than rail, but the trip may not be as comfortable. The main London terminal is Victoria Coach Station, Buckingham Palace Road (near Victoria Station), SW1, tel: 020-7730 3499 (reservations), 0990 808080 (for general information about National Express services). For some trips, tickets are purchased on board.

Rail The national network, formerly run by British Rail, is now in the hands of 25 private operators, each covering a different area. You can buy through tickets from any point in the country, even if it means traveling on services of more than one operator. Staff selling you tickets must sell you the cheapest ticket for that route, but the complexity of ticketing means they sometimes make mistakes. Always check services before you travel, and beware that you may not be quoted for the cheapest possible fare. Beware of weekend engineering works: regional maps showing affected services for each weekend ahead may be posted at stations. Special bus services fill in for the closed sections of line, but they add significantly to the journey time. Train tickets are subject to numerous special deals; day return or saver tickets (return within a given period) are much cheaper than two single tickets for the same journey, but are subject to time restrictions (typically not to be used before 9 am); Saver tickets are more expensive on Fridays and certain other days. Apex tickets give discounts for booking seven days or more in advance on InterCity (long-distance) journeys. A BritRail pass is a good buy if you intend to make more than one train journey. This is only available to non-U.K. residents, and gives unlimited travel over the whole network for a certain number of days. Young Persons' Railcards (for under-26s and students) and Senior Citizens' Railcards (for over-60s) give one-third off the full ticket price. Bicycles are carried free of charge on most services. Apart from the London–Scotland and London–Cornwall lines at peak periods, it is seldom necessary to reserve. Train information can be obtained by telephone: look in the *Yellow Pages* under "Railways."

Season tickets and memberships
Those intending to visit a number of stately homes and castles should consider taking out a membership for the **National Trust** (N.T.) and **National Trust for Scotland** (N.T.S.) (see panel, page 102; note that membership in the N.T. entitles you to entry to N.T.S. properties, and vice versa) and/or **English Heritage** (E.H.), **Cadw** (for Wales), **Historic Scotland** (H.S.) (see panel, page 124). Membership is available in all of these at any staffed property. Many other houses are under the umbrella of the Historic Houses Association (2 Chester Street, London SW1X 7BB, tel: 020-7259 5688).

Senior citizens
Anyone aged 60 or over is entitled to a Senior Citizen's Railcard and can get discounts on admission fees.

Student and youth travel
Youth hostels These offer bargain-basement accommodations. The Youth Hostels Association (Y.H.A.) has an excellent network of hostels ranging from primitive converted primary schools to manor houses and medieval castles. Some have stunning locations, such as in the Lake District, Snowdonia, and the Scottish Highlands. There is no maximum age restriction. Accommodations are simple, usually in dormitories, although some hostels have family rooms; food is served at most hostels, at set times, although it is always possible to bring your own. Few establishments allow hostelers to stay in during the day; at peak times and weekends reserve ahead. You must join the Y.H.A. (unless you hold a youth hostel card from another country) in order to stay.

The central London information outlet is the Y.H.A. Shop and Y.H.A. Travel, both at 14 Southampton Street, WC2E 7HY, tel: 020-7379 0597;

the head office is at 8 St. Stephen's Hill, St. Albans, Hertfordshire AL1 2DY, tel: 01727-845047. The Scottish Y.H.A. is based at 7 Glebe Crescent, Stirling FK8 2JA, tel: 01786 891400. **International student cards** These useful IDs help you gain reduced admission to tourist sights and places of entertainment. Young Persons' Railcards give a third off the price of under-26s and student rail tickets.

Telephones
In emergencies tel: **999** (police, fire, and ambulance); calls are free. Operator for national calls tel: **100**; for international calls tel: **155** (both free). Directory inquiries (Information) for national calls tel: **192**; for international calls tel: **153** (both free from payphones only). Calls on numbers prefixed **0800** are free.

To make a call from a public telephone, put the money in before dialing (if you put in large-denomination coins, beware: you will not get change), and collect any unspent coins when you hang up. Phone cards are useful, as many booths no longer take coins; cards can be bought from post offices and newsdealers in denominations of £3, £5 and £10. Mercury phonecards enable calls to be made using the Mercury network to any British Telecom number.

The dial tone is a continuous purr, the ringing tone is a repeated *brr-brr*, and a repeated single tone tells you the line is busy; a continuous tone means the number dialed is "unobtainable" or else you will get an automated message.

To call abroad, dial 00 followed by the country's code, followed by the local number minus the initial 0.

Australia 61	New Zealand 64
Canada 1	U.S. 1
Republic of Ireland 353	

Time
When it is 12 noon in Britain between the last Sunday in October and the last Saturday in March it is 8–10 PM in Australia, 4–8:30 AM in Canada, 12 noon in the Republic of Ireland, midnight in New Zealand and 4–7 AM in the U.S. The rest of the year, clocks go forward one hour to British Summer Time.

273

CONVERSION CHARTS

FROM	TO	MULTIPLY BY
Inches	Centimetres	2.54
Centimetres	Inches	0.3937
Feet	Metres	0.3048
Metres	Feet	3.2810
Yards	Metres	0.9144
Metres	Yards	1.0940
Miles	Kilometres	1.6090
Kilometres	Miles	0.6214
Acres	Hectares	0.4047
Hectares	Acres	2.4710
Gallons	Litres	4.5460
Litres	Gallons	0.2200
Ounces	Grams	28.35
Grams	Ounces	0.0353
Pounds	Grams	453.6
Grams	Pounds	0.0022
Pounds	Kilograms	0.4536
Kilograms	Pounds	2.205
Tons	Tonnes	1.0160
Tonnes	Tons	0.9842

MEN'S SUITS

UK	36	38	40	42	44	46	48
Rest of Europe	46	48	50	52	54	56	58
US	36	38	40	42	44	46	48

DRESS SIZES

UK	8	10	12	14	16	18
France	36	38	40	42	44	46
Italy	38	40	42	44	46	48
Rest of Europe	34	36	38	40	42	44
US	6	8	10	12	14	16

MEN'S SHIRTS

UK	14	14.5	15	15.5	16	16.5	17
Rest of Europe	36	37	38	39/40	41	42	43
US	14	14.5	15	15.5	16	16.5	17

MEN'S SHOES

UK	7	7.5	8.5	9.5	10.5	11
Rest of Europe	41	42	43	44	45	46
US	8	8.5	9.5	10.5	11.5	12

WOMEN'S SHOES

UK	4.5	5	5.5	6	6.5	7
Rest of Europe	38	38	39	39	40	41
US	6	6.5	7	7.5	8	8.5

Toilets

Normally marked "W.C." or "Toilets," these are divided into "Men" or "Gents" and "Women" or "Ladies." With a few exceptions, entry is free. Public restrooms, or "loos," are generally in fair supply.

Tourist offices

There are over 800 tourist informa-tion centers in Britain, run by regional tourist boards for England, Wales, and Scotland: most are well-marked (look for the i sign). National park visitor centers also have good local information.

The British Tourist Authority's web-site is www.visitbritain.com, linking on to attractions, events and accom-modations. It has a U.S. office at 7th Floor, 551 Fifth Avenue, New York, NY 10176-0799, tel: 1-800 GO 2 BRITAIN or 212-986 2200. The English Tourist Board and British Tourist Authority are at Thames Tower, Black's Road, Hammersmith W6 9EL, tel: 020-8846 9000, fax 020-8563 0302. English Tourist Board website:www.TravelEngland.org.uk. The Scottish Tourist Board is at 23 Ravelston Terrace, Edinburgh EH4 3EU, tel: 0131-332 2433, fax: 0131-343 1513. Their website is found at: www.holiday.scotland.net. The Wales Tourist Board, is at Brunel House, 2 Fitzalan Road, Cardiff CF2 1UY, tel: 02920 499909, fax: 02920 485031. Website: www.visitwales.com. For details of any tourist information center in Britain, tel: 0800 192192.

Walking and hiking

England and Wales are served by public rights of way open to walkers; Scotland has an informal rule tolerat-ing access to open land except in the shooting season (see page 266). Foot-paths (marked with yellow arrows) are for walkers only; bridle paths (marked in blue) are open to horse-back riders and cyclists too. Long-distance paths are indicated with acorn motifs. Guided walks are offered by numerous bodies (contact information offices for details). If you devise your own walks, you need a good map and appropriate equip-ment: do not underestimate the perils of the mountains (see page 168).

ACCOMMODATIONS

Tourist information centers hold local accommodations lists, and many provide a reservation service. Bed-and-breakfast ("B&B") is ubiquitous and great value: typically it consists of a room in a private house (some have separate bathrooms) and use of a living room ("lounge"). Regional tourist boards publish lists of farmhouses, inns and guesthouses offering B&B (including the English Tourist Board's book *Where to Stay*). Country house hotels give you the chance to stay in period country homes; many are privately run by families. Many pubs have a few rooms for overnight visitors. Generally, supply outstrips demand: provided you are prepared to drive to the next town, you will always find a bed, although be warned that the most popular resort towns and the Scottish Highlands get very busy in season. The following recommended hotels and inns are divided into three price categories, based on bed and breakfast for one person sharing a double- or twin-bedded room:

($) = budget: generally under £35.
($$) = moderate: generally £35–£60.
($$$) = expensive: generally over £60.

276

LONDON

Chelsea, Knightsbridge, and Victoria
Basil Street ($$$)
8 Basil Street, SW3 1AH tel: 020-7581 3311
Formal, old-fashioned yet stylish.
Quality Eccleston Hotel ($$$)
80–83 Eccleston Square, SW1V 1PS
tel: 020-7834 8042
A well-maintained, comfortable hotel.
The Rubens at the Palace ($$$)
Buckingham Palace Road, SW1W 0PS
tel: 020-7834 6600
Luxury in an enviable location overlooking the Royal Mews behind Buckingham Palace.

Bayswater, Kensington, and Hyde Park
Delmere Hotel ($$$)
130 Sussex Gardens, W2 1UB
tel: 020-7706 3344
Friendly staff, well-equipped rooms, jazz-themed bar and a comfortable lounge.
Kensington Manor Hotel ($)
8 Emperor's Gate, SW7 tel: 020-7370 7516
The late Victorian terraced house has been transformed into a modest hotel. Ideally placed for South Kensington museums and Knightsbridge shopping.
The Millennium Gloucester Hotel ($$$)
4–18 Harrington Gardens, SW7 4LH
tel: 020-7373 6030
Cosmopolitan, stylish hotel; marble bathrooms, air conditioning.
Parkwood ($$)
4 Stanhope Place, W2 2HB
tel: 020-7402 2241
Pretty hotel overlooking Hyde Park.

The Thistle White's Hotel ($$$)
90–92 Lancaster Gate, W2 3NR
tel: 020-7262 2711
Elegant well-cared-for "town house" style hotel.

Regent's Park
Hotel Ibis Euston ($$)
3 Cardington Street, NW1 2LW
tel: 020-7388 7777
Popular and convenient for Euston Station, this good-value hotel also has a secure parking lot.
Kennedy Hotel ($$$)
Cardington Street, NW1 2LP
tel: 020-7387 4400
Modern hotel close to Euston Station. Bar with satellite TV and all-day snacks, Spires Restaurant, meeting rooms.

Bloomsbury and West End
Bloomsbury Park ($)
126 Southampton Row, WC1B 5AD
tel: 020-7430 0434
Cozy hotel catering to all markets.
Thistle Royal Trafalgar ($$$)
Whitcomb Street, WC2H 7HG
tel: 020-7930 4477
Popular hotel adjacent to the National Gallery and convenient for many West End theaters.

Beyond the center
The Barbican Hotel ($$)
Central Street EC1V 8DS tel: 020-7251 1565
Large, modern, near arts complex and the City.
Sandringham ($$–$$$)
3 Holford Road NW3 1AD tel: 020-7435 1569
Small, friendly, with garden, on edge of Hampstead Heath.
Thistle Tower ($$$)
St. Katherine's Way E1 9LD
tel: 020-7481 2575
Modern hotel very convenient for City; fine views of Tower Bridge.

THE WEST COUNTRY

Bath, Somerset
Paradise House ($)
86–8 Holloway, BA2 4PX tel: 01225 317723
Quietly located in an elevated position, minutes from the center.
Royal Crescent ($$$)
16 Royal Crescent, BA1 2LS
tel: 01225 823333
On Bath's famous street; the interior matches the setting.

Bradford-on-Avon, Wiltshire
Bradford Old Windmill ($)
4 Masons Lane, BA15 1QN
tel: 01225 866842
Converted windmill with amusing decor.

Bristol
Berkeley Square Hotel ($$$)
15 Berkeley Square, Clifton, BS8 1HB
tel: 0117-925 4000
Smart Georgian hotel with tastefully decorated rooms. Near the university and art gallery.

Rodney Hotel ($$)
4 Rodney Place, Clifton, BS8 4H7
tel: 0117-973 5422
Attractive terraced hotel with brightly decorated rooms. Convenient for the city center and M5.

Cornwall
Carbis Bay Hotel ($$$)
Carbis Bay, St. Ives, TR26 2NP
tel: 01736 795311
Family-run hotel in fine seaside location.
Pedn-Olva Hotel ($$)
The Warren, St. Ives, TR26 2EA
tel: 01736 796222
Friendly hotel affording glorious views across the bay.
Port Gaverne ($$)
Port Gaverne, nr. Port Isaac, PL29 3SQ
tel: 01208 880244; free-phone 0500 657867
Pleasant inn by a cove on an unspoiled coast.
Skidden House Hotel ($$$)
Skidden Hill, St. Ives, TR26 2DU
tel: 01736 796899
The oldest hotel in St. Ives. Cozy bedrooms, modern facilities.

Dartmoor, Devon
Holne Chase ($$$)
nr. Ashburton, TQ13 7NS tel: 01364 631471
Peacefully located by the River Dart; well-appointed rooms.
Oxenham Arms ($$)
South Zeal, nr. Okehampton, EX20 2JT
tel: 01837 840244
Pleasant 15th-century inn in village street.

Dartmouth, Devon
Royal Castle ($$$)
11 The Quay, TQ6 9PS tel: 01803 833033
17th-century coaching inn on the quayside.

Dorset
Plumber Manor ($$$)
Hazelbury Bryan Road, Sturminster Newton, DT10 2AF tel: 01258 472507
Jacobean manor with 16 bedrooms.
Priory ($$$)
Church Green, Wareham, BH20 4ND
tel: 01929 551666
An 800-year-old priory with riverside gardens.

Exeter, Devon
St. Olaves Court ($$$)
Mary Arches Street, EX4 3AZ
tel: 01392 217736
Georgian-style house near cathedral.

Exmoor, Somerset and Devon
Ashwick House Hotel ($$$)
Dulverton, TA22 9QD tel: 01398 323868
Grand turn-of-the-century country house in large grounds on the edge of Exmoor.

Barnstaple
Halmpstone Manor ($$)
Bishop's Tawton, EX32 0EA
tel: 01271 830321
Lovely manor house surrounded by farmland.

The Oaks Hotel ($$$)
Porlock, TA24 8ES tel: 01643 862265
Enchanting Edwardian country house overlooking Porlock Bay.

Salisbury, Wiltshire
Milford Hall Hotel ($$)
206 Castle Street, SP1 3TE
tel: 01722 417411
A personally managed Georgian mansion house close to the town centre.

Scilly, Isles of, Cornwall
Island Hotel ($$$)
Tresco, TR24 0PU tel: 01720 422883
Modern hotel; island a refreshing getaway.

SOUTHERN ENGLAND

Brighton, East Sussex
Adelaide ($$$)
51 Regency Square, BN1 2FF
tel: 01273 205286
Small hotel in elegant square facing on to the seafront.
Courtlands ($$)
21–27 The Drive, BN3 3JE
tel: 01273 731055
Quietly situated, easy walk to town and seafront; swimming pool.

Canterbury, Kent
Ebury Hotel ($$)
65-67 New Dover Road, CT1 3DX
tel: 01227 768433
Fine period detailing, a very comfortable lounge and the restaurant is recommended.
Falstaff ($$)
8–12 St. Dunstan's Street, CT2 8AF
tel: 01227 462138
Old coaching inn near Westgate Tower.

Dover, Kent
Wallett's Court ($$$)
West Cliffe, St. Margaret's at Cliffe, nr. Dover, CT15 6EW tel: 01304 852424
Old-fashioned rooms in manor house, newer ones in barn annex.

Isle of Wight
George Hotel ($$)
Quay Street, PO41 0PE tel: 01983 760331
This historic townhouse between the pier and the castle has been elegantly transformed; the restaurant is highly rated and the brasserie is good for less formal meals.
Seaview Hotel ($$)
High Street, Seaview, PO34 5EX
tel: 01983 612711
First-class, ideal for families; nautical trappings.

Rye, East Sussex
Jeake's House ($$)
Mermaid Street, TN31 7ET
tel: 01797 222828
Gabled, part tile-hung 17th-century house in cobbled street.

The Weald, Kent
Kennel Holt Hotel ($$$)
Goudhurst Road, Cranbrook, TN17 2PT
tel: 01580 712032
Homey yet distinguished country house set in five acres of lovely gardens.
Tanyard ($$)
Wierton Hill, Boughton Monchelsea, nr. Maidstone, Kent ME17 4JT
tel: 01622 744705
Fine 14th-century house in charming grounds; ultra rural.

Tunbridge Wells
Hotel du Vin & Bistro ($$)
Crescent Road, TN1 2LY tel: 01892 526455
Pleasantly old-fashioned hotel offering spacious, simply decorated bedrooms.

HEART OF ENGLAND

Chiltern Hills, Oxfordshire
Beetle and Wedge ($$$)
Moulsford-on-Thames, Oxfordshire OX10 9JF
tel: 01491 651381
Ideally placed for exploring the Thames Valley; by the river.
Stonor Arms ($$–$$$)
Stonor, Henley-on-Thames, Oxfordshire RG9 6HE tel: 01491 638866
18th-century inn in peaceful village near deer park and walks. Two restaurants.

Cotswolds
Bibury Court ($$)
Bibury, nr. Cirencester, Gloucestershire GL7 5NT tel: 01285 740337
Old-world Jacobean mansion by River Coln, offering a relaxed retreat.
Buckland Manor ($$$)
Buckland, nr. Broadway, Hereford & Worcester WR12 7LY tel: 01386 852626
Top class hotel in a medieval manor.
Collin House ($$)
Collin Lane, Broadway, Hereford & Worcester WR12 7PB tel: 01386 858354
Exemplary country house hotel.
Cotswold House ($$$)
The Square, Chipping Campden, Gloucestershire GL55 6AN
tel: 01386 840330
Formal elegance with murals and antiques.

Dorchester on Thames
White Hart Hotel ($$$)
High Street, OX10 7HN tel: 01865 340074
Charming friendly inn located in historic Thameside village.

Ludlow, Shropshire
Cliffe Hotel ($$)
Dinham, SY8 2JE tel: 01584 872063
Friendly hotel with castle views.
Overton Grange ($$)
Hereford Road, SY8 4AD tel: 01584 873500
An Edwardian mansion set in attractive gardens and surrounded by the Welsh Marches. The restaurant is highly rated.

Malvern Hills, Herefordshire
Feathers Hotel ($$)
High Street, Ledbury, HR8 1DS
tel: 01531 635266
Striking, black-and-white timber-framed coaching inn with traditional interior decor.

Oxford, Oxfordshire
Linton Lodge ($$)
13 Linton Road, OX2 6UJ tel: 01865 553461
Large hotel comprising several houses close to colleges and river.
Randolph ($$$)
Beaumont Street, OX1 2LN
tel: 01865 247481
Large, comfortable hotel in city center.

Stratford-upon-Avon, Warwickshire
Billesley Manor Hotel ($$$)
Alcester, B49 6NF tel: 01789 279955
Peacefully located 16th-century manor house.
Falcon Hotel ($$$)
Chapel Street, CV37 6HA tel: 01789 279953
Traditional inn in the heart of town. Pretty gardens, cozy restaurant.
White Swan ($$$)
Rother Street, CV37 6NH tel: 01789 297022
Half-timbered building with modern facilities.

EASTERN ENGLAND

Cambridge, Cambridgeshire
Arundel House ($–$$)
53 Chesterton Road, CB4 3AN
tel: 01223 367701
Victorian terrace by Jesus Green.
Garden House ($$$)
Granta Place, Mill Lane, CB2 1RT
tel: 01223 259988
Modern riverside hotel, close to colleges.
Gonville ($$$)
Gonville Place, CB1 1LY tel: 01223 366611
Traditional hotel by Parker's Piece park.

Constable Country, Essex/Suffolk
Great House ($$)
Market Place, Lavenham, Suffolk CO10 9QZ
tel: 01787 247431
Georgian exterior belies an ancient timber-framed structure. Only four bedrooms.

Lincoln, Lincolnshire
D'Isney Place ($$)
Eastgate, LN2 4AA tel: 01522 538881
Red-brick house (1735), near cathedral; B&B.

North Norfolk coast
Beaumaris Hotel ($$$)
South Street, Sheringham, Norfolk NR26 8LL
tel: 01263 822370
Five minutes from seafront and town.
Morston Hall ($$$ inc. dinner)
Morston, Holt, Norfolk NR25 7AA
tel: 01263 741041
By marshes, a 17th-century brick-and-flint house; four bedrooms; great restaurant.

Norwich, Norfolk
Maid's Head ($$)
Tombland, NR3 1LB tel: 01603 209955
Dating from 1272, England's oldest hotel in continuous use; the best bet in the city.
Quality Hotel ($$$)
2 Barnard Road, Bowthorpe, NR5 9JB tel: 01603 741161
Modern hotel on outskirts of the city.

Southwold, Suffolk
Swan ($$$)
Market Place, IP18 6EG tel: 01502 722186
Traditional hotel; good standards of comfort.

Stamford, Cambridgeshire
George ($$$)
71 St. Martins, PE9 2LB tel: 01780 750750
Splendid coaching inn; elegant public rooms, good restaurant.

WALES

Brecon Beacons, Powys
Gliffaes ($$)
nr. Crickhowell, Powys NP8 1RH tel: 01874 730371
Traditional family-run hotel, overlooking River Usk and set in parkland; good fishing nearby.
Llangoed Hall ($$$)
Llyswen, Powys LD3 0YP tel: 01874 754525
Stylish Edwardian with personal touches; classic cooking.

Gower Peninsula, Swansea
Fairyhill ($$$)
Reynoldston, Swansea SA3 1BS tel: 01792 390139
Mansion with own trout stream; local dishes feature on an ambitious menu.

Llangammarch Wells, Powys
Lake Country House ($$$)
LD4 4BS tel: 01591 620202
A graceful retreat near Llandrindod Wells.

Snowdonia
Maes-y-Neuadd ($$$)
Talsarnau, nr. Harlech, Caernarfonshire LL47 6YA tel: 01766 780200
Ancient building with splendid vistas.
Old Rectory ($$$)
Llanwrst Road, Llansanffraid Glan Conwy, Conwy LL28 5LF tel: 01492 580611
Fine views of mountains and Conwy Castle; gourmet dinners.
Portmeirion Hotel ($$$)
Portmeirion, Caernarfonshire LL48 6ER tel: 01766 770000
Hotel fronts estuary and has lavish interior.
Princes Arms Hotel ($$)
Trefriw, Conwy, LL27 0JP tel: 01492 640592
Family-run hotel with splendid views across the Conwy Valley. A wonderful place to stay.
St. Tudno ($$$)
Promenade, Llandudno, Conwy LL30 2LP tel: 01492 874411
Oustanding hospitality on the seafront.

Tenby, Pembrokeshire
Penally Abbey ($$$)
Penally, nr Tenby, SA70 7PY tel: 01834 843033
Georgian Gothic house, close to coast, four-poster beds; French-influenced cooking.

Wye Valley, Monmouthshire
Celtic Manor Hotel ($$$) *Coldra Woods, Newport, NP6 2YA tel: 01633 413000*
Magnificently restored 19th-century manor house with three championship golf courses.
Crown at Whitebrook ($$–$$$)
Whitebrook, Monmouthshire NP5 4TX tel: 01600 860254
Small with pretty rooms, comfortable lounge; in densely wooded valley.
Parva Farmhouse ($$)
Tintern, nr. Chepstow, Monmouthshire NP6 6SQ tel: 01291 689411
Cozy without being cute.
Three Salmons ($$-$$$)
Bridge Street, Usk, NP5 1BQ tel: 01291 672133
Charming town centre coaching inn that has a stylish appeal.

NORTHWEST ENGLAND

Chester, Cheshire
Grosvenor ($$$)
Eastgate Street, CH1 1LT tel: 01244 324024
Four-star luxury hotel at the heart of the city.

The Lake District, Cumbria
Mill ($$–$$$)
Mungrisdale, nr Penrith, CA11 0XR tel: 01768 779659
Cozy, informal former mill cottage.
Old Vicarage ($$$)
Church Road, Witherslack, nr. Grange-over-Sands, LA11 6RS tel: 015395 52381
Fine cooking, very comfortable; beneath Whitbarrow Scar.
Patterdale Hotel ($$)
Patterdale, nr. Penrith, CA11 0NN tel: 017684 82231
Fine views of the valley and fells.
Sharrow Bay ($$$)
Ullswater, nr. Penrith, CA10 2LZ tel: 017684 86301
One of Lakeland's most celebrated hotels, highly rated for comfort and its cuisine.
Skiddaw Hotel ($$)
Main Street, Keswick, CA12 5BN tel: 017687 72071
Pleasant hotel in the heart of town. Cheerful restaurant.
The Trout Hotel ($$$)
Crown Street, Cockermouth, CA13 0EJ tel: 01900 823591
Long established, cozy hotel by the banks of the River Derwent. Attractive restaurant.
Wasdale Head Inn ($$)
Wasdale Head, nr. Gosforth, CA20 1EX tel: 019467 26229
Long-established haunt of walkers and climbers; in spectacular isolated position.

White Moss House *($$$ inc. dinner) Rydal Water, Grasmere, LA22 9SE*
tel: 015394 35295
Elegant house (formerly owned by Wordsworth family); English cuisine.

The Peak District, Derbyshire
Cavendish *($$$)*
Baslow, Derbyshire DE45 1SP
tel: 01246 582311
High-class comfort in a civilized retreat in the Chatsworth estate.
Riber Hall *($$$)*
nr. Matlock, Derbyshire DE4 5JU
tel: 01629 582795
Elizabethan manor perched above Derwent Gorge; period character but modern facilities.

NORTHEAST ENGLAND

Co. Durham and Northumberland
The Postchaise Hotel *($$)*
36 Market Place, Bishop Auckland, DL14 7NX
tel: 01388 661296
Old town-center hostelry; lively atmosphere and good value. Home-cooked meals.
White Swan Hotel *($$$)*
Bondgate, nr. Alnwick, NE66 1TD
tel: 01665 602109
Elegant 300-year-old hotel in town center.

Durham
Royal County *($$$)*
Old Elvet, DH1 3JN tel: 0191-386 6821
Ample, comfortable hotel, on the river bank.
Three Tuns Swallow Hotel *($$$)*
New Elvet, DH1 3AQ (0191-386 4326
Old-established, comfortable city center hotel.

North York Moors, North Yorkshire
Lastingham Grange *($$$)*
Lastingham, YO6 6TH tel: 01751 417345
Old-fashioned, welcoming, in tranquil village.
Mallyan Spout *($$$)*
Goathland, nr. Whitby, YO22 5AN
tel: 01947 896486
Located in a village in fine walking country.

York, North Yorkshire
Abbots Mews *($)*
6 Marygate Lane, YO3 7DE
tel: 01904 634866
Just outside city walls, quiet former coachman's cottage.
Cottage *($$)*
3 Clifton Green, YO3 6LH tel: 01904 643711
Attractive, friendly 10 minutes from center.
Mount Royale *($$$)*
The Mount, YO2 2DA tel: 01904 628856
Two early 19th-century houses with antiques, plants, and a welcoming atmosphere.

Yorkshire Dales, North Yorkshire
Amerdale House *($$$)*
Arncliffe, nr. Skipton, BD23 5QE
tel: 01756 770250
Manor house in beautiful setting; run with flair.

Ashfield House *($$)*
Grassington, nr. Skipton, BD23 5AE
tel: 01756 752584
Small hotel off the Square: rustic décor.
Miller's House *($$$)*
Middleham, Wensley-dale, DL8 4NR
tel: 01969 622630
Off an enchanting village square; elegantly furnished rooms and accomplished cooking.

SOUTHERN SCOTLAND

Borders (Scottish)
Burts Hotel *($$)*
The Square, Melrose, TD6 9PN
tel: 01896 822285
Family-run country town hotel within easy drive of 16 golf courses. Welcoming atmosphere.
Cringletie House *($$$)*
Duncan Road, Peebles, Peeblesshire EH45 8PL
tel: 01721 730233
Romantic-looking country house, family-run.

Dumfries and Galloway
Balcary Bay *($$$)*
Auchencairn, nr. Kirkcudbright, DG7 1QZ
tel: 01556 640217
Small, lone hotel by shore of Solway Firth.
Knockinaam Lodge *($$$)*
Portpatrick, Rhinns of Galloway, DG9 9AD
tel: 01776 810471
Looks toward Mountains of Morne in Ireland.

Edinburgh
Caledonian *($$$)*
Princes Street, EH1 2AB tel: 0131-459 9988
90-year-old former railroad hotel; grand lobby, attractive rooms, friendly service.
Howard *($$$)*
32–6 Great King Street, EH3 6QH
tel: 0131-557 3500
A Georgian row house in the city's New Town.
Rothesay *($$)*
8 Rothesay Place, EH3 7SL
tel: 0131-225 4125
Reasonably priced, family-run hotel.
Roxburghe *($$$)*
38 Charlotte Square, EH2 4HG
tel: 0131-225 3921
Fine example of Adam architecture minutes from Princes Street; range of bedrooms.

Firth of Forth
Greywalls *($$$)*
Gullane, Muirfield, East Lothian EH31 2EG
tel: 01620 842144
Designed by Lutyens, overlooks golf links.

Glasgow
Ewington *($$$)*
132 Queens Drive, Queens Park, G42 8QW
tel: 0141-423 1152
Well-equipped, friendly, overlooks the park.
Malmaison *($$$)*
278 West George Street, G2 4LL
tel: 0141 5721000
Striking, stylish bedrooms with state-of-the-art equipment – ISDN lines and CD players.

280

One Devonshire Gardens ($$$)
1 Devonshire Gardens, G12 0UX
tel: 0141-339 2001
Elegant hotel occupying a row of houses.

St. Andrews, Fife
St. Andrews Old Course ($$$)
Old Station Road, KY16 9SP
tel: 01334 474371
By the famous golf course and the sea;
elegant, well-equipped and comfortable.
Scores ($$$)
76 The Scores, KY16 9BB
tel: 01334 472451
In two 1880s row houses; seafront view.
Convenient for Old Course.

Trossachs, Stirling
Roman Camp ($$$)
Main Street, Callander, Perthshire FK17 8BG
tel: 01877 330003
Manor house on River Teith.
Terraces Hotel ($$)
4 Melville Terrace, KK8 2ND
tel: 01786 472268
Welcoming hotel convenient for the center.

NORTHERN SCOTLAND

Deeside
Banchory Lodge ($$$)
Banchory, Aberdeenshire AB31 5HS
tel: 01330 822625
Rambling Georgian house in secluded gardens;
antiques, and hearty Scottish fare.
Kildrummy Castle ($$$)
Kildrummy, Aberdeenshire AB33 8RA
tel: 019755 71288
Victorian mansion by castle ruin.

Inverness, Highland
Dunain Park ($$$)
nr. Inverness, IV3 6JN tel: 01463 230512
Friendly house with good country cooking.
Knockie Lodge ($$$)
Whitebridge, IV1 2UP tel: 01456 486276
Restful and "lived in" rather than elegant.

Lochaber, Highland
Ardsheal House ($$$)
Kentallan, Glencoe, Argyllshire PA38 4BX
tel: 01631 740227
Good base for Loch Linnhe and Glen Coe.
Arisaig House ($$$)
Arisaig, Inverness-shire PH39 4NR
tel: 01687 450622
Austere exterior, attractive interior. Imaginative
menu.
Kilcamb Lodge ($$$)
Strontian, Acharacle, Highland PH36 4HY
tel: 01967 402257
Friendly hotel with fine views of Loch Sunart.

Oban and Argyll and Bute
Airds ($$$ including dinner)
Port Appin, Appin, Argyllshire PA38 4DF
tel: 01631 730236
Small hotel with views of Loch Linnhe.

Isle of Eriska ($$$)
Eriska, Ledaig by Oban, Argyllshire PA37 1SD
tel: 01631 720371
Idyllic island setting (bridge to mainland); putt-
ing green, croquet lawn. Pretty rooms.

Perth and Kinross
Guinach House ($$)
By the Birks, Urlar Road, Aberfeldy, PH15 2ET
tel: 01887 820251
Edwardian house, off A826, open fire, books;
fine cooking, own produce.
Killiekrankie Hotel ($$)
Killiekrankie, PH16 5LG tel: 01796 47320
Delightful hotel in extensive grounds.
Bedrooms are light, and public rooms include a
sun lounge and a bar.

Shetland
Busta House Hotel ($$$)
Brae, ZE2 9QN tel: 01806 522506
Charming 16th-century former laird's home in
its own grounds.

Skye, Highland
Kinloch Lodge ($$$)
Isle Ornsay, Sleat, IV43 8QY
tel: 01471 833214
Friendly Gaelic hotel; small and peaceful.
Royal Hotel ($$)
Portree, IV51 9BU tel: 01478 612525
Hotel with health and leisure facilities.

Spey Valley and Cairngorms
Columba House ($$)
Manse Road, Kingussie, Inverness-shire
PH21 1JF tel: 01540 661402
Comfortable 19th-century manse in elevated
grounds; good home cooking.

Sutherland, Highland
Ceilidh Place ($$)
14 West Argyll Street, Ullapool, IV26 2TY
tel: 01854 612103
Bookshop, gallery, coffee and wine bar as well
as hotel; friendly owners; simple bedrooms.

281

RESTAURANTS

Meals at the following restaurants are divided
into three price categories:
($) = budget: probably under £15 per head.
($$) = moderate: probably £15–£30 per head.
($$$) = expensive: probably over £30 per
head.

LONDON

For further suggestions, see page 59.

Alastair Little ($$–$$$)
49 Frith Street, W1 tel: 020-7734 5183
Unassuming Soho restaurant, minimalist
décor, but high-quality dishes with Asian and
Mediterranean flavors.

Accommodations and Restaurants

Alfred ($$$)
245 Shaftesbury Avenue, WC2
tel: 020-7240 2566
English, Welsh, and Scottish dishes; range of
traditional beers.
Coast Restaurant ($$$)
Albermarle Street, W1 tel: 020-7495 5999
Daring, eclectic menu—beetroot and sweet
potato risotto—in a modern, space-age décor.
Le Gavroche ($$$)
43 Upper Brook Street, W1
tel: 020-7408 0881
Superlative restaurant; a friendly atmosphere.
The Hothouse ($)
78–80 Wapping Lane, E1 tel: 020-7488 4797
Modern and traditional English cuisine in a con-
verted warehouse.
The Ivy ($$)
1 West Street, WC2H 9NE tel: 0171 8364751
A fashionable brasserie where regulars return
again and again; classic dishes. Book ahead.
J Sheekey ($$)
28-32 St Martin's Court, WC2
tel: 0171 240 2565
One of London's best-known seafood restau-
rants. Expect traditional English fish dishes.
Lindsay House *($$)*
21 Romilly Street, W1V 5TG
tel: 0171 4390450
A fine Georgian town house. Irish chef Richard
Corrigan's Celtic roots are very evident in a
gutsy, almost robust style.
Mirabelle ($$-$$$)
56 Curzon Street, W1Y 8DL
tel: 0171 4994636
Marco Pierre White's first-rate classic French
cooking is especially good-value at lunch. It is
essential to book.
St John ($$)
26 St John Street, EC1M 4AY
tel: 0171 2510848/2514998
Fergus Henderson reworks traditional English
recipes and explores Mediterranean dishes.

THE WEST COUNTRY

Bath, Somerset
The Moody Goose ($$)
7A Kingsmead Square, BA1 2AB
tel: 01225 466688
A stylish restaurant with modern English food.
No 5 Bistro ($$)
5 Argyle Street tel: 01225 444499
Inventive mix of French and Far Eastern dishes,
with English specialties.

Bristol, Bristol
River Station ($$)
The Grove, BS1 4RB tel: 0117 9144434
A relaxed bistro as well as an upbeat restau-
rant. The food has a Mediterranean slant.

Cornwall
Old Custom House ($$)
South Quay, Padstow tel: 01841 532359
Situated in the center of the town, this attrac-
tive restaurant has an imaginative fixed-price
menu.

The Kitchen ($$)
The Coombes, Polperro tel: 01503 272780
Cozy cottage featuring fresh fish caught locally.

Dartmoor, Devon
Gidleigh Park ($$$)
Chagford tel: 01647 432367
Idyllic mock-Tudor hotel on edge of moor; cook-
ing of international repute.
Holne Chase Hotel ($$$)
Ashburton, Newton Abbot tel: 01364 631471
Former hunting lodge; specialities include lamb
and seafood.
22 Mill Street ($$)
22 Mill Street, Chagford, TQ13 8AW
tel: 01647 432244
The restaurant is comfortable, though small,
and the cooking is assured.

Dartmouth, Devon
Carved Angel ($$$)
2 South Embankment tel: 01803 832465
French regional and British cuisine, with personal touches. A national institution.

Dorset
Bistro on the Beach ($$)
Solent Promenade, Southbourne,
Bournemouth,H6 4BE tel: 01202 431473
Fresh seafood that draws the crowds. Reserve
some weeks in advance.
Three Horseshoes ($–$$)
Powerstock, nr. Beaminster
tel: 01308 485328
Pleasant inn in center of thatched village.

Exmoor, Devon
Chough's Nest ($$)
North Walk, Lynton tel: 01598 753315
Interesting dinners in a bright, airy dining room.
Old Rectory Hotel ($$$)
Parracombe, Barnstaple tel: 01598 763368
Stylish décor and delicious home-cooked meals.
Rising Sun ($–$$)
Lynmouth tel: 01598 753223
Former smugglers' inn, now a paneled restau-
rant and bar, attractive bedrooms.

SOUTHERN ENGLAND

Brighton, East Sussex
Black Chapati ($$)
12 Circus Parade, New England Road
tel: 01273 699011
Indian, Thai and Chinese influences inspire the
truly adventurous and creative menu.
Terre à Terre ($$)
7 Pool Valley tel: 01273 729051
Innovative vegetarian meals.

Whitstable, Kent
Whitstable Oyster Fisher Co ($$)
Horsebridge Beach, CT5 1BU
tel: 01227 276856
The best seafood restaurant in the area. Look
out for native Whitstable oysters. Book a table,
especially at weekends.

Eastbourne, East Sussex
Star ($$)
Alfriston, nr. Eastbourne tel: 01323 870495
Famous old-world inn/hotel, in charming village. Soup, ploughman's lunch, hot dishes.

Hastings, East Sussex
Roser's ($$)
64 Eversfield Place tel: 01424 712218
Intimate restaurant; small French-inspired menu, excellent wines.

New Forest, Hampshire
Le Poussin ($$)
The Courtyard, Brookley Road, Brockenhurst tel: 01590 623063
Delicious well-presented ingredients.

The Weald, Kent
Honours Mill ($$)
87 High Street, Edenbridge, TN8 5AU tel: 01732 866757)
Carefully prepared French-based cooking; dress up to come here. Pretty river views.
Rankins ($$)
Sissinghurst tel: 01580 713964
English dishes with a hint of the Mediterranean and Middle Eastern, using local produce.
Soho South ($$)
23 Stone Street, Cranbrook, TN17 3HF tel: 01580 714666
Country-pine chic; French-based menu that ranges from snacks to three-course meals.
Thackeray's House ($$)
85 London Road, Tunbridge Wells tel: 01892 511921
Historic house linked with William Thackeray; accomplished, uncomplicated cooking.

Windsor, Berkshire
Waterside ($$$)
River Cottage, Ferry Road, Bray tel: 01628 620691
Splendid restaurant with rooms; French/Mediterranean style.

HEART OF ENGLAND

Cotswolds
Feathers ($$)
Market Street, Woodstock tel: 01993 812291
A gracious old hotel with daily menu; close to Blenheim Palace.
Harry Hare's ($-$$)
3 Gosditch Street, Cirencester, GL7 2AG tel: 01285 652375
Popular all-day eatery, from breakfast (brunch at weekends) to supper. There's a Mediterranean bias, but fish and chips too.
Inn for all Seasons ($$)
The Barringtons, Burford tel: 01451 844324
Generous portions of home-cooked food are served in both character bar and stone-walled restaurant.
The Lygon Arms ($$$)
Broadway tel: 01386 852255
Traditional fare served in the stunning Great Hall of this distinctive hotel.

Herefordshire and Worcestershire
The Evesham Hotel ($$)
Coopers Lane, Evesham tel: 01386 765566
Friendly, with acclaimed menu and wine list.
Olde Salutation ($-$$)
Weobley, nr. Hereford tel: 01544 318443
Medieval inn in picturesque village; good-value Sunday lunch.

Oxford, Oxfordshire
Le Manoir aux Quatr' Saisons ($$$)
Great Milton tel: 01844 278881
Some of the finest, most inspired cooking in the land. Splendid bedrooms.
Liason ($$)
29 Castle Street tel: 01865 242944
Chinese restaurant; good dim sum.
Munchy Munchy ($)
6 Park End Street tel: 01865 245710
Idiosyncratic Southeast Asian gem.

Stratford-upon-Avon, Warwickshire
The Boathouse ($)
Swan's Nest Lanetel: 01789 297733
Robust, flavorful meals for the theater crowds.

283

EASTERN ENGLAND

Cambridge, Cambridgeshire
Cambridge Lodge Hotel ($$)
139 Huntingdon Road tel: 01223 352833
Classic cuisine in comfortable surroundings.
Midsummer House ($$–$$$)
Midsummer Common tel: 01223 369299
A short walk from the center; excellent wines and cheeses.
Old Fire Engine House ($$)
25 St. Mary's Street, Ely tel: 01353 662582
Eat in the quarry-tiled rear garden in summer.

Constable Country, Essex
White Hart Hotel ($$)
Colchester (01376 561654
Traditional Italian; home-made pasta specialty.
White Hart ($-$$)
Halstead, Great Yeldham, CO9 4HJ tel: 01787 237250
Old Tudor pub serving good food and a selection of wines.

Lincoln, Lincolnshire
Wig and Mitre ($–$$)
30 Steep Hill tel: 01522 535190
Brasserie-style 14th-century inn close to the cathedral.

Norwich, Norfolk
Adlard's ($$$)
79 Upper Giles Street tel: 01603 633522
Friendly service; fixed-price French menus; good-value lunches.
Brasted's ($$)
8-10 St Andrews Hill, NR2 1AD tel: 01603 625949
Mediterranean influences mixed with classic European, and the wine list is excellent.

Southwold, Suffolk
Crown ($–$$)
90 High Street tel: 01502 722275
Elegant inn with excellent fish; reserve.

WALES

Brecon Beacons, Powys
Griffin Inn ($$$)
Llyswen tel: 01874 754241
Local produce features strongly in the dishes of this very popular country inn.

Snowdonia National Park, Gwynedd
Castle Cottage Hotel ($)
Pen Llech, Harlech tel: 01766 780479
Highly acclaimed cooking in delightful 16th-century cottage.
The Hotel Portmeirion ($$$)
Penrhyndeudraeth, Portmeirion, LL48 6ET tel: 01766 770000
Menus are in Welsh (with English subtitles).

NORTHWEST ENGLAND

284

The Lake District, Cumbria
Appleby Manor Country House Hotel ($$$)
Roman Road, Appleby-in-Westmorland tel: 017683 51571
Imaginative dishes and generous portions.
The Punchbowl ($–$$)
Crossthwaite, Kendal, LA8 8HQ tel: 015395 68237
A 17th-century coaching inn. Fine wines and modern British cooking. Must book.

Cheshire
Broxton Hall Country House Hotel ($$)
Whitchurch Road, Broxton tel: 01829 782321
A fine collection of dishes; lovely gardens.

Manchester
Yang Sing ($)
34 Princess Street tel: 0161-236 2200
Superb dim sum.

The Peak District, Derbyshire
Fischer's Baslow Hall ($$–$$$)
Baslow Hall, Carver Road, Baslow tel: 01246 583259
Innovative cuisine with Japanese touches.

NORTHEAST ENGLAND

Northumberland
Lord Crewe Arms ($$)
Blanchland, Nr Consett, DH8 9SP tel: 01434 675251
A 13th-century lodging house for monks.

North York Moors
Appleton Hall Country House Hotel ($$)
Appleton-le-Moors tel: 01751 417227
Reliable English dishes.
Milburn Arms Hotel ($$)
Rosedale Abbey, Pickering tel: 01751 417312
Imaginative use of local ingredients.

York, North Yorkshire
Devonshire Arms Country House Hotel ($$$)
Bolton Abbey, Skipton tel: 01756 710441
Chef Andrew Nicholson produces quality dishes featuring local produce.
Melton's Restaurant ($$)
7 Scarcroft Road, TO23 1ND tel: 01904 634341
The cooking is Anglo-French and everything is made on the premises, including the bread.

SOUTHERN SCOTLAND

Borders (Scottish)
Burt's Hotel ($–$$)
The Square, Melrose tel: 01896 822285
Fine 18th-century inn with fixed-price and à la carte menus.

Edinburgh
Iggs ($$)
15 Jeffrey Street tel: 0131-557 8184
Spanish and Scottish dishes.
Bonars at L'Auberge ($$)
56 St. Mary's Street tel: 0131-556 5888
Authentic French cuisine.
Martin's ($$)
70 Rose Street North Lane tel: 0131-225 3106
Unpretentious, accomplished cooking.

Glasgow
Buttery Restaurant ($$)
652 Argyle Street tel: 0141-221 8188
Nouvelle cuisine in opulent Victorian décor.
Ubiquitous Chip ($–$$)
12 Ashton Lane tel: 0141-334 5007
Ex-warehouse off Byres Road; Scottish dishes (but no chips!).
Yes ($$)
22 West Nile Street tel: 0141-221 8044
Ultra-modern dining, featuring an eclectic mix of Japanese and Scottish fare.

St. Andrews, Fife
Peat Inn ($$$)
Peat Inn, by Cupar tel: 01334 840206
One of the best-known restaurants in Scotland. French cuisine.

NORTHERN SCOTLAND

Perth and Kinross
Killiecrankie ($–$$)
Pass of Killiecrankie, nr. Pitlochry tel: 01796 473220
Scottish game, meat, and fish.

Skye
Hotel Eilean Iarmain ($–$$)
Isle Ornsay tel: 01471 833332
Small inn looking over Sound of Sleat; home cooking; good wines.

Sutherland and Wester Ross
Altnaharrie Inn ($$$)
Ullapool tel: 01854 633230
Former drovers' inn; virtuoso dinners.

A

A la Ronde 78
Abbey Dore 122
Abbeydale Industrial
    Hamlet 21, 192
Abbotsbury 77
Abbotsford 36, 218–219
Aberdeen 239
Aberfeldy 253
Aberystwyth 159
Aboyne 241
accommodations 276–281
Adam, Robert 51
Aira Force 178
Aldeburgh 146
Alfriston 99
Allerford 79
Alloway 216
Alnwick 199–200
Altarnun 67
Althorp 137
Alton Towers 189
Amberley 20, 97
American Museum 65
Anglesey, Isle of 154
Anglesey Abbey 17, 138
Angus 215
Anstruther 230
Antony 71
Arbor Low 186
Arbroath 215
architecture 22, 28–31
Arnside Knott 175
Arran 215
Arreton Manor 100
artists 38–39, 149
Arundel 97
Ashburton 73
Ashdown Forest 89, 92
Ashmolean Museum 126
Audley End House 143
Austen, Jane 36, 77, 108
Avebury 65
Aviemore 256
Axbridge 85
Ayr 36, 216
Aysgarth Falls 209

B

Bakewell 186
Balmoral Castle 241
Bamburgh 199
Bannockburn Heritage
    Centre 231
Barnard Castle 209
Barnsley House Garden
    118
Barra 261
Bateman's 103
Bath 63, 65–66
Battle 99
Beachy Head 98–99
Beamish: North of England
    Open Air Museum 21,
    192, 194
Beaulieu Abbey 101
Beaumaris 154
Bedfordshire 137
Bedruthan Steps 68
Beinn Lora 238
Belvoir Castle 137
Ben Nevis 244
Berkeley Castle 119
Berkshire 89
Berwick-upon-Tweed 199
Betws-y-coed 167
Beverley 192, 194
Bewdley 115

Bewl Water 92
Bibury 119
Big Pit Mining Museum 20,
    156
Bignor Roman Villa 97
Birmingham 114,
    184–185
Black Country 111–112
Black Country Museum 20
Black Isle 242
Blackpool 95, 176
Blaenau Ffestiniog 20, 167
Blair Castle 253
Blenheim Palace 30, 115
Blickling Hall 142
Blists Hill Victorian Town
    123
Bluebell Railway 90
Bodiam Castle 99
Bodmin Moor 67
Bodnant Gardens 17, 169
Bolderwood 101
Bonawe Iron Furnace 248
Bonnie Prince Charlie 246
Borders, The (Scottish)
    217, 218–219
Boscastle 68
Bosham 96
Bothwell 220
Bourton-on-the-Water 120
Bowhill House 218
Bradford 192, 194–195
Bradford on Avon 67
Braemar 240
Branklyn Garden 17, 252
Brechin 215
Brecon Beacons National
    Park 153, 155
Bridgewater Canal 128
Bridgnorth 115
Brighton 88, 90–91, 94,
    95
Bristol 63, 72
British Library 47
Broadstairs 91
Broadway 120
Brodick Castle 215
Brontë Parsonage Museum
    197
Brontë sisters 36, 198
Buckfastleigh 73–74
Buckie 257
Buckinghamshire 113
Buckland Abbey 74
Bucklers Hard 101
Bude 68
Burford 120
Burghley House 147
Burnham Overy Staithe
    142
Burnham Thorpe 142
Burns, Robert 36, 216
Burrell Collection 229
Buscot Park 118
buses and coaches 272
Bute 215
Buttermere 175, 178
Buxton 187
Byland Abbey 202

C

Cadw (Welsh Historic
    Monuments
    Commission) 167
Caerlaverock Castle 221
Caernarfon 167, 169
Caerphilly Castle 157
Calderdale 195
Caldey Island 165
Callander Crags 214
Callanish 260

Cambrian Mountains 159
Cambridge 137, 138–139
camping 264
canals 128–129
Canterbury 93
Cape Wrath 259
Cardiff 157
Carisbrooke Castle 100
Carlisle 176–177
Carreg Cennen Castle 155
Cartmel 179
Castell Coch 157
Castle Acre 140
Castle Bolton 209
Castle Drogo 73
Castle Howard 30, 195
Castle Kennedy Gardens
    222
Castle Museum, York 206
Castle Rising 140
castles and manors 26–27
Castleton 186
Cawdor Castle 242
Centre for Alternative
    Technology 164
Cerne Abbas 76
Chalfont St. Giles 36, 116
Channel Tunnel 98, 264
Charleston Farmhouse 91
Charlestown 71
Chartwell 102–103
Chastleton House 120
Chatham Dockyard 20, 96
Chatsworth House 17, 187
Chawton 36
Cheddar Gorge 64, 85
Chedworth Roman Villa
    119
Chee Dale 175
Cheltenham 117
Chenies 116
Chepstow 171
Cheshire 174
Chesil Beach 77
Chester 177
Cheviot Hills 201
Chichester 96–97
Chiddingstone 107
children 264–265
Chilham 93
Chillingham Castle 201
Chiltern Hills 113, 115
Chipping Campden 120
Chipping Norton 120
churches and monasteries
    28–29
Cinque Ports 34, 105
Cirencester 118
clans and tartans 233
Cley 142
climate 265–266
Clovelly 72
Clyde Valley 220
Coalbrookdale Furnace and
    Museum of Iron 123
Cockermouth 178
Coldharbour Mill 20
Constable, John 38, 148
conversion charts 274
Conwy 167, 169
Cook, Captain James 203
Cookham 39, 109
Corfe Castle 77
Cornwall 62
Corrieshalloch Gorge 258
Cotehele 71
Cotswold Wildlife Park 119
Cotswolds 113, 118–121
Coventry 112
Coxwold 36, 202
Cragside 201
Craignethan Castle 220
Cramond 226
Craster 199

Crathes Castle 17, 241
crime 266
Crinan Canal 248
Croft Castle 122
Cromarty 242
Cromford 21, 40, 186
Cuillins 254
Culloden 242
Culross 226–227
Culzean Castle 216
Cumbria 173
customs 266, 267

D

D-Day Museum 104
Dalby Forest 203
Dalmeny 226
Dan-yr-ogof Caves 155
Dartmoor 37, 62, 73–74
Dartmouth 74
Deal 98
Dedham 148
Deeside 240–241
Dent 209
Dentdale 209
Derbyshire 174
Derwent Water 178
Devon 62
Dickens, Charles 50, 91,
    104
Dinas Island 158
disabilities, visitors with
    266–267
Dolaucothi Gold Mines 159
Dolgellau 167–168
Dorchester 37, 75
Dornoch 258, 259
Dorset 63
Doune 231
Dounreay 259
Dove Cottage 36, 178
Dove Dale 186
Dover 88, 98
Down House 103
Drake, Sir Francis 80
Drewsteignton 73
driving 267–268
Drum Castle 241
Drumlanrig 222
Dryburgh Abbey 219
Dumfries and Galloway
    212, 221–222
Dunblane 231
Duncansby Head 238, 259
Dunfermline Abbey 227
Dungeness 105
Dunkeld 252
Dunkery Beacon 79
Dunrobin Castle 259
Dunstanburgh Castle 199
Dunster 79
Duntisbournes 119
Dunvegan Castle 255
Durham 196
Durham, County 192
Duxford Air Museum 138

E

285

Earth Centre 192
East Anglia 136
Eastbourne 98–99
Eastwood 137
economy 14
Edinburgh 213, 223–225
Edzell 17, 215
E.H. (English Heritage) 124
Eildon Hills 218
Eilean Donan Castle 258

Index

Elan Valley 159
Elgar, Sir Edward 125
Elgin 257
Ely 140
English Heritage 124
English Marches 112–113
Erddig 159
Eskdale 178
Eton 109
European Union 14
events 18
Exeter 62, 78
Exmoor National Park 78–79

F

Fairford 119
Falkland Palace 227
Felbrigg 142
Fens 136
Finchcocks 103
Finchingfield 148
Fingal's Cave 247
Firth of Forth 226–227
Fishbourne Roman Palace 96, 97
Fishguard 165–166
Fitzwilliam Museum 138
Flag Fen 147
Flamborough Head 192
Flatford Mill 148
Floors Castle 219
Fort William 244
Fortrose 242
Fountains Abbey 29, 197
Fowey 71

G

gardens 16–17
Gardens of the Rose 146
Gatehouse of Fleet 222
Glamis Castle 215
Glasgow 228–229
Glastonbury 80
Glen Coe 244–245
Glen Nevis 238
Glendurgan 16
Glenelg 258
Gloucester 117
Gloucestershire 113
Golf 230
Gordonstoun 256
government 11
Gower Peninsula 153, 162
Grasmere 175, 179
Grassington 208
Great Coxwell Tithe Barn 118
Great Malvern 125
Grey Cairns of Camster 259
Grey Mare's Tail 214
Grime's Graves 140
Guisborough Priory 202

H

Haddo House 239
Haddon Hall 187
Hadleigh 148
Hadrian's Wall 193, 201
Hailes Abbey 120
Halifax 195
Hampshire 89
Hardknott Pass 178
Hardy, Thomas 37, 63, 75

Harewood House 197
Harlech 167, 169
Harris 260–261
Hartland Quay 72
Hastings 99
Hatfield House 146
Hawes 209
Hawkshead 179
Haworth 36, 197, 198
Hay-on-Wye 155
health 268
Hebden Bridge 195
Helmshore Textile Museums 21
Helmsley 202
Henley-on-Thames 109
Heptonstall 195
Hereford 122
Herefordshire 112–113
Hertfordshire 137
Hesket Newmarket 178
Hever Castle 17, 102
Hexham 201
Hidcote Manor 120
High Force 208
Higher Bockhampton 75
Highland Folk Museum 256–257
Highlands 236–237, 262
Hill House 229
Historic Houses Association 273
Historic Scotland 124
history of Britain
  Industrial Revolution 40–41
  maritime history 34–35
  monarchs 32–33
  prehistoric Britain 24–25
Holkham Hall 142
Holy Island 193, 199
Hopetoun House 226
Houghton Hall 142
H.S. (Historic Scotland) 124
Hughenden Manor 116
Hull 192
Hunterian Art Gallery 228–229
Hutton-le-Hole 202
Hythe 105

I

Ightham Mote 103
industrial museums 20–21
Ingleborough 209
Ingleton Waterfalls 193
Inner Hebrides: see Mull, Skye and islands off Oban
insurance 269
Inveraray 248
Inverewe Garden 258
Inverness 242
Iona 247
Ironbridge Gorge 20, 123
Islay 249
Isle of Man 176
Isle of Wight 89, 92, 100

J

Jamaica Inn 67
Jarlshof 251
Jedburgh 218
Jervaulx Abbey 209
John O'Groats 259
Johnson, Dr. 122
Jura 249

K

Kellie Castle 230
Kelso 219
Kendal 179
Kenilworth Castle 133
Kenmore 238, 253
Kent 88
Keswick 178
Kiftsgate Court Gardens 120
Kilmartin 249
Kilpeck Church 122
Kingley Vale 97
King's College Chapel 28
King's Lynn 140
Kings and queens 32–33
Kingussie 256
Kirkcudbright 222
Knockan Cliff 258
Knole 103

L

Lacock Abbey 67
Lake District 36, 39, 173, 174, 175, 178–181
Lancashire 173–174
Land's End 69
Lanhydrock House 67
Lanreath 67
Laugharne 36, 160
Launceston 67
Lavenham 148
Ledbury 125
Leeds 195
Leeds Castle 103
Legoland 109
Leicester 137
Leicestershire 137
Lewes 91
Lewis and Harris 260–261
Lichfield 122
Lincoln 141
Lindisfarne Castle 199
Linlithgow Palace 226
Linn o'Dee 240
literary heritage 36–37
Little Moreton Hall 30, 189
Little Walsingham 142
Liverpool 174, 182
Lizard Peninsula 64, 70
Llanberis 20, 167
Llandrindod Wells 162–163
Llandudno 94, 167
Llangollen, Vale of 163
Llechwedd Slate Caverns 20, 167
Lochaber 244–245
Lochaline 245
Loch Awe 248
Loch Lomond 232
Loch Morar 245
Loch Ness 242
Loch Tay 253
Logan Botanic Garden 222
London
  2 Willow Road 51
  accommodations 58, 276
  airports 264
  Apsley House 50
  art exhibitions 48
  BBC Experience 48
  Bethnal Green Museum of Childhood 49
  Britain at War Experience 49
  British Library 47

British Museum 45, 47
Buckingham Palace 43, 51
Cabinet War Rooms 49
cemeteries 50
Chiswick 46
Chiswick House 46, 51
churches 54
City 45
Courtauld Institute 47
Covent Garden 44, 47, 52
day-trips from 47
Design Museum 49
Dickens' House 50
Docklands 46
Dr. Johnson's House 50
Dulwich Picture Gallery 49
embassies and consulates 268
Estorick Gallery of Modern Italian Art 49
Fenton House 51
Freud's House 51
Geffrye Museum 49
Globe Theatre 49
Greenwich 46, 47
Ham House 46, 51
Hampstead 46
Hampton Court 30, 51
historic houses 50–51
history 44, 45
Houses of Parliament 44
Imperial War Museum 49
Keats' House 51
Kensington Palace 50–51
Kenwood House 51
Kew 16, 51
Leighton House 51
London Aquarium 49
London Dungeon 49
London Transport Museum 47
London Zoo 48
Madame Tussaud's 48
Millennium Dome Millennium Experience 47
Museum of London 46, 49
Museum of the Moving Image 49
museums and art galleries 47–49
National Gallery 43, 47
National Maritime Museum 46, 47
National Portrait Gallery 47
Natural History Museum 48–49
nightlife and entertainment 55
Osterley Park 51
Public Record Office 45
pubs 59
Regent's Park 45
Richmond 46
Royal Air Force Museum 49
Serpentine Gallery 48
Shakespeare's Globe Theatre 49
St. Bartholomew the Great 46, 54
St. James's Park 43
St. Martin-in-the-Fields 43, 54
St. Paul's Cathedral 46, 54
Science Museum 49

shopping 56–57
Sir John Soane's
  Museum 50
Smithfield 46
Soho 44
Southwark Cathedral 54
Speakers' Corner 57
Spencer House 51
street markets 57
Syon House 31, 51
Tate Gallery 49
tours, organized 271
Tower Bridge 45, 53
Tower of London 45, 49
Trafalgar Square 42–43
Victoria and Albert
  Museum 48
views 56
Wallace Collection 48
Wembley Stadium 48
West End 42–43
Westminster Abbey 37,
  44, 54
Westminster Cathedral
  54
Whitehall 45
Wimbledon Lawn
Tennis Museum 48
Long Man of Wilmington
  99
Long Melford 148
Longleat 80
Lost Gardens of Heligan
  71
Lower Broadheath 125
Lower Slaughter 120
Lowry, L. S. 39, 183
Ludlow 124
Lullingstone 92, 103
Lulworth Cove 64, 77
Lundy Island 78
Lydford Gorge 64, 73
Lyme Hall 187
Lyme Regis 77

Machynlleth 164
Mackintosh, Charles
  Rennie 229
Maes Howe 250–251
Maiden Castle 75
Malham 208
Mallaig 245
malt whisky 240
Malvern Hills 125
Manchester, 183, 185
Mapledurham 116
maps 270
  see also Contents
Matlock Bath 187
media 270
Mellerstain House 219
Melrose 219
Mevagissey 71
Midland Motor Museum
  115
Milford Haven 166
Milton Abbas 76
Milton, John 36, 116
Milton Keynes 137
Minsmere 146
Minster Lovell 120
Minterne Magna 76
Moel Fammau 158
monasteries 28–29
money 270
Monk's House 91
Monmouth 171
Monsal Dale 175, 186
Montgomery 166
Montrose 215

Morecambe Bay 173
Moretonhampstead 73
Morwenstow 68
Mount Edgcumbe 71
Mount Grace Priory 202
Mousa Broch 251
Mousehole 69
Mull 247

National Gallery of
  Scotland 224
National Gardens Scheme
  17
national holidays 269
National Lighthouse Centre
  70
National Motor Museum
  101
National Museum of
  Photography, Film and
  Television 194
National Museum of Wales
  157
National Parks 145
National Railway Museum
  206
National Tramway Museum
  187
National Trust 102, 144
National Trust for Scotland
  102, 213
National Waterways
  Museum 17
National Wireless Museum
  100
Near Sawrey 178
Nelson, Lord Horatio 35,
  142
Nether Stowey 82
New Forest 101
New Lanark 214, 220
New Lanark Mills 21
Newcastle-upon-Tyne 200
Newquay 69
Nidderdale 208
Norfolk 136, 142
Norfolk Broads 141
North Bovey 73
North of England Open Air
  Museum 21, 194
North and South Uist 261
North York Moors National
  Park 202–203
North Yorkshire Moors
  Railway 202
Northamptonshire 137
Northleach 119
Northumberland 192
  Coast 199–200
  National Park 200–201
Norwich 143, 149
Nottingham 137
Nottinghamshire 137
N.T. (National Trust) 102
N.T.S. (National Trust for
  Scotland) 102, 213

Oban 248
Offa's Dyke Path 153
Okehampton 74
Old Man of Hoy 251
Old Radnor Church 162
Old Sarum 83
opening hours 270–271
Orkney Islands 250
Osborne House 100

Outer Hebrides 260–261
Owletts 103
Oxford 113, 126–127

Padstow 19, 68
Painswick 17, 118, 119
Paradise Silk Mill and
  Museum 21
Parham House 97
Parracombe 78
Paul Corrin Musical
  Collection 67
Peak Cavern 187
Peak National Park 174,
  186–187
Peebles 218
Pembroke 165
Pembrokeshire 153
Pembrokeshire Coast
  National Park 165–166
Penjerrick 16, 71
Pennines 191
Penrhyn Castle 169
Penshurst Place 102
Penwith 68, 69
Penzance 70
Perth 252
Perth and Kinross
  252–253
Peterborough 147
Petworth 101
Pevensey Castle 99
pharmacies 271
Pickering 203
Pistyll Rhayader 164
Pitlochry 252–253
Plas Newydd (Anglesey)
  154
Plas Newydd (Llangollen)
  164
Plockton 258
Pluscarden Abbey 257
Plymouth 80
Poldark Mine 20
Polesden Lacey 102
police 272
Polperro 71
Pontcysyllte Aqueduct 129
Port Isaac 68
Port Sunlight 188
Portloe 71
Portmeirion 169
Portsmouth 104
post offices 272
Postbridge 73
Potter, Beatrix 145, 178
Powis Castle 17, 166
Preseli Hills 166
Presteigne 163
Princetown 73
Prinknash Abbey 119
public transportation 272
pubs 15

Quantock Hills 62, 82
Quarry Bank Mill 21, 189
Quebec House 103

Raasay 255
rail services 272–273
Ramsey Island 165
Ramsgate 91

Reeth 207, 208
restaurants 281–282
Restormel Castle 67
Ribblesdale 209
Richborough Castle 105
Richmond 208–209
Ridgeway Path 115
Rievaulx Abbey 202
Ring of Brodgar 250
Ripon 197
Rob Roy 232
Robert the Bruce 231
Robin Hood's Bay 203
Rochester 96
Romney Marsh 105
Romsey 108
Rosemarkie 242
Ross-on-Wye 171
Royal Yacht Britannia,
  former 224
Royal Society for the
  Protection of Birds 144
Rum 255
Runswick Bay 193, 203
Rye 104–105

Saffron Walden 143
St. Abb's Head 214, 219
St. Albans 146
St. Andrews 230
St. David's 165
St. Ives 39, 69
St. Just in Roseland 71
St. Michael's Mount 70
St. Neot 67
Salisbury 83, 82–83
Saltaire 194
Sandringham 142
Sandwich 105
Scarborough 203
Scilly, Isles of 83
Scone Palace 252
Scott, Sir Walter 36,
  218–219, 232
Scottish Mining Museum
  21
seaside resorts 94–95
season tickets (historic
  houses) 273
Selborne 36
Selkirk 218
Selworthy 79
senior citizens 273
Seven Sisters 98, 99
Severn Valley Railway 115
Sezincote 120
Shakespeare, William 36,
  131, 132
Sheffield 21, 192
Shetland Islands 250, 251
Shobdon 122
Shrewsbury 130
Shropshire 112
Shropshire Hills 130
Sissinghurst Garden 17
Skara Brae 250
Skegness 95
Skokholm 165
Skomer 165
Skye 254–255
Slimbridge 113, 119, 144
Smailholm Tower 219
Snowdon 167, 168
Snowdonia National Park
  153, 167–170
Snowshill 120
Solva 166
Somerset 62–63
South Downs 87–88
South Uist 261

Index

Southampton 89
Southsea 104
Southwell 146
Southwold 146
Spalding 141
Spey Valley 256–257
Spurn Head 192
Staffordshire 174
Staithes 193, 203
Stamford 147
Standen 102
Stinsford 75
Stirling 231
Stoke-by-Nayland 148
Stoke-on-Trent 21, 189
Stokesay Castle 27, 124
Stonehenge 63, 84
Stonor House 116
Stott Park Bobbin Mill 21, 179
Stourhead 16, 84
Stourport-on-Severn 115
Stratford-upon-Avon 36, 131–132
student/youth travel 273
Studley Royal 17, 197
Sudbury 148
Sudeley Castle 120
Surrey 89
Sussex 88–89
Swaledale 208–209
Sweetheart Abbey 222
Sygun Copper Mine 20, 167
Symonds Yat 158

Teesdale 208
telephones 273
Tenby 165
Tewkesbury 117
Thames Valley 109
Thaxted 148
Thirlmere 178
Thomas, Dylan 36, 160
Thornton Dale 202
Thorpeness 146
Threave Castle and Gardens 221–222
Three Peaks 209
Tintagel 62, 68
Tintern Abbey 171
tipping 270
Tissington 186
toilets 274
Tolpuddle 76
Torridon 258
Totnes 74
tourist offices 274
Traquair House 218
Trebah 16, 71
Trelissick 16
Trerice 69
Tresco 83
Tretower 155
Trewithen 16
Tring Reservoir National Nature Reserve 115
Trossachs 232
Trooping the Colour 18
Tunbridge Wells 107
Tyne and Wear 192

Valle Crucis Abbey 163
Valley of Rocks 64, 78
Verulamium 146
Veryan 71

Waddesdon Manor 132
Wakehurst Place 17
Walberswick 146
Walker Art Gallery 182
walking, hiking 145, 274
Walmer 98
Walpole St. Peter 140
Walsoken 140
Warkworth 200
Warwick 133
Warwickshire 113
Wast Water 178
Watercress Line 108
Watersmeet 79
The Weald 87, 103, 107
Weald and Downland Open Air Museum 96–97
Wells 84–85
Wells-next-the-Sea 142
Welsh Folk Museum 157
Welsh language 160–161, 269
Welsh Slate Museum 20,167
Wensleydale 209
West Highland Line 245
West Highland Way 245
West Somerset Railway 82
West Wycombe 116

Western Isles 260–261
Westonbirt Arboretum 118
Weymouth 77
Wharfedale 208
Wheal Martyn 20
Whipsnade Wild Animal Park 116
Whitby 37, 202, 203
Whithorn 222
Wicken Fen 140
Widecombe in the Moor 73
Wilton House 83
Wiltshire 63
Wimpole Hall 138
Winchcombe 120
Winchelsea 105
Winchester 89, 107–108
Windermere 179
Windsor 109
Winkworth Arboretum 17
Wisley Garden 16–17
Woburn Abbey 147
Woodstock 114
Wookey Hole 85
Worcester 125
Wordsworth, William 36, 82, 178
Wren, Sir Christopher 54
Wye Valley 171

Yarmouth, Isle of Wight 100
York 204–206
Yorkshire 191–192
Yorkshire Dales National Park 192, 207, 208–209

Tarn Hows 179
Tarr Steps 79

Ullswater 175, 178
Ullapool 258

Picture credits

The Automobile Association would like to thank the following for their assistance in the preparation of this book.
BRIDGEMAN ART LIBRARY 38a *Fitting Out, Mousehole Harbour, 1919* by Stanhope Alexander Forbes (1857–1947) (Bradford Art Galleries and Museums/Bridgeman Art Library, London), 149a *Wood Scene 1810* by John Crome (1768–1821) (By courtesy of the Board of Trustees of the V & A/Bridgeman Art Library, London), 149b *Fishing Boats off Yarmouth* by John Sell Cotman (1782–1842) (Christie's London/Bridgeman Art Library, London). **BRITISH WATERWAYS BOARD** 128a Buckby Locks. **LLANGOLLEN INTERNATIONAL MUSICAL EISTEDDFOD** 152 dancers. **MARY EVANS PICTURE LIBRARY** 32a Charles II, 32b Elizabeth I, 32c Henry VIII, 33 Charles I, 39a J. M. W. Turner, 40a Manchester 1870, 94b bathing machine at Brighton, 94c Hastings. J. MORGAN 160a Royal National Eisteddfod of Wales, 161 Rhymney Valley. RITZ HOTEL 59b tea at the Ritz. **THE MANSELL COLLECTION** 216a Robert Burns, 246b Charles Stuart.

All remaining pictures are held in the Association's own picture library (A.A. PHOTO LIBRARY) with contributions from: M. **ADELMAN** 36a, 41, 227a, 238, 261a, 262b. **M. ALLWOOD-COPPIN** 26–7, 130a, 130b. **P. AITHIE** 151b. **A. BAKER** 4, 20b, 64b, 69b, 112, 123c, 179, 198a, 198b, 198c, 208a, 212a, 230a, 230b, 231, 232, 236, 252, 256. **P BAKER** 21b, 23b, 26b, 44, 60, 63, 68, 73, 75a, 75b, 77, 106b, 140, 173, 186a, 187, 197a, 203a, 206a. **J. BEAZLEY** 16a, 186c, 190, 194a, 194b, 196b, 199, 200, 214, 216b, 217, 221, 222b, 237, 249a, 259. **A. W. BESLEY** 5b, 70c, 71a. **M. BIRKITT** 5c, 28b, 65a, 84, 95a, 111b, 115, 131, 135b. **E. A. BOWNESS** 18a, 173b, 243. **P. & G. BOWATER** 229b. **P. BROWN** 12b, 86, 88b, 90, 91, 97a, 99, 104a, 105. **D. BURCHILL** 174, 176a. **I. BURGUM** 110a, 123a, 123b, 124b, 150, 155a, 156a, 157a, 157b, 162, 164a, 165a, 165b, 167, 168, 169a, 169b, 171b, 269. **J. CARNIE** 233a, 245a, 245b, 253c, 258. **T. COHEN** 263b. **D. CROUCHER** 225, 233b. **D. CROUCHER** 159a, 163, 164b, 222a. **J. CROWE** 145, 147. **S. DAY** 8a, 176. **P. EDEN** 100b. **R. ELLIOTT** 224, 226–7. **P. ENTICKNAP** 108. **R. FLETCHER** 34b. **D. FORSS** 15a, 30b, 50, 81b, 89, 92, 95b, 98, 102b, 103, 109a, 109b, 128b, 142a. **S. GIBSON PHOTOGRAPHY** 213, 220, 228, 229a. **J. GRAVELL** 166. **V. GREAVES** 132. **S. GREGORY** 202a. **A. GRIERLY** 154b. **J. HENDERSON** 211b, 235. **A. J. HOPKINS** 25, 82–3, 171a, 193. **R. JOHNSON** 250, 251. **C. JONES** 177. **P. KENWARD** 275b. **A. LAWSON** 23, 61b, 69a, 70a, 70b, 74a, 74b, 116, 126–7, 144b. **S. & O. MATHEWS** 191b. **J. McCRAE** 125b. **E. MEACHER** 5a, 65b. **C. MOLYNEUX** 209a. **R. MORT** 12a, 14a, 54b, 272. **J. MORRISON** 192, 209b. **R. NEWTON** 21a, 37, 80a, 85, 143a, 158, 160b, 189, 206b. **D. NOBLE** 17, 93, 104b, 106. **K. PATERSON** 215, 249b. **A. PERKINS** 156. **J. PERRIN** 153. **N. RAY** 19, 62, 67. **P. SHARPE** 3, 175, 178, 219, 240, 248. **M. SHORT** 110b, 118a, 119. **B. SMITH** 11a, 45, 56a, 59a. **A. SOUTER** 10a, 24a, 72, 81a, 118b, 120, 136. **F. STEPHENSON** 18b. **R. STRANGE** 11b, 13b, 14b, 43b, 46, 48, 51, 57a, 57b, 185. **R. SURMAN** 28a, 113. **D. TARN** 207. **M. TAYLOR** 223. **T. TEEGAN** 79. **T. D. TIMMS** 222a. **M. TRELAWNY** 7a, 47, 54a, 58b, 96, 241, 271. **P. TRENCHARD** 35b. **R. VICTOR** 13a. **W. VOYSEY** 9b, 16b, 22b, 34a, 35a, 38–9, 49, 53b, 78, 82b, 87, 88a, 101a, 107b, 156b. **R. WEIR** 6, 7b, 239, 244a, 254, 257, 260. **J. WELSH** 114, 184. **L. WHITWAM** 10b, 30a, 40b, 129, 138a, 138b, 143, 177, 182, 183a, 183b, 184a, 185a, 186b, 188a, 188b, 188c, 195, 201, 204, 206c, 208b, 266, 268, 275. **H. WILLIAMS** 24b, 29, 64a, 122a, 122b, 207. **P. WILSON** 55, 56b, 58a. **T. WOODCOCK** 9.

Contributors

Revision copy editor: Grapevine Publishing Services   Original copy editor: Sue Gordon

Revision verifier: Tim Locke